Considering Anthropology and Small Wars

This book includes a variety of chapters that consider the role and importance of anthropology in small wars and insurgencies.

Almost every war since the origins of the discipline at the beginning of the nineteenth century has involved anthropology and anthropologists. The chapters in this book fall into the following myriad categories of military anthropology:

- Anthropology for the military. In some cases, anthropologists participated directly as uniformed combatants, having the purpose of directly providing expert knowledge with the goal of improving operations and strategy.
- Anthropology of the military. Anthropologists have also been known to study state militaries. Sometimes this scholarship is undertaken with the objective of providing the military with information about its own internal systems and processes in order to improve its performance. At other times, the objective is to study the military as a human group to identify and describe its culture and social processes.
- Anthropology of war. As a discipline, anthropology has also had a long history of studying warfare itself.

This book considers the anthropology of small wars and insurgencies through an analysis of the Islamic State's military adaptation in Iraq, Al Shabaab recruiting in Somalia, religion in Israeli combat units, as well as many other topics.

The chapters in this book were originally published as a special issue of the journal *Small Wars & Insurgencies*.

Montgomery McFate is Professor in the Department of Strategic and Operational Research, US Naval War College, Newport, RI, USA. Dr. McFate received a BA from Berkeley, University of California, USA, a PhD in Anthropology from Yale University, USA, and a JD from Harvard Law School, USA. She is the author of *Military Anthropology* (2018) and editor of *Social Science Goes to War* (2015).

Considering Anthropology and Small Wars

Edited by
Montgomery McFate

LONDON AND NEW YORK

First published 2021
by Routledge
2 Park Square, Milton Park, Abingdon, Oxon OX14 4RN

and by Routledge
605 Third Avenue, New York, NY 10017

Routledge is an imprint of the Taylor & Francis Group, an informa business

© 2021 Taylor & Francis

All rights reserved. No part of this book may be reprinted or reproduced or utilised in any form or by any electronic, mechanical, or other means, now known or hereafter invented, including photocopying and recording, or in any information storage or retrieval system, without permission in writing from the publishers.

Trademark notice: Product or corporate names may be trademarks or registered trademarks, and are used only for identification and explanation without intent to infringe.

British Library Cataloguing in Publication Data
A catalogue record for this book is available from the British Library

ISBN 13: 978-0-367-53817-0 (hbk)

Typeset in Myriad Pro
by Newgen Publishing UK

Publisher's Note
The publisher accepts responsibility for any inconsistencies that may have arisen during the conversion of this book from journal articles to book chapters, namely the inclusion of journal terminology.

Disclaimer
Every effort has been made to contact copyright holders for their permission to reprint material in this book. The publishers would be grateful to hear from any copyright holder who is not here acknowledged and will undertake to rectify any errors or omissions in future editions of this book.

Contents

Citation Information vii
Notes on Contributors ix

Introduction: Considering anthropology and small wars 1
Montgomery McFate

1 Combat anthropologist: Charles T. R. Bohannan, counter-insurgency pioneer, 1936-1966 9
Jason S. Ridler

2 Archaeology and small wars 28
Christopher Jasparro

3 Identity wars: collective identity building in insurgency and counterinsurgency 55
Heather S. Gregg

4 Lost in translation: anthropologists and Marines in Iraq and Afghanistan 76
Paula Holmes-Eber

5 Beyond faith and foxholes: vernacular religion and asymmetrical warfare within contemporary IDF combat units 95
Nehemia Stern and Uzi Ben Shalom

6 Doing one's job: translating politics into military practice in the Norwegian mentoring mission to Iraq 121
Kjetil Enstad

7 'The perfect counterinsurgent': reconsidering the case of Major Jim Gant 139
David B. Edwards

8 Francis FitzGerald's *Fire in the Lake*, state legitimacy and
    anthropological insights on a revolutionary war   164
    Paul B. Rich

9 Accidental ethnographers: the Islamic State's tribal engagement
    experiment   191
    Craig Whiteside and Anas Elallame

10 The anthropology of Al-Shabaab: the salient factors for the
    insurgency movement's recruitment project   213
    Mohamed Haji Ingiriis

    Index   235

Citation Information

The chapters in this book were originally published in *Small Wars & Insurgencies*, volume 31, issue 2 (March 2020). When citing this material, please use the original page numbering for each article, as follows:

Introduction
Considering anthropology and small wars
Montgomery McFate
Small Wars & Insurgencies, volume 31, issue 2 (March 2020), pp. 211–218

Chapter 1
Combat anthropologist: Charles T. R. Bohannan, counter-insurgency pioneer, 1936-1966
Jason S. Ridler
Small Wars & Insurgencies, volume 31, issue 2 (March 2020), pp. 267–285

Chapter 2
Archaeology and small wars
Christopher Jasparro
Small Wars & Insurgencies, volume 31, issue 2 (March 2020), pp. 313–339

Chapter 3
Identity wars: collective identity building in insurgency and counterinsurgency
Heather S. Gregg
Small Wars & Insurgencies, volume 31, issue 2 (March 2020), pp. 381–401

Chapter 4
Lost in translation: anthropologists and Marines in Iraq and Afghanistan
Paula Holmes-Eber
Small Wars & Insurgencies, volume 31, issue 2 (March 2020), pp. 340–358

Chapter 5
Beyond faith and foxholes: vernacular religion and asymmetrical warfare within contemporary IDF combat units
Nehemia Stern and Uzi Ben Shalom
Small Wars & Insurgencies, volume 31, issue 2 (March 2020), pp. 241–266

Chapter 6
Doing one's job: translating politics into military practice in the Norwegian mentoring mission to Iraq
Kjetil Enstad
Small Wars & Insurgencies, volume 31, issue 2 (March 2020), pp. 402–419

Chapter 7
'The perfect counterinsurgent': reconsidering the case of Major Jim Gant
David B. Edwards
Small Wars & Insurgencies, volume 31, issue 2 (March 2020), pp. 420–444

Chapter 8
Francis FitzGerald's Fire in the Lake, state legitimacy and anthropological insights on a revolutionary war
Paul B. Rich
Small Wars & Insurgencies, volume 31, issue 2 (March 2020), pp. 286–312

Chapter 9
Accidental ethnographers: the Islamic State's tribal engagement experiment
Craig Whiteside and Anas Elallame
Small Wars & Insurgencies, volume 31, issue 2 (March 2020), pp. 219–240

Chapter 10
The anthropology of Al-Shabaab: the salient factors for the insurgency movement's recruitment project
Mohamed Haji Ingiriis
Small Wars & Insurgencies, volume 31, issue 2 (March 2020), pp. 359–380

For any permission-related enquiries please visit:
www.tandfonline.com/page/help/permissions

Notes on Contributors

David B. Edwards, Department of Anthropology and Sociology, Williams College, Williamstown, MA, USA.

Anas Elallame, Nonproliferation and Terrorism Studies, Middlebury Institute of International Studies, Monterey, CA, USA.

Kjetil Enstad, Department of Land Power, The Norwegian Defence University College/The Military Academy, Oslo, Norway.

Heather S. Gregg, Department of Military Planning, Strategy and Operations, US Army War College, Carlisle, PA, USA.

Paula Holmes-Eber, Jackson School of International Studies, University of Washington, Seattle, WA, USA.

Mohamed Haji Ingiriis, Faculty of History, St Peter's College, University of Oxford, UK.

Christopher Jasparro, National Security Affairs, US Naval War College, Newport, RI, USA.

Montgomery McFate, Department of Strategic and Operational Research, Center for Naval Warfare Studies, US Naval War College, Newport, RI, USA.

Paul B. Rich, Editor, *Small Wars & Insurgencies*.

Jason S. Ridler, Krieger School of Arts and Sciences, Advanced Academic Programs, Johns Hopkins University, Sacramento, CA, USA.

Uzi Ben Shalom, Department of Sociology and Anthropology, Ariel University, Israel.

Nehemia Stern, Department of Sociology and Anthropology, Ariel University, Israel.

Craig Whiteside, US Naval War College Monterey and US Naval Postgraduate School, Monterey, CA, USA.

INTRODUCTION

Considering anthropology and small wars

Montgomery McFate

ABSTRACT
Almost every war since the origins of the discipline at the beginning of the 19th century has involved anthropology and anthropologists. In some cases, anthropologists participated directly as uniformed combatants. Following the philosopher George Lucas, one might call this 'anthropology *for* the military,' having the purpose of directly providing expert knowledge with the goal of improving operations and strategy. In some cases this scholarship is undertaken, anthropologists have also studied State militaries, which following George Lucas might be considered 'anthropology *of* the military.' Sometimes this scholarship is undertaken with the objective of providing the military with information about its own internal systems and processes in order to improve its performance. At other times, the objective is to study the military as a human group to identify and describe its culture and social processes. Both 'anthropology *for* the military' and 'anthropology *of* the military' tend to have a practical, applied aspect, whether the goal is improving military effectiveness or influencing national security policy. On the other hand, anthropology as a discipline has also had a long history of studying warfare itself, known as 'the anthropology of war.' The papers in this special edition fall into these myriad categories of military anthropology.

Almost every war since the origins of the discipline at the beginning of the 19th century has involved anthropology and anthropologists. My recent book, *Military Anthropology: Soldiers, Scholars and Subjects at the Margins of Empire*, explored the dangers inherent in the military implementation of foreign policy and the role of anthropologists in this enterprise. Very often the anthropologists warned the military (generally unsuccessfully) that exporting Western models would fail in non-Western contexts; that inaccurate perceptions about the culture and society of host nations would hinder their ability to govern; and that military objectives that ignore the local society would undercut strategic objectives. The examples that I chose for *Military*

Anthropology were neither systematic, nor up-to-date, nor comprehensive. This special edition broadens the inquiry by inviting scholars from a variety of disciplines to expand the inquiry of how anthropology and the military intersect.

The contributors to this special edition held a writer's workshop at the US Naval War College in March 2019, which was supported by the US Naval War College Strategic and Operational Research Department and the Center for Irregular Warfare and Armed Groups. One topic that arose during our discussions was: how have anthropologists participated in war? In some cases (as my book explored), anthropologists participated directly as uniformed combatants. Anthropologists serving in uniform frequently participated in civil affairs or unconventional operations where their skills were valuable for working closely with civilian populations, including Edmund Leach, Gregory Bateson and David Prescott Barrows. In other cases, they advised the military as civilians about the culture and society of local civilian populations. The US Army Human Terrain System used anthropologists (among other academic disciplines) to provide socio-cultural information to military units in Iraq and Afghanistan. Following the philosopher George Lucas, one might call this 'anthropology *for* the military,' having the purpose of directly providing expert knowledge with the goal of improving operations and strategy.

For this special edition, historian Jason Ridler contributed a paper on Charles Ted Routledge Bohannan (1914–1982), who was considered one of America's premier experts in unconventional warfare in his day but is now largely forgotten. Using a historian's tools of interviews and archival research, Jason Ridler details Bohannan's early years as an archaeologist studying Native Americans and his subsequent service in the Philippines conducting intelligence and reconnaissance behind enemy lines. After the war, Bohannan stayed in the Philippines as an advisor to the Joint US Military Assistance Group (JUSMAG) where he became friends and colleagues with Air Force Intelligence officer and CIA operative Major Edward Lansdale. As Ridler observes, whereas Lansdale's acumen was in what might be called 'influence operations,' Bohannan 'brought a deeper appreciation of the current political-military and cultural realities of the Philippines based on his life amongst the guerrillas (1944–1950) and rooted in his anthropological training.' After their success in the Philippines, Bohannan and Lansdale were involved a number of covert counterinsurgency programs during the early years of the Vietnam War. Their friendship ended when Bohannan criticized Lansdale's extra-legal methods on the grounds that they were ineffective. Ridler's assessment of Bohannan is that 'COIN required cultural acumen, shared risk, and sage appreciation of local conditions if any strategy or solution was to succeed' and Bohannan 'proved that true in combat against the Japanese, an advisor against the Huk, and a last-ditch attempt against the Viet-Cong.'

Bohannan offers a very clear cut case of an anthropologist participating as a uniformed combatant. However, the relationship of anthropology and the military is sometimes more ambiguous and obscure. Christopher Jasparro's paper for this special edition, 'Archaeology and Small Wars,' traces the history of the role of archaeologists in small wars and the use of archaeology for and by militaries (and other combatants) during and after conflict, including the use archaeological resources as targets and resources. Jasparro observes that during the colonial era state militaries often exploited archaeological materials and cultural heritage to achieve their strategic goals including intelligence collection, survey mapping, geopolitical posturing and legitimation of colonial claims. In the post-Cold War era, insurgent groups are now exploiting archaeological resources and cultural heritage – for example, the destruction of the Bamian Buddhas – to achieve their strategic goals, including legitimation of territorial claims, intimidate opponents, and procurement of resources. As Jasparro notes, 'Instead of western colonial and imperial powers employing archaeological methods and research to achieve their aims or profiting from the expropriation artifacts and antiquities, it is their non-western opponents.'

Another paper in this special edition that falls into the category of anthropology *for* the military is Heather Gregg's contribution, 'Identity Wars: Collective Identity Building in Insurgency and Counterinsurgency.' Rather than detailing the contributions of a single anthropologist or the discipline as a whole to the military enterprise, Gregg uses her knowledge of identity theory and anthropology to argue that counterinsurgencies devote inadequate attention to identity building in population groups. 'The U.S. model of counterinsurgency, specifically in Iraq,' argues Gregg 'focused on building the structure of the state, including competent security forces, a modern democracy, a functioning economy based on Iraq's oil wealth, and rule of law. The assumption was that a functioning state would be sufficient for a happy and loyal population and that there was no need to build a collective identity. This lack of national unity building opened the door for Sunni Islamist insurgents to create a divisive identity.'

As these papers illuminate, anthropology has been used by military actors to attain their objectives. Yet, that is not the only role for anthropology and anthropologists in the military domain. In some cases, anthropologists have also studied State militaries, which following George Lucas might be considered 'anthropology *of* the military.' Sometimes this scholarship is undertaken with the objective of providing the military with information about its own internal systems and processes in order to improve its performance, such as the work of Margaret Harrell or Donna Winslow. At other times, the objective is to study the military as a human group to identify and describe its culture and social processes, as in the work of Anne Irwin and Charles Kirke. Another strain of 'anthropology *of* the military' is critical of the institution as a whole, such as the work of Hugh Gusterson and Katherine Lutz. This type of critical military anthropology sometimes offers public policy insights but rarely offers practical organizational suggestions.

In this volume, anthropologist Paula Holme-Eber offers a humorous and insightful take on anthropology *of* the military. She draws on survey results and ethnographic data obtained working among the US Marine Corps to describe how 'the contrasting worldviews of the Marines and anthropologists frequently led to misunderstandings, frustrations and garbled interpretations as the two struggled to work together to help resolve conflicts in Iraq and Afghanistan.' One area of misunderstanding between scholars and Marines concerned the yearning of most academics to fully understand the manifold complexity of a given problem before offering any analysis or solution. But, as Holmes-Eber notes, the military does not have time to spend on research. In the words of a USMC general officer, 'Part of the problem we had at (a joint headquarters command) was that we just sat around admiring the problem. But we who are in the military have to do something. We have to go out and deal with the tsunami, the insurgent, whatever. We can't just sit there.' As Holmes-Eber's research demonstrates, when academics work with the military, both military personnel and anthropologist must develop cross-cultural skills.

Also in this special edition, anthropologists Nehemia Stern and Uzi Ben Shalom offer an example of anthropology *of* the military. Using interview data, Stern and Ben Shalom explore the vernacular roles that religious practices and experiences play within contemporary combat units of the Israel Defense Forces, highlighting 'a broad range of instrumental functions that religious practices and experiences may serve, including morale boosting, unit solidarity, and more talismanic functions.' Their perspective runs counter to the 'fox hole paradigm,' in which faith offers soldiers a means of overcoming the stress of combat. On the contrary, they argue, IDF 'soldiers often turn to rituals (wearing skullcaps, putting on phylacteries, or reciting psalms) to produce certain practical outcomes, such as creating a sense of order out of a chaotic situation, building morale, creating unit cohesion, and other esoteric forms of experiences.'

In this special edition, Kjetil Enstad also offers an anthropological view on how Norwegian political ambitions were translated into military practice in the Norwegian contingent of the International Coalition against Islamic State of Iraq and the Levant (ISIL). Enstad notes that while Norway may 'play an insignificant role through its small advise-and-assist mission,' for Norway, the contribution to the US-led Coalition part of a defense strategy aimed at 'bolstering transatlantic and NATO relations to ensure US and NATO support should there ever be a threat to Norwegian territory.' Relying on interviews with Norwegian commanders, Enstad observes that the disconnect between Norway's political aims and its military objectives in Iraq transformed military practices into symbolic functions. 'Although an allied field exercise in northern Norway is clearly beneficial to the allied defense of Norway, it is less clear what kinds of military activities in an advise-and-assist operation in Iraq will bolster the alliance.' Frequently prevented from participating in the core military activities for which they had been trained and equipped, the Norwegians were forced back on military basics such as 'being professional, of diligently maintaining the equipment, and of always going through the checks and inspections thoroughly in preparation for operations, even if they would never get past the camp gate.' As Enstad notes, 'somehow, the act of buttoning your shirt properly in the Iraqi heat constitutes defense of the cold Norwegian North.' Enstad concludes by noting that core military practices ('doing military things') needs to be expanded and reconstituted to accommodate the unique features of advise and assist missions.

Both 'anthropology *for* the military' and 'anthropology *of* the military' tend to have a practical, applied aspect, whether the goal is improving military effectiveness or influencing national security policy. On the other hand, anthropology as a discipline has also had a long history of studying warfare itself, known as 'the anthropology of war.' Much of this research has pertained to the nature of humanity itself (are humans generally peaceful or violent? Does this result from nature or nurture?), often relying on the archeological record as evidence for or against various claims. Another strain of the anthropology of war has attempted to identify the origins of war, offering as potential origins the rise of agricultural societies, the 'bad neighbor problem,' politics of small-scale societies, and contact between colonial states and indigenous cultures. This type of inquiry tends to be highly theoretical and generally has limited application to military issues and problems.

Within the anthropology of war, there are a group of scholars who have studied small wars and insurgencies, such as Allen Feldman and David Lan. In many cases, ethnographic fieldwork is conducted in dangerous places and involves grave physical risks. This research is often ethnographic in nature, meaning the researcher conducts participant observation while living among a group of people. (It is worth noting, however, that anthropologists do not have a monopoly on ethnographic research, an approach that has a long tradition in political science, such as the work of Karl Jackson in Indonesia.) Where fieldwork is not possible sometimes secondary source documents have been used to illuminate the world of enemy combatants, such as Ruth Benedict.

A number of contributors to this special edition fall within the sphere of the anthropology of war. Anthropologist David Edwards offers a reconsideration of the case of Major Jim Gant, who General Petraeus called 'the perfect counterinsurgent.' In a moment when the US military believed that operating within the framework of local culture would improve their counterinsurgency efforts in Iraq and Afghanistan, Jim Gant's efforts to integrate himself and his Special Forces into the life of the Afghan village of

Mangwal was seen as exemplary. Not surprisingly, Gant encouraged resistance from within the Pentagon and was found guilty of a variety of regulations (including wearing a beard, using drugs, and living with his lover on base). Edwards draws on his own fieldwork in Afghanistan and his ethnographic informants to argue that Gant's understanding of the tribal system in Afghanistan was flawed, as was his notion of *pakhtunwali* as a rigid code of behavior. Edwards observes that Gant's 'understanding of the people with whom he was interacting was pre-determined by his conception of his military world and, most of all, himself. With regard to tribes, Gant saw them as essentially identical to his own team of soldiers, each bonded by its sense of honor and its adherence to a warrior ethos.'

Also in the category of anthropology of war is the paper by Paul Rich, which examines Frances Fitzgerald's *Fire in the Lake* through the prism of ethnological research in Vietnam stretching back to the Francophone era research of Paul Mus in the 1930s and 1940s. Frances FitzGerald was a freelance reporter who first went to Vietnam in 1966, later becoming a devotee of French ethnologist and Buddhist scholar Paul Mus. The core theme of *Fire in the Lake* is that the South Vietnamese state lacked any serious claim to the Confucian concept of a 'Mandate of Heaven,' which had effectively passed to the Marxist regime of the North under Ho Chi Minh. Rich's paper falls in the domain of the intellectual history of anthropology, as it provides cultural and historical context for Lake's book and the various concepts of revolution and legitimacy that appear within the work. Rich suggests that 'The chief importance of the book really lies in the way it attempted to tackle the issue of political legitimacy during military conflict and to pinpoint this as a crucial to the success or failure of any counterinsurgency campaign. Even now, there is a remarkably limited anthropological focus on issues of state legitimacy during COIN campaigns such as those in Iraq and Afghanistan.'

Craig Whiteside and Anas Elallame's paper, 'Accidental Ethnographers: The Islamic State's Tribal Engagement Experiment,' can also be considered an example of the anthropology *of* war. The authors note that the wars in Afghanistan and Iraq required that NATO forces adjust to the tribal social structures of these environments. Local tribal partners were recruited as adjunct counterinsurgents and the US made efforts at tribal engagement. By 2006, these efforts effectively shifted the views of Iraqi tribal leaders to a pro-American and anti-al-Qaeda position. This cognitive shift by both the Americans and the Sunni tribal leaders, as Whiteside and Elallame note, allowed them to join together to fight against al-Qaeda in Iraq in the 2006–7 period. The period of the Awakening which saw 'Sunni tribes siding with infidel occupiers over fellow Muslims,' prompted some confusion within the Islamic State as to why the tribes had sided with the Coalition. The Islamic State eventually recognized that its troubles centered on tribal relations, and developed a strategy of unification known as the *Strategy to Improve the Political Position of the Islamic State of Iraq*. As Whiteside and Elallame observe, 'This document reveals the beginning of a sociological approach to understanding the tribal problem.' Going forward, the Islamic State stole 'a page from the American's playbook,' and established 'Awakening Jihadist Councils' and a Tribal Engagement Office tasked with gaining detailed information about the Sunni tribal structure in their assigned areas. 'The leaders in the Islamic State displayed no qualms about adopting U.S. methods and even terminology in its plan to turn things around after 2009.' Whiteside and Elallame note that the Islamic State's adoption of US methods for tribal engagement was the result of their initial failure to capture the loyalty of the tribes, much as the Coalition's failure to secure the loyalty of the tribes led to their initial counterinsurgency failures in Iraq.

Another contribution in this special edition to the anthropology *of* war is Mohamed Haji Ingiriis' paper on Al Shabaab recruitment. Based on research with defectors in Somalia, Ingiriis argues that while economic factors play a role, local political and security concerns are much more salient motivations for young men to become members of Al-Shabaab. Many recruits are radicalized through a jihad discourse, although the deeper reason is frequently political grievances against the Mogadishu government and other clan-based federal states. Wounded by the status of Somalia as a failed state, many young men join Al Shabaab to change the situation in southern Somalia by punishing those Somalis and non-Somalis they hold accountable for contributing to the collapsed state. Recruits also join Al Shabaab because the organization abhors the notion of clan-based representation (unlike the government). In turn, Al-Shabaab exploits the grievances expressed by clans and communities who feel marginalised by the federal government. 'The existence of unequal political power and socio-economic status has made young local Somali men prone to extremist ideologies of empowering marginalised clans and communities and punishing those who accumulated wealth through the government's patronage system.'

All of the papers that comprise this special edition offer insights into the variety of ways in which anthropology and the military intersect. They also point to a variety of questions that remain to be addressed: First, what advantages does an ethnographic or archeological research approach that seeks to understand the adversary, civilian population or partner government *in situ* provide the military? Second, what contributions have anthropologists made to the military by virtue of their knowledge, approach, or methodology that could not (or has not) been offered by scholars from different disciplines? Third, what is the future of military anthropology (if indeed such a field exists)?

Disclosure statement

No potential conflict of interest was reported by the author.

Bibliography

Feldman, Allen. *Formations of Violence: The Narrative of the Body and Political Terror in Northern Ireland*. Chicago: University of Chicago Press, 1991.
Gusterson, Hugh. *Nuclear Rites*. Berkeley, CA: University of California Press, 1996.
Harrell, Margaret C. *Invisible Women: Junior Enlisted Army Wives*. Washington: RAND, 2001.
Irwin, Anne. "Diversity in the Canadian Forces: Lessons from Afghanistan." *Commonwealth & Comparative Politics* 47, no. 4 (Nov 2009): 494–505. doi:10.1080/14662040903375067.
Kirke, Charles. *Red Coat, Green Machine: Continuity in Change in the British Army 1700 to 2000*. Birmingham: Continuum Press, 2012.
Lan, David. *Guns and Rain: Guerrillas & Spirit Mediums in Zimbabwe*. Berkeley, CA: University of California Press, 1985.
Lucas, George. *Anthropologists in Arms: The Ethics of Military Anthropology*. Lanham, MD: AltaMira Press, 2009.
Lutz, Catherine A. *Homefront: A Military City and the American Twentieth Century*. Boston, MA: Beacon Press, 2002.
McFate, Montgomery. *Military Anthropology: Soldiers, Scholars and Subjects at the Margins of Empire*. New York: Oxford University Press, 2018.
Winslow, Donna. *The Canadian Airborne Regiment in Somalia: A Socio-Cultural Inquiry*. Ottowa, ON: Canadian Government Pub Centre, 1997.

Combat anthropologist: Charles T. R. Bohannan, counter-insurgency pioneer, 1936-1966

Jason S. Ridler

ABSTRACT
Charles T. R. Bohannan was an instrumental figure in US successes in counter-insurgency in the immediate post-war era. These successes were not just vested in his wartime combat experience, but his pre-war training in archeology and anthropology. Brilliant, tough, and eccentric, Bohannan parlayed his extensive work with foreign and distant cultures into a view of guerrilla warfare that bolstered US successes in the Philippines and Vietnam, alongside his more celebrated boss Edward Lansdale. Here, we see how Bohannan's view of war, culture, and statehood were impacted by a career among Native Americans, ancient peoples, and challenging orthodoxy at every turn.

All during the war I figured that if I lived through it I would go into Graves Registration picking up US bones officially in New Guinea, and unofficially collecting Japanese bones for the Smithsonian, and then revert to my prewar trade, anthropology. However, I found that what I was doing seemed so much more important and worthwhile that I stayed on in the service. Am damn glad that I did, if for no other reason than that my pension makes me independent as a hog on ice.[1]

Lieutenant-Colonel (ret'd) Charles Bohannan, 1981

In 2006, strategist Colin S. Gray argued that the United States faced many challenges in reconciling its preferred way of warfare with the development of strategy to face irregular enemies. Among these weaknesses was cultural awareness. 'From the Indian Wars on the internal frontier, to Iraq and Afghanistan today, the American way of war has suffered from the self-inflicted damage growing out of a failure to understand the enemy of the day.'[2] Ironically, these points coincide with robust years of US Army experience in irregular warfare.[3] These experiences, as historian Andrew Birtle points out, were valuable at the moment, but the expertise was at the fringe of the Army's core ethos of conventional warfare. The knowledge fell into disuse and obscurity, as pursuing the study and practice of these conflicts were professional dead ends. Soldiers were to re-learn these lessons on the job.[4]

Given this context, it is intriguing that America's post-war practitioners of irregular warfare brought discrete knowledge from substantial civilian careers to their military service to fill this gap. Most celebrated is General Edward Lansdale, whose career as an advertising executive in the 1930s became critical to his own mastery of psychological operations and appreciation of cultural symbols and psychology in the Philippines and Vietnam.[5] But equally important was Lansdale's chief partner in both the Philippines and Vietnam, archeologist Lieutenant-Colonel Charles Ted Routledge Bohannan (1914–1982).

Bohannan served in combat with the 32d Division during the New Guinea and Philippines campaigns. During the early Cold War, he joined the Army's Counter Intelligence Corps (CIC) and worked with Lansdale and Filipino Secretary of Defense (and future President) Ramon Magsaysay to defeat the communist Huk insurgency. He led part of the US Special Survey Team to Colombia in 1959 during the period known as *La Violencia*, and found himself working off and on with Lansdale in Vietnam from 1954 to 1965. He wrote *Counter Guerrilla Operations: the Philippines Experience* (1962), one of the best American treatise on the subject, with his colleague Colonel Napoleon Valeriano. In his day, Bohannan was considered one of America's premier experts in unconventional warfare until his death to esophagus cancer in 1982. He is now largely forgotten or dismissed.[6]

Bohannan's military success was predicated on his rather unorthodox nature, upbringing, and professional career as an anthropologist and archeologist. They were integral aspects of his approach to irregular warfare. As a fiercely individualistic teenager, he became an amateur archeologist in the American west. This life afforded him the chance to deal with non-white cultures, foremost the Native Americans. In four professional digs, he demonstrated the command of skills and leadership required to unearth lost cultures from American soil. When he came to military affairs, he viewed war as a phenomenon that required cultural acumen as well as tactical excellence. He held no bones about his loathing for US soldiering and training, describing Officer Candidacy School as an 'unmitigated pain in the ass ... The levels of instruction and achievement would not pass muster in an NCO academy 20 years later. Compared to what was given in ROTC 10 years before it was pathetic.'[7] Like rank, the title also was no proof of intelligence, 'I had known so many highly intelligent people who could barely write their own name,' he recalled at the end of his life. 'I had known PhDs who probably needed assistance in dressing themselves. I could see absolutely no significant difference in ability based on education.'[8] For Bohannan, ability trumped all. And in warfare, the ability to appreciate other cultures and their history trumped tactics and technology.

Education of a nomad

The Bohannans were from pioneer stock, Sons of the Revolution, and had made a name for themselves in soldiering, education, and medicine. His father worked in rural education, was a statistician, and the co-creator of the IQ test. His mother's failing health led to a nomadic childhood to find a healthier environment.[9] Charles Ted Rutledge Bohannan was born on 23 December 1914 while his father worked at the University of Kentucky, co-creating the first tobacco co-op in the state as a means to stifle industry corruption.[10] From 1914 to 1931 they moved from Kentucky to New York, Ohio and Montana, Washington, Colorado and New Mexico, and, finally to Washington D.C.[11] In 1931, Dr. Bohannan joined the Bureau of Public Roads as the first advisor on economic strategies to improve the rural road system, and moved the family to Kensington, Maryland.[12] By 17, young Charles Bohannan had seen more of the US than some people would in a lifetime.

He became a rangy six-foot-two teenager with rusty-red hair and poor eyesight, and took to educating himself. He devoured books 'in a single gulp,' reading Darwin, Plato, and Bacon as well as popular fiction for young men his age. Bohannan found kindred spirits among C. S. Forester's heroes, especially Rifleman Dodd, hero of *Death to the French*, an abandoned guerrilla in Portugal during the Napoleonic Wars. He considered it 'mandatory reading' on guerrilla warfare.[13] Rudyard Kipling's novel *Kim* was also essential. The abandoned son of an Irish soldier in India, Kim grows up in the Indian street culture, and uses his native cunning and knowledge to help a Tibetan Lama find the 'River of Arrows.' 'If there were one book that I would ask you to read,' he told USAID workers headed to Vietnam in 1966, 'it might very well be *Kim*.'[14] Kim's life along foreign peoples mirrored his own. Other favorites were the memoirs of future colleague Clyde Kluckhohn, a leading ethnographic scholar of the Navajo. Klucholn's emerging scholarship on values orientation within cultures, and how people view their own experience as normal and challenged by others, likely informed Bohannan's own view of understanding foreign cultures in small wars.[15] Bohannan prepared himself to lead a 'strenuous life' as Theodore Roosevelt called it, one where the 'splendid ultimate triumph' rested with the man who 'does not shrink from danger, from hardship, or from bitter toil.'[16] When 14, his father gave him a gun and some cash. 'If you run out of money or ammunition,' he told his son, 'come home.'[17] Bohannan spent months on his own in the wild, working in New Mexico or Colorado, the two states he loved most. He earned a living collecting rare snakes and Native artifacts and selling them to locals or the Smithsonian. He trained himself as a marksmen, hunter, and cartographer, and picked up smatterings of Spanish, German, and Quebec French from the people he had met while working in New Mexico and Colorado. He learned much from the Mexican and Spanish laborers, including a courtly version of Spanish.[18]

Bohannan also learned to handle himself physically. He was strong, tough, and well versed in wrestling, though he had no time for boxing. 'I think it's a very stupid sport,' he recalled later. 'Karate, judo, plain alley fighting – they are all right if you don't have a knife or a club. But boxing – asinine.'[19] From Native Americans, he learned combat arts, tracking, and how to move silently.[20] Of all the people in the west, he held the Native Americans in highest regard.

Native culture and warfare

Bohannan received an informal education on unconventional warfare from participants who ended up around the camp fires of archeological digs, including Native Americans. As he told USAID workers in 1966:

> [In] my boyhood, I spent a very great many nights out on the high desert, listening to the tales of men who had fought, as guerrilla or as regulars in wars ranging from our Indian Wars on the High Plains – both sides, men from both sides – to the men who rode with Pancho Villa in Mexico. During part of this time I was with revolutionary forces in Mexico.[21]

Native Americans captivated Bohannan's imagination. The past three generations of his family were friends of Native Americans, as doctors, educators, and colleagues.[22] By the time he received his degree in 1938, he accounted himself as a specialist in their culture and folklore, and later told historian Alfred McCoy that he was an expert on 'the Navajo.'[23] Cultural awareness was critical to understanding a people's psyche, something he honed as a student of archeology, understanding that people unlike him had a frame of reference that was as important to them as being a white American was to his seniors. This affection did not endear the Bohannan family to many in Washington, DC. When Bohannan was initially hired to make the first official census on the Indian reservations for the Bureau of Census in 1940, his name was revoked when, according to him, the family name was mentioned to the Bureau chief. The family's sympathy for Native Americans ensured that 'no damn Bohannan' would get the job.[24]

From roughly 1930–1934, Bohannan amassed a deep knowledge Native culture, including warfare from the campfire talks and readings.[25] When he served in the Philippines, he had a much greater appreciation of guerrilla warfare than his contemporaries.[26] He would serve with a mix of US, Filipino, and indigenous peoples fighting in similar fashion to the Natives of the Indian Wars: raids, hostages and prisoner trades; avoiding direct combat against superior numbers and firepower, but then striking with bold courage.[27] In the

American West, he was inoculated against the prevailing US Army bias that viewed guerrilla warfare as a necessary evil, instead of a school of war itself.[28]

Mentors and expeditions

In the summer of 1934, Bohannan was bound for George Washington University, and was selected for an expedition to Alaska headed by the renowned Czech-born anthropologist Aleš Hrdlička, who had been awarded the T.H. Huxley Award in 1927.[29] Hrdlička's early research focused on the remains of Asians and Native Americans and generated the first well documented theory of the colonization of the American continent by the peoples of East Asia, across the Bering Strait, some 15,000 years ago.[30] Hrdlička also fostered a Euro-centric view of civilization, following a race-based lineage that began with white Europeans (and some of his later theories reflected a deeper racial bias). Yet within the 'three-race' paradigm he dismissed notions of purity or homogeneity and embraced variation within populations that lead to *types* of people that also reflected an anti-imperialist streak within this racial frame of reference.[31]

Reduced funds meant Hrdlička's 1934 expedition required cost cutting.[32] Bright and cheap students would work for less. Bohannan was among them.[33] He worked as laborer, hunter, and note-taker on several burial digs of Koniag and Pre-Kongia peoples and life, how they worked, hunted, cooked, lived, fought, and died, including evidence of massacres and cannibalism.[34] Hrdlička was impressed with Bohannan and made him his laboratory assistant at the Smithsonian.[35] In 1935, Bohannan worked at Lindenmeier site in the north of Colorado. Located near Fort Collins, the Lindenmeier Site contained one of the richest deposits of Folsom findings, a Paleo-indian archeological culture that occupied much of central North America around 8,000 B.C.[36] John L. Cotter, noted archeologist, worked alongside Bohannan.[37] Cotter recalled Bohannan hated 'being photographed, washing, changing his clothes, or taking his glasses off at any time ... Stetson perpetually on his head, he appeared like a frontiersmen.'[38] Bohannan was '... a total romantic ... dedicated to doing all the things the most difficult way possible, and with maximum discomfort.'[39] They would work together an another dig in New Mexico in 1935, unearthing materials of Clovis peoples.[40]

After graduating from George Washington University in 1938, Bohannan was given a leadership position at the Hardin Village Site in Kentucky, administered by President Franklin D. Roosevelt's Works Progress Administration (WPA). He was only 24-years old.[41] The work was painstaking, the crews were difficult, and the results and successes appropriated by the site's administrator William S. Webb.[42] When the war ended his career, Bohannan's efforts became somewhat buried.[43] But they endured.[44] Modern archeologist John Pollock, having used Bohannan's research from Hardin, noted

Bohannan was an excellent archaeologist. In particular, his excavations are well-documented and he took excellent notes ... It was his attention to detail that enhanced the scientific significance of the sites he excavated. Many of his colleagues at that time did not pay as much attention to record keeping and other details as Bohannan did.[45]

When the war began in 1939, Bohannan worked for the Census Bureau and organized his notes for a PhD in anthropology should he survive. He enlisted in June 1941, months before Pearl Harbor.

The Second World War

From 1941 to 1945, Bohannan fought his way through the Second World War. Initially, he served as a radar rig mechanic in Australia but ditched his unit to fight with the 32nd Division at 'Bloody Buna' on New Guinea. He bought his 'peer review' at Officer Candidate School in 1943. Commissioned as a lieutenant of the 128th Regiment of the 32nd Division on April Fool's Day, 1943, he received a decoration for bravery during the Battle of Aitap before finding his true calling as platoon leader of an Intelligence and Reconnaissance (I&R) unit during the liberation of the Philippines. I&R units worked alongside guerrillas in gathering details behind enemy lines for their unit, and engaged in combat operations. Bohannan became part of a small cadre of the US soldiers focused on unconventional war.[46]

From Leyte to Luzon, Bohannan led a mixed unit of American, Filipino and Igorot guerrillas, and soldiers on intelligence and combat operations, initially acting as the lynchpin between Filipino Ruperto Kangleon's guerrillas and Gen. MacArthur's invasion force. The US Army viewed the Filipino guerrillas as necessary but often useless, and many soldiers held the racist beliefs of the era as exemplified in I&R veteran Norman Mailer's short story, *The Dead Gook*: Filipinos were liars, cheaters, and cowards.[47] Not Bohannan. He made Felix Jabillo, former member of the Philippine Constabulary and later a guerrilla with the Philippine Scouts, the unit's 'chief of staff ... all around guide, counselor, and tail-kicker ... closer to me than any brother could be.'[48] Bohannan built empathy with Filipinos, who had fought for years without quality gear or footwear, by going barefoot in the jungle.[49]

Bohannan's academic work taught him that human beings came from common origins. Differences were not biological as much as cultural. Culture was constructed and could be understood and used. And cultural ignorance and belief in American superiority could lead to hardships.[50] One example: Bohannan survived near-fatal moments at Breakneck Ridge and Limon on Leyte and spent nearly a month behind enemy lines.[51] Jabillo noted he must have an *'anting anting'* (a talisman containing indigenous, Catholic and often freemason symbols, worn to protect one from danger, made famous by Filipino folk heroes and bandits). Wary of offending his chief of staff, Bohannan quietly dismissed the notion. Some mystic allure was fine for impressing locals that he was a 'head man' to be listened to, but it was poison to the unit. First, his courage became bankrupt. An *anting-anting* meant he was bullet proof although he sent other men to face death. Second, it increased the idea that Americans were capable of anything, but not Filipinos. 'To this day,' he wrote in 1945,

> my people look at me and I can hear them thinking: 'Look, old man, you can do these things, you can take all kinds of chances; you can go places where it would be too dangerous for anyone else, you have anting-anting!' And dammit, I have felt like a heel every time I have sent a man who knows the story into a dangerous situation. They have never said it in so many words; they have certainly never hesitated to go where I've asked them to, but I know they are thinking: 'I wish you would loan me your anting-anting.'

Such a talisman was fine for bandits, 'but they are no good for the man who wants the troops he leads to feel that he is sharing the danger with them so far as his duties allow.'[52]

Bohannan led his mixed-race team to a series of successes from Leyte to Luzon until a near fatal wound on the Villa Verde Trail near war's end. He joined the Army Counter Intelligence Corps as a trained investigator in 1946 and briefly hunted Japanese war criminals, but was ordered to the Philippines.[53]

The Philippines

The post-war Philippines government was independent but devastated from the war and liberation campaign, riddled with corruption, and uninterested in stopping abuses by the landholding *illustrado* class who used guerrillas as private armies.[54] It also faced a growing threat to its legitimacy on Luzon. The *Hukbong Bayan Laban sa mga Hapon* ('People's Army Against the Japanese') or Huk, were a wartime guerrilla group made of the pre-war socialist and communist parties. Trained by veteran Chinese communists, the Huk were brutal, refused to serve under US leadership or disarm after Japan's defeat, and their leadership was barred from power in post-war elections despite popularity. Initially dismissed as a criminal threat, they gained support from the oppressed peasants. President Manuel Roxas' 'mailed fist' strategy focused on conventional tactics and hurting the peasants in Japanese fashion. Both failed. The result of punishing the peasantry was a rise of Huk influence throughout 6000 square miles in Central Luzon that they ruled as a separate power called Huklandia (home of their external HQ, Politburo-Out).[55] After Communist victory in China in 1949 and North Korean success in the Korean War in fall 1950, Huk Supreme military commander Luis Taruc succumbed to pressure from senior party leadership and declared a revolutionary state had been achieved. Huk forces would now try to take Manila.[56]

During this period, Captain T. R. Bohannan struck a friendship with Air Force Intelligence officer and CIA operative Major Edward Lansdale, former advertising executive, veteran of the Office of Strategic Services, and early pioneer of psychological warfare. Both men viewed Roxas efforts early as disastrous. It ignored strategic, political, and historical realities and relied on Japanese tactics. They decided to work together to change the strategy as advisors within the Joint US Military Assistance Group (JUSMAG) that stewarded US military aid.[57]

Each man brought complimentary skills to counter-guerrilla warfare. Lansdale's greatest gifts were in strategic outlook, diplomatic influence with powerbrokers, and the ability to employ other nation's cultures in psychological operations. Never a combat soldier, Lansdale's acumen was in what might be called 'influence operations' or strategic-messaging. Lansdale specialized in building relationships with senior leadership, appreciating other cultures, and advising across a broad spectrum of strategic to tactical psychological operations. In these areas he had great mastery.[58] To this Bohannan brought a deeper appreciation of the current political-military and cultural realities of the Philippines based on his life amongst the guerrillas (1944–1950) and rooted in his anthropological training. He also had deeper experience and thinking on unconventional warfare. His skillset dovetailed with his actual combat experience of the Filipino struggle. For Bohannan, this insurgency could not be separated from culture, politics, or history. Lansdale agreed.[59] Conventional soldiers often recused themselves from two of these three ideas, but for 'Ed and Boh' they were synonymous. Bohannan would later call it 'irregular political activity' since it represented 'a contest, a relationship, between individuals that touches on every sphere, every form of human relations.' Such work was plagued with semantic difficulties on the psychological and irregular warfare side. '[F]or all the ways of acting against an enemy, these two fields of warfare appear most properly to belong to the social sciences.' Soldiers involved in this kind of work had to think like social scientists, minus ridiculous jargon.[60] Proving his point after the fact, Bohannan published his views of counter guerrilla warfare in the academic journal *Annals of Political and Social Science* after he and Lansdale put them into practice.[61]

It remains difficult to dissect just who was responsible for what ideas that became the strategy to defeat the Huk. And this was by design.[62] Lansdale and Bohannan spent careers putting most of the focus on the Filipinos and Vietnamese they worked with, and Bohannan actively disdained the spotlight, preferring to be 'Johnny Behind the Door' to Lansdale's more public presence.[63] The brain-trust, however, were Lansdale, Bohannan, and Magsaysay. Additional ideas were contributed by innovative thinkers in the Filipino armed forces like Captain Napoleon Valeriano, commander of the Nenita Unit who Bohannan helped to reshape as a legitimate counter-guerrilla force.[64] 'How did they operate?' Bohannan asked in an unpublished analysis of guerrilla warfare.

> By working, in one way or another all the time; by spending virtually (this is literally true) a minimum of 20 hours a day with Filipinos who had something to do with, or contribute to, the solution of the problem; by poking their noses into everything, and trying to get it all working in the same direction, whether it be the press, or the army, or the business community, or politicians from the President down to ward-heelers, or any of the dozen churches in the country. By never leaving the key man alone except when he went to bed with his wife, until he was thoroughly indoctrinated. By having friends or contacts on every side of every fence, including the leader of the insurgents, his mother, and several of his past or present mistresses. By letting everyone know that they were personally committed, and that they believed he too was equally dedicated (so that he would lose face if he proved himself not to be). By never asking anyone to do anything unless he believed it was right and in the interest of his country, but making unlimited (at times shameless) demands on him to do what was right.[65]

His dedication bought saliency for the three main pillars of their strategy: political, military, and psychological. Lansdale was master of the political, building strategies with Magsaysay on recasting the government as an honest legal broker, correcting economic practices, reducing corruption, and securing Magsaysay as the next leader of the country (he eventually became president in 1953). Lansdale and Magsaysay engineered the program of 'civic action' for the defense departments, which included a series of counter measures (civic works, hospitals, legal recourse for land dispute, reducing civilian casualties) that recast government forces as legitimate. Bohannan lead the military side of adapting the post-war Philippine Armed Forces away from the Japanese-based techniques that brutalized the peasantry into an effective counter-guerrilla organization. He developed novel operations alongside Valeriano to defeat, confuse, and terrify the Huk. Their tactics included counterfeit Huk units, use of disguises, employment of ruses, and building the reputation of the armed forces as pro-peasant and anti-Huk. That said, each man's opinion was wanted in each sphere of expertise.[66]

Both men believed that psychological warfare was rooted in cultural norms. Bohannan had seen its power with the *anting-anting* and spoke afterwards that the counter-guerrilla must 'Learn, and capitalize on local customs and beliefs among the troops, but do not hope completely to eradicate them, even if they are as senseless and counter-productive as fear of the dark.'[67] The most controversial operation involved using Filipino superstition. These included the using of a dead Huk, drained of blood, to be left as a victim of the *Asuang* (a mythical creature similar to a Western vampire), with rumors that such creatures lived in Huk territory.[68] Another operation involved using a picture of an eye enclosed in a triangle, a leaflet that spoke to fears of being watched by a supernatural force. 'This was secretly posted in places Huk were known to pass or take shelter. The picture bore the connotations of ethical and/or religious groups not well known to the average Huk, but respected by them and most people.' But it generated unease and concern about its purpose and its origins. It killed no Huk, or made anyone surrender, but it made them avoid their favorite shelters and avoid spaces where the eye was laid. 'It did contribute to the feeling of harassment that lessens the offensive spirit; to the feeling of frustration and futility that can ultimately lead to the dissolution of a guerrilla unit and the surrender or submergence of its members.'[69] The only thing it should not do is ruin the reputation of the government and armed forces as 'honest men dedicated to public welfare.'[70] Bohannan likely contributed to all of these ideas, alongside Valeriano as well as Lansdale.[71]

The most successful operation that combined the political, military, and psychological was the creation of the Economic Development Corps (EDUCOR) project. EDUCOR was designed as a surrender program that would give former Huks land, thus removing active Huk from guerrilla operations and providing a counter-message to the Huk's slogan of 'land for the landless.' Lansdale said it emerged from a morning strategy session between him, Magsaysay, and others, when the idea of the Roman military colonies was discussed. Soon EDCOR became part of first a military and then a national program of both Huk rehabilitation and then agricultural reform.[72] As Bohannan was the best read member of this cadre when it came to military history, it is likely he was the one who originated the idea.[73] EDCOR was a symbolic victory for helping turn the peasantry against the Huk, and was among the key successes that helped secure Magsaysay's presidency, though its success as agrarian reform has been contested.[74]

Between 1950 and 1954 the Magsaysay strategy of 'All Out Friendship or All Out Force' began breaking support for the Huk and transformed military failures into a Huk route. Constant counter-guerrilla operations pressed the Huk out of Huklandia. While on the run, Taruc surrendered in 1954.[75] Lansdale and Magsaysay received most of the credit, but much is due to Bohannan. Among the breakthroughs that turned the tide against the Huk was discovering the Politburo-IN. One of Bohannan's informants who worked as a janitor discovered their trash in Manila in late 1950 and informed the authorities. The raid of the Huk HQ found almost all of their intelligence material intact. It was a goldmine of information on support systems, locations, and government supporters among others that led to the stampede of victory after 1950.[76] All thanks to a Filipino janitor who worked for Bohannan. 'Ed [Lansdale] hit the grassroots,' noted Bohannan's wife Dorothy, 'but they were the educated grassroots. It was the educated level. Bo, on the other hand, was like a pied piper. He hit the uneducated grassroots as well and tried to educate them and help them up into another position.'[77] They would try and employ similar skills and tactics in Vietnam.

Vietnam

Bohannan served as Magsaysay's advisor while Lansdale went to Vietnam during the dying days of French rule in 1954. The success of the anti-Huk campaign allowed Lansdale to perform a similar function, where he became instrumental in the formation of South Vietnam and the early political and military actions of the government of President Ngô Đình Diệm.[78] Bohannan supported Lansdale's efforts in many ways, from close protection against kidnapping to bull sessions on ideas, but two programs reflected his cultural approach. Operation Brotherhood was a joint effort of Lansdale and Bohannan, originating at Lansdale's Saigon Military Mission (SMM). The SMM was run by the CIA, but was presented as a strictly Filipino initiative of Magsaysay compatriot and member of the Filipino Junior Member of Commerce, Oscar J. Arellano. Filipino doctors and nurses would be sent to the emergent state of Diệm's South Vietnam to provide aid and medical assistance in sections troubled by the Viet Cong. It quickly evolved into an international 'project of preventive medicine in terms of programmed instruction and social health projects.'[79] Bohannan knew the value of medical aid to build trust for the government, from first aid to surgical teams, and of having Asians seeing other Asians succeed. Operation Brotherhood was largely a success, treating 700,000 Vietnamese, and knowledge of its good work spread to almost three million.[80]

But Operation Brotherhood, and its facilities also acted as a cover for a sharper project: Freedom Company. South Vietnam was desperately weak in military training, weapons, and vehicle maintenance, even counter guerrilla warfare theory. Freedom Company was led by former guerrilla Frisco 'Johnny' San Juan, who organized a cadre of ex-Hunter College ROTC guerillas to join. These men had fought the Japanese and the Huk, and were trained by Bohannan and San Juan to mentor the South Vietnamese Army. Bohannan selected, supported, and organized all the men who made up the initial spearhead of Freedom Company, holding the initial strategy sessions at his home in Manila. Bohannan believed in the value of different cultures working together, but the similar challenges facing the Vietnamese made using former Huk fighters a natural fit. By and large, both projects were a success, largely with Bohannan supplying and supporting them from Manila.[81] Freedom Company's efforts were initially resisted by Diệm, but he eventually relented to being taught COIN by 'inferior' Asians. Bohannan believed this was best done not with US advisors but with other South-East Asian experts, 'Brown face to brown face,' he noted.[82]

Bohannan left South East Asia in 1956 to teach at Fort Riley Infantry School, though he would return in two bursts after his retirement from the Army in 1961. As an advisor with RAND, he worked with Rufus Philips in early 1963 on the Chieu Hoi 'surrender' program, and in the wake of the failure of Saigon's counter-guerrilla effort added his voice to efforts in public and within the Pentagon to have Lansdale return.[83] When Diem was assassinated, all three men started a campaign to shift the US war effort from increasing militarization, emphasizing their success in similar operations in the Philippines. Lansdale would return to South Vietnam in 1965 as an advisor to the Johnson administration, but his influence had waned due to his personality clash with Secretary of Defense Robert McNamara and his reputation for covert and often extra-legal methods.

When Lansdale assembled his fact-finding mission in 1965, Bohannan was among those chosen to participate. However, he was soon working outside of Lansdale's own control, conducting operations independently, and according to one source Bohannan attempted to start a small rebellion to shake up the losing strategy.[84] For many, Bohannan had become more difficult than before, with men like Daniel Ellsberg and Lou Conein viewing him as a liability.[85] What sunk his efforts, however, was asking mission members and officials to follow his orders instead of Lansdale. He had personally criticized Lansdale's strategy and operations, on the basis that they were just not making a difference. According to Lansdale's recent biographer, Bohannan was right. Surprised and upset at his former partner's conduct, Lansdale ordered Bohannan out of the country. It was a critical blow to their friendship, one that was only rekindled thanks to Ellsberg's 'betrayal' of leaking the Pentagon Papers, which initiated a correspondence between the two until Bohannan's death.[86] Lansdale's mission failed to find purchase with senior Pentagon leadership, and he was soon viewed as an old hand and outsider whose opinion was no longer relevant and whose reputation as a rule breaker was not needed.[87] His influence, then, followed Bohannan's out of Vietnam as the Tet Offensive challenged America's message of victory and peace in the near future.

Conclusion

In three wars and other missions, Bohannan brought an anthropologist's skills to military affairs. For him, the war was fundamentally a cultural as much as a physical enterprise. In his major work on counter-guerrilla operations, *Counter-Guerrilla Warfare: The Philippines Experience*, Bohannan wrote of psychological, cultural, economic, legal, and combat factors that bled into each other's domain. He believed that the guerrillas had to be separated from the population through a variety of means; that the guerrillas who could not be bargained with had to be fought; and that peace had to come at some point, or the problems of the people (almost all of which were socio-economic and culturally based) had to be addressed. Bohannan referred to this last factor as 'steal their thunder – taking political, psychological, economic, and social actions affecting both the civilians and guerrillas designed to draw support away from the guerrillas and to attract it to the government, accompanied by continuing closely coordinated combat operations against the active guerrillas.' This final factor, the most culturally oriented, was under utilized despite its potential. He warned that 'only the fourth has succeeded in achieving the objectives of antiguerrilla forces while respecting the human rights of the civilian population.'[88]

In this regard, he also indicted US soldiers in the Philippines. 'American officers were guilty of the worst crimes,' he once noted, including ones of 'moral decency (witness the signs on apartment houses requisitioned for quarters for American dependents: *Dogs and Filipinos Keep Out*).'[89] Bohannan championed Filipino clothing, learned their language, and lived among them until the day he died (in part to protest the abandoning of South Vietnam, which thoroughly disgusted him).[90] COIN required cultural acumen, shared risk, and sage appreciation of local conditions if any strategy or solution was to succeed. He proved that true in combat against the Japanese, an advisor against the Huk, and a last-ditch attempt against the Viet-Cong. Cultural empathy was never provided by the US Army, but in a career among other cultures Bohannan brought this skill to bear. His unique view of warfare was largely forgotten as the defeat of Vietnam ended the romance of counterinsurgency in US military circles. Yet, even now his career is overshadowed by his own inclination and Lansdale's fame,[91] in part to keep the shine on the foreign peoples he served.[92]

Although he was a trained archeologist, Bohannan never became a professional anthropologist. He was bound for a PhD at Harvard when the war began but never returned. And, indeed, his weaponization of culture in the service of the state may make him a marked man in some anthropological circles. Worse, his championing of using superstition against the Huk can certainly be viewed as ghoulish misuse of the ethics and standards of anthropologists of his era and today. In that regard, he was an American soldier first, amateur anthropologist second. But, his approach to warfare was shaped and bolstered by an anthropological appreciation of the value of foreign culture that removed him from the herd of most conventional soldiers of his era, and even Lansdale. From his time among the Native Americans of the Plains and New Mexico, to the headhunters of Luzon, to the working poor of Manila and Saigon, Bohannan may have arrived with the biases of a white American, but was inoculated from the worst of those biases by his training in the field and school. Anthropological understanding informed his view of war. What successes he had were predicated on this training and are impossible to consider without them.

Notes

1. Bohannan to Joseph Starr, 3 August 1981, transcribed by Claring Bohannan, Charles Ted Rutledge Bohannan Personal Papers (hereafter cited as CTRB Papers).

2. Gray, "Irregular Warfare and the Essence of Strategy," 34 http://www.strategic studiesinstitute.army.mil/pdffiles/pub650.pdf.
3. Birtle, *US Army Counterinsurgency*, 3.
4. Andrew Birtle noted the bias against COIN helped created 'amnesia within the military's corporate memory by discouraging frank and open examinations of the Army's experiences ... A final influence upon the position of small wars in Army thought was the officer corps' own self-image. American political philosophy was one factor that shaped this image. Another was the concept of officer professionalism that arose during the nineteenth century. Many officers believed that soldiers should devote themselves exclusively to purely military subjects to the exclusion of nonmilitary activities, especially politics. Such an attitude reinforced the Army's predisposition to relegate the highly political realm of small wars to the periphery of professional thought.' Birtle, 272–3.
5. The best selling though flawed work by Max Boot is the latest. See Boot, *The Road Not Taken*; Lansdale, *In the Midst of Wars*; Currey, *Edward Lansdale*; and Nashel, *Edward Lansdale's Cold War*.
6. For key texts in his career, see Carlisle, *The Red Arrow Men*; Currey, *The Unquiet American*; Bohannan and Valeriano, *Counter-Guerrilla Warfare*; Rempe, "The Past as Prologue?"; and Toland, *Captured by History*, 157.
7. Charles Bohannan, *I Am Ashamed: Confessions of a Citizen Soldier*, n.d., unpublished memoir. CTRB Papers.
8. Ibid.
9. "Charles Dudley Bohannan" *Evening Star* 18 October 1956.
10. "A Preliminary Study," 161–96.
11. *Month Catalogue of United States Government Publications*, 687, 1059. http://openlibrary.org/books/OL14029252M/Monthly_catalog_of_United_States_Government_publications.
12. Ibid.
13. Bohannan and Valeriano, 215.
14. Bohannan Lecture to AID workers, Hawaii, 14 December 1966, page 5, Rufus Philips Papers (hereafter cited as RPP).
15. Papers of Clyde Kluckhohn, University of Iowa, http://www.lib.uiowa.edu/speccoll/MSC/ToMsC650/MsC640/kluckhohn.html Kluckhohn," The Way of Life," *The Kenyon Review*
16. Roosevelt, "The Strenuous Life," 1.
17. Claring Bohannan interview by Jason S. Ridler, 10 May 2011.
18. Comments from Dorothy Bohannan on rough Draft of Unquiet America, n.d. Cecil Currey Collection, Fort Hayes State University Kansas, Forsyth Library Special Collections, Bohannan File (hereafter cited as CCC).
19. Bohannan, *I Am Ashamed*.
20. Claring Bohannan interview, 19 December 2012.
21. Bohannan, "Lecture to USAID, 13 December 1966," RPP. This author has no data on his efforts in Mexico.
22. See note 19 above.
23. McCoy interviewed Bohannan for his book *Policing America's Empire*, where he described himself in these terms. McCoy, 377.
24. See note 19 above.
25. Bohannan, "Lecture to USAID, 13 December 1966," 1.
26. Bergerud, *Touched with Fire*.

27. Bob Utley, the official historian of the national parks and expert on Native warfare, surmised these elements of how Native Americans waged war with US soldiers at the turn of the twentieth century. Despite cultural diversity, the tribes shared certain characteristics that had important military implications. Utley, *Frontier Regulars*, 5.
28. Birtle, Passim.
29. Ortner, "Aleš Hrdlička and the Founding of the *American Journal of Physical Anthropology: 1918*,"; Michael A. Little and Kenneth A. R. Kennedy, eds, *Histories of American Physical Anthropology*, 87–104; and Montgomery, *Register to the Papers of Aleš Hrdlička*, 4–11.
30. Ortner, "Aleš Hrdlička and the Founding of the *American Journal of Physical Anthropology: 1918*," passim.
31. Oppenheim, "Revisiting Hrdlička and Boas," 92–103.
32. John L. Cotter, et al., *Clovis Revisited*, 2.
33. Hrdlička, *The Anthropology of Kodiak Island*, 204.
34. ibid., 204–38.
35. CTRB papers, File: Kodiak 1934.Aleš Hrdlička 22 April 1935.
36. Gantt, "The Claude C. And Lynn Coffin Lindenmeier Collection," passim.
37. John L. Cotter letter to Dorothy Bohannan, CTRB Papers, undated, transcribed by Claring Bohannan, 27 May 2011.
38. John L. Cotter letter to Dorothy Bohannan, 19 January 1984, CTRB Papers, transcribed by Claring Bohannan on 8 July 2011.
39. CTRB Papers.
40. John L. Cotter et al., *Clovis Revisited*: 1.
41. Lyon, *A New Deal for Southeastern Archeology*, 63–7.
42. William S. Webb, quoted in Lyons, 97. CTRB Papers.
43. CTRB Papers, "Collins Letter to Dorothy Bohannan, undated."
44. Lyons, 106–107; and Lee E. Hanson, *The Hardin Village Site*, n.p.
45. Pollock interview, 15 May 2011.
46. Bohannon, *I am Ashamed*, 15 August 1944, Headquarters 128th Infantry, Roll for Infantry Man's Badge, 7 September 1944, National Archive, College Park, hereafter NARA, RG 407 WWII Operations Reports, 1940–1946 32nd Infantry Division 332 INF (128) 1.2–332 INF (128) 2.1 Box 8056, Runde, "The US Army Intelligence and Reconnaissance Platoon," 26.
47. Mailer, "The Dead Gook," *Advertisements for Myself*, 148.
48. Bohannan, "That Damn Anting-Anting," article for *Veterans Federation of the Philippines*, CTRB Papers. The identity of Jabillo was provided by his niece.
49. Interview with Claring Bohannan, August 2015.
50. Bohannan, "That Damn Anting-Anting," MacArthur pressed all the guerrillas of the Philippines to be intelligence gathering elements only and, when the official history of the guerrilla campaign was produced by the US Army (a work that is largely a collection of documents and weak on narrative and analysis), much of it bemoans the poor quality of the intelligence gathering of the Filipino guerrillas. See Willoughby, *The Guerrilla Resistance Movement in the Philippines*.
51. Carlisle, *The Red Arrow Men*, passim.
52. Interview with Bohannan's goddaughter, 2015.
53. Ridler, "The Fertile Ground of Hell's Carnival," 15–20.
54. Ibid., 15–29.
55. Bohannan and Valeriano, ebook location 446.

56. See Luis Taruc, *He Who Rides a Tiger*.
57. There are three major works on Lansdale's life, and many lesser efforts. See Currey, *The Unquiet American*; Nassell, *Edward Lansdale's Cold War*; and Max Boot, *The Road Not Taken*.
58. Ibid.
59. See the reading list for his book, *Counter-Guerrilla Warfare* for a clue to the depth of his reading on this subject. Lansdale never included such lists in his own efforts, though he was also well read.
60. Bohannan and Valeriano, location 106.
61. Bohannan, "Anti-Guerrilla Warfare," 19–29.
62. Bohannan removed any reference to his own name in *Counter-Guerrilla Warfare*, though Lansdale appears once. Bohannan makes almost no appearance in Lansdale's *In the Midst of Wars*. Writing to Bohannan after the release of the Pentagon Papers, Lansdale said, 'If only my book were being published soon, it would help. Our friends come out smelling like roses, untainted and heroic in it and against a proper background. As you know, from long ago, I decided that Asia needed its own heroes – so I've given them a whole bookfull of them, with us … merely being companionable friends to some great guys.' 18 July 1971, CCC.
63. See note 19 above.
64. This is detailed in Bohannan and Valeriano.
65. Quoted in Ridler, "A Lost Work of El Lobo," 92–312.
66. Boot, *The Road Not Taken*; and Bohannan and Valeriano, *Counter-Guerrilla Warfare*, passim.
67. Ridler, "A Lost Work of El Lobo," 300.
68. Boot, *The Road Not Taken*, 130.
69. Bohannan and Valeriano, location 1898.
70. Currey, *Edward Lansdale*, 101–2; and, Bohannan and Valeriano, location 1904.
71. See note 69 above.
72. Currey, 98.
73. For an excellent discussion of Lansdale's command of history, see Nashel, *Edward Lansdale's Cold War*, passim.
74. Kerkvliet, *The Huk Rebellion*, 239.
75. There is no effective or authoritative single volume of this campaign. Please see the following: Bohannan and Valeriano, *Counter-Guerrilla Warfare*; Kerkvliet, *The Huk Rebellion*; Lansdale, *In the Midst of Wars*; and, Boot, *The Road Not Taken*.
76. Bohannan and Valeriano, location 2057; Boot, 124–5; and Bohannan, "Lecture to USAID, December 1966."
77. Currey, 93–95; and, Dorothy Bohannan interview with Cecil Currey, 27 July 1985.
78. Bernard Fall, *The International Position of South Viet-Nam*, Part 3, 19.
79. Lansdale and Bohannan's efforts were revealed in the Pentagon Papers, referencing meetings in August 1954. See Philips, *Why Vietnam Matters*, 44; Witek, "Review, *Adventures in Viet*-Nam; Michael Bernard," 67–9; and Fall, *The International Position of South Viet-Nam*, Part 3, 19, Bernard Fall Papers, John F, Kennedy Library, Box P-1 Papers and Reports by Fall.
80. HIA Edward Geary Lansdale (EGL) Papers, Box 35, File: OPERATION BROTHERHOOD.
81. Lansdale, *In the Midst of Wars*, 95; and, interview with Claring Bohannan, August 2015.
82. Boot, 242, author interview with Bohannan, August 2015.
83. Philips, *Why Vietnam Matters*, 133–4.

84. Philip interview.
85. Currey, passim. Rufus Philip interview.
86. CTRB PP, Correspondence with Lansdale.
87. Philips, *Why Vietnam Matters*, 157; J. A. Koch, *The Chieu Hoi Program In South Vietnam, 1963–1971*; and Boot, 436, 465, 483.
88. Bohannan, "Antiguerrilla Operations," 20.
89. Bohannan, "US Objectives in the Philippines, 1946–1950," likely from 12 to 16 December 1964, 1–7. HIA Charles T. R. Bohannan Papers, Box 4, "File Bo's Drafts."
90. See note 19 above.
91. Boot's recent work on Lansdale sees Bohannan as a tough, eccentric but otherwise secondary character in the drama of Lansdale's life. It is my contention that such readings are misleading on how much these men were partners with each other and Magsaysay. See Boot, *The Road Not Taken*.
92. Bohannan, *I Am Ashamed*. Writing to Bohannan near the end of his life, Lansdale claimed "I decided that Asia needed its own heroes–so I've given them a whole book full of them, with us … merely being companionable friends to some great guys." CCC, Edward G. Lansdale to Charles T. R. Bohannan, 18 July 1971.

Acknowledgments

The author would like to thank Claring Bohannan, Rufus Philips, Mike Benge, Andrew Birtle, and Kalev Sepp for their support of this work. All errors, however, are his own.

Disclosure statement

No potential conflict of interest was reported by the author.

Funding

This paper could not have been executed without the support of the Smith Richardson Foundation 2014 Fellowship for Foreign Policy and National Security.

Bibliography

Bergerud, Eric M. *Touched with Fire: The Land War in the South Pacific*. New York: Penguin, 1997.
Birtle, Andrew J. *US Army Counterinsurgency and Contingency Operations Doctrine, 1860–1941*. Washington: Center for Military History, United States Army, 2003.

Bohannan, Charles D., and D. P. Campbell. "A Preliminary Study on the Marketing of Burley Tobacco in Central Kentucky." In *Twenty Eighth Annual Report of the Kentucky Agricultural Experiment Station for the Year 1915, Part II, Bulletin,* 161–196.

Bohannan, Charles T. R. "Anti-Guerrilla Warfare." *Annals of Political and Social Science* 341 (May 1962): 19–29. doi:10.1177/000271626234100104.

Bohannan, Charles T. R, and Napoleon Valeriano. *Counter-Guerrilla Warfare: The Philippines Experience*. Westport: Praeger Security International, 1962. Republished 2006.

Boot, Max. *The Road Not Taken: Edward Lansdale and the American Tragedy in Vietnam*. New York: Liveright, 2018.

Carlisle, John M. *The Red Arrow Men: Stories of the 32d Division on the Villa Verde Trail*. Detroit: Arnold-Powers, inc., 1945.

Cotter, John L., and Anthony T. Boldurian. *Clovis Revisited: New Perspectives on Paleoindian Adaptation from Blackwater Draw, New Mexico*. Ephreta: Science Press, 1999.

Currey, Cecil. *Edward Lansdale: The Unquiet American*. New York: Brassey's Inc, 1988.

Gantt, Erik. "The Claude C. And Lynn Coffin Lindenmeier Collection: An Innovative Method for Analysis of Privately Held Artifact Collection and New Information on a Folsom Campsite in Northern Colorado." Master's Thesis, Colorado State University, Fort Collins, 2002.

Gray, Colin S. "Irregular Warfare and the Essence of Strategy: Can the American Way of War Adapt?" *US Army Strategic Studies Institute* (March 2006): 34. http://www.strategicstudiesinstitute.army.mil/pdffiles/pub650.pdf

Hanson, Lee E. *The Hardin Village Site*. Studies in Anthropology Series Number 4. Lexington: University of Kentucky Press, 1966.

Hrdlička, Aleš. *The Anthropology of Kodiak Island*. Philadelphia: The Wistar Institute of Anatomy and Biology, 1944.

Koch, J. A. "The Chieu Hoi Program In South Vietnam, 1963–1971." *Report for the Advanced Research Project Agency*. Santa Monica: Rand Publication, 1973.

Lansdale, Edward. *In the Midst of Wars: An American's Mission to Southeast Asia*. Fordham: Fordham University Press, 1991. originally published 1972.

Linebarger, Paul. *Psychological Warfare*. Darke: Coachwhip Publications, 1947. Reprinted 2010.

Little, Michael A., and A. R. Kenneth, eds. *Histories of American Physical Anthropology in the Twentieth Century*. Lanham: Lexington Books, 2010.

Lyon, Edwin A. *A New Deal for Southeastern Archeology*. Tuscaloosa: The University of Alabama Press, 1996.

Mailer, Norman. *Advertisements for Myself*. Boston: Harvard University Press, 1959. Reprinted 1992.

McCoy, Alfred. *Policing America's Empire: The United States, the Philippines, and the Rise of the Surveillance State*. Madison: University of Wisconsin Press, 2009.

Montgomery, Robert Lynn. *Register to the Papers of Aleš Hrdlička*. Washington, DC: Smithsonian Institute, 1996. Revised by Jennifer Chien, 2006.

Nashel, Jonathan. *Edward Lansdale's Cold War*. Boston: University of Massachusetts Press, 2005.

O'Brien, Michael John, and W. Raymond Wood. *The Prehistory of Missouri*. Independence: University of Missouri Press, 1998.

Oppenheim, Robert. "Revisiting Hrdlička and Boas: Asymmetries of Race and Anti-Imperialism in Interwar Anthropology." *American Anthropologist*, 112 (March 2010), 92–103.

Parsons, T. and E. A. Shils eds., *Toward a General Theory of Action*. Cambridge, MA: Harvard University Press, 1951.

Philips, Rufus. *Why Vietnam Matters: An Eyewitness Account of Lessons Not Learned*. Annapolis: Naval Institute Press, 2008.

Rempe, Dennise. 2002. "The past as Prologue? A History of US Counterinsurgency in Colombia, 1958–1966." *Occasional Paper from the Strategic Studies Institute*, Strategic Studies Institute, March.

Reynolds, Michael. *The Young Hemingway*. New York: Norton, 1996.

Ridler, Jason S. "A Lost Work of El Lobo Lieutenant-Colonel Charles T.R. Bohannan's Unpublished Study of Guerrilla Warfare and Counterinsurgency in the Philippines, 1899–1955." *Small Wars and Insurgencies* 26, no. 2 (2015): 292–312. doi:10.1080/09592318.2015.1008088.

Ridler, Jason S. "The Fertile Ground of Hell's Carnival: Charles T. R Bohannan and the US Army Counter Intelligence Corp's Investigation of War Criminals, Collaborators, and the Huk, in the Philippines, 1945–1947." *Defense and Security Analysis* 33, no. 1 (2017): 15–29. doi:10.1080/14751798.2016.1269391.

Roberts, Frank H. H, Jr. "Edgar Billings Howard." *American Anthropologist* 45, no. 3 (1943): 452–454. doi:10.1525/aa.1943.45.3.02a00100.

Roosevelt, Theodore. *The Strenuous Life: Essays and Addresses*. New York: The Century, 1902.

Runde, Richard. "The US Army Intelligence and Reconnaissance Platoon, 1935–1965." Master's Thesis, US Army Command and General Staff College, Leavenworth, 1994. doi:10.3168/jds.S0022-0302(94)77044-2

Taruc, Luis. *He Who Rides A Tiger: A Story of an Asian Guerrilla Leader*. Melbourne: Geoffrey Chapman, 1967.

Toland, John. *Captured by History: One Man's View of Our Tumultuous Century*. New York: St. Martin's Press, 1997.

Utley, Bob. *Frontier Regulars: The United States Army and the Indian, 1866–1891*. Lincoln: University of Nebraska Press, 1973. Reprinted 1984.

Willoughby, Charles Andrew. *The Guerrilla Resistance Movement in the Philippines: 1941–1945*. US Army, Far East Command, 1948.

Witek, John. "Review, *Adventures in Viet-Nam. The Story of Operation Brotherhood, 1954–1957*, by Michael Bernad." *The Catholic Historical Review* 63, no. 1 (January 1977): 67–69.

Archaeology and small wars

Christopher Jasparro

ABSTRACT
The protection, destruction, utilization and manipulation of cultural property and material heritage, especially archaeological sites and artifacts, by state and non-state actors has become commonplace in contemporary small wars and hybrid conflicts. The U.S. and its western allies have taken a limited and largely legalistic and limited approach to this development in contemporary warfare to the advantage of adversaries who have made control of the past a key part of their strategies and operations. This paper traces the role of cultural heritage in small warfare from ancient times through its contemporary re-emergence and what the implications are for future small wars.

Introduction

In May of 2015, international audiences watched anxiously as Islamic State (IS) fighters swept towards the ancient Syrian city and UNESCO World Heritage site of Palmyra. Cultural heritage groups unsuccessfully lobbied the U.S.-led coalition to conduct air strikes to blunt IS's advance.[1] Russian President Vladimir Putin seized the opportunity to exploit this, criticizing the U.S. and its allies: 'Everything that is happening in Palmyra is the result of the uncoordinated actions between the so-called international coalition with the Syrian authorities and Russia, I have said many times that in order for the fight with terrorism to be effective we must unite our efforts.'[2] The Assad regime also saw an opportunity here, viewing the city's fall as tactical defeat but a strategic gain that might 'encourage Washington to review its Syria policy, would make U.S.-allied Jordan take greater notice of the Islamic State threat, and force Iraq to cooperate more with Syria ... '[3]

As IS fighters edged closer, Palmyra's museum staff frantically prepped their collection including Greco-Roman statuary, jewelry, ancient glass, and mosaics for evacuation as IS fighters edged closer.[4] Three were shot as they loaded the trucks that would spirit much of the collection to safety.[5] Shortly after capturing the city, IS beheaded on video 25 captives in Palmyra's Roman amphitheater.[6] In August 2015, IS beheaded Professor Khaled al-As'ad, former general manager of museums and antiquities in Palmyra, for not offering allegiance and refusing 'to reveal the location of archaeological treasures and two chests of gold the terrorists thought were in the city.'[7]

IS destroyed several of Palmyra's temples, its Arch of Triumph, part of its Roman amphitheater along with statues, monuments and nearby Sufi structures.[8] IS also exploited pre-existing looting networks to profit from antiquities trafficking. After Russian backed Syrian troops retook Palmyra in spring 2016, reports emerged of off-duty soldiers looting.[9] Russian forces helped clear mines and unexploded ordinance (they were also accused of building a base within the archaeological zone).[10] During the initial clean-up several mass graves were reportedly found. To celebrate the city's recapture, Moscow organized a concert by St. Petersburg's Mariinsky Symphony Orchestra in the Roman amphitheater (Putin looked on via a giant video screen) to demonstrate Russia's contribution to stabilizing Syria, combatting international terrorism, and protecting world heritage.[11] An international restoration effort, funded by UNESCO, Italy, Poland, and Russia is now underway. In August 2018, the Syrian government stated it hoped to re-open the site, which before the war attracted 150,000 visitors a year, to tourism in 2019.[12]

The story of Palmyra encapsulates how the material (i.e. archaeological) past has become a domain in the modern small war battlespace. The destruction or preservation of a society's material culture can be of strategic utility for combatants while threats to a group's heritage can spur resistance to occupiers. Looting may help fund combatants. Archaeological sites and investigations may become resources for post-conflict stabilization and reconstruction. The Palmyra case also illustrates many of the facets and tensions in the relationship between archaeology and the military in today's small wars which, archaeology being a cognate discipline of anthropology, parallel many features of the wider anthropology of small wars addressed in this Special Edition. This paper traces the history of the role of archaeologists in small wars and the use of archaeology for and by militaries (and other combatants) during and after conflict including the use archaeological resources as targets and resources from the small wars of the 19th century to those of today.

Two broad conclusions are drawn. First, the main facets of the archaeology-military relationship in small wars have persisted over time but the contexts and actors have changed. One key change has been a role reversal between western countries and non-state and non-western actors in places such as the Middle East. Furthermore, in western countries (particularly anglophone ones) the military-archaeology relationship has bi-furcated. The second reflects this role reversal and bifurcation. So while, the U.S. and other western militaries are improving their capability to not harm cultural heritage sites, they have yet to systematically consider the material past from a strategic point of view or as key terrain in the contemporary battlespace unlike many of their state and non-state adversaries now do. These adversaries thus have an advantage in contemporary small and hybrid wars that western militaries and archaeologists are ill-prepared to counter.

Ancient antecedents

The destruction and looting of material cultural heritage by combatants to reinforce victors' physical and cultural dominance and to remind the vanquished of the loss of their political, cultural and religious freedom dates back to antiquity.[13] Indeed, it is fitting that much of the drama enacted out in Palmyra took place in a Roman theater since the Romans were sophisticated practitioners of destroying and manipulating material heritage in small wars. The Romans essentially re-organized and re-wrote entire landscapes to pacify indigenous resistance.[14] (Roman emperor Aurelian razed Palmyra in 273 AD as part of putting down several local rebellions). Contemporary debates about the propriety and utility of destroying cultural heritage have their roots in Roman times.[15]

The Romans destroyed Jerusalem's Second Temple in 70 AD, while crushing a Jewish insurgency. The decision-making around the destruction illustrates the enduring tension between heritage protection and destruction (and how to portray it) that, as the Palmyra case attests, still persists. Jewish historian and eye-witness Josephus Flavius (first an opponent and then ally of Rome), claimed Roman general Titus was against destroying the temple because, 'burning down so vast a work as that was, because this would be a mischief to the Romans themselves, as it would be an ornament to their government while it continued.'[16] Josephus blames the destruction on Roman soldiers' detestation of the insurgents and desire for loot.[17] The 4th century AD Christian historian Severus conversely claimed that Titus debated but favored destruction

> Titus summoned his council, and before taking action consulted it whether he should overthrow a sanctuary ... For if preserved it would testify to the moderation of the Romans, while if demolished it would be a perpetual sign of cruelty. On the other hand, others, and Titus himself, expressed their opinion that the Temple should be destroyed without delay, in order that the religion of the Jews and Christians should be more completely exterminated.[18]

Whatever the truth, it is significant that even, 'ancient historians recognized that both the destruction of the Temple and its preservation had discrete advantages to a victorious power.'[19]

Twins are born: 19th-early 20th centuries

Although the destruction, manipulation and protection of archaeological resources in war has ancient ancestry, its present manifestation, along with other elements of the archaeology-military relationship in small wars, was birthed in the late 19th and early 20th centuries. Many scholars date the origin of modern concepts for using and protecting cultural heritage in war and the discipline of archaeology to the Napoleonic Wars. The looting of art and heritage protection provisions can be found in postwar conventions and codes of conduct. Whilst the first systematic survey of Egypt's archaeological remains was conducted by scientists attached to Napoleon's invasion force; their work became the foundation 'for the eventual institutionalization of the discipline.'[20] Western concepts and theories of small wars and insurgency/counterinsurgency (COIN) harken to the 19th century[21] with the rise of the modern state, imperialism, and decolonization.[22] Similarly, the academic discipline of archaeology emerged from 19th century scientific advances (particularly in geology and evolutionary biology), industrialism, and imperialism. War and archaeology have remained relatives ever since, especially in the Middle East. The practices of modern archaeology and small warfare can thus be thought of as fraternal twins of a sort.

This relationship matured and became tightest during the heyday of European imperial expansion and colonialism in the 19th and early 20th centuries. Archaeological excavation and the acquisition of antiquities became a grey area of imperial competition. Archaeological research was employed to legitimize colonial occupation and battlefield archaeology and provided lessons for the conduct of colonial small warfare. For instance, 'in French Algeria and Tunisia archaeology was used to fasten the ancient past of an unrelated culture to the historical identity of the metropole and legitimize the act of colonization itself.'[23] The examination of the archaeological remains of ancient campaigns by French officers, ' ... would provide the means through which France could learn the colonizing methods of their classical forbearers. As one military official stated, "every vestige of [Roman] domination in this country is a lesson for us."'[24]

The contemporary convergence between war and antiquities trafficking has antecedents in the 19th century and early 20th century looting by military forces, the removal of artifacts from excavations in colonial and conquered territories to imperial metropoles, and in the diplomats, soldiers (many of whom were amateur archaeologists), and archaeologists who engaged with looters and smugglers to acquire antiquities for museums. By the 1920's growing anger at this appropriation of antiquities helped stoke anti-western nationalist movements which, in turn, spurred many 20th century anti-colonial insurgencies. This nationalism also led to constraints being placed upon western excavations by indigenous archaeologists fed up with the days when 'imperial writ [could] uproot another nation's past.'[25] That animosity and suspicion towards foreign researchers has persisted today and its effects undergird present debates concerning the archaeology-military relationship.

> I say, have you seen this – they want you [Sir Mortimer Wheeler] as – "Director General of Archaeology in India!" – Why, you must be rather a king-pin at this sort of thing! You know, I thought you were a regular soldier![26]

This quotes highlights how blurred the line between military (and intelligence) officers and archaeologists was. Where one role ended and the other began was not always clear while the interpretation and physical appropriation of the material past were woven into the conduct of military operations.

For Britain, imperial expansion following the Napoleonic Wars 'brought with it incessant "policing actions" and colonial wars ... and throughout the nineteenth century there were only nine years when the nation was not campaigning in one way or another.'[27] Imperial service provided opportunities for antiquarian and archaeological activities amongst officers who were encouraged and given leave for travel and research to pursue scientific interests such as writing for journals and collecting for museums.[28] According to Cambridge University archaeologist, Christopher Evans, the military contribution to social sciences 'particularly one such as archaeology that is so bound up with both topographic mapping and the large-scale deployment of labour' is underappreciated yet fundamental.[29] Officers had training trained in skills such as survey, mapping, and landscape sketching on which much of the scientific basis for archaeological fieldwork was subsequently built. Some of these officers became important figures in the establishment of archaeology as a scientific discipline and/or notable small warriors.

An illustrative case is that of Lieutenant-General Pitt-Rivers, oft referred to as the 'father of scientific archaeology'[30] who began his career in artillery and engineering, fields in which industrialization and advances in science, required officers with a degree of technical competence and scientific acumen.[31] His military service as a quartermaster, artillery officer, and engineer developed skills he later applied to archaeological fieldwork: logistics, surveying and mapping, accuracy in topographic description and landscape analysis, and systematic typological collection.[32] Pitt-River's systematic approach to excavation was a major influence on the aforementioned Sir Mortimer Wheeler who, although a career solider, is also 'considered one of the world's first professional archaeologists' helped establish modern archaeology by bringing military rigor and discipline to archaeological practice.[33] As archaeology began formalizing as discipline, scholars obtained more overseas field experience developing skills useful for intelligence work and irregular warfare. A World War I Italian officer noted, 'Archaeologists were found particularly useful in "I" [intelligence] work, because their training rendered them thoroughly capable of weighing, sifting, and coordinating evidence, deducing accurate or at least reasonable conclusions.'[34] Archaeologists also spoke local languages, had experience leading host nation workers, understood local political dynamics, and possessed survey and mapping skills. Facility with deciphering ancient languages was also useful for codebreaking. Many also possessed tactically relevant skills and experience such as land navigation, riding, shooting and combatting bandits or hostile locals.

The story of the Palestinian Exploration Fund (PEF) encapsulates the closeness of the relationship for the British in the Middle East. The PEF was founded in 1867 by a group of academics and clergy whose purpose 'was investigating the Archaeology, Geography, Geology and Natural History of Palestine.'[35] The PEF had close ties to the British Army which was interested in surveying and mapping the region. The PEF ultimately produced a ten volume series covering archaeological features, fauna, flora, Jerusalem, and place names (including maps of Jerusalem and transliteration) surveyed from Tyre to Wadi Ghazza on 1:63,360 scale maps that proved useful in later military campaigns. Numerous British small warriors and intelligence officers including Horatio Kitchener, Charles Warren, Charles Wilson, Claude Conder, David Hogarth, Stuart Newcombe, and T.E. Lawrence worked with the Palestine Exploration Fund (PEF) early in their careers. For Victorian small warriors such as Kitchener, Warren, Wilson and Condor archaeological survey and excavation in Palestine provided opportunities to hone skills in mapping, sketching, surveying, and working with indigenous populations.

PEF expeditions and civilian archaeologists were used as cover for intelligence purposes. In 1914 a survey of Ottoman territory in southern Palestine and the Sinai was conducted under cover of a PEF archaeological expedition, led by then Captain Stuart Newcombe of the Royal Engineers with Leonard Wooley and T.E. Lawrence (they later produced a scholarly publication called *The Wilderness of Zinn*). The ruse was suggested by then Major C.E. Caldwell (better known today as the author of *Small Wars Their Principles and Practice*) in order to 'increase the likelihood that the Ottomans would grant permission for the expedition.'[36] Prior to the expedition, Wooley and Lawrence had been excavating at Carchemish (the permit was secured by David Hogarth then Keeper of Oxford's Ashmolean Museum in Oxford) in 1910 where they 'seemed more focused on the progress of the Bagdad Railway than on digging.'[37]

France also combined military and archaeological activity in the Middle East. For example, in 1855 it dispatched Biblical scholar Ernest Renan to survey ancient Phoenicia and acquire antiquities for the Louvre with a division of pickaxe and spade-wielding soldiers at his disposal.[38] In 1868 fighting erupted between tribesmen backing a French attempt to document a Moabite stone (now in the Louvre) with Bedouin, aided by the stones' Prussian discoverer.[39] In 1869 when France occupied Lebanon to quell a civil war and protect Maronite Christians, the 7000-man strong French force included a scientific corps tasked with, among other things, archaeological survey.[40]

North Africa, however, was where the French mastered the application of archaeology to support colonial conquest and COIN. 'As the principal instrument of French imperialism the military directly interacted with the ancient past, physically appropriated it, politicized it, and created narratives in which the Armée d'Afrique became the direct' heir to Roman garrisons.[41] France saw itself as the successor of Rome and archaeological research was used to create narratives to justify occupation of former Roman territories. Furthermore, French officers saw that the Romans offered a strategic blueprint for conquest and tactical insights for occupying key terrain.

> Archaeological reconnaissance became vital to the success of the Armée d'Afrique's campaign and it was common practice for French units to establish strongholds within Roman forts or use Roman grain silos as stores for provisions. Additionally, Roman aqueducts and cisterns provided a thirsty army with water and the extensive network of Roman roads provided the infantry and their artillery with relatively uninterrupted access across uneven terrain.[42]

French officers and entire units were involved in archaeological work such as when the Foreign Legion's 2nd Regiment was ordered to conduct an archaeological survey of a Roman site at Lambaesus in 1848.[43]

In Central Asia during the late 19th and early 20th centuries archaeology was deeply intertwined with intelligence activities and small wars in Central Asia. Archaeological expeditions in Central Asia became extensions of the Great Game.[44] Archaeological discovery and imperial prestige went hand in hand as countries such as Russian, Britain, France, Germany, Japan and others competed for influence in Central Asia. Expeditions provided opportunities for mapping that supported geopolitical posturing as well as small war campaigning. Another aim of European and western expeditions was to rediscover ancient Asian civilizations and prove how the western civilization like ancient Greece influenced them.[45] This, in turn, was used to support imperial claims on grounds of cultural superiority and precedence.

Imperial prerogative sanctioned the expropriation of antiquities as 'caravan loads of artefacts made their way west to museums in London, Paris, Berlin and St Petersburg.'[46] One representative illustration of the blurring of imperial competition, intelligence, archaeology, and looting occurred in 1890. British Indian Army intelligence officer Captain Hamilton Bower discovered evidence of an ancient Buddhist civilization in the Taklamakan Desert which spurred competition for antiquities amongst European, America, and Japanese diplomats and scholars that then birthed an industry for counterfeiting old books.[47]

The lines between war and archaeology and soldier-archaeologist-spy were often blurred amongst players of the Great Game. Charles Masson (pseudonym of James Lewis) excavated around 50 sites in the Kabul-Jalalabad region of Afghanistan in the 1820s and 1830s and was first European to find Harappa. He was a British Army deserter and was co-opted to spy for the Britain in exchange for pardon.[48]

Sir Marc Aurel Stein (named appropriately after Roman Emperor Marcus Aurelius) learned surveying and cartography as a young man in the Hungarian military, became a civil servant in the Indian Archaeological Service and an overt player of the Great Game who also became the 'preeminent Western scholar, explorer and excavator of Central Asia' in the late 19th and early 20th centuries. He was also a pioneer of using aerial photography to locate sites (a technique which would also become valuable for military intelligence).[49] His first major expedition surveyed the ancient Graeco-Buddhist kingdom of Gandhara in 1897–98 while attached to General Blindon Blood's 'butcher and beat it' raid into the North-West Frontier.[50]

Although Stein was a scholar, his research provided the Raj with strategic intelligence and many of his maps were classified; throughout his career he was dogged by the suspicions of local rulers who deemed him a spy.[51] Wooley called Stein's achievements as 'the most daring and adventurous raid on the ancient world that any archaeologist had attempted.'[52] The metaphor of the raid is apt (though Wooley undoubtedly meant in in complimentary fashion). The take from his expeditions filled rooms in the British Museum and the Museum of Central-Asian Antiquities in Delhi, 182 packing cases were required to transport the finds of his 1913–1916 expedition alone.[53]

The military-archaeology line was blurry for Russians too. The Russian General Staff established its own Scientific Military Committee and dispatched surveying expeditions for topographic mapping, intelligence collection and charting 'the ruins of old temples and fortresses.'[54] The Russian Geographical Society was founded in 1845 in part to study 'foreign countries, primarily those that border on Russia, i.e. Turkey, Persia, China, etc.' with the Russian Archaeological Society being established in its wake in 1847. Many of the expeditions undertaken by the solider-intelligence officer-explorer Nikolai Przhevalsky were done on behalf of the Russian Geographical Society (often using military funds). He asserted that his 'scientific research will camouflage the political goals of the expedition and should discourage any interference by our adversaries' and argued for archaeological investigations to be conducted in places of strategic interest such as Eastern Turkestan.[55]

Another Russian soldier-archaeologist, Colonel (later General) Mikhail Pevtsov continued Przhevalsky's work in the 1889–1890 expedition to Tibet that mapped southern Turkestan and surveyed archaeological ruins and ancient monuments.[56] The diplomat and archaeologist Nikolai Petrovsky became Russian Consul in Kashgar backed by a small Cossack force in 1882 and became the *de facto* ruler of Turkestan for over 20 years.[57] Called the 'New Genghis Khan' by locals,[58] he was also a prolific excavator and collector of antiquities known for his 'brilliant finds [that] ushered in a new era in the archaeological study of Eastern Turkestan.'[59]

World War I was arguably the heyday for archaeologists as intelligence agents and irregular warriors. The most famous of these was T.E. Lawrence who began his career and garnered his knowledge of Arab culture and language as an archaeologist in the Middle East. Other British professional and amateur archaeologists also served in the Middle East theater as soldiers and intelligence or political officers including: Gertrude Bell, J.E. Taylor (one of the first to study the Sumerians), Henry Rawlinson (decipherer of cuneiform), and A.H. Ledyard (who surveyed Nineveh)[60] as well as D.G. Hogarth. James Henry Breasted, an American Egyptologist, was recruited by General Allenby 'to provide advice to the British government on how best to work with, control, and govern the native Arab peoples to whom they had promised so much in return for Arab support during the War' and in 1920 collected intelligence while conducting an epigraphic survey spanning Egypt to India via Iraq, Syria, and Lebanon.[61]

German archaeologists were similarly engaged. Diplomat and amateur archaeologist, Count Max von Oppenheim discovered the Neolithic ruins of Tel Halaf and helped bring Turkey into the War on the side of the Central Powers. He subsequently directed subversion and sabotage efforts in the Middle East and Central Asia including an attempt to foment an anti-British Muslim insurrection.[62]

Archaeologists played a role in the irregular and intelligence competition between the Germans and Americans in Latin America. Mayan specialist Sylvanus Morley has been called 'the finest American spy of World War I'[63] for his work as an Office of Naval Intelligence (ONI) agent. Other U.S. Central American specialists served as ONI operatives including: John Alden Mason, Samuel Lathrop, Thomas Gann, and Herbert Spinden.[64]

Following World War I, the archaeology-military relationship began to weaken and bifurcate as the high point of colonial conquest and imperial competition waned and resistance to external excavations and appropriation of antiquities grew. Academic archaeology and post-war officer corps were developing and maturing as separate and increasingly professionalized disciplines. By World War II, archaeological cover had also worn thin for military and intelligence operations.

During World War II archaeologists served in irregular and unconventional operations, although in less prominently than their World War I predecessors. American archaeologists in Greece, for instance, were recruited by the Office of Strategic Services (OSS) to conduct intelligence and unconventional warfare and partisan operations in the Balkans.[65] Harvard archaeologist-anthropologist Carleton Coon, fought with the OSS in North Africa while fellow archaeologist-anthropologist Charles Bohannan proved adept as an unconventional solider in the Philippines and later became a key COIN operator during the early Cold War (see the article by Jason Ridler in this issue). Louis Dupree also fought behind the lines in the Philippines and then attended Harvard after the war as a student and protégé of Coon's. Dupree became the preeminent American archaeologist on Afghanistan whose book *Afghanistan a Cultural and Political History* is still recommended reading for deploying American troops.[66] Others served as intelligence analysts and regional specialists for the military and OSS.[67] The Federal Bureau of Investigation (FBI) also recruited American archaeologists working in Guatemala to keep tabs on Germans.

The main military-archaeology tie in WW II was a conventional one with the establishment of allied Monuments, Fine Arts, and Archives (MFAA) sections (aka Monuments Men). However, their formation heralded a shift in the role of archaeology and archaeologists in western militaries from the exploitation of cultural heritage and archaeology to its protection and its use to support information operations and post-war reconstruction Furthermore, after WWII, a series of international humanitarian conventions were established in hopes of avoiding future devastation, including the 1954 Hague Convention on the Protection of Cultural Property in the Event of Armed Conflict.[68] The key provisions oblige signatories to safeguard cultural property by refraining from using it in ways that could expose it to destruction or directing hostility against it unless required by 'military necessity' (a term which is not specifically defined).[69] The convention also contains somewhat unspecific language for military forces to prevent theft, looting, and vandalism. These developments became the basis for how military-archaeology issues have been approached in recent small wars in western militaries.

As the Cold War progressed, cultural heritage protection considerations in the west fell by the wayside and military MFAA capabilities atrophied further weaken the connection between militaries and the discipline of archaeology and by the Korean War no MFAA section or equivalent unit was available in the U.S. military.[70] However, the Soviets did keep up the Tsarist practice of appropriating and (re) interpreting archaeological sites for supporting nationalist cultural and territorial claims (along with attempts to profit from cultural tourism by controlling sites and appropriating artworks).[71] In China archaeology was, similarly, used to bolster historical claims and regime strategic communications.[72]

In the U.S. the main Cold War impact on the military-archaeology relationship stemmed from controversy over the manner in which anthropological information and anthropologists were employed in support of COIN operations in Vietnam. This led the American Anthropological Association to establish a code of ethics (eschewing engagement with the military). Subsequent academic research critiqued the discipline's colonial origins and complicity in imperialism.[73] By the end of the Cold War the relationship could be considered one of bi-furcation and estrangement.

Reversal and bifurcation: late 20th-early 21st centuries

In the small wars of the post-Cold War era the nexus between archaeology and war as well as controversies around the military-archaeology relationship have re-surfaced. There has been a role reversal with non-state and non-western actors targeting and exploiting archaeological resources and cultural heritage to achieve their goals in ways similar to how former imperial powers did. Western powers, on the other hand, have been slow to respond to the renewed importance of the material past in contemporary conflict. In general their response has been focused first on minimizing their own impacts on cultural sites and secondarily on protecting sites and combatting looting and trafficking while post-conflict uses of archaeology have also become relatively more important. Meanwhile the relationship between the military and academic archaeology has remained largely bifurcated, aside from a small network of officers and archaeologists working on cultural heritage protection issues.

The intentional destruction of cultural heritage to humiliate and dominate enemies has returned and become more frequent and intense.[74] Archaeological sites have become objects of low-intensity conflict such as the 2008 border skirmishes that erupted between Cambodia and Thailand over the ruins of Preah Vihear Temple. Insurgents and terrorists target cultural heritage (including archaeological sites, museums and artifacts) to promote their cause, intimidate and incite opponents, build territorial legitimacy and procure resources.[75] In the Balkan conflicts of the 1990s all intentionally targeted heritage sites. For instance, Croat forces destroyed the 16th century Stary Most bridge, a symbol of both Bosnian culture and interethnic unity, to ' ... destroy the enemy's cultural identity ... '[76] Elsewhere in the Balkans foreign jihadists targeted Christian sites and traditional local mosques and ceremonies and Bosnian forces attacked Serbian Orthodox churches.[77]

In 2001 the Taliban destroyed the Bamian Buddhas to 'erase evidence of pluralism in Afghan culture, within Islam, and between civilizations'[78] and to humiliate local populations.[79] These decisions were not foregone acts of mindless iconoclasm. They were debated and contested within the Taliban and between the Taliban and al-Qaeda. Like Titus, the Taliban leadership had to weigh the pros and cons of destruction versus preservation. At one point, Mullah Omar himself proclaimed the statues would be protected.[80]

When jihadist fighters overran northern Mali in 2012 they deliberately destroyed tombs to erase 'the physical legacy of Sufi Islam.'[81] The tension between destruction and preservation also played out amongst jihadist leaders when Al Qaeda in the Islamic Maghreb leader Abdelmalek Droukdel admonished his fighters and other jihadist leaders for their shortsightedness.[82] Local populations turned against the invaders and residents and cultural heritage personnel took great risks to save thousands of religious manuscripts from possible destruction.[83]

IS has conducted the most systematic and extensive campaign against cultural heritage in recent times. IS strategically targeted and, as Boston University archaeologist Michael Danto explains, manipulated material heritage to tie 'it into history, providing a back story to itself and showing it is part of this massive unstoppable force to appeal to young fighters.'[84] The group destroyed Mesopotamian, Byzantine, Roman, Ottoman, Christian and Shia sites in order to intimidate opponents, re-write history, mark territory and incite sectarian conflict. IS destroyed Christian, Shia and Sufi sites in Mosul to erase competing religious symbols from the landscapes and terrorize their adherents. The strategic thinking underlying IS' campaign against cultural heritage was foreshadowed during the earlier American occupation of Iraq. U. S. Army Lieutenant General Daniel Bolger called Al-Qaeda in Iraq's 2006 bombing and destruction of the Askariya shrine's Golden Dome its greatest single attack because it plunged the country into sectarian war undermining the U.S. effort in Iraq in a single blow.[85]

Mohamed Ahmad al-Sayani, chair of Yemen's General Organization of Antiquities and Museums, claims over 60 sites have been damaged or destroyed since 2015 mainly from Saudi airstrikes in an deliberate attempt to destroy Yemen's heritage and demoralize its citizens. This is despite UNESCO having given the Saudis detailed coordinates of significant heritage sites which some archaeologist fear were used for targeting rather than protection.[86]

Archaeology has become a feature of the proxy and hybrid conflicts in the gray zone between conventional conflict and irregular warfare. Russia has the use of archaeology to support nationalist and territorial claims (along with profiting from cultural tourism by controlling sites and appropriating artworks).[87] Russia's connection to classical Greek sites has been spun to validate Putin's argument that 'Russia should continue its civilizing mission on the Eurasian continent.'[88] In 2011 Putin made international headlines in a staged scuba dive in which he 'recovered' two ancient Greek urns from the site of Phangoria, a submerged classical city on the Black Sea across the Kerch strait from Crimea whose kings Russian nationalists have adopted as proto-Russians.[89] In March 2014, Putin referenced Khersones to help justify the annexation of Crimea[90] and in 2015 he joined a survey of a Byzantine wreck off Sevastopol (an event which was also timed to celebrate the Russian Geographical Society's 170th year anniversary)[91] to further promote Russian ties to Crimea.

The use and control of the past have again become an important tool of Chinese statecraft and conflict. President Xi Jinping 'has cloaked himself in the mantle of tradition more thoroughly than any Chinese leader since the imperial system collapsed in 1911'[92] and his ideological program explicitly employs traditional cultural imagery. Underwater archaeology is being employed in China's hybrid and gray area campaign to control the South China Sea to bolster China's claims that it discovered, named, and explored the Paracel and Spratly islands first and thus has historic rights.[93] Like 19th century Great Game competitors, the Chinese are now evoking the Silk Road as a subject of archaeological research and are conducting seaborn archaeological expeditions focused on the 'Maritime Silk Road' to validate Beijing's maritime and naval aspirations.[94] China launched its first first-purpose built archaeological research vessel in 2014, which in addition to state of the art scientific capabilities is 'armed to the teeth.'[95]

Antiquities trafficking is a lucrative transnational criminal activity garnering an estimated US$2.2 billion per year.[96] The trade has converged with insurgency and terrorism; archaeological sites are vulnerable to opportunistic looting when state authority collapses. Systematic exploitation by armed groups seeking funding or profit and 'operations against terrorist organizations are now more likely to intersect with antiquities looting and trafficking as well.'[97] For example, decades of conflict in Afghanistan has made antiquities looting and trafficking commonplace and more organized, mostly for subsistence reasons but with some involvement by armed groups as well.[98]

During civil unrest following the 1991 Gulf War, numerous Iraqi regional museums were looted while previously opportunistic pilfering at archaeological sites evolved into organized criminal enterprises.[99] The 2003 invasion of Iraq unleashed an outbreak of looting which impacted up to 10% of the country's 10,000 recognized archaeological sites per year by 2008,[100] with insurgents joining the trade. In the Syrian civil war, insurgents (IS in particular) turned to antiquities trafficking as a major source of funding and looting became a form of employment ISIS could offer in occupied areas.[101] Captured documents indicate that IS had gone as far as formally integrating antiquities trafficking into its bureaucracy and finances.[102]

Insurgent and terrorist groups in Yemen including the Houthis, al-Qaeda and IS are profiting from antiquities trafficked from Yemen to western markets terrorist organizations in the region. Al-Qaeda has been blamed for raiding museums in Yemen while receipts for around $5 million worth of antiquities sold were found in a raid on an IS financier's house.[103] In the Philippines, looters excavate coastal and estuarine sites, among the looters are rumored to be New People's Army guerilla seeking to finance their insurgency.[104]

Archaeology has also become important in the aftermath of war. Archaeological-based heritage tourism has been used to facilitate postwar reconstruction and development and archaeological remains have served as symbols of reconciliation and national unity.[105] The recruitment of former combatants to serve in site protection forces or as guides can also be used to facilitate disarmament, demobilization, and reintegration (DDR) programs by providing jobs for demobilized government forces and former combatants.[106]

As in conflict, there is tension post-conflict between what to protect and for what purposes. Cases from Bosnia, Kosovo, Israel and elsewhere show that 'if managed by local groups sensitively, heritage sites can advance reconciliation and reunification. Equally the past can be misused in the present to deny previous atrocities or inflame inter-communal tensions.'[107] For example, Angkor Wat, Cambodia's main tourist attraction, has played a role in symbolic and economic reconstruction.[108] Tourism is now the largest sector of the economy exceeding 12% of GDP.[109] In 2017, Angkor Archaeological Park generated US$100 million from 2.5 million visitors.[110] Conversely disagreements have arisen between over how to balance protection and development pitting international, national, and local interests against each other.[111] Similarly, the reconstruction of Kabul's archaeological museum in the aftermath of the Taliban's defeat raised questions over whether this reflected the desires of ordinary Afghans wanted or foreigners and Afghan elites. (This issue was made more complicated by early 20th century efforts of ruling elites to use archaeology and the establishment of the national museum for state building generated popular resentment and helped spur the replacement of a secular oriented king with and Islamist government).[112]

With the end of the Cold War and the eruption of ethnic small wars in the Cold War's aftermath, missing persons investigations 'have become a central feature in societies emerging from conflict ... [and] Forensic archaeology has become a key part of such investigations'[113] for a mix of reasons from prosecution and attribution, truth and reconciliation, human rights and humanitarian (i.e. helping families of victims).

Forensic archaeology and archaeologists have been used to investigate mass killings and find victims of Cold War era conflicts in places such as Cyprus, Guatemala, El Salvador Guatemala, Colombia, and Angola. For instance, the Guatemalan Forensic Anthropology Foundation (FARG) has uncovered more than 10,000 sets of human remains with the goal of determining cause of death and identity to return the remains 'to families who have been searching for their mothers, fathers, sons and daughters for decades.'[114] Evidence gathered by FARG (and others) has also been used to help prosecute former high-ranking military officials.[115] Forensic archaeologists deployed to the Balkans and Rwanda in support of UN International Criminal Tribunals for the former Yugoslavia (ICTY) and Rwanda.[116] Forensic teams from 14, mainly NATO, countries operating on behalf ICTY exhumated over 4000 bodies between 1999 and 2000 in Kosovo.[117] U.S. Army Corps of Engineer archaeologists supported COIN operations and the U.S. Department of Justice Iraq Mass Graves Teams following the overthrow of the Hussein regime.[118]

Forensic and traditional archaeology are being used to treat the physical and emotional wounds of small war veterans and their families. The Defense

POW/MIA Accounting Agency is tasked with accounting for all missing U.S. service men and women from large and small wars alike. In furtherance of this task it employees mixed teams of active duty military personnel and forensic anthropologists and archaeologists. The identification and recovery of missing Vietnam War serviceman plays an important role for the emotional healing of families and veterans alike while improving relations between the U.S. and Vietnam.[119]

'Rehabilitation archaeology' is a new approach that applies training and participation in archaeological fieldwork to help veterans of Iraq and Afghanistan recover from wounds and trauma and to reintegrate into civilian life. Such programs are in effect the flip side of the historic use of archaeologists' skills for and in the military. According to the British MoD, 'There is a close correlation between the skills required by the modern soldier and those of the professional archaeologist. These skills include surveying, geophysics (for ordnance recovery or revealing cultural heritage sites), scrutiny of the ground (for improvised explosive devices or artifacts), site and team management, mapping, navigation and the physical ability to cope with hard manual work in often-inclement weather conditions.'[120]

Former Air Force captain and co-founder of American Veterans Archaeological Recovery (AVAR) of Stephen Humphreys explains

> A large number of veterans struggle with isolation and disempowerment, either because of their injuries or disabilities, or because the rules and experiences in the civilian world are so different from what they have been through. The adventure, camaraderie, and sense of accomplishment that come from participating in archaeological digs directly address these problems.[121]

Operation Nightingale (now Operation Nightingale Heritage) was started by the British Ministry of Defence (MoD) to help rehabilitate soldiers returning from Afghanistan. . Similarly, the Task Force Dagger Foundation (which provides support to wounded veterans of US Special Operations Command) and East Carolina University, for example, have developed a rehabilitation program for special operators who have served in Iraq and Afghanistan using underwater archaeological surveys of WWII sites in the Northern Mariana Islands.

Due to advances in technology, methods and theory since the late 1980s, battlefield archaeology matured and emerged as a 'legitimate field of inquiry in archaeology, anthropology and history.'[122] Battlefield archaeology contributes insights to the wider anthropology and archaeology of war as well as decision-making in battle[123] (as the French colonial forces discovered in North Africa). The corrective information and new lessons derived from battlefield archaeology can help ensure that the wrong lessons are not learned from history and applied to contemporary operations.

Battlefield archaeology, for instance, is adding to (and in some cases helping re-write) the histories and lessons learned about small wars and insurgencies across time and space from Roman fights with Germanic tribes to Indian Wars in North America to the Zulu War in Africa. For example, underwater archaeological investigations into the sinking of the USS Housatonic by the confederate semi-submersible Hunley in 1864 during the U.S. Civil War demonstrated the attack was an early example of asymmetric maritime warfare by insurgents (foreshadowing the contemporary use of stealthy, semi-submersible and explosive craft to attack conventional ships by the Sea Tigers of the LTTE and Al-Qaeda and smuggling operations of Colombian cartels and Chinese organized crime). Nonetheless, the bi-furcation of the military and academic archaeology has limited the dissemination to, and application of, such results into professional military education and contemporary operational thinking.

The demand for social scientists to provide cultural expertise engendered by the wars in Iraq and Afghanistan and other theaters in the war on terror led to archaeologists volunteering to assist and advise military forces. For example, after 911, U.S. government agencies reached out to Near Eastern Archaeology and Egyptology programs in hopes of hiring translators and interpreters. A small number of archaeologists served on Human Terrain Teams (HTTs) in the Middle East. Unlike in earlier conflicts, however, archaeologists only played a minor role in these areas. The main use of archaeologists in this conflict has been in advising and assisting military forces to identify and avoid targeting and damaging cultural property, combatting antiquities trafficking, and in support of forensic investigations.

The involvement of archaeologists with the military in all three of these areas re-opened previously mentioned ethical debates. Debate over archaeologists as cultural specialists occurred within the larger context of debate over the participation of anthropologists in war, so will not be discussed in detail here. The employment of archaeologists as forensic investigators[124] and in CHP has spurred specific debate in archaeological circles which parallels wider debates in anthropology but some archaeologically specific angles. The debates have served to reflect and sustain the bifurcation in the military-archaeology relationship.

Critics focus on three main concerns. First, that support of military operations expose academic archaeologists to being perceived and targeted as spies. Second, that any work for the military shows, by default, political advocacy for specific wars or policies. A subset of this argument is that archaeologists working for the military privilege the protection of sites over human life.[125] Third, critics argue that practice of archaeology reinforces western domination of others due to its imperial past and roots in western culture, thus western archaeologists working with them military perpetuate 'structural violence'[126] against other cultures.

On the other side, pragmatists contend protecting cultural heritage is a goal in its own right and neither requires or implies support for military objectives. For example, Laurie Rush argues that the goals of archaeologists working with the military are stewardship and preservation and fulfilling legal requirements under the Hague Convention and other statutes which are thus inherently different than providing cultural expertise to combat forces.[127] She also posits that the military-archaeology partnership has been based on archaeological not military terms and has included professional organizations such as the AIA along with local archaeologists and communities.[128] Some pragmatists argue that allowing the destruction of cultural heritage by refusing to work with the military is itself unethical. There is also a small third camp, consisting mainly of serving military personnel with archaeological backgrounds, who argue protecting cultural heritage makes good military sense and thus should be pursued for both preservationist and military reasons.

Conclusion

The role of archaeology and its relationship to military operations has been reprised and fused in the small wars of the post-Cold War era, where once again the material past has become and object and resource of war. For many non-state actors (insurgents, terrorists, criminals) as well as emerging powers like Russia and China, the past is again a domain in the battlespace and archaeology and archaeological resources have become strategic and military ways and means. Instead of western colonial and imperial powers employing archaeological methods and research to achieve their aims or profiting from the expropriation artifacts and antiquities, it is their non-western opponents.

In practice, the focus of U.S. and other western militaries and security establishments has been legalistic and defensive focused primarily on primarily on impact avoidance and minimizing the damage to sites from their own actions (and the potential blowback that results) and compliance with the Hague Convention and secondarily on countering antiquities trafficking that supports insurgent and terrorist groups. Serious attention to post-Cold war heritage protection issues did not happen until the looting of the Baghdad Museum in 2003 and subsequent threats to Iraqi archaeological sites came to light in the wake of the U.S. invasion of Iraq. The later actions by IS added attention and urgency. Initial actions were largely bottom-up ones pushed by military officers with archaeological and other related backgrounds, civilian archaeologists working for the military (mainly on domestic bases in compliance with environmental and cultural resource regulations), and concerned academics. Most of the effort had been on identifying sensitive sites for inclusion on 'no-strike' lists and for inclusion in intelligence preparation of the battlespace (IPB) products. Other actions being taken (to varying degrees in different militaries) include the formation of specialized cultural protection units or inclusion of archaeologists and relates specialists into civil affairs units, training for deploying troops, education (cultural heritage protection is included in the U.S. Army ROTC curriculum and electives are on the books at the U.S. Naval War College and U.S. Air War College), and development of doctrine (by NATO for instance).

Broader governmental initiatives are also being pursued in various western countries. There are also international efforts under the aegis of UNESCO, Blue Shield, and other organizations which space limitations preclude from discussions here. For example the U.S. has stood up an interagency Cultural Antiquities Task Force (CATF) in 2004 to 'coordinate efforts across federal agencies, including law enforcement, to block trafficking in cultural property.'[129] The Department of Defense recently institutionalized responsibility for cultural heritage protection to the Office of the Deputy Assistant Secretary of Defense (ODASD) for Stability and Humanitarian Affairs. The U.S. finally rarified the Hague Convention in 2009. The *Protect and Preserve International Cultural Property Act* (HR1493) to restrict importation of Syrian antiquities was signed into law in 2016 and the *Illicit Art and Antiquities Prevention Act* bill was introduced to Congress in May 2018.

Despite these strides, U.S. and key allied militaries have yet to systematically consider the material past as a strategic element or domain of contemporary and emerging future small war and hybrid battlespaces above the operational and tactical levels or beyond legal and protectionist (mainly avoidance of inadvertent destruction) lenses. Archaeology, as a discipline, has also yet to seriously wrestle with either the strategic, ethical or scientific implications of non-western actors systematic targeting of cultural heritage and weaponizing of archaeological sites and research in a post-factual world dominated by 'fake news.'

Although the ties between the military and archaeology have grown closer, the overall relationship between the military and the discipline of archaeology remains heavily bifurcated and given the vehemence of ethical debates will remain so. This limits the expertise available needed by militaries to operate in the domain of material culture, as well as the ability of archaeologists and other cultural heritage professionals to influence the military and to apply scientific rigor to counter spurious historical claims and narratives. Similarly, this also limits the transference and application of lessons learned from battlefield archaeology into military education and doctrine.

The U.S. and its main western allies, thus, remain ill-postured to counter or proactively respond to adversaries' attempts to manipulate, destroy or exploit archaeological and heritage sites and resources or to leverage opportunities that local resistance to such attempts may engender. Consequently, while it appears likely that the archaeological domain will remain and perhaps even grow important in the small wars and hybrid conflicts of the future, it is equally likely, barring a significant shift in thinking, that the U.S. and other western allies will cede momentum in this domain to their adversaries. Equally, archaeology may be ceding scientific and scholarly integrity in some areas of the world if it refuses to join the fight against actors willing to destroy and post-factually manipulate sites and research.

Notes

1. McGirk, "Syrians Race to Save Treasures."
2. Shakov, "Putin Blames U.S."
3. Westfall, "Syrian Insurgent Advances."
4. See note 1 above.
5. Ibid.
6. Alshami, "Between Bombs."
7. Melvin, "ISIS Beheads."
8. Katz, "Ancient City Damaged."
9. "Syrian Troops Looting."
10. Contact Reporter, "Russians Building Base."
11. Rosenberg, "Gergiev Conducts Concert."
12. Cascone, "Nearly Destroyed by ISIS."
13. Gerstenblith, "Archaeology in Context of War," 19.
14. Williams, *Archaeology of Roman Surveillance*.
15. See note 13 above.
16. Brandfon, "Arch of Titus."
17. "The Romans Destroy Temple."
18. See note 16 above.
19. Ibid.
20. Bellisari, *Raiders of the Lost Past*, xi.
21. Rid, "Nineteenth Century Origins," 727.
22. Gates, *Counterinsurgency*.
23. Bellisari, *Raiders of the Lost Past*.
24. Ibid.
25. Brysac, 54.
26. Chadha, "Visions of Discipline," 378.
27. Evans, "Soldiering Archaeology," 2.
28. Ibid.
29. Evans, "Soldiering Archaeology."
30. Bowden, *Life and Work*.
31. See note 29 above.
32. Ibid.
33. Monuments Men Foundation, *"Sir Mortimer Wheeler"*.
34. Shapland, "British Salonika Force," 88.
35. "Palestine Exploration Fund".
36. Mohs, *Military Intelligence*, 172.
37. Desplatt, "Digging for Country".
38. Bellisari, *Raiders of the Lost Past*, 126.
39. Ibid.
40. Ibid., 100.

41. Ibid., 125–6.
42. Ibid., 113.
43. Ibid.
44. Franz, "Archaeology and Great Game".
45. Ibid.
46. Ibid.
47. Meyer and Brysac, *Tournament of Shadows*, 351–2.
48. "Charles Masson".
49. Meyer and Brysac, *Tournament of Shadows*, 346, 349, 358, 376.
50. Ibid., 352.
51. Ibid., 376.
52. Brysac, "Last of Foreign Devils," 53.
53. Ibid.
54. Popova, Russian Explorations, 106.
55. Ibid, 110.
56. Ibid., 111–112.
57. Meyer and Brysac, *Tournament of Shadows*, 271.
58. Ibid., 217.
59. Popova, Russian Explorations, 114.
60. Stewart, "Queen of Quagmire," 12.
61. Sheppard, "Not all Spies".
62. Anderson, *Lawrence in Arabia*, 30, 36–9.
63. Harris and Sandler, *Archaeologist was a Spy*, xiii.
64. Ibid., 295–300.
65. Allen, *Classical Spies*.
66. The story of Luis Dupree and his wife Nancy in many ways encapsulates the arch of this paper's subject matter. During the Cold War Louis was suspected by many to be a U.S. spy and he later served with the mujahedeen in Pakistan during the war against the Soviets, Nancy an Afghan expert in own right became heavily engaged in preserving Afghan culture and restoring the National Museum after the Taliban's fall. See https://magazine.atavist.com/love andruin for their story.
67. Allen, *Classical Spies* and Martin, *American Geography*.
68. Gerstenblith, "Archaeology in Context of War," 21.
69. Ibid.
70. Edsel, 422.
71. Joyce, "Politics and Archaeology".
72. Lewis, "Chinese Civilization".
73. Price, *Anthropology and Militarism*.
74. Pollock, "Archaeology and War," 223.
75. Jasparro, "Case for Cultural Heritage Protection," 92.
76. Nuhefendic, "Mostar."
77. Jasparro, "Case for Cultural Heritage Protection," 93.
78. Jasparro, "Human Security," 9.
79. Semple, "Why Buddhas Destroyed."
80. Jasparro, "Case for Cultural Heritage Protection," 99.
81. Ibid., 100.
82. Ibid.
83. Ibid.
84. Ibid.

85. Bolger cited in Jasparro, "Case for Cultural Heritage Protection," 101.
86. Lawler, "War Savages Sites."
87. See note 71 above.
88. Aridici, "How Putin Russian."
89. Campbell, "Shipwrecks to War."
90. Ibid.
91. Feldschreiber, "Putin Takes Submarine."
92. Johnson, "China's Memory."
93. Erickson and Bond, "Archaeology and South China Sea."
94. Henderson, Chinese Underwater Archaeology.
95. See note 93 above.
96. Campbell, "Illicit Antiquities Trade",113.
97. Howard, Elliot, and Prohow, *IS and Cultural Genocide*, 3.
98. Wendle, "Whose Stealing."
99. Rothfield, *Antiquities under Siege*, 6.
100. Ibid.
101. Drennan, Black-Market Battleground.
102. Howard, Elliot, and Prohow, *IS and Cultural Genocide*, 2.
103. Fadel, "Robbing Them."
104. Byrne, *Counterheritage*, 148–150.
105. Jasparro, "Human Security," 10.
106. Jasparro, 107.
107. Winter, *Post-conflict Heritage*, 21.
108. Legendre de Koninck, "Reviving Angkor Wat."
109. Southern, "The Future of Cambodia."
110. Spiess, "Ticket Revenue at Angkor."
111. Candelaria, "Angkor Sites," 254.
112. Kila, "Military Cultural Experts," 203.
113. Mekellide, "Recovery and Identification," 30.
114. Jones, "The Secrets."
115. Ibid.
116. Koff, *Bone Woman*, 7–8.
117. Mekellide, "Recovery and Identification," 34.
118. White and Livoti, "Preserving Cultural Heritage," 203.
119. Dyhouse, "We find Bones," 14–8.
120. Op Nightingale Heritage, *About*.
121. Brady, *Veterans Turning to Archaeology*.
122. Scott and McFeaters, "Archaeology of Battlefields," 116.
123. Conlin and Russel, "Archaeology of a Naval Battlefield," 21.
124. For balanced reviews of this debate and challenges to practice of forensic archaeology in war see: Steele, "Archaeology and Forensic Investigation" and Ferllini, "Forensic Archaeology".
125. Stone, *Cultural Heritage Ethics*, 6.
126. Bernback quote in Stone, *Cultural Heritage Ethics*, 7.
127. Rush, *Military Archaeology*, 145.
128. Ibid.
129. Office of Spokesperson, *State Announces New Initiatives*.

Disclosure statement

No potential conflict of interest was reported by the author.

Bibliography

n.d. "After Examining the Ancient Shipwreck near the Entrance to Balaklava Bay in Sevastopol, Vladimir Putin Talked to Journalists about His Submersion on Board the Bathyscaphe and Answered Some of Their Questions." http://en.kremlin.ru/events/president/transcripts/50148

Allen, Susan Heuck. *Classical Spies: American Archaeologists with the OSS in World War II Greece*. Ann Arbor: University of Michigan Press, 2011.

Alshami, Belal. 2017. "Between Bombs and Beheadings: Palmyra after the ISIS Takeover." *Syria Deeply*, July 21. Accessed February 20, 2019. https://www.newsdeeply.com/syria/articles/2015/07/21/between-bombs-and-beheadings-palmyra-after-the-isis-takeover

2015. "Answers to Journalists' Questions." August 18. Accessed November 6, 2018. http://en.kremlin.ru/events/president/transcripts/50148

Bellisari, Andrew. 2019. "Raiders of the Lost past Nineteeth-Century Arcaheology and French Imperialism in the near East 1798–1914." *Honors Thesis Submitted to History and French Depaetments of Rutgers University*. April. (Campbell, Could Shipwrecks Lead the World to War? 2015).

Bohstrom, Philippe. 2017. "Diving Robbers Are Looting Underwater Treasures." *Haaretz*, March 15. Accessed October 28, 2018. https://www.haaretz.com/archaeology/diving-robbers-looting-underwater-treasures-1.5449229

Bowden, Mark. *The Life and Archaeological Work of Lieutenant-General Augustus Henry Lane Fox Pitt-Rivers, DCL, FRS. FSA*. Cambridge: Cambridge University Press, 1991.

Brady, Heather. 2018. "Why Military Veterans are Turning to Archaeology." August 30. Accessed October 19, 2018. https://www.nationalgeographic.com/culture-exploration/2018/08/military-veterans-archaeology-shaker-dig-explorer-digventures/?user.testname=none

Brandfon, Fredric. n.d. "'The Arch of Titus in the Roman Forum A Case Study of Vandalism and History,' Change over Time." *International Journal of Conservation and the Built Environment* (Spring 2016). https://cot.pennpress.org/special-article

Browley, Graham. 2015. "Antiquities Lost, Casualties of War." *New York Times*, October 5, 20.

Browne, Klm. "Traffikcing in Pacific World War II Sunken Vessels." *GSTF International Journal of Law and Social Sciences* 3, no. 2 (2014): 67–74.

Brysac, Shareen Blair. 1997. "Last of the Foreign Devils." *Arcaheology Magazine*, November/December, 53.

Byrne, Dennis. *Counterheritage Critical Perspectives on Heritage Conservation in Asia*. New York, NY: Routledge, 2014.

Campbell, Peter. "The Illicit Anqituities Trade as a Transnational Criminal Network: Characterizing and Anticipating Trafficking of Culutral Heritage." *International Journal of Cultural Property* 20 (2013): 113-153. doi:10.1017/S0940739113000015.

Candelaria, Maria, and Fe. Aurora. "The Angkor Sites of Cambodia: The Conflicting Values of Sustainable Tourism and State Sovereignty." *Brooklyn Journal of International Law* 31, no. 1 (2005): 254.

Cascone, Sarah. 2018. "Nearly Destroyed by ISIS, the Ancient City of Palmyra Will Reopen in 2019 after Extensive Renovations." *ArtNet News*, August 27. Accessed February 5, 2019. https://news.artnet.com/art-world/syria-isis-palmyra-restoration-1338257

Chadha, A. "Visions of Discipline: Sir Mortimer Wheeler and the Archaeological Method in India 1944-1948." *Journal of Social Archaeology* 2, no. 3 (2002): 378-401. doi:10.1177/146960530200200305.

2019. "Charles Masson Biographical Detail." British Museum. Accessed February 1, 2019. sahttps://www.britishmuseum.org/research/search_the_collection_data base/term_details.aspx?biold=138885

Christopher, Jasparro. "Culture and Human Security Now." *Regional Develoment Dialogue* 24, no. 2 (Autumn 2003): 11-21.

Conlin, David, and Matthew Russell. "Archaeology of a Naval Battlefield: H.L. Hunley Amd USS Housatonic." *The International Jounral of Arcaheology* 35, no. 1 (2006): 20-40.

Conn, Carleton. *A North Africa Story, the Anthropologist as an OSS Agent 1941-1943*. Ipswith, MA: Gambit, 1980.

Desplat, Juliet. n.d. "Digging for King and Country." Accessed February 27, 2019. https://blog.nationalarchives.gov.uk/blog/digging-king-country/

Dillon, Dana. 2011. "Countering Beijing in the South China Sea." *Hoover Institution Policy Review*, June 1. Accessed October 30, 2018. https://www.hoover.org/research/countering-beijing-south-china-sea

Drennan, Justine. 2014. "The Black-Market Battlegroung." October 17. Accessed October, 2014. www.foreignpolicy.com/articles/2014/10/17_the_black_market_syria_iraq_isis

Dyhouse, Tim. 2004. "At the Tactical Level We Find Bones." *VFW, Veterans of Foreign Wars Magazine*, June/July, 14-18.

Edsel, Robert. *The Monuments Men*. New York, NY: Center Street, 2009.

Erickson, Andrew, and Kevin Bond. 2015. "Archaeology and the South China Sea." July 20. Accessed January, 2018. https://thediplomat.com/2015/07archaeology-and-the-south-china-sea/

Evans, Christopher. "Soldiering Archaeology: Pitt Rivers and 'Militarism'." *Bulletin of the History of Archaeology* 24, no. 4 (2014): 1-20.

"Exclusive: Odyssey Explorer Cargo Seixed Because OMEX Violated Cypriot Customs Laws." January 20, 2016. Accessed November 5, 2018. http://thepipeline.info/blog/2016/01/20/exclusive-odyssey-explorer-cargo-seized-because-omex-violated-cypriot-customs-laws/

Fadel, Leila. 2019. "Robbing Them Of Their Future." *NPR*, January 6. Accessed February 15, 2019. https://www.npr.org/2019/01/06/682532244/yemens-loss-of-antiquities-is-robbing-them-of-their-future

Feldschreiber, Jared. 2018. "Putin Takes Submarine on Shiprwreck Expedition in Black Sea." August 18. Accessed November, 2018. Byzantine vessel that sank near the entrance to Balaklava Bay in Sevastopol in the Crimea, which was annexed by Moscow last year. The subsea expedition was timed to coincide with the anniversary of the Russian Geographical Society's establishment 170 yea.

Ferillini, Roxanna. "Forensic Anthropology in Crisis Settings: A Required Component of Investigation in the World's Trouble Spots." *Human Remains and Violence* 3, no. 2 (2017): 98–116. doi:10.7227/HRV.3.2.7.

Flecker, Michael. 2015. "Archaeology Could Wreck China's Sea Claims." May 5. Accessed November, 2018. https://www.todayonline.com/world/asia/archaeology-could-wreck-chinas-sea-claims

Franx, Paris. 2014. "Archaeology and the Great Game: Explorers on the Silk Road." *Decoded Past.com*, November 17. Accessed February 20, 2019. http://decodedpast.com/archaeology-great-game-explorers-silk-road/14024

Gates, Scott, and Kaushik Roy. 2017. " Counterinsurgency in the Modern World ." *Oxford Bibiliographies*, April 28. Accessed February 5, 2019. http://www.oxfordbibliographies.com/view/document/obo-9780199791279/obo-9780199791279-0075.xml

Gerstenblith, Patty. "Archaeology in the Context of War: Legal Frameworks for Protecting Cultural Heritage during Armed Conflict." *Arcaheologies: Journal of the World Arcaheological Congress* 5 (2009): 19–31.

Grantham, David. "Antiquities and Conflict: Changing Military Strategy." *Norwich Review of International and Transnational Crime* 1, no. 2 (2016): 28–42.

Harris Charles, III, and Louis Sadler. *The Archaeologist Was a Spy*. Albuquerque: University of New Mexico Press, 2003.

Henderson, Jon. 2014. "Underwater Archaeology in China." November 26. Accessed November, 2018. http://blogs.nottingham.ac.uk/underwaterarchaeology/2014/11/26/underwater-archaeology-in-china/

Hosty, Kieran, and Paul Hundley. *PRELIMINARY REPORT on the Australian National Maritime Museum's Participation in the Rhode Island Marine Archaeology Project's Search for HMB Endeavour August 200*. Sydney Australia: Archaeological, Auatralian National Maritime Museum, 2003.

Howard, Russell, Marc Elliot, and Jonathan Prohiv. *IS and Cultural Genocide: Antiquities Trafficking in the Terrorist State*. Tampa: Joint Special Operations University Press, 2016.

Jasparro, Christopher. "The Case for Culutral Heritage Protection as an Element of COIN." In *The Future of Counterinsurgency: Contemporary Debares in Internal Security*, edited by Lawrence and Paul Shemella, 91–120. Cline: Praeger, 2015.

Johnson, Ian. 2016. "China's Memory Manipulators." *The Guardian*, June 8. Accessed October 12, 2018. https://www.theguardian.com/world/2016/jun/08/chinas-memory-manipulators

Jones, Maggie. 2016. "The Secrets in Guatemala's Bones." *The New York Times*, June 30. Accessed February 1, 2019. https://www.nytimes.com/2016/07/03/magazine/the-secrets-in-guatemalas-bones.html

Joyce, Rosemary. 2011. "Politics and Archaeology,Russian Style." August 18. Accessed January, 2018. http://blogs.berkeley.edu/2011/08/18/politics-and-archaeology-russian-style/

Katz, Brigit. 2018. "Ancient City of Palmyra, Gravely Damaged by ISIS, May Reopen Next Year." *Smithsonian.com*, August 29. Accessed February 20, 2019. https://www.smithsonianmag.com/smart-news/ancient-city-palmyra-gravely-damaged-isis-may-reopen-next-year-1-180970160/#T36G0p4WzIGgYGL5.99

Kila, Joris. "Utilizing Military Cultural Experts in Times of War and Peace: An Introduction." In *Culture and International Law*, edited by P. Meerts, 183–228. The Hague: Hague Academic Coalition, 2008.

Koff, Clea. *The Bone Woman A Forensic Anthropologists Search for Truth in the Mass Graves of Rwanda, Bosnia, Croatia and Kosovo*. New York, NY: Random House, 2004.

Lawler, Andrew. 2018. "War Savages Ancient Sites in Yemen and Iraq, Destroying Archaeological Record ." *Science Magazine*, April 10. Accessed February 1, 2019. https://www.sciencemag.org/news/2018/04/war-savages-ancient-sites-yemen-and-iraq-destroying-archaeological-record?r3f_986=https://www.google.com/

Legendre de Koninck, Helen. 1997. "Hopes Pinned on Reviving Angkor Wat." *Jarkata Post*, June 29.

Lewis, Ricardo. 2016. "Does Chinese Civilization Come from Ancient Egypt?" *Foreign Policy*, September 2. Accessed September 14, 2016. https://foreignpolicy.com/2016/09/02/did-chinese-civilization-come-from-ancient-egypt-archeological-debate-at-heart-of-china-national-identity/

Long, Doug. n.d. "Hiroshima: Henry Stimonson's Diary and Papers: Part 8 July 21 Thru July 25, 1945." Accessed October 29, 2018. http://www.doug-long.com/stimson8.htm

Luke, Christina. "U.S. Policy, Cultural Heritage, and U.S. Borders." *International Journal of Cultural Property* 19 (2012): 175–196. doi:10.1017/S094073911200015X.

Martin, Geoffrey. *American Geography and Geographers: Toward Geographical Science*. Oxford: Oxford University Press, 2018.

McGirk, Tim. 2015. "Syrians Race to Save Ancient City's Treasures from ISIS." *National Geographic.com*, July 10. Accessed January 25, 2018. https://news.nationalgeographic.com/2015/07/150710-palmyra-syria-isis-looting-museum-archaeology/

Melvin, Don, Ralph Ellis, and Salma Abdelaziz. 2015. "ISIS Beheads Expert Who Refused to Reveal Location of Valuable Antiquities." *CNN.com*, August 18. Accessed February 20, 2019. https://www.cnn.com/2015/08/18/middleeast/isis-executes-antiquities-expert/index.html

Meyer, Karl, and Shareen Blair Brysac. *Tournament of Shadows*. Washington, DC: Counterpoint, 1999.

Mikellide, Maria. "Recovery and Identification of Human Remains in Post-conflict Environments: A Comparative Study of the Humanitarian Forensic Programs in Cyprus and Kosovo." *Forensic Science International* 279 (2017): 33–40. doi:10.1016/j.forsciint.2017.07.040.

Milmo, Cahal. 2016. "Odyssey Explorer: Cyprus to Examine Suspect Cargo of Antiquties from Offshore Supply Ship." January 16. Accessed November 2018. https://www.independent.co.uk/news/world/europe/odyssey-explorer-cyprus-to-examine-suspect-cargo-of-antiquities-from-offshore-supply-ship-a6816691.html

Mohs, Polly. *Military Intelligence and the Arab Revolt, the First Modern Intelligence War*. New York, NY: Routledge, 2008.

2012. "North African Salafists Turn on Sufi Shrines in Mali." May 18. Accessed May, 2014. http://www.jamestown.org/single/?tx_ttnews%5Btt_news%5D=39387&tx_ttnews%5BbackPid%5D=588&no_cache=1#.U4YrS3JdX-s

Nuhefendic, Azra. "Mostar: The Old One Twenty Years Later." November 8, 2013. Accessed May, 2014. www.balcanicaucaso.org/eng/Regions-andcountries/Bosnia-Herzegovnia/Mostar-the-Old-One-twenty-years-later-143828

Nuray, Aridici. 2014. "How Vladmir Putin Has Changed the Meaning of Russian." The Conversation, April 9. Accessed October 10, 2018. http://theconversation.com/how-vladimir-putin-has-changed-the-meaning-of-russian-24928

2016. "Op Nightingale Heritgae About." Accessed October 19, 2018. https://www.opnightingaleheritage.com/about-1

Page, Jeremy. 2013. "Chinese Territorial Strife Hits Archaeology." *The Wall Street Journal*. December 2. Accessed November, 2018. https://www.wsj.com/articles/chinese-territorial-strife-hits-archaeology-1385954351

n.d. "Palestine Exploration Fund (PEF)." https://zochrot.org/en/article/56409

Pinker, Steven. *The Better Angels of Our Nature, Why Violence Has Declined*. New York, NY: Viking, 2011.

Pollock, Sudan. "Archaeology and Contemporary Warfare." *Annual Review of Anthropology* 45 (2016): 215–231. doi:10.1146/annurev-anthro-102215-095913.
Popova, Irina. 2008. "Russian Explorations in Central Asia at the Turn of the 20th Century." St. Petersburg. Russian Explorations in Central Asia at the Turn of the 20th Century, St Petersburg, 2008. http://www.iop.or.jp/Documents/1727/12_%5B104-126%5DI.F.Popova.pdf104-126
Price, David. 2013. "Anthropology and Militarism." July 24. Accessed October 29, 2018. http://www.oxfordbibliographies.com/view/document/obo-9780199766567/obo-9780199766567-0094.xml
Rathavong, Ven. 2018. "Mortars Found in Preah Vihear Temple." *Khmer Times*, September 14.
Reporter, Contact. 2017. "Russians Building Army Base at Syria's Palmyra Site ." *Chicago Tribune*, May 17. Accessed February 5, 2019. https://www.chicagotribune.com/news/nationworld/ct-russia-palmyra-base-20160517-story.html
Rid, Thomas. "The Nineteenth Century Origins of Counterinsurgency Doctrine." *Journal of Strategic Studies* 33 (2019): 727–758. doi:10.1080/01402390.2010.498259.
Roach, John. 2017. "The Ttanic Was Found During Secret Cold War Navy Mission." November. Accessed November 5, 2018. https://news.nationalgeographic.com/2017/11/titanic-nuclear-submarine-scorpion-thresher-ballard/
2005. "The Romans Destroy the Temple at Jerusalem, 70 AD." *EyeWitness to History*. Accessed February, 2019. www.eyewitnesstohistory.com
Rosenberg, Steve. 2016. "Russia's Valery Gergiev Conducts Concert in Palmyra Ruins." *BBC News*, May 5. Accessed February 5, 2019. https://www.bbc.com/news/world-middle-east-36211449
Rothfield, Lawrence. *Antiquities under Siege: Cultural Heritage Protection after the Iraq War*. Plymouth: AltaMira, 2008.
Rubin, Michael. 2017. "Strategies Underlying Iranian Softpower." *American Enterprise Institute. AEI*, March 15. Accessed March 2017. https://www.aei.org/publication/strategies-underlying-iranian-soft-power/
Rush, Laurie. "Cultural Protection as a Force Multiplier in Stabilty Operations." *Military Review* 92 no. March–April (2012): 36–43.
Rush, Laurie. "Military Archaeology in the U.S." In *Cultural Heritage Ethics and the Military*, edited by Peter Stone, 139–146. Woodbridge, UK: Boydell Press, 2013.
Rush, Laurie, and Luisa Benedettini Millington. *The Caribineieri Command for the Protection of Cultural Property*. Woodbridge, UK: Boydell Press, 2015.
Scarfuri, Michael. "H.L. Hunley Revealed: Documentation, Deconcretion, and Recent Developments in the Investigation of an American Civil War Submarine from 1864." *The International Journal of Nautical Archaeology* 46, no. 2 (2017): 306–316.
Scott, Douglas, and McFeaters. Andrew. "The Archaeology of Historic Battlefields: A History and Theoretical Development in Conflict Archaeology." *Journal of Archaeological Research* 19, no. 1 (2011): 103–132. doi:10.1007/s10814-010-9044-8.
Seidel, James. 2016. "Beijing Details Historic Claim to South China Sea." *news.com*.au, November 4. Accessed October 17, 2018. https://www.news.com.au/world/beijing-details-historic-claim-to-south-china-sea/news-story/8aab3eedb376ced913201871b9e84893
Semple, Michael. n.d. "Why the Bamian Buddhas Were Destroyed." Accessed November, 2014. http://www.afghanistan-analysts.org/guest-blog-why-the-buddha
Shakov, Damien. 2016. "Putin Blames Lack of U.S.-Assad Cooperation for Loss of Palmyra ." *NewsWeek*, December 12. Accessed February 20, 2019. https://www.newsweek.com/putin-blames-lack-us-assad-cooperation-losing-palmyra-532696

Shapland, Andrew. "The British Salonika Force Collection at the British Musuem." In *Archaeology behind the Battle Lines, the Macedonia Campaign and Its (1915–1919)*, edited by Andrew Shapland and Evamgelia Sefani, 85–120. Legacy, NY: Routledge, 2017.

Sheppard, Kate. 2014. "doctorkate.wordpress.com." December 1. Accessed February 1, 2019. https://doctorkate.wordpress.com/2014/12/01/not-all-archaeologists-are-spies

n.d. "Sir Robert Eric Mortimer Wheeler (1890–1976)." Accessed February 10, 2019. https://www.monumentsmenfoundation.org/the-heroes/the-monuments-men/wheeler-mortimer

Southern, Paul Nathan. 2017. "The Future of Cambodia: Tourism." October 16. Accessed November 2018. http://sea-globe.com/cambodia-future-tourism/

Spiess, Roman. 2018. "Ticket Revenue Jumps 72% After Ticket Price Hike." January 2. Accessed 2018 November. https://www.phnompenhpost.com/business/ticket-revenue-angkor-wat-jumps-72-percent-after-price-hike

Steele, Caroline. "Archaeology and the Forensic Investigation of Recent Mass Graves: Ethical Issues for a New Practice of Archaeology." *Archaeologies: Journal of the World Archaeological Congress* 4, no. 3 (2008): 414–428. doi:10.1007/s11759-008-9080-x.

Stewart, Rory. 2007. "Queen of the Quagmire." *New York Review of Books*, October 25, 12. doi:10.1094/PDIS-91-4-0467B.

Stone, Peter. *Cultural Hertiage Ethics and the Military*. Woodbridge, UK: Boydell Press, 2013.

2016. "Syrian Troops Looting Ancient City Palmyra, Says Archaeologist." *The Guardian.com*, June 1. https://www.theguardian.com/world/2016/jun/01/syrian-troops-looting-ancient-city-palmyra-says-archaeologist

2018. "Task Force Dagger Foundation Veterans Do Underwater Archaeology in the Pacific." July 23. Accessed October 28, 2018. https://www.prweb.com/releases/task_force_dagger_foundation_veterans_do_underwater_archaeology_in_the_pacific/prweb15643365.htm

2017. "Ukraine and Russia Fight over Crimean Heritage." *France24.com*, September 28. Accessed October 17, 2018. http://www.france24.com/en/20170928-ukraine-russia-fight-over-crimean-heritage

UNESCO. 2017. "Tourism between Chance and Threat." Accessed November, 2018. http://www.unesco.org/new/en/culture/themes/underwater-cultural-heritage/protection/threats/tourism/

Wagener, Martin. "Lessons from Preah Vihear: Thailand, Cambodia, and the Nature of Low-Intensity Border Conflicts." *Journal of Southeast Asian Affairs* 3 (2011): 27–59. doi:10.1177/186810341103000302.

Wendle, John. 2013. "Whose Stealing Afghanistian;s Cultural Treasures." *National Geographic News*, August 1. Accessed November 23, 2014. http://nationalgeographic.com/news/whose-stealing-afghanistan-cultural-treasures/

Westfall, Sylvia. 2015. "Syrian Insurgent Advances Put Assad under Pressure." *Reuters*, June 2. Accessed February 20, 2019. https://uk.reuters.com/article/uk-mideast-crisis-syria-military/syrian-insurgent-advances-put-assad-under-pressure-idUKKBN0OI1W520150602

White, Cheryl, and Thomas Livoti. "Preserving Cultural Heritage in Time of Conflict: A Tool for Counterinsurgency." In *Cultural Heritage in the Crosshairs Protecting Cultural Property during Conflic*, edited by Joris Kila and James Zeidler, 195–218. Leiden: Brill, 2013.

Williams, Joey. *The Archaeology of Roman Surveillance in Central Altentejo, Portugal*. Berkeley: Dept of Classics UC Berkeley, 2017.

Winter, Tm. *Post-conflict Heritage Postcolonial Tourism: Culture, Politics and Development and Angkor*. New York, NY: Routledge, 2007.

Identity wars: collective identity building in insurgency and counterinsurgency

Heather S. Gregg

ABSTRACT
Collective identity building is a critical component of most insurgent movements, including constructing a compelling cause with which individuals can identify and a sense of purpose and camaraderie. Counterinsurgencies, by contrast, devote surprisingly little attention to creating identities that compete with insurgents. Instead, they tend to focus on providing goods and services to vulnerable populations with the assumption that emotional resources, such as a sense of identity and purpose, are not necessary. This article draws from theoretical work on identity building to outline how collective identities are constructed, what they include, and how they shape human behavior. It then considers the U.S. led operations in Iraq from 2003–2011, and compares these efforts to the emergence of Sunni Islamist insurgencies in Iraq to investigate how insurgents used identity building, but counterinsurgents did not. It then applies this theoretical literature to construct a program for how counterinsurgents could include identity construction as part of its strategy to undermine insurgent movements.

In 2015, French-American anthropologist Scott Atran addressed the UN Security Council on his research of violent extremist groups around the globe. Rather than focus on poverty or lack of opportunity as the cause of extremism, Atran pointed to a deeply human need that draws individuals to extremist groups – the need to belong a group and to find identity. Atran argues,

> Violent extremism represents not the resurgence of traditional cultures, but their collapse, as young people unmoored from millennial traditions flail about in search of a social identity that gives personal significance and glory ... They radicalize to find a firm identity in a flattened world: where vertical lines of communication between the generations are replaced by horizontal peer-to-peer attachments that can span the globe.[1]

Atran's observations touch on the important role that collective identity plays in attracting and retaining recruits to insurgent movements. Specifically, collective identity helps give purpose and meaning to individuals' lives, bonds members together, and inspires them to join the group and stay in it through difficult times. Insurgencies ranging from communist based movements to Islamist groups today have used collective identity building to draw recruits, maintain units, and differentiate supporters from dissenters. Counterinsurgencies (COIN), by contrast, devote surprisingly little attention to creating compelling causes and identities aimed at attracting support from populations. Rather, counterinsurgents tend to focus on providing goods and services to vulnerable populations, including security, food and water, and utilities, as a means of drawing populations away from insurgents and towards governments and security forces. Within this COIN strategy, the assumption appears to be that providing for physical needs are sufficient for winning the support of populations and that emotional resources, such as a sense of identity and purpose, are not necessary.

This article draws from theoretical work on identity building to consider how collective identities are constructed, what they include, and how they shape human behavior. It then considers the U.S.-led operations in Iraq from 2003–2011, and compares these efforts to the emergence of Sunni Islamist insurgencies to investigate how they used collective identity to build their movement, but counterinsurgents did not. It concludes by suggesting how counterinsurgents can include identity construction as part of a strategy to undermine insurgent movements.

The study of identity

The study of identity spans across several academic disciplines, including psychology, social psychology, anthropology, and political science. These fields focus on different aspects of identity, ranging from the individual to the collective, the unconscious to the conscious, and identity as constant to dynamic and ever changing. Several of these approaches are particularly useful for investigating how collective identity construction plays an important role in insurgency and counterinsurgency, including group dynamics, the interplay between culture and identity, and the politicization of identity.

Perhaps the most work on identity formation comes from the field of psychology, which focuses specifically on how individual identities are created, and the conditions under which these identities are either healthy or dysfunctional. For example, psychologist Erik Erikson's work on adolescents and deviant behavior considers what he calls the 'ego-identity,' or the process whereby individuals must navigate stages of develop to create a healthy sense of self in relation to the society around them.[2] Several scholars of terrorism[3] build on Erikson's work in an attempt to identify personality types that are prone to join insurgent groups. Psychologist Lorenz Böllinger, for example, used Erikson's stages of development to conclude that individuals who joined terrorist groups in 1980s Germany had pathological identities.[4] Similarly, Martha Crenshaw drew from Erikson to posit that individuals who join terrorist groups have weak identities and are seeking meaning.[5] Others, such as psychologist John Horgan and Fathali Mohammad Moghaddam, consider the process of individual radicalization, rather than identity formation, as a cause of extremist behavior.[6] This expansive body of literature focuses almost exclusively on how individual identities are formed, and the conditions under which individuals become radicalized and join insurgent movements, rather than how insurgent groups themselves develop identities, the cultural resources they use, and how these identities attract active and passive support for their cause.

The field of anthropology, and its focus on the connection between culture and identity, is particularly useful for thinking about how insurgent groups formulate collective identity. Within this literature, a debate exists over what exactly culture is, and how it is produced and maintained. Specifically, does culture shape individuals and groups, or do individuals and groups produce culture? Margaret Mead, for example, observed that 'education' through culture and society shape personality, as opposed to genetics or human nature, and accounts for differences in behavior across cultures and society.[7] In *Patterns of Culture*, Ruth Benedict further investigated the nexus between individual personality, and the complex mixture of nature and culture that makes it, focusing particularly on the role customs play in indoctrinating individuals into society.[8] By contrast, Norenzayan, Schaller and Heine argued that collective identities produce culture – practices and beliefs that are shared horizontally across individuals and that are passed vertically from generation to generation, preserving both individuals and groups. They assert that, 'Human cultures are ... well-coordinated social groups in which the individuals share massive amounts of common goals, desires, values, beliefs and other forms of knowledge.'[9] Cultural artifacts, such as visual art, mythology, and religion all play a role in distinguishing one group's beliefs and practices from another's.[10]

Anthropologist Clifford Geertz takes a different approach, focusing on shared symbols and their meaning as culture. Geertz is particularly interested in the role that symbols play in communicating culture to members of the group. Geertz describes that symbols 'are extrinsic sources of information ... they lie outside the boundaries of the individual organism as such in that intersubjective world of common understandings into which all human individuals are born ...'[11] Geertz further contends that, 'culture patterns have an intrinsic double aspect: they give meaning, i.e. objective conceptual form, to social and psychological reality both by shaping themselves to it and by shaping it to themselves.'[12] Symbols, therefore, become an important dimension of shared meaning, including identity.

Building off of Geertz and others, sociologist Ann Swidler offers a somewhat similar analysis of culture, suggesting that 'culture influences actions not by providing the ultimate values towards which an action is oriented but a shaping a repertoire or "tool kit" of habits, skills and styles from which people construct "strategies of action."'[13] Swidler further proposes that these cultural toolkits function differently between 'settled' periods, when culture and social structure reinforce one another to influence action, and 'unsettled' periods, when 'explicit ideologies' play a role influencing 'strategies of action.'[14] Swidler suggests that, overall, making this distinction allows us to see two very different ways in which culture shapes behavior and, especially, how certain cultural tools are used (or not) in unsettled periods.

Alongside the role that culture and symbols play in collective identity, another particularly important aspect of group identity formation is the emotional and cognitive role that belonging and acceptance in a group play in human interaction. For example, anthropologist Scott Atran notes the importance of camaraderie as a condition that attracts supporters to insurgent groups. Atran writes, 'It is the larger family, or "tribe," and not the mostly ordinary individuals in it, that increasingly has seemed to me the key to understanding the extraordinary violence of mass killing and the murder of innocents.' Atran further explains that his use of 'tribe' does not refer to the anthropological sense of connection through kinship, but 'a group of interlinked communities that largely share a common cultural sense of themselves, and which imagine and believe themselves to be part of one big family and home.'[15] Through his fieldwork in Palestine and Indonesia, Atran proposes, 'Maybe people don't kill and die simply for a cause. They do it for friends – campmates, schoolmates, workmates ... ' Echoing Anthropologist Benedict Anderson's seminal work on nationalism and the 'imagined communities' it builds, Atran calls this 'imagined kin.'[16]

Political theorist Keally McBride contends that communal identities and the need to belong is not a new phenomenon but, in the modern era, 'the desire for belonging is the impetus behind a great deal of political imagination,' that is in response to 'liberal individualism and capitalism.'[17] In this new era of political imagining, communities – voluntary groups that bridge the gap between the individual and the nation and that give people a sense of belonging – have taken on new importance: 'Communities are both personal and interpersonal: they engage ways of being involved with others without losing what makes oneself distinct.'[18] McBride suggests that communities are increasing in importance and political aspirations. As this occurs, communities will come into conflict with one another over their political imaginings of how society and government ought to be.[19]

Finally, collective identities can distinguish one group from another. Anthropologist Jack David Eller considers specifically the role that differentiating group identities plays in ethnic conflict.[20] He posits that ethnicity is less about a fixed set of criteria, and more about why groups build identities and how they use culture to do this. 'Cultural differences alone do not ethnicity make; culture or cultural differences become ethnicity if and when a group takes it up and uses it in certain specific and modern ways.'[21] Collective identity building, in other words, is a powerful tool for differentiating groups for specific political and social purposes.

Given this discussion, the next section investigates the role of collective identity in insurgency and counterinsurgency, especially: how do insurgents and the counterinsurgents build collective identity, if at all? Which cultural resources do they use to create it? How do they differentiate their group from other groups, and who do they include and exclude? And what are the rewards for joining and the punishments for not joining?

Insurgency, counterinsurgency and collective identity

Understanding the importance of collective identity building in insurgency and counterinsurgency requires first delineating how these conflicts differ from conventional wars. Typically, conventional wars are fought between uniformed forces controlled by a country's government, and victory is usually defined as one government's forces defeating another's, or one government imposing its will on another.[22] Insurgencies, by contrast, involve an 'irregular' force, also known as non-state actors, challenging a government and its forces, usually (but not always) within its own borders. Irregular forces typically emerge in response to particular grievances, and build their forces from like-minded individuals and groups from within the population. They often are not uniformed, particularly in the beginning, and not well known to the government. Insurgents also need the population's support, active and passive, to hide from the government and to gain recruits and other resources. Robert Taber notes, for example, 'Without the consent and active aid of the people, the guerilla would be merely a bandit and could not long survive.'[23]

Governments also need a population's active and passive support to thrive, especially in irregular wars. Populations support governments in a number of ways, including by following its laws, paying taxes and, in the case of democracies, through voting and other forms of civic participation. Even dictators need the population's support, as Gene Sharpe duly notes, and will quickly crumble if the population no longer fears a dictator's power and are unwilling to comply with its leadership.[24]

Several scholars identify the importance of 'the cause' for attracting and building popular support for insurgencies.[25] 'The first basic need for an insurgent who aims at more than simply making trouble is an attractive cause,' according to David Galula, 'particularly in view of the risks involved and in view of the fact that the early supporters and the active supporters – not necessarily the same persons – have to be recruited by persuasion.'[26]

Furthermore, the insurgent needs a cause with which large numbers of individuals and groups can identify. Galula states: 'the insurgent must, of course, be able to identify himself [sic] totally with the cause or, more precisely, with the entire majority of the population theoretically attracted by it.'[27] The insurgent's cause, therefore, is the first step in identity building.

Along with the cause, political scientist Daniel Byman specifically names identity building as a critical component for developing what he calls 'proto-insurgencies' or insurgencies in their earliest stages. Specifically, Byman notes that identity building is the first of five key tasks nascent insurgent groups must perform (along with identifying a cause, managing rivals, finding sanctuary and securing support) to 'gain the size and capabilities of an insurgency.'[28] Byman asserts that creating identity is 'a surprisingly difficult task,' and that insurgents must compete with other forms of identity, including national (the state identity, which they are often fighting), and other competing sub- and super-identities.[29] Byman further notes that, 'culture becomes intensely political' in this process.[30]

The U.S. Army and Marine Corps' Field Manual 3-24, *Counterinsurgency*, addresses the role of identity in counterinsurgency as part of a broader chapter on the need to understand local culture.[31] It defines identity as 'a broad term used to describe how people conceive of themselves and how they are perceived by others. Identity shapes how people view themselves and the world.' The manual goes on to note that, 'In times of conflict, people may choose to emphasize certain group identities such as nationality or religion, while at other times different identities, such as one's profession or gender, may matter more.' The manual further notes that social structure and identity 'affect people's allegiances and influence how groups and individuals will interpret and respond to U.S. actions.'[32] Counterinsurgency expert David Kilcullen echoes these points, stressing that 'populations in insurgency negotiate a complex process of continuously morphing contingent identity, where each person's or group's status (friend, enemy, neutral, ally or opponent, bystander, sympathizer) changes moment by moment, depending on the nature of the groups with which it is interacting.'[33]

Insurgents also need mechanisms that create internal cohesion within their movement. Galula, for example, notes the importance of organizational structure and discipline to achieve this cohesion.[34] The use of identity to achieve this cohesion, however, has been addressed by only a few scholars. Atran, for example, posits that when fused with 'the cause', a grand scenario that includes macro-level ideas like religion and salvation, belonging to a group creates a sense of purpose that can propel individuals to do almost anything.[35] Atran asserts, 'It is a combination of imagined kinship and religion ... that made large scale human cooperation (and competition) possible, with war a main motor for realization of these large scale social developments.'[36]

Political anthropologist and former Australian Army officer David Kilcullen notes the importance of social networks as a form of identity and belonging, and the role they play in propelling individuals to join insurgent groups. In *The Accidental Guerilla*, Kilcullen argues that rise of transnational Islamist groups, like Jemaah Islamiya in Southeast Asia, has more to do with social ties than Islam, and that similar dynamics are at play across insurgent movements with different causes.[37] In a 2006 interview with journalist George Packer about insurgencies, Kilcullen argued, 'There are elements in human psychological and social makeup that drive what's happening ... It's about human social networks and the way that they operate.' Kilcullen goes on to argue, 'The thing that drives these guys [is] a sense of adventure, wanting to be part of the moment, wanting to be in the big movement of history that's happening now ...'[38]

Just as insurgents need individuals to identify with the cause, so too do governments need the support of their people. Creating collective identity is one important way to ensure support. However, literature on counterinsurgency is surprisingly thin on the creation of collective identity as a means to build support for the government's side of the conflict. Galula is perhaps the one exception. He makes mention of the need for national identity, and contends that the counterinsurgent needs a compelling cause and identity to compete with and defeat the insurgent. Specifically, Galula names 'national consensus' as an important ingredient, and that 'the solidity of a regime is primarily based upon this factor.'[39]

However, aside from Galula, surprisingly little is said about the importance of identity building in COIN literature. For example, FM 3–24 makes no mention of the need to build identity for a successful counterinsurgency, despite noting the importance of understanding identity as part of the culture and that social structure and identity 'affect people's allegiances and influence how groups and individuals will interpret and respond to U.S. actions.'[40] Rather, the manual focuses heavily on establishing good governances and providing resources to the population, such as security, infrastructure, and rule of law. Similarly, Kilcullen does not address the importance of building identity in his works on counterinsurgency, nor does Taber.[41]

Furthermore, most literature on state stabilization and 'nation building,' which are the interim and long-term goals of counterinsurgencies, does not discuss collective identity building as a critical component.[42] For example, the RAND Corporation has produced several volumes on nation building in the modern era but does not address national identity as a necessary ingredient.[43] Economist Francis Fukuyama's work on state building asserts: 'If a nation arises from this, it is more a matter of luck than design.'[44] Although Ghani and Lockhart name the importance of investing in human capital and delineating citizens' rights and responsibilities as important tasks in stabilization and state building, they do not elaborate beyond this point.[45] Yet another example can be found in a stabilization framework developed by the U.S. Government that names five desired end states in stability operations ('a safe and secure environment, the rule of law, a stable democracy, a sustainable economy, and social well-being') but does not name national identity construction as one of its pillars.[46]

As will be discussed, the U.S. model of counterinsurgency, specifically in Iraq, focused on building the structure of the state, including competent security forces, a modern democracy, a functioning economy based on Iraq's oil wealth, and rule of law. The assumption was that a functioning state would be sufficient for a happy and loyal population and that there was no need to build a collective identity. This lack of national unity building opened the door for Sunni Islamist insurgents to create a divisive identity.

Operation Iraqi freedom and Sunni Islamist insurgencies

In 2003, the United States, together with a coalition of around 30 other countries, invaded Iraq with the aim of deposing its dictator, Saddam Hussein, and ridding the country of its alleged weapons of mass destruction (WMD) program. Alongside these ambitions, the U.S. government sought to replace Saddam Hussein with a liberal democracy, and to make Iraq prosper as an oil-rich country with competent security forces and adherence to the rule of law.[47] While the invasion began as a conventional war, with U.S. and Coalition forces confronting the Iraqi military, several insurgent groups emerged following the overthrow of Saddam Hussein with the aim of challenging both the presence of coalition forces in the country and the emerging Iraqi government.[48]

Prior to the invasion, the U.S. Department of Defense (DoD) made tentative plans for what it called 'Phase IV' of Operation Iraqi Freedom, which focused on rapidly stabilizing the country and setting it on the road to democracy. The DoD planned to bring Iraqi exiles into the country after toppling Saddam Hussein and have them run an interim government until elections could be held. The ex-patriot-led interim government, the Iraqi Governing Council, was unknown and unsupported by the population, forcing the creation of a new interim body, the Iraqi Interim Government in 2004.[49] The U.S.-led civilian agency responsible for the occupation, the Coalition Provisional Authority (CPA), also initiated a massive 'de-Baathification' program as its first order, which aimed to rid the country of all senior- and mid- level Baath party members (Saddam Hussein's party), which disproportionately affected Sunnis.[50] When provincial and national elections were held in the country, they largely broke out along ethnic lines, which gave the Shia, as the numerical majority, the upper hand.[51] Ultimately, the Sunnis, who enjoyed considerable advantages under Saddam Hussein, were all but left out of the political process.

Coalition powers also focused on rapidly standing up a new military, and retraining other security forces. The CPA decided to disband the Iraqi Army in CPA Order No. 2, and rebuild it from scratch. This decision put roughly 350,000 men out of work, destroyed a national symbol that dated back to the 1920s, and created a security vacuum in the country. Efforts to rebuild the army and retrain security forces were hindered by high desertion rates, unrealistic timelines, and poor training.[52] Ultimately, when ISIS took Mosul in 2014 Iraqi forces either shed their uniforms and fled, or ISIS slaughtered the forces by the thousands.[53]

The U.S.-led invasion further prioritized establishing essential services and restoring the country's economy; however, these efforts also ran into difficulties. The DoD overestimated the state of the country's physical infrastructure, which made providing basic services, especially electricity, very difficult.[54] Plans to turn the country's vast oil reserves into the lifeblood of the economy and a resource that would pay for the rebuilding of the state also proved difficult. Moreover, the fledgling Iraqi government could not create a system for sharing the oil wealth among the various ethnic groups in the country, making it more a source of conflict than stability.[55]

Finally, the CPA made the creation of a constitution and rule of law a priority in the first year of the occupation. U.S. led attempts to draft a constitution ran into opposition from the country's highest Shia cleric, the Grand Ayatollah Sistani, who issued a *fatwah* insisting that a national referendum be held to determine the drafters of the constitution. After stalled talks and protests, the CPA held a national referendum to select a body to write the constitution, and the draft was approved in October 2005.[56]

In the midst of efforts to build the state, the U.S. government and military could no longer deny that the conventional invasion of Iraq had produced multiple insurgencies against Coalition forces and the fledgling Iraqi government. This realization, which was slow to come, compelled U.S. forces to adopt a new strategy, counterinsurgency, to address the conflict. Prior to its formal adoption, several commanders began implementing COIN approaches in their areas of operation. For example, then U.S. Army Colonel H.R. McMaster used a population-centric approach to countering insurgents in the city of Tal Afar, pushing U.S. forces off bases and placing them around the clock with local security forces. Then Major General David Petraeus focused on economic development and local governance in his area of operation with the 101st Airborne.[57] Coalition forces expanded these efforts as part of the 'surge,' which began in 2006, and included an increase in overall troop numbers, extended deployments, and pushing troops out to Joint Security Stations throughout populated areas with the goal of improving security and contact with local communities.[58] Overall, these approaches focused more on building relationships with the population in an effort to better understand their needs and vulnerabilities than on enemy-centric raids that tended to alienate the population.

In 2006, Sunni tribal leaders began working with U.S. forces in the province of Anbar to push out Al Qaeda in Iraq (AQI), a Sunni Islamist group. As part of what became known as the 'Sunni Awakening,' U.S. forces helped stand up ad hoc security forces beginning in 2006, which became known as the 'Sons of Iraq' (SOI). While initially successful in putting down AQI, these forces became a problem for Coalition forces and the Iraqi government, which were left with the difficult choice of either disbanding the forces or integrating them into already large national security forces. In some cases, the Iraqi military put SOI units down with force.[59] Throughout these major efforts to switch from a more conventional mindset and occupation to a counterinsurgency, the United States and its allies did little to help build Iraqi identity. As will be described in the conclusion, Coalition forces, at the direction of key individuals in Iraqi society and government, could have helped create programs to shape and strengthen Iraqi identity that would have competed with Sunni insurgents.

The Sunni Islamist insurgencies

Initially, the U.S.-led invasion appeared to go off without a significant reaction from the population or the Iraqi military, prompting President George Bush to declare 'mission accomplished' on 1 May 2003, just six weeks after the invasion began. However, within a year, multiple insurgent groups – including secular, nationalist, tribal, Shia, and transnational Sunni Islamist – succeeded in destabilizing the country and forcing Coalition forces to switch from a conventional war to a counterinsurgency.[60]

Sunni Islamist insurgent groups in particular, specifically AQI and later ISIS, created a compelling identity that not only challenged the Iraq government and Coalition forces, but also provided a positive course of action for those who joined or supported the movement. First, as Galula notes, Sunni Islamist insurgents built an identity that focused on what they were fighting against. AQI and its earlier predecessors[61] targeted three broad enemies in particular: Coalition forces, the fledgling government, and Shia Muslims. As with most insurgents, AQI formed its broadest identity around fighting the occupation. Political scientist Ahmed S. Hashim notes, 'Sunni Arab opposition to and dislike for the occupation was evident from the very beginning. This is not surprising, because they saw themselves as targets of the invasion.'[62] The most persistent of Sunni insurgent groups used Islam and religious resources to build its identity. Hashim, for example, notes that Sunni clerics helped form the initial resistance to the U.S. led occupation, using mosques and other venues to articulate grievances, including a cleric in Fallujah, who praised an attack against U.S. forces in May 2003, and another cleric who called for jihad against U.S. forces in October of that same year.[63] Hashim notes that the U.S. military's arrest of clerics and Sunni sheikhs (tribal leaders) enraged the population, contributing to Fallujah becoming one of the centers of the Sunni insurgency, and infusing it with religious significance.[64]

Sunni Islamist insurgents further identified Coalition forces as not only occupiers, but also as immoral, Christian 'infidels,' connecting their identity to a wider narrative purported by transnational Islamist groups. This narrative stretches back almost a century and includes Islamists like Hassan al-Banna, Sayyid Qutb, Sayyid Abul a'la Maududi, Abdullah Azzam and later Osama bin Laden and Abu Bakr al-Baghdadi. Specifically, these ideologues argue that the U.S. (and western powers more broadly) aims to destroy Islam through the spread of its 'bankrupt' culture and its foreign policy objectives. These leaders call for 'True Muslims' to not only resist these advances through boycotts and other efforts, but also by engaging in defensive jihad to protect the faith.[65] This narrative also emerged within the first year of the war in Iraq. Hashim quotes a Sunni insurgent as saying, 'We fight the Americans because they are nonbelievers and they are coming to fight Islam ... and we want this country to be ruled by Tawhid [the indivisibility of God] and the Sunna [the sayings and tradition of the Prophet Muhammed].'[66] He quotes another insurgent as saying, 'In invading a Muslim territory, the objective of the infidels has always been to destroy the cultural values of Islam. With them they bring nationalism, democracy, liberalism, communism, Christianity ... '[67]

Sunni Islamist insurgent groups also stressed an anti-Shia identity that shaped both social and political dynamics in the country. Hashim notes, 'For many of Iraq's Sunni Arabs ... there is something ineluctably non-Arab or anti-Arab – indeed even anti-Iraqi – about the Shia of their country.'[68] AQI, under its first leader Abu Mus'ab al-Zarqawi, and later ISIS claimed that killing Shia was not only permissible, branding them as apostates, but necessary to purify the Islamic community.[69] This narrative, and the identity it produced, had disastrous consequences for the country. Sunni-Shia violence erupted with the 2006 bombing of the al-Askari mosque in Samarra, one of AQI's opening attacks against Shia, and culminated with the mass slaughter of Shia in ISIS-held territory in Iraq and Syria.[70]

As important, Sunni Islamist insurgents formed an identity based not just on what they were fighting against, but also on what they were fighting for. Hashim asserts that, from the beginning, Sunni insurgents were fighting for the defense of their identity. 'Ultimately, the shock and resultant anger, as well as Coalition policies that struck at the Sunni Arabs' identity and self-worth, have contributed to the emergence and perpetuation of the insurgency.'[71] Hashim concludes, 'We cannot wish away the role of identity crisis as a grievance and as a primary cause of the insurgency, but we do because identity is such an intangible commodity ... '[72]

AQI and ISIS also called for the recreation of the caliphate to communicate purpose and identity. AQI briefly declared a state in Anbar, Iraq, in 2006, just after U.S. forces killed its leader, Zarqawi. That same year, Sunni leaders and U.

S. forces drove AQI out during the Anbar awakening.[73] After remnants of AQI reemerged and joined forces with other element to create ISIS, Adnani, the spokesperson for ISIS, claimed in 2013 that 'Our goal is to establish an Islamic state that doesn't recognize borders, on the Prophetic methodology.'[74] ISIS realized its goal of creating a modern-day caliphate in 2014, after it successfully captured Mosul, and began to implement what it claimed to be the most pure form of Islam.

Sunni Islamist insurgent groups further fought for what it meant to be a true Muslim, based on an identity shaped by an extreme interpretation of Islam and by invoking jihad to defend and promote their identity. Religious extremist groups like AQI and ISIS, therefore, provided a powerful identity that not only articulated what one is against, but what one is for, and what one's purpose is in life. This identity was a call to action and – at its most extreme – promised to change the world.

Finally, insurgent groups like AQI, and later ISIS, used well-known symbols to build their identity and communicate with target populations. Specifically, these groups drew from Salafism, a strict and literalist understanding of Islam that claims the Qur'an and the example of the Prophet provide a complete guide for Islam today, and that human reason is *biddah*, or innovation.[75] This understanding of Islam seeks to unify and purify the worldwide Muslim community; it is an ideology and identity known to many Sunni Muslims around the globe, thus expanding the group's identity beyond immediate circumstances in Iraq.

Furthermore, AQI and ISIS drew heavily from the Prophet Muhammed as a symbol to communicate identity and meaning to its followers.[76] All Muslims know the example of the Prophet and consider him a guide for life. Muslim studies scholar John Renard argues, for example, 'From a spiritual perspective, Muhammad functions as the progenitor par excellence, for God created him first of all creatures.'[77] AQI, and later ISIS, used the symbol of the Prophet to communicate the group's intent and identity. Islamic extremism expert William McCants notes that, after taking parts of Iraq, ISIS created billboards that called it 'A caliphate in accordance with the Prophetic method,' and included this slogan on their uniforms.[78] AQI and especially ISIS, therefore, drew from the example of the greatest Muslim to communicate its actions, goals, and identity to the worldwide Muslim community, the *ummah*.

Ultimately, AQI and ISIS were driven from the territory they held by a combination of international military intervention and the local population no longer supporting their presence. AQI did little to provide resources to the populations it controlled during its insurgent operations against Coalition forces in Iraq and, combined with its mercurial and parasitic practices, it lost the support of the population. ISIS made a greater attempt to work with the local populations it controlled under the Islamic State, particularly in Raqqa and Mosul, but it also lost the support of local populations over time.[79] The downfall of these insurgent groups suggests that, while identity may be important to garnering support and gaining recruits, other more material factors like access to basic resources, are also important for sustaining support of an insurgent movement in the long run.

Conclusion: a plan for collective identity building in COIN

If counterinsurgents want to compete holistically with insurgents to win the support of local populations, then consciously taking efforts to help build collective identity is an important undertaking in this effort. Helping to build national identity, if done effectively, could act as a force multiplier that inoculates the population from insurgents' agendas and gives them a competing sense of belonging and purpose. However, counterinsurgents should not be the driving force in this initiative, which would undoubtedly reflect their own cultural biases and priorities, thus making these efforts likely to fail, if not unethical. Rather, collective identity building must come from the people. Specifically, counterinsurgents could work through key individuals in society and government – community activists, artists, politicians, sports figures and other 'national entrepreneurs'[80] – to help create a sense of shared destiny among the population and connect that sentiment in a way that builds hope for the future.[81]

Counterinsurgents, at the direction of national entrepreneurs, can create this sense of common destiny by structuring tasks of their stabilization efforts in specific ways. First, development projects, if properly structured, are a useful way of building a shared identity among the population. For example, the Afghan government and international advisors launched the National Solidarity Program (NSP) in 2003 as a means of using development projects to build ties among community members and to connect villages and districts to the central government. The NSP required villages to build Community Development Councils – local leaders and other key figures – that would decide how to spend $60,000 grants through the creation of a project with a timeline and a budget that included ten percent from the community through monetary contributions, materials, or labor. The NSP aimed to build community, and a shared sense of destiny through decision-making, consensus building, and community ownership of development projects. These projects also had the added benefit of being 'insurgent-proof' because attacking these initiatives would destroy projects that the population had created, potentially alienating the very support the insurgents needed. The NSP created schools, bridges, roads, irrigation systems and water pumps, to name a few projects.[82] Ultimately, this approach to development could build a common destiny and social capital, or trust, within communities in addition to improving infrastructure.

Another COIN initiative that could include collective identity building as part of its overall aims is security force assistance. Training security forces provides necessary security against insurgent attacks, but could also be an opportunity to build a common identity through a shared understanding of what volunteers are fighting for, not just what they are fighting against. This common identity could be built through a collaborative effort between COIN forces and national entrepreneurs to provide a basic education of the country, its laws and ideals, and through an oath of office. For example, Colonel Stephen Townsend, commander of 3–2 Stryker Brigade in Iraq during the 2007 Battle of Baqubah, proposed seven rules and one oath for the Iraqi military fighting alongside U.S. forces:

> 1) Protect your community from AQI, JAM and other terrorist militia. 2) Accept both peaceful Sunni, Shia and others. 3) Stay in your neighbourhood/AO [area of operations] for your safety. 4) Take an oath of allegiance to the Constitution of Iraq. 5) Register with Iraqi Security Forces and Coalition Forces [biometrics for CF]. 6) For your safety, wear a standard uniform and markings. 7) Reserve hiring preference for Iraqi Police and Army.

And the proposed oath was:

> 1) I will support and defend the Constitution of Iraq. 2) I will cooperate fully with the Iraqi government. 3) I will guard my neighborhood, community and city. 4) I will bear no arms outside my home without coordination of Iraqi Security Forces or Coalition Forces. 5) I will bear no arms against the Government of Iraq, Iraqi Security Forces or Coalition Forces. 6) I will not support sectarian agendas.[83]

This oath is important because it required volunteers to identify what they were fighting against, namely specific insurgent groups and sectarian agendas, but also what they were fighting for, including the constitution and, as importantly, one's neighbors and community.

Yet another way that counterinsurgents could foster collective identity is by working with local communities and national entrepreneurs to create an inspiring national cause that effectively competes with insurgents. Atran argues, for example, that to compete with ISIS and other movements like it, governments and communities need to 'offer youth something that makes them dream, of a life of significance through struggle and sacrifice in comradeship ... which gives them a sense of special destiny and the will to fight; offer youth a positive personal dream, with a concrete chance of realization; and offer youth the chance to create their own local initiatives.'[84] Atran further argues that merely providing job opportunities is not sufficient inspiration. 'What dreams may come from most current government policies that offer little beyond promises of comfort and security? Young people will *not* choose to sacrifice everything, including their lives – the totality of their self-interests – just for material rewards.'[85] In other words, building a collective identity that successfully competes with insurgents requires more than just providing public goods and the chance to earn a living; national entrepreneurs, governments and communities need to foster 'a cause' that inspires individuals to participate in the destiny of the country.

Finally, counterinsurgents should work with national entrepreneurs and populations to create symbols that communicate collective unity and identity. These symbols could range from sports teams to inspiring pieces of architecture to national parks to television shows that highlight a country's collective identity, such as cuisine or music. As Geertz and other anthropologists assert, symbols create a shared sense of meaning and communication among a group. In Iraq, these symbols of shared meaning could have come from various national entrepreneurs and coalition powers could have helped elevate them and give them a national platform through grants or other initiatives.

Conclusion

This article has argued that collective identity building is a critical component of most insurgent movements but, by contrast, counterinsurgents devote surprisingly little attention to creating compelling identities that compete with insurgents. U.S. led operations in Iraq from 2003–2011 illustrate this dynamic: Sunni Islamist insurgencies in Iraq placed considerable importance on identity building, but counterinsurgents did not, focusing rather on building the structure of state. Ultimately, a counterinsurgent approach to collective identity building should include initiatives that help foster a sense of unity while stabilizing the state, including working through national entrepreneurs to identify unifying cultural tools and using them to reinforce a sense of common destiny among a country's population.

Notes

1. Atran, 2015.
2. Erikson, *Identity, Youth and Crisis*.
3. This article defines terrorism as a tactic that threatens or uses violence, usually against civilians, with the aim of gaining publicity or making governments look weak and ineffective. Insurgency is the wider strategy designed to challenge existing governments, overthrow governments, or secede from states. Therefore, terrorism is a tactic that insurgents can use to further their overall political goals.
4. Arena and Arrigo, "Social Psychology, Terrorism and Identity."
5. Arena and Arrigo, "Social Psychology, Terrorism and Identity"; and Crenshaw, "The Psychology of Political Terrorism."
6. Horgan, *Walking Away from Terrorism*; and Moghaddam, "The Staircase to Terrorism."
7. Meade, *Coming of Age in Samoa*.

8. Benedict, *Patterns of Culture*.
9. Norenzayan, Schaller, and Heine, "Evolution and Culture," 345.
10. Ibid., 346.
11. Geertz, "Religion as a Cultural System," 80.
12. Ibid., 81.
13. Swidler, "Culture in Action," 273.
14. Swidler, "Culture in Action," 278.
15. Atran, *Talking to the Enemy*, 8–9.
16. Anderson, *Imagined Communities*; and Atran, *Talking to the Enemy*, 11.
17. McBride, *Collective Dreams*, 1.
18. Ibid., 3.
19. Ibid., 1–22.
20. Eller, *From Culture to Ethnicity to Conflict*.
21. Eller, *From Culture to Ethnicity to Conflict*, 11.
22. Clausewitz, *On War*.
23. Taber, *The War of the Flea*, 12.
24. Sharpe, *From Dictator to Democracy*.
25. Taber, *The War of the Flea*.
26. Galula, *Counterinsurgency Warfare*, 12.
27. Ibid., 13.
28. Byman, *Understanding Proto-Insurgencies*, 11.
29. Ibid.
30. Ibid., 12.
31. U.S. Department of the Army, *Insurgencies and Counterinsurgencies*.
32. U.S. Department of the Army, *Insurgencies and Counterinsurgencies*, 3-3.
33. Kilcullen, "Intelligence," 144.
34. Galula, *Counterinsurgency Warfare*, 31.
35. Atran, *Talking with the Enemy*, 32–40.
36. Ibid., 39.
37. Kilcullen, *Accidental Guerilla*, xxiv-xxvii.
38. Packer, "Knowing the Enemy," 2.
39. Galula, *Counterinsurgency Warfare*, 14.
40. See note 32 above.
41. Kilcullen, "Intelligence"; Kilcullen, *Accidental Guerilla*; and Taber, *War of the Flea*.
42. Gregg, "Beyond Population Engagement."
43. Dobbins, et al, *America's Role in Nation Building*; Dobbins, et al, *The UN's Role in Nation Building*; and Dobbins, et al, *The Beginner's Guide to Nation Building*.
44. Fukuyama, *State Building*, 99.
45. Ghani and Lockhart, *Fixing Failed States*, 144.
46. Perito, ed., *Guide for Participants in Peace*, xxxiv.
47. Gregg, *Building the Nation*.
48. Gregg, Arquilla and Rothstein, eds. *The Three Circles of War*.
49. Bensahel, et al, *After Saddam*, 175–176. Chandrasekaran, "Interim Leaders Named in Iraq"; and Wright, "Iraqis Back New Leaders."
50. "Coalition Provisional Authority Order Number One."
51. Makia, "The Iraqi Elections of 2010 – and 2005."
52. Bensahel et al, *After Saddam*, 142–147.
53. Al-Salhy and Arango, "Sunni Militants Drive Iraqi Army Out of Mosul."
54. Department of Defense, "Measuring Stability and Security in Iraq."
55. "Iraq's Oil War"; and Blanchard, "Iraq: Oil and Gas Legislation."

56. "Constitution of the Republic of Iraq."
57. Packer, "The Lessons of Tal Afar."
58. Anderson, "Inside the Surge."
59. Clayton and Johnson, "The Enemy of My Enemy is My Friend"; and Porter, "Iraqi Prime Minister."
60. Hashim, *Insurgency and Counterinsurgency*, 59–124.
61. The Sunni Insurgent movement went through several iterations, mergers and name changes, See: Kilcullen, *Blood Year*, 21–23.
62. Hashim, *Insurgency and Counterinsurgency*, 18.
63. Hashim, *Insurgency and Counterinsurgency*, 23–24, 28.
64. Hashim, *Insurgency and Counterinsurgency*, 29.
65. Gregg, "Jihad of the Pen"; Lia, *The Society of Muslim Brothers*, 54–60; Esposito, *Islamic Threat*, 121; Adams, "Mawdudi and the Islamic State"; and Maududi, "Self-Destructiveness of Western Civilization."
66. Hashim, *Insurgency and Counterinsurgency*, 115–116.
67. Ibid., 116.
68. Ibid., 71.
69. Wood, *The Way of Strangers*, 118–120; Williams, *Counter Jihad*, 201–202; Kilcullen, *Blood Year*, 29–36; and McCants, *ISIS Apocalypse*, 7–15.
70. Kilcullen, *Blood Year*, 29.
71. Hashim, *Insurgency and Counterinsurgency*, 68.
72. Ibid., 69.
73. Kilcullen, *Blood Year*, 32–35; and McCants, *ISIS Apocalypse*, 15.
74. Wood, "What ISIS Really Wants," 20.
75. Wictorowicz. "Anatomy of the Salafi Movement," 207.
76. Wood, "What ISIS Really Wants."
77. John Renard, *Islam and the Heroic Image*, 105.
78. McCants, *ISIS Apocalypse*, 126.
79. Caris and Reynolds, "ISIS Governance in Syria," 4; and Irving, "What Life Under ISIS Looked Like from Space."
80. See note 47 above.
81. See note 47 above.
82. Ghani and Lockhart, *Fixing Failed States*, 206–211; and Humayun, Exum, and Nagl, "A Pathway to Success in Afghanistan."
83. "7 Rules, 1 Oath."
84. Atran, "The Role of Youth," Emphasis his.
85. Ibid.

Disclosure statement

The views expressed are those of the author and do not reflect the official policy or position of the U.S. Army War College, the Department of Defense, or the U.S. government.

Bibliography

"7 Rules, 1 Oath." *Michael Yon Online Magazine*, July 19, 2007. Accessed August 15, 2019. https://www.michaelyon-online.com/7-rules-1-oath.htm

Adams, Charles J. "Mawdudi and the Islamic State." In *Voices of Resurgent Islam*, edited by J.L. Esposito, 99–133. New York: Oxford University Press, 1983.

Al-Salhy, Suadad, and Tim Arango. "Sunni Militants Drive Iraqi Army Out of Mosul." *New York Times*, June 11, 2014. Accessed August 15, 2019. https://www.nytimes.com/2014/06/11/world/middleeast/militants-in-mosul.html

Anderson, Benedict. *Imagined Communities*. New York: Verso, 1991.

Anderson, Jon L. "Inside the Surge: The American Military Finds New Allies, but at What Cost?" *New Yorker*, November 19, 2007. Accessed August 25, 2019. https://www.newyorker.com/magazine/2007/11/19/inside-the-surge

Arena, Michael P., and Bruce A. Arrigo. "Social Psychology, Terrorism and Identity: A Preliminary Re-examination of Theory, Culture, Self, and Society." *Behavioral Sciences and the Law* 23 (2005): 485–506. doi:10.1002/bsl.653.

Ashraf, Ghani, and Clare Lockhart. *Fixing Failed States: A Framework for Rebuilding A Fractured Word*. New York: Oxford University Press, 2008.

Atran, Scott. *Talking to the Enemy: Faith, Brotherhood and the Unmaking of Terrorists*. New York: Ecco, 2010.

Atran, Scott. "On Youth, Violent Extremism, and Promoting Peace. Address to UN Security Council, April 23, 2015." *UNISA*, Accessed August 16, 2019. https://www.unisa.edu.au/siteassets/episerver-6-files/global/eass/mnm/publications/address_un_security_council_scott_atran.pdf

Benedict, Ruth. *Patterns of Culture*. New York: Houghton Mifflin, 1934.

Bensahel, Nora, Olga Oliker, Keith Crane, Richard R. Brennan, Heather S. Gregg, Thomas Sullivan, and Andrew Rathmel. *After Saddam: Prewar Planning and the Occupation of Iraq*. Santa Monica: RAND, 2008.

Blanchard, Christopher M. "Iraq: Oil and Gas Legislation, Revenue Sharing, and U.S. Policy." *Congressional Research Services*, November 3, 2009.

Byman, Daniel. *Understanding Proto-Insurgencies*. Santa Monica: RAND, 2007.

Caris, Charles C., and Samuel Reynolds. "ISIS Governance in Syria." *Institute for the Study of War, Middle East Security Report* 2 (2014): 1–43. Accessed August 25, 2019. http://www.understandingwar.org/sites/default/files/ISIS_Governance.pdf.

Chandrasekaran, Rajiv. "Interim Leaders Named in Iraq." *Washington Post*, June 2, 2004. Accessed August 16, 2019. http://www.washingtonpost.com/wp-dyn/articles/A7879-2004Jun1.html

Clausewitz, Carl. *On War*, Translated by M. Howard and P. Parret. Princeton, NJ: Princeton University Press, 1976.

Clayton, Govinda, and Andrew Thompson. "The Enemy of My Enemy Is My Friend ... the Dynamics of Self-Defense Forces in Irregular Warfare: The Case of the Sons of Iraq." *Studies in Conflict and Terrorism* 37, no. 11 (2014): 920–935. doi:10.1080/1057610X.2014.952262.

"Coalition Provisional Authority Order Number One: De-Ba'athification of Iraqi Society." *National Security Archive, George Washington University*, Accessed August 16, 2019.

https://nsarchive2.gwu.edu/NSAEBB/NSAEBB418/docs/9a%20-%20Coalition%20Provisional%20Authority%20Order%20No%201%20-%205-16-03.pdf
"Constitution of the Republic of Iraq." October 15, 2005. Accessed August 16, 2019. https://www.constituteproject.org/constitution/Iraq_2005.pdf?lang=en
Crenshaw, Martha. "The Psychology of Political Terrorism." In *Political Psychology*, edited by M. Hermann, 379–413. San Francisco: Jossey-Bass, 2006.
Dobbins, James, John G. McGinn, Keith Crane, Seth G. Jones, Rollie Lal, Andrew Rathmell, Rachel M. Swanger, and Anga R. Timilsina. *America's Role in Nation Building: From Germany to Iraq*. Santa Monica: RAND, 2003.
Dobbins, James, Seth G. Jones, Keith Crane, Andrew Rathmell, Brett Steele, Richard Teltschik, and Anga R. Timilsina. *The UN's Role in Nation Building: From the Congo to Iraq*. Santa Monica: RAND, 2005.
Dobbins, James, Seth G. Jones, Keith Crane, and Beth Cole DeGrasse. *The Beginner's Guide to Nation Building*. Santa Monica: RAND, 2007.
Dobbins, James, Seth G. Jones, Keith Crane, Christopher S. Chivvis, Andrew Radin, F, Stephen Larrabee, Nora Bensahel, Brooke Stearns Lawson, and Benjamin W. Goldsmith. *Europe's Role in Nation Building*. Santa Monica: RAND, 2008.
Eller, Jack D. *From Culture to Ethnicity to Conflict: An Anthropological Perspective on International Ethnic Conflict*. Ann Arbor: University of Michigan Press, 1999.
Erikson, Erik. *Identity, Youth and Crisis*. New York: W.W. Norton, 1968.
Esposito, John. L. *Islamic Threat: Myth or Reality?* New York: Oxford University Press, 1992.
Fukuyama, Francis. *State-Building, Governance and World Order in the 21st Century*. Ithaca: Cornell University Press, 2004.
Galula, David. *Counterinsurgency Warfare: Theory and Practice*. Westport, CN: Praeger, 2006.
Geertz, Clifford. "Religion as a Cultural System." In *Reader in Comparative Religions: An Anthropological Approach*, edited by W.A. Lessa and E.Z. Vogt, 78–89. Fourth ed. New York: Harper Collins, 1979.
Gregg, Heather S. "Beyond Population Engagement: Understanding Counterinsurgency." *Parameters* 39, no. 3 (2009): 18–31. Accessed August 25, 2019. https://ssi.armywarcollege.edu/pubs/parameters/articles/09autumn/gregg.pdf.
Gregg, Heather S. "Jihad of the Pen: Countering Al Qaeda's Revolutionary Ideology." *Terrorism and Political Violence* 22, no. 2 (2010): 292–314. doi:10.1080/09546551003597584.
Gregg, Heather S. *Building the Nation: Missed Opportunities in Iraq and Afghanistan*. Lincoln, NE: Potomac/University of Nebraska Press, 2018.
Gregg, Heather S, John Arquilla, and Hy. S. Rothstein, eds. *The Three Circles of War: Understanding the Dynamics of Conflict in Iraq*. Lincoln, NE: Potomac/University of Nebraska Press, 2010.
Hashim, Ahmed S. *Insurgency and Counterinsurgency in Iraq*. Ithaca: Cornell University Press, 2006.
Horgan, John. *Walking Away from Terrorism: Accounts of Disengagement from Racial and Extremist Movements*. New York: Routledge, 2009.
Humayun, Ahmed A., Andrew M. Exum, and John A. Nagl. "A Pathway to Success in Afghanistan: The National Solidarity Program." *Center for New American Security*, March 2009. Accessed August 16, 2019. http://www.cnas.org/files/documents/publications/CNAS%20Policy%20Brief%20-%20Supporting%20Afghanistans%20NSP%20March%202009.pdf

Irving, Doug. "What Life under ISIS Looked like from Space." *RAND Review*, January 9, 2018. Accessed August 16, 2019. https://www.rand.org/blog/rand-review/2018/01/what-life-under-isis-looked-like-from-space.html

Johnson, Keith. "Iraq's Oil War." *Foreign Policy*. January 17, 2014. Accessed August 16, 2019. http://foreignpolicy.com/2014/01/17/iraqs-oil-war/

Juergensmeyer, Mark. *Terror in the Mind of God: The Global Rise of Religious Violence*. Berkeley: University of California Press, 2000.

Kilcullen, David. "Intelligence." In *Understanding Counterinsurgency: Doctrine, Operations and Challenges*, edited by Thomas Rid and Thomas Keaney, 141–159. London: Routledge, 2010.

Kilcullen, David. *Blood Year: The Unraveling of American Counterterrorism*. New York: Oxford University Press, 2016.

Killcullen, David. *The Accidental Guerilla: Fighting Small Wars in the Midst of a Big One*. New York: Oxford, 2009.

Lia, Brinyar. *The Society of Muslim Brothers in Egypt*. Ithaca: Ithaca Press, 1998.

Makia, Kanan. "The Iraqi Elections of 2010—And 2005." *Middle East Brief*, no. 42 (2010): 1–8. Accessed August 25, 2019. https://www.brandeis.edu/crown/publications/meb/MEB42.pdf.

Maududi, Abul A'la. "Self-Destructiveness of Western Civilization." In *Modernist and Fundamentalist Debates in Islam: A Reader*, edited by Mansoor Moaddel and Kamran Talattof, 325–331. New York: Palgrave, 2000.

McBride, Keally D. *Collective Dreams: Political Imagination and Community*. University Park: Pennsylvania State Press, 2005.

McCants, William. *ISIS Apocalypse: The History, Strategy and Doomsday Vision of the Islamic State*. New York: St. Martins, 2015.

Meade, Margaret. *Coming of Age in Samoa*. New York: William Morrow, 1928.

Moghaddam, Fathali M. "The Staircase to Terrorism: A Psychological Explanation." *American Psychologist* 60, no. 2 (2005): 161–169. doi:10.1037/0003-066X.60.2.161.

Norenzayan, Ara, Mark Schaller, and Steven. J. Heine. "Evolution and Social Psychology." In *Evolution and Culture*, edited by T. Douglas, Kendrick Mark Schaller, and Jeffry A. Simpson, 343–366. New York: Taylor and Francis, 2006.

Packer, George. "Knowing the Enemy." *New Yorker*, December 10, 2006. Accessed August 25, 2019. https://www.newyorker.com/magazine/2006/12/18/knowing-the-enemy

Packer, George. "The Lessons of Tal Afar." *New Yorker*, April 10, 2006. Accessed August 25, 2019. https://www.newyorker.com/magazine/2006/04/10/the-lesson-of-tal-afar

Perito, Robert M, ed. *Guide for Participants in Peace, Stability and Relief Operations*. Washington, DC: U.S. Institute of Peace, 2007.

Porter, Gareth. "Iraqi Prime Minister Al-Maliki Draws U.S. Troops into Crackdown on Sunnis." *Washington Report on Middle East Affairs* 28, no. 4 (2009): 24–25 May/June. https://www.wrmea.org/009-may-june/iraqi-prime-minister-al-maliki-draws-u.s.-troops-into-crackdown-on-sunnis.html

Renard, John. *Islam and the Heroic Image*. Macom, GA: Mercer University Press, 1999.

Sharpe, Gene. *From Dictator to Democracy*. Boston: Albert Einstein Institute, 2002.

Swidler, Ann. "Culture in Action: Symbols and Strategies." *American Sociological Review* 51, no. 2 (1986): 273–286. doi:10.2307/2095521.

Taber, Robert. *The War of the Flea: The Classic Study of Guerilla Warfare*. Washington, DC: Potomac Press, 2002.

U.S. Department of Defense. "Measuring Stability and Security in Iraq." *November 2006 Report to Congress*, Accessed August 16, 2019. https://archive.defense.gov/pubs/pdfs/9010Quarterly-Report-20061216.pdf

U.S. Department of the Army. *FM 3-24/MCWP 3-33.5: Insurgencies and Counterinsurgencies*. Alexandria, Virginia: Department of the Army, May 2014.

Wictorowicz, Qunitan. "Anatomy of the Salafi Movement." *Studies in Conflict and Terrorism* 29, no. 3 (2006): 207–239. doi:10.1080/10576100500497004.

Williams, Brian G. *Counter Jihad: America's Military Experience in Iraq, Afghanistan and Syria*. Philadelphia: University of Pennsylvania Press, 2017.

Wood, Graeme. "What ISIS Really Wants." *Atlantic*, March 2015, Accessed August 15, 2019. https://www.theatlantic.com/magazine/archive/2015/03/what-isis-really-wants/384980/

Wood, Graeme. *The Way of Strangers: Encounters with the Islamic State*. New York: Random House, 2017.

Wright, Robin. "Iraqis Back New Leaders, Poll Says." *Washington Post*. June 25, 2004. Accessed August 16, 2019. http://www.washingtonpost.com/wp-dyn/articles/A3433-2004Jun24.html

Lost in translation: anthropologists and Marines in Iraq and Afghanistan

Paula Holmes-Eber

ABSTRACT
Drawing upon ethnographic data gathered over a six year period, this paper illustrates how the contrasting worldviews of US Marines and anthropologists frequently led to misunderstandings, frustrations, and garbled interpretations as the two struggled to work together to help resolve conflicts in Iraq and Afghanistan. I examine three key military domains where cultural experts and Marines attempted to work together to understand the cultural factors at play in both Iraq and Afghanistan: first as interpreters or experts in pre-deployment language and culture training programs; secondly in theater on the Human Terrain Teams; and third as cultural SMEs (experts) in military planning rooms. As the case studies and interviews illustrate, while both sides thought they were working together to understand the foreign cultures where they were operating, the real cross-cultural misunderstanding was ironically between the cultural experts and Marines.

In 2009, a power point slide, affectionately nicknamed the 'noodle' or 'spaghetti' slide, was circulated around Washington D.C. and the Department of Defense.[1] The slide, which attempted to summarize on one page – through a complex spaghetti web of lines and nodes – -the complexity of the social and cultural factors affecting the war in Afghanistan, brought quite a few laughs and comments, including a column in the *New York Times*.[2] Headed by the tongue-in-cheek title, 'We have met the enemy and he is power point,'[3] the column poked fun at the absurd lengths to which power point presentations had seemingly devolved in the military. 'When we understand that slide, we'll have won the war,' General McCrystal was quoted as saying upon seeing the slide – a comment which apparently brought laughter from his staff.

Curiously, while members of the American academic – and especially anthropological–community laughed at the slide as a parody of how the military simplified the cultural issues involved in the war in Afghanistan, several of the Marines I was working with at the time viewed the slide quite differently. 'You know that noodle diagram that was published in the *New York Times*?' commented Major Neal,[4] an intelligence officer conducting research on the situation in Afghanistan. 'Well everyone on the outside thought it was ridiculous. But those of us on the receiving end actually found it useful in thinking about the issues at work in the situation.'

These two differing perspectives are not simply differences of opinion or personal taste. As I will argue in this paper, they reflect a significant cultural division between anthropologists (and other cultural experts) and the U.S. military, indicating two separate worldviews and understandings of both the concept of culture and its appropriate representation and analysis. Drawing upon ethnographic data gathered over a six year period (2006-12), this article illustrates how the contrasting worldviews of the Marines and anthropologists frequently led to misunderstandings, frustrations, and garbled interpretations as the two struggled to work together to help resolve conflict in Iraq and Afghanistan.

In the following pages, I examine three key military domains where cultural experts and Marines attempted to work together to understand the cultural factors at play in both Iraq and Afghanistan: first as interpreters or experts in pre-deployment language and culture training programs; secondly in theater on the Human Terrain Teams; and third as cultural SMEs (experts) in military planning rooms. As the case studies and interviews illustrate, while both sides thought they were working together to understand the foreign cultures where they were operating, the real cross-cultural misunderstanding was – ironically – between the cultural experts and Marines.

Background and method

Within a few years after the invasions of Afghanistan (2001) and Iraq (2003), the U.S. military began turning to anthropologists and other 'cultural experts' to help explain the complex cultural factors fueling a clearly unconventional war for the 'hearts and minds' of the local populations. Cultural Subject Matter Experts (SMEs) were brought into the planning rooms, as advisors to commanders in theater, and as experts to help design and teach culture and language training programs for deploying service members.

Realizing that cultural understanding required time, study and experience, the Marine Corps (which had none of these) turned to outside specialists to quickly translate and explain the situation in terms that would make sense to Marines. In January 2006, three years after the initial invasion of Iraq, the Marine Corps Culture Center, CAOCL, received its official charter from General James Mattis (at the time, Lieutenant General at the Marine Corps Combat Development Command). The Center's initial purpose was to provide culture and language training for Marines deploying to Iraq. However, fairly quickly the Center's leadership realized that teaching a few phrases in Arabic along with some basic courtesies (or 'do's and don'ts' as the Marines called it) was not sufficient to provide the in-depth cultural understanding required to solve the problems the U.S. was facing in the new irregular warfare environment. So the Marine Corps University (MCU) founded a new and unique position: a 'professor of operational culture' who would teach graduate level courses on anthropology, Islam and the Middle East to the officers at the University.

In September 2006, I was hired for this new position at the Marine Corps University with additional responsibilities supporting the new Marine Corps Center for Advanced Operational Culture Learning (CAOCL). As an anthropologist with no background or understanding of the military, I quickly realized that in order to design a culture curriculum that would fit the needs of the Corps, I needed to understand the culture of the Marines in my classes. This study thus first began as research on how Marines' internal military culture influenced their ability to learn about and make sense of the new DoD cultural directives in the classroom.

My research approach focused initially on the resident Marine Corps officer and enlisted education programs. I not only taught my own classes at the four officer and one enlisted officer schools at the University, but I devoted significant time to observing classes taught by other faculty. Furthermore, I observed and interviewed instructors and their classes at the Officers' Candidate School (OCS) and the Basic School (TBS) as well as the Infantry Officers' course (IOC).

Over time, however, the project expanded to focus not only on ways that culture was being incorporated into education programs, but how the new culture requirements were being interpreted and implemented into Marine Corps training – from the recruit depots to training prior to deployment to Afghanistan, Iraq, and other locations that Marines were being sent. Thus in addition to conducting ethnographic observations and interviews at seven of the resident Marine Corps schools, I also traveled to the different MEFs (Marine Expeditionary Forces) on the east and west coast. With the support from several Marine Corps educational programs, I was sent to observe Marine Corps cultural training programs and pre-deployment exercises at Camp LeJeune, NC, 29 Palms, CA, 8th and I in Washington D.C. and on base at Quantico, V.A. Observations included watching simulated cultural exercises such the Mojave Viper CAX (Combined Arms Exercises) which prepared Marines for combat in Iraq and observing culture lectures and briefs to battalions preparing for deployment. Finally, I spent an intense week of observation and interviews with the leadership, instructors, and recruits at Parris Island Recruit Depot in South Carolina. These experiences form the basis for this paper.

To make sense of what I was observing, I also conducted in-depth interviews with over 80 commissioned, non-commissioned, and retired Marines at all levels from second lieutenant to general officer, as well as from recruits to sergeant majors. A number of Marines who had returned from recent deployments to Iraq and Afghanistan also volunteered to discuss their cultural challenges while operating in the field.[5] Thus the study not only included data on programmatic challenges and processes but also individual Marines' on-the-ground views of their need for and use of culture 'in theater.'

Last, but not least, I led the design, implementation and analysis of an online survey by CAOCL focusing on attitudes towards culture and language learning.[6] Launched in February 2010, with the assistance of the Marine Corps Center for Lessons Learned,[7] CAOCL sent out an anonymous survey to 15% of all Marines (except general officers) with addresses on the Global Address List (GAL). The survey sample consisted of predominantly career Marines (with ranks of lieutenant or corporal and above): in other words, those Marines who had been in the Marine Corps long enough to have been deployed and to have received culture and language training in the past four years.[8]

We received 2406 valid responses from active duty Marines from every rank (except general officer), and every military occupational specialty (MOS). 83% of the respondents had deployed at least once during their careers and 20% were currently deployed at the time they filled out the survey. The survey asked Marines basic demographic questions regarding their rank, military occupational specialty, age, gender, education, language and cultural background, and deployment experience. Marines were also requested to answer a series of questions about their use of culture and language skills while deployed, their pre-deployment culture and language training, the usefulness and value of culture and language training for preparing them for the mission, and how important they thought culture and language skills were, in general, for mission effectiveness. In addition to a set of standardized questions, Marines had several opportunities to provide open ended answers and suggestions.[9]

This wide range of fieldwork over such a long period of time provided a unique opportunity to examine firsthand the challenges that anthropologists and other 'cultural experts' faced in assisting the Marine Corps in understanding the cultural factors influencing military operations in Iraq and Afghanistan.

Teaching culture: anthropologists, terps and other cultural 'experts' try to communicate

One of the first steps the Marine Corps (and other services) took at the beginning of the invasion in Iraq was to hire or locate individuals within the Marine Corps and other services who understood the culture and language of

Iraq. This early solution to the problem reflected the military's and Marine Corps' assumption that culture and language were virtually synonymous and interchangeable.

Thus, some of the first outsiders to be employed by the military during the Iraq war were, not unexpectedly, interpreters who not only translated words, but also often provided cultural explanation and advice. 'Terps' (as Marines referred to them) were hired to assist units in speaking to both Iraqi leaders and others in the population. Usually these interpreters were heritage speakers from Iraq or other Arabic speaking countries and were assigned to specific Marine units during their deployment. As one interpreter, Sayyid, observed, 'They knew it was very important. They needed to have language and culture there. But they were kind of on the lazy side – they wanted someone else to do the translation, handle the culture for them.'

During my research, numerous Marines commented on the importance of their 'terps in teaching them the language and culture of the area. 'I cannot forget the interpreters. My interpreters were always teaching us words and ways of the Iraqi people,' noted a gunnery sergeant and radio chief in his response to the CAOCL survey. Similarly, a Marine captain and ground supply officer stated on the survey, 'Having the services of a local interpreter is invaluable in interacting with locals (people from the local population). Interpreters can understand more than U.S. service members what is actually being said, cultural nuances and exactly what locals are trying to convey based on their cultural understanding.'

In addition to hiring interpreters and native speakers from the region, anthropologists, and other 'cultural experts' were also hired in the United States to develop and provide language and culture training to the troops prior to departure. In part, due to the Marine Corps' predilection for quick execution and action, and in part reflecting its inherent flexibility in responding to the mission, initially there was no centralized organization hiring and training these experts. Reflecting the Marine Corps' respect for leadership and decision making at all levels, unit leaders and higher level commanders were given an immense amount of discretion in selecting what pre-deployment training they conducted, how much time to devote to that training, and who would provide the training. The result was an extraordinary flourishing of many kinds of culture and language training programs, provided by a range of different contracting companies.

Since the U.S. government was reluctant to hire new permanent personnel, in order to meet the sudden and urgent need for interpreters and instructors, most were hired through private contracting companies (the U.S. government equivalent of temporary employment agencies). As a result, initially Marines were receiving interpreters and training from many different organizations and individuals, each with their own approaches and ideas as to how culture and language should be taught, interpreted and understood. Some were contracted by Marine Corps organizations such as CAOCL (Center for Advanced Operational Culture), MCIA (the Marine Corps Intelligence Activity), the former SCETC (Security Cooperation Education and Training Command) or the ATG (Advisor Training Group). Others were contracted out from DoD organizations (for example the Defense Language Institute, DLI) or other U.S. military services such as the Army. Yet, many other private contracting companies were also providing their own translators, instructors, and materials directly to specific Marine units. And in certain cases, local community colleges or universities were also offering classes taught by their faculty or graduate students.

Since the contracting companies hired the interpreter or instructor, by law it was up to the contractor – not the U.S. government – to screen and train applicants and determine if they were qualified to interpret or teach. This created a number of practical problems in providing Marines with culture and language support in ways that worked for them. First, while a number of these pre-deployment training instructors were natives from Iraq – and later Afghanistan – due to the difficulty in locating sufficient heritage speakers and culture experts, in the initial years (2003–2008) these instructors came from a great range of backgrounds. Some were Middle Eastern expatriates or their children; others were anthropologists or other regional experts who had a background in the Middle East; and a few were simply Marines who had completed a deployment in Iraq and could talk about their experiences.

As several Marines observed in their responses to the CAOCL survey, the hodgepodge of instructors and interpreters was extremely varied in their quality and ability to communicate and teach. A number of them were outstanding. One Chief Warrant Officer, for example, stated, 'the best was during a MOUT [military operations on urban terrain] training in 2007 before an OIF deployment where Iraqi nationals lived in the town we trained in aboard Camp LeJeune. They cooked for us, sang songs and broke us down into small groups where we discussed cultural issues.'

However, other instructors and interpreters were not adequately qualified or prepared to work with Marines. On occasion, Marine units would deploy with an interpreter who was not capable of translating. Sometimes the interpreter or instructor did not speak either English or the native language well. In other cases, particularly in areas where many languages are spoken, the interpreter or instructor did not speak the language of the area to which the Marines were deploying. 'We deployed to Nuristan province – where no one speaks Pashto or Dari – only Nuristani. Even our interpreters didn't speak the language,' noted a logistics officer in his comments on the survey.

'We had a situation where an Afghan SME (subject matter expert) was supposed to do role playing for a KLE [key leader engagement]. And he didn't speak a word of Pashtu. So he was speaking Dari and the students were speaking Pashtu and it didn't work,' Lieutenant Colonel Jones stated about a negotiation exercise. In another case, one staff sergeant wrote in frustration in his response to the CAOCL survey, '[Our instructor] had not yet mastered the English language and we couldn't understand 50% of what he was saying.'

Language and verbal interpretation skills however, were not the only problem. In my interviews and in the CAOCL survey, a number of Marines expressed concerns about the reliability of the cultural information they were receiving or the bias of their teachers. 'Instructors need to be screened and teach fact, and not preach their personal academic/moral/religious agenda,' commented a Marine captain on the survey:

> Academics and expatriates are not necessarily the best or up-to-date. I had multiple instructors talk to me *ad nauseum* about Afghan culture, Pashtunwali (an Afghan ethical code), do's and don'ts etc. After nine months with the Afghans, I know that these instructors were grossly out of touch with the current state of Afghan 'culture.'

A Marine lieutenant colonel and infantry officer echoed these sentiments when he stated, 'Don't rely on culture learning from expatriates who have lived in the U.S. for too many years. They are out of touch with their own people often.'

The importance of receiving instruction from individuals who have had recent experience in theater was emphasized by one captain who commented in the survey, 'I highly recommend finding instructors that have been to Afghanistan in the past ten years, particularly interpreters who have been expatriated and know how to communicate to Marines. And [also hiring] Marines that have deployed to these theaters in recent years.'

Even so, some Marines in the survey cautioned that simply having experience in theater was not sufficient for someone to teach about the culture of the country. As one captain wrote in his response to the CAOCL survey, 'I felt that the instructor, who was a prior corporal with PTT (Police Transition Team) experience, had no business being a cultural instructor and ... knew little more than myself.'

While the Marines sometimes found their translators and instructors unable to provide what they thought they needed, on the other side, the instructors had their own challenges. Muhammad, a native Arabic speaker who was hired to teach language and culture to Marines, explained his initial frustration in working with the Corps:

> I saw an ad looking for an Arabic instructor three months after I got here [Muhammad had just moved to the U.S.]. By chance. The interesting thing was when I came [to the Corps] – the culture shock. It wasn't that big with adjusting to the U.S. But here the first thing that struck me was I realized how I didn't know that much about the Marine Corps. I was really surprised. Here there are Marines and they don't know anything about the Middle East!

> The second shock was they think they don't need it, they don't care. [They would say to me],'Why do I need to learn Arabic? They all speak English'.
>
> From that I started to learn what they need, what they want. I began to learn how to communicate with them because I had to learn *their* language. Another point that I learned about Marines. They are standing there and they are thinking, 'What do you know?' You have to sell yourself. If you don't know the tools you need to communicate in a few words, you either lose them or win them.
>
> I was put with a Marine sergeant to see how he taught culture. He showed me tricks, being a Marine – how he taught the class, how he went around .... I learned how to speak – just jumping in, to challenge them without making it sound personal. The sergeant taught me by observing him. It's all about bonding with them. I share with them stories from other Marines and they like it. They see that you are speaking their language and you understand what they need.

As I will elaborate in the next sections, this cross-cultural dance between Marine and SMEs (especially the difficulty in translating from Marine culture to outside experts they have turned to for help) was more than simply a case of learning each other's traditions or 'do's and don'ts.' It reflected fundamental cultural differences in the ways that Marines and their cultural experts viewed their roles and purpose in understanding culture in the battlespace.

Culture SMEs in theater: translation challenges of the Human Terrain Teams

In addition to hiring interpreters and instructors to assist with culture and language training for Iraq and Afghanistan, the U.S. government and military engaged a second set of academic experts to aid in understanding the social and cultural issues in theater: SMEs. While these SMEs worked in many roles, ranging from positions on the joint staffs to contractors in the field, the most publicized and controversial engagement of SMEs was with the Army's Human Terrain Teams (HTTs).[10]

Started in 2007, the Army's HTTs were intended to provide a new critical cultural capacity to the military battalions stationed in Iraq and Afghanistan. According to the HTT Handbook, 'HTTs are five to nine person teams deployed by the Human Terrain System to support field commanders by filling their cultural knowledge gap in the current operating environment and providing cultural interpretations of events occurring within their area of operations.'[11] These teams were expected to go out among the population and assess the situation from the local people's perspective, reporting back to the commander on what they had seen and heard.

The Marine Corps never actually funded or deployed any of their own HTTs, which were under the direction of the Army. However, a number of

Marine units, working in conjunction with the Army, were assigned their own HTTs, funded by the Army. The HTTs received considerable negative attention in the media from individuals belonging to the American Anthropological Association (AAA) who complained that the use of anthropologists on the teams violated ethical standards of the discipline.[12] (An official report on the issue by the AAA, found that these teams were not conducting anthropology, thus sidestepping the conflict.)[13] Ironically, given that most of the complaints came from members of the AAA, very few cultural anthropologists[14] actually ever deployed on the five to nine person teams, which were typically composed of a team leader, one to two social scientists (who typically held a master's or doctoral degree in *any* social science discipline, not just anthropology), two to four analysts and a research manager. The majority of the team members were retired or active duty military with an occasional political scientist or international relations specialist as the 'social scientist' rather than an anthropologist.[15] These teams were intended to assist military commanders in understanding the cultural situation in the area.

One of the major challenges for these teams was that the social scientists were ostensibly hired to provide a general understanding of what was going on in the area – offering openly accessible information (not intelligence) about overall attitudes and concerns faced by the population. However, to the Marines and soldiers working with these teams, the academics on the HTTs were typically seen as 'combat assets,' assisting the commander in applying cultural knowledge to the battlespace. Thus while the social scientists on these teams tended to view their role as providing research data and studies of the local communities in order to advance the military's basic cultural understanding and knowledge, Marines and soldiers working with the social scientists tended to see them as just another kind of 'intelligence asset' – providing secret information that could be used to locate and target possible insurgents and prevent their hostile activities.

This differing interpretation of the use of cultural information from the SMEs was described by Colonel James, who worked closely with an HTT during his deployment to Iraq, '[Sometimes] there were translation issues. One afternoon I was trying to work out a predictive tool, so I needed info. I looked over the room and asked Mary (the social scientist on the team), "Can you give me this information?" She said, "I can't do that. That would be targeting".'

The translation problem worked both ways, however, as Mary Fielding (the HTT social scientist mentioned above) later added:

> [I have to emphasize the] importance of understanding the culture of the military you're working with. There may be someone who knows more about the subject than you, but if you are able to talk to the commander and explain in a way that he wanted, you would be the one listened to. There were a lot of social scientists with PhDs who were walking around telling everyone about

their degrees and their universities and how important they were. And they would talk to the military commander as if he was barely out of kindergarten. It turned out that three of the commanders had PhDs from Ivy League universities.

She continued, noting that over time, the SMEs and the military officers slowly began to understand what the other was trying to accomplish, 'What was important was when they started trying to understand academics. We went from eggheads to becoming a member of the team.'

This difficult dance between the Marines and their cultural experts was not simply a matter of learning to communicate properly and work together, however. As my observations and efforts to support Marines in the planning room revealed, these challenges reflected important differences between two significantly different worldviews – between the perspectives of those with 'hard skills' (tangible, concrete visible skills such as mapping the battlespace) and 'soft skills' (those intangible, hard to quantify understandings of human relationships and interactions).

Cultural analysis in the planning room: power point, maps and 'human terrain'

The windowless room in the Marine Corps Battle Staff Training Facility (BSTF) looked to me just like something straight out of a Star Wars movie. Five enormous video screens filled the walls. A colorful map of the conflict area, showing its mountains, rivers, roads, rail lines and ports filled the two corner screens. Three other screens portrayed a second map, showing the same landscape but overlaid with strange symbols – colored rectangles with X's and circles inside, black lines connecting the rectangles, and big blue arrows emanating from the boxes and converging on a set of red arrows. Pasted on the walls between the screens were sheets of butcher block paper and computer printouts with diagrams and charts providing a dizzying array of information: anything from the location of police stations, names of local mayors, tables of local imports and exports, plans of sewer systems and diagrams of relationships between known insurgent groups in the area.

Below the screens and charts, a large U-shaped table lined with laptop computers and stacks of papers followed the walls of the room. Along the table, twenty- four Marine majors and lieutenant colonels sat hurriedly working on their computers in front of them. Every now and then one of them would stand up to hand a paper or diagram to his colleague and speak in rapid, but quiet tones. At the back of the room stood several colonels, chatting unconcernedly to a couple of civilians, who stuck out distinctly in their suits and ties. Seated at a separate table in the middle of the 'U,' two general officers shuffled a stack of papers, shared a quiet joke and stared periodically at the five enormous screens on the walls, waiting.

The screens flickered. In front of the screens stood a Marine lieutenant colonel, slightly tense in the shoulders but composed.

'The slides?' he queried a Marine to his right sitting at the table. "Generals. Colonels. This is Lieutenant Colonel Hastings. My team and I will be briefing you on the cultural IPB [intelligence preparation of the battlefield] for exercise Mojave Sting."

Today, whether or not Marines or other staff members like it (and many do not), the primary medium for communicating in the military is by providing summaries of one's work through power point. As General Taylor advised the students in the planning exercise described above, '[You must] become a student of briefing. Man has evolved to power point. That's the way of military life. We use briefing.'

From a cultural perspective, the use of power point to communicate in the military reflects a uniquely visual way of thinking about and conceptualizing the world. In my work, both at Marine Corps University and with Marine Corps organizations, it was expected that we would not only use power point presentations, but also maps, diagrams, charts, tables, graphs, videos, and even dynamic fading and appearing pictures or words to represent the problems we were discussing. For example, Dr. Green described a lecture he had just prepared to me: 'Visual representation of information is essential – [for example in this lecture I use a] hierarchy map, networks maps, photos, videos and aerial photos.'

This emphasis on conceptualizing the world visually was explained to me by Colonel Simons, 'We just love to look at things in maps and pictures. That's the way we were brought up. We just love that.' Elaborating further, he explained how the physical environment – or 'terrain' – is a central part of the way that Marines look at the world, 'We think about everything in terms of terrain. I can't drive home without thinking of everything in terms of terrain – how the road rises, where the river is. It's something that Marines can relate to.'

In traditional battlefield analyses, the military preference for information that is transmitted visually is quite logical. Conventional military battles are fought on clearly defined physical spaces (or terrain) which are well suited to analysis using geographic techniques such as mapping. Not surprisingly, then, early on in the culture venture (and congruent with this visual way of thinking about conflict), culture became translated into the military metaphor of *'human terrain.'* Like physical terrain, which could be mapped and understand graphically, putting humans *on the map* made sense.

Explaining why 'human or cultural terrain' was a useful way for the military to think about people who were in the battlespace, Major Neal stated, 'Culture is a tool that can be used in any environment. That's why we focus on cultural terrain as a concept that fits within the military. [It provides a] process of how to use cultural information in a diagram we are familiar with.' In a demonstration of the 'Mapping the Human Terrain Project' called Map H-T, one of the leaders of the project emphasized its value to the military by stating, '[Our] product is a battlefield information sharing system that shows cultural information on a map. It helps inform my planning on a macro level.' He continued by noting that this system would help, 'to get your arms around all that plethora – to get human data into a format that is useful. How do you help manage what the commander on the ground needs to know? [With this product] you can visually predict in layers.' His comments thus emphasized the way that mapping 'human terrain' could help commanders quickly grasp and constrain the complex, 'soft' and unfamiliar concept of culture in a structure that was familiar to them.

Although 'human terrain' is a metaphor that makes sense to a military culture that views the world through maps, this two dimensional, static way of conceptualizing culture produced some rather unusual interpretations of human behavior (from my academic and scholarly perspective), especially when used to analyze a non-conventional battlespace. This strange 'mis'-translation became very clear to me during a final cumulative wargaming exercise at Command and Staff College (CSC) called 'Nine Innings.'

Deviled eggs?: Eggheads and devil dogs share plans

Requiring the preparation of a fictive operational/strategic plan for stabilizing the Philippines, the final wargame of Nine Innings at CSC involved the entire school of two hundred students plus faculty and numerous outside experts (SMEs) from Marine Corps University. Over a two week period, students were split up into planning cells (or groups) and were assigned different issues to research and report on to the commanding general for the exercise. Cells and teams were distinguished by colors (blue for friendly forces, red for hostile forces and green for the 'neutral' population). Indeed, the military convention of labeling various actors in the battlespace by a color rather than a number or a name, immediately emphasized the visual nature of the exercise.

Most interesting from a cultural point of view, however, were the products of the exercise. Each day, students produced power point slides that visually summarized their findings. Economic, political, social, cultural, ethnic, linguistic and militarily strategic information was depicted through colorful graphs, charts, and maps. Words were primarily reduced to a few key terms below the slide, definitions of symbols or occasionally, bulleted lists.

Students creatively found ways to summarize the information they had collected over the day, using signs such as arrows, lines, color coding, circles, flags and numerous other symbols that were initially unintelligible to me. Many of these strange symbols, it turned out, were a standard set of military symbols which all students study in the Joint Marine-Army publication *Operational Terms and Graphics* best known as FM101-5-1.[16] Like the symbols one learns for reading geographic or nautical maps, these symbols are part of the military language and integrally tied to mapping functions.

A particularly interesting case example was the power point produced by the 'green cell'[17] with which I was working. Students in the cell (which analyzed the local population) were assigned the task of briefing the commanding general on the ethnic and linguistic composition of the Philippines and then relating this composition to levels of income or poverty. The students in the cell were initially rather overwhelmed by the ethnic and linguistic data: the Philippines consist of well over one hundred ethnic and linguistic groups scattered over more than seven thousand islands. Furthermore, maps of poverty and income levels were incomplete across the country, making any kind of meaningful correlation unlikely.

To my great surprise on the day of the briefing, the students had succeeded in reducing an immense amount of complex data into one simple slide. The slide agglomerated the more than one hundred ethnic and linguistic groups into three simple categories. Then, on the basis of the simpler, reshaped ethnographic landscape, a map of poverty across the Philippines was overlaid upon the ethnic data suggesting a weak relationship between the two. From my perspective as a SME, it seemed I had failed in assisting the students in conducting an effective analysis of a complex situation: one where the culture and characteristics of the local population were not fixed and easily measurable and where meaningful relationships between factors would require careful statistical, not visual analysis. However, the students' power point slide was received quite well by the military leadership for the exercise who saw the slide as providing exactly what they needed.

What had happened in the translation? Why would visual analyses such as the noodle slide described at the beginning of the article or the Philippines cultural summary in Nine Innings 'hit the target' for its military viewers while seeming extremely simplistic and reductionist to me or other anthropologists? As I learned through my later observations and interviews, from my students' point of view, it would have been professional suicide to provide the general officers with reams of confusing and even conflicting information (which is what I, as a scholar, thought appropriate). Due to Marine Corps (and general military) cultural ideals of decisiveness and the ability to respond quickly in ambiguous situations, my students understood that successful communication and briefs to the general required them to be succinct and provide only the most essential information in a short period of time.

'Give it to me Barney style': time, speed and simplification

In his practical, terse and direct way, General Taylor explained to me one day why the military did not have time to spend hours researching and analyzing issues, 'Part of the problem we had at (a joint headquarters command) was that we just sat around admiring the problem. But we who are in the military have to do something. We have to go out and deal with the tsunami, the insurgent, whatever. We can't just sit there.'

Given the rapid 'churn' or tempo of operations when deployed, Marines often have very little time to conduct anything more than a quick surface assessment of an issue. Describing the frantic pace and time pressure on one of the organizations evaluating cultural issues in Afghanistan while he was deployed, Lieutenant Colonel Lyons observed, 'Their problem was partly that they were expected to put out a product each day. I don't blame them, if I had to put out a report every day that's what I'd do [simplify the issue]. So you end up with a report that's an inch deep and a mile wide. It's a check-in-the-box.'

Echoing this concern with lack of time, at one of the warfighting exercises, a Marine intelligence analyst commented to me, 'We don't have time for the complex analysis. So what we need to do is extract the important information, download it to a system and then input it into a map. We're all about maps.'

This sense of urgency and the need to take action and be decisive often leads to a disconnect between Marines and the PhDs working with them, who are often accused of losing sight of the main objective. In leading a working group composed of Marines and academics, Colonel Irons reflected this concern, 'I don't want this to be an academic discussion – no offense to you academics – but those tend to just get going and going and (lifts arms wide). We need to get something done. So if we can try to focus the discussion and get some outputs.'

Conversely, the expectation that SMEs could provide a hastily assembled, simplistic analysis of a problem also led to frustration on the academics' part. As Mary Fielding commented to me about her work on a Human Terrain Team in Iraq, 'Power point briefings. You really have to know the language of your audience. Sometimes you would be asked to provide one slide with five points and only two seconds to tell what it means. It was an incredible experience to me to walk in and have someone from the Marines tell me that, "You have ten minutes to tell me how you are value-added, and if you don't you can leave."'

Marines and anthropologists not only have different expectations regarding the appropriate amount of time necessary to research a problem, but as Ms. Fielding notes above, they both also diverge on the kinds and amount of information that needs to be provided. Most of the Marines I interviewed subscribed to the KISS (Keep It Simple Stupid) approach to communicating information, especially in briefs to general officers. In numerous presentations,

I have heard the commanding officer chide a presenter who was talking too long, or providing too much information, state, 'Give it to me Barney-style' – indicating he wanted a very basic simple explanation. 'I think less is more,' stated one of the lieutenant colonels regarding his brief on culture for one of the Pacific Challenge planning exercises, 'If I put too much in the slide, I'll confuse them.'

Frequently, because so many people are contributing an immense amount of information in a brief to a general officer, even if they would like to include more information, both Marines and SMEs are rarely given the opportunity to provide more than one power point slide on their work. During the Command and Staff College Nine Innings exercise, for example, students in the 'green cell' were expected to summarize an entire day's worth of information and research into one slide for their brief to the Commanding General. As one student explained, 'We cannot afford to get down into the details. We have a very defined endstate.'

Limited time and slide space, however, are not the only reason that Marines might condense the information into a few power point slides. As Major Davis observed about his role on a planning team in Iraq, 'If you can't put it up on a wall and you can't visualize it – it goes away. I had a forty page document but if I hadn't put it up on the wall, they wouldn't have understood any of it.' The need to present simple, concise, visually clear information was also expressed by one of the majors in a Nine Innings exercise. 'How you display the system is very influential in understanding it. We try to map the problem or create a framework to constrain the problem.'

In another conversation about a culture training brief, Lieutenant Colonel Jones stated, 'A picture is worth a thousand words. That's ten times more important for the operator. Yes, there's more details [that should be included] and a lot of information is left out. But the operator isn't going to read that.'

However, while virtually all of the Marines I talked to were clear that the military system left little time or space for complex analyses, several of them expressed their concerns that such analyses were not always sufficient. In the Nine Innings exercise, for example, one of the team leaders expressed his difficulty with reducing a large amount of cultural information into a slide, 'Graphic tools are great, but we're having the problem of trying to depict it. We can conceptualize the problem but we're having difficulty representing it.' Similarly, a Marine major who was working on a computer modeling program for tribal structures in Iraq also observed, 'Demographics are changing rapidly. Tribal movements, people movements change everything in six months. It changes daily even. To try to map it is improbable.'

And in discussing his experiences in the brigade command staff in Afghanistan, Colonel Chase remarked about the cultural aspects of the situation, 'I think we're too quick to propose solutions before we understand the problem. I think we need to be taking more time, studying and understanding the problems and making less power points.'

Discussion and conclusion

Whether during pre-deployment language and culture training, in theatre on Human Terrain Teams or in the planning room, Marines assumed that the cultural experts working with them had the necessary expertise (which was not always the case), viewed the cultural experts as additional intelligence assets (a major ethical issue that most anthropologists could not explain to their military counterparts), and shared their military values and goals of accomplishing the mission quickly and effectively. From the anthropologists' perspective, on the other hand, they were frustrated and puzzled as to why they were being asked to provide information and analyses in ways that watered down or even invalidated the scholarly validity of their input. Failing to understand the language and culture of the Marine Corps, anthropologists' assistance often failed to explain the cultural issues in ways the Marines expected, providing limited value or applicability for the Marines. Culture, then, frequently became 'lost in translation' despite the many millions of dollars invested in developing culturally relevant programs and projects.

This cultural disconnect between anthropologists and the military is not a new phenomenon. As Montgomery McFate[18] illustrates in great detail, the efforts of anthropologists to assist the US in developing culturally effective military operations over the past century have left behind a trail of misguided and failed cooperation spanning the globe from Siberia to Palau to Kenya to Burma to Vietnam to contemporary conflicts in Iraq and Afghanistan. During World War II, David Price[19] argues, despite the enormous number of anthropologists who supported the war effort in many forms, the partnership was so fraught with ethical and scholarly difficulties that anthropologists and the military parted ways on such inimical terms that many anthropologists today still view the military as 'the Evil Empire.' During the Vietnam War, a concerted effort was made by the military to recruit anthropologists and social scientists to assist in understanding the Vietnamese culture with similarly doomed results: the institutional and cultural differences between government and social scientists proved so great that despite major efforts on both sides, Congress scrapped the so-named Project Camelot and similar programs, viewing them as a waste of money and resources.[20] In the current round of military-anthropology cooperation in Iraq and Afghanistan, anthropologists have shared their puzzlement and frustration as they have attempted to create culturally based courses at the Naval Academy,[21] develop culturally appropriate research among the intelligence community[22] or work with the military to preserve archaeological sites and artifacts.[23]

The difficulties faced by the military and anthropologists in understanding what the other needs in order to translate successfully between the different cultures provides a fascinating challenge. As the examples above illustrate, while Marines and anthropologists (and other cultural experts) may both originate from the same American culture, that does not mean they view or interpret the world in the same way. Paradoxically, the problem suggests that cultural challenges may not simply exist 'out there' between the U.S. and other countries, but between our own subcultures: whether they are military cultures, NGO cultures, government cultures or civilian and academic cultures.

Notes

1. Portions of this paper have been adapted from the author's book, Holmes-Eber, *Culture in Conflict*.
2. Bumiller, "We Have Met the Enemy."
3. Ibid.
4. To protect the individuals in this study, all names are pseudonyms.
5. It is important to note that due to ethical and professional considerations I have never applied for or received a security clearance. Thus all data in this study, including interviews and discussions with military personnel, by definition, contain no sensitive information. With the exception of removing personally identifying information, then, no 'scrubbing' of data from my interviews or fieldnotes has been necessary prior to their publication. Furthermore, no personal benefit has been gained by the author as a result of this research.
6. A separate IRB was obtained for this statistical study.
7. A large portion of the survey implementation, design and analysis was conducted by Erika Tarzi and Basma Maki at CAOCL and I am indebted to them for their diligent work. I am also deeply indebted to the hard work and support of MCLL (Marine Corps Lessons Learned) who programmed and sent out the survey online for CAOCL.
8. Almost all Marines of higher ranks are included in the GAL. However entry level Marines (E-1s privates, E-2s lance corporals and O-1s second lieutenants) often do not obtain email addresses until they have completed their MOS (military occupational specialty) training. General Officers were excluded. A few Marine reservists who were currently on active duty did respond to the survey as well as 7 Navy medical, engineering and chaplain MOS who were embedded with Marine units.
9. A complete description of the survey questionnaire, sampling frame and methodology are available from CAOCL upon request.
10. For an in-depth discussion of anthropologists' experiences and challenges in working on the Human Terrain Teams see McFate, *Social Science goes to War*.
11. U.S. Human Terrain System, *Human Terrain Team Handbook*, 2.
12. AAA Commission, "Final Report"; Cohen, "Panel Criticizes Military's Use"; Fluehr-Lobban, "Anthropology and Ethics"; Gonzalez, "Towards Mercenary Anthropology?"; Gusterson, "The U.S. Military's Quest"; and Vergano and Weise, "Should Anthropologists Work?"
13. AAA Commission, "Final Report."

14. According to correspondence with Dr. Montgomery McFate, who participated in these teams, anthropologists averaged at most 30% of the team memberships.
15. U.S. Human Terrain System, *Human Terrain Team Handbook*.
16. U.S. Army Headquarters, "Operational Terms and Graphics."
17. The green cell was added to planning to represent the general population in conflict scenarios. Thus, planning includes blue forces (friendly), red (hostile) and green (neutral/civilians).
18. McFate, *Military Anthropology*.
19. Price, *Anthropological Intelligence*.
20. Deitchman, *The Best Laid Schemes*.
21. Fujimura, "Culture In/Culture of."
22. Fosher, "Pebbles in the Headwater."
23. Rush, "Archaeological Ethics."

Acknowledgments

This project was supported by several US Marine Corps educational organizations: CAOCL under the guidance of Col (ret) George Dallas; the Marine Corps University under the Director of the Vice President of the University, Dr. Jerre Wilson; and TECOM (Training and Education Command) under Jeffry Bearor, SES and Deputy Director. Their assistance and support are gratefully acknowledged.

Disclosure statement

No potential conflict of interest was reported by the author.

Bibliography

AAA Commission on the Engagement of Anthropology with the U.S. Security and Intelligence Communities, CEAUSSIC. 2009. "Final Report on the Army's Human Terrain System Proof of Concept Program." *American Anthropological Association*, October 14.

Bumiller, Elisabeth. 2010. "We Have Met the Enemy and He is Power Point." *The New York Times*, April 26. http://www.nytimes.com/2010/04/27/world/27power point.html?_r=1&ref=world

Cohen, Patricia. 2009. "Panel Criticizes Military's Use of Embedded Anthropologists." *New York Times*, December 4.

Deitchman, Seymour J. *The Best Laid Schemes: A Tale of Social Research and Bureaucracy*. 2nd ed. Quantico, VA: MCU Press, 2014.

Fluehr-Lobban, Carolyn. "Anthropology and Ethics in America's Declining Imperial Age." *Anthropology Today* 24, no. 4 (2008): 18–22. doi:10.1111/anth.2008.24.issue-4.

Fosher, Kerry. "Pebbles in the Headwater: Working within Military Intelligence." In *Practicing Military Anthropology: Beyond Expectations and Traditional Boundaries*, edited by Robert Rubenstein, Kerry Fosher, and Clementine Fujimura, 83–100. New York, NY: Kumarian Press, 2013.

Fujimura, Clementine. "Culture in/Culture of the United States Naval Academy." In *Anthropologists in the Securityscape: Ethics, Practice and Professional Identity*, edited by George E. Robert Albro, Laura A. McNamara Marcus, and Schoch-Spana Monica, 115–128. Walnut Creek, CA: Left Coast Press, 2012.

Gonzalez, Roberto J. "Towards Mercenary Anthropology?: The New US Army Counterinsurgency Manual FM 3-24 and the Military-Anthropology Complex." *Anthropology Today* 23, no. 3 (2007): 14–19. doi:10.1111/j.1467-8322.2007.00511.x.

Gusterson, Hugh. "The U.S. Military's Quest to Weaponize Culture." *Bulletin of the Atomic Scientists* (June 20, 2008). http://www.thebulletin.org/print/web-edition/columnists/hugh-gusterson/the-us-militarys-quest-to-weaponize-culture

Holmes-Eber, Paula. *Culture in Conflict: Irregular Warfare, Culture Policy, and the Marine Corps*. Stanford, CA: Stanford University Press, 2014.

McFate, Montgomery. *Social Science Goes to War: The Human Terrain System in Iraq and Afghanistan*. Oxford, UK: Oxford University Press, 2015.

McFate, Montgomery. *Military Anthropology: Soldiers, Scholars and Subjects at the Margins of Empire*. Oxford, UK: Oxford University Press, 2018.

Price, David H. *Anthropological Intelligence: The Deployment and Neglect of American Anthropology in the Second World War*. Durham, NC: Duke University Press, 2008.

Rush, Laurie. "Archaeological Ethics and Working for the Military." In *Practicing Military Anthropology: Beyond Expectations and Traditional Boundaries*, edited by Robert Rubenstein, Kerry Fosher, and Clementine Fujimura, 9–28. New York, NY: Kumarian Press, 2013.

U.S. Army Headquarters, and U.S. Marine Corps Combat Development Command. 2010. "Operational Terms and Graphics. FM 1-02 (FM 101-5-1) and MCRP 5-12a."

U.S. Human Terrain System. 2008. *Human Terrain Team Handbook*. KS: Fort Leavenworth. September.

Vergano, Dan, and Elizabeth Weise. 2008. "Should Anthropologists Work Alongside Soldiers? Arguments Pro, Con Go to Core Values of Cultural Science." *USA Today*, December 9.

Beyond faith and foxholes: vernacular religion and asymmetrical warfare within contemporary IDF combat units

Nehemia Stern and Uzi Ben Shalom

ABSTRACT
This paper explores the vernacular roles that religious practices and experiences play within contemporary combat units of the Israel Defense Forces (IDF). We argue for an anthropological perspective that highlights the modes through which rituals serve efficacious – as opposed to semiotic – ends. In this way, we seek to push back against what we term the 'faith in a foxhole' paradigm, where religion is primarily seen as a meaning-making system whose nearly sole function is to aid soldiers in coping with the chaos and uncertainty of combat. We demonstrate how amidst the low-level and long-term style of contemporary asymmetrical warfare, ritual practices can often function less as the matrix for broader meaning making systems but are rather mobilized in ways that are meant to support certain practical and pragmatic goals. The article concludes that while scholars have mostly focused attention on the institutional forces and political consequences of 'religionization' within Israeli society, they have missed the many vernacular ways in which Israelis mobilize and instrumentalize their use of ritual and religious practices in both military and civilian contexts.

Introduction

In late February of 2018, at the summation of the Israel Defense Force's combat commander's course, graduates on the parade ground began singing a ritual staple of Jewish religious liturgy known as '*Ani Maamin*' (I believe). The lyrics read, 'I believe with complete faith in the coming of the Messiah, and even though he may tarry, I still wait expectantly for him every day that he will come.'[1] This spontaneous incident was neither endorsed nor organized by the IDF Command and it came at a moment of rising concerns that the Israeli army was becoming more religious, nationalist, and loyal to particular right-wing rabbinic elements within Israel society.[2]

The incident sparked a brief but powerful storm of media comment and controversy. Some took umbrage at how the specific religious connotations of the liturgy excluded secular Israelis or the minority of non-Jewish servicemen and women. Others, however, applauded the seemingly spontaneous rendition of one of the most evocative verses in the Jewish liturgy. Perhaps in an attempt to calm the waves, the IDF's official response to the episode read 'This was an unusual incident, and it will be followed up with a clarification of procedures in this [specific] base and the units to which the soldiers are assigned.'[3]

It is difficult to underestimate the widespread emotional significance of the *Ani Maamin* liturgy. The current version of the song is taught in nearly every Jewish religious elementary school and can be found in most Jewish prayer books.[4] Students are regularly taught that the catechism was intoned by Jewish inmates in the Nazi death camps and at other catastrophic moments in Jewish history.[5] Most notably, religious tunes are commonly sung – unofficially – within IDF combat units in various contexts, from field exercises to the moments immediately before or after combat operations. Soldiers who self-identify as both religious and secular can often be observed huddling in spontaneous circles and dancing in ecstatic fashion to classic liturgical verses.

These spontaneous liturgical rituals highlight what some anthropologists and religious studies scholars would term 'vernacular' modes of religious expression. 'Vernacular religious' expressions point to 'fluidity, flexibility and innovation in religious traditions,'[6] and reflect the multivalent ways in which religion is practiced on the ground in people's day-to-day lives, as well as the importance of the geographical and cultural context in which belief and praxis occur.[7]

The power and popularity of the many liturgical or ritual practices expressed within combat units reflect a vernacular undercurrent of religious expressions that have yet to be properly appreciated by scholars of faith in the military. These vernacular modes of religious experience are expressed by both self-identifying religious and secular soldiers, and – we argue – are poignantly felt in the staging areas, roadblocks, and forward military camps from which the IDF engages in ongoing asymmetrical warfare against non-state actors on multiple fronts.

This paper explores these vernacular roles that religious practices and experiences play within contemporary combat units of the Israel Defense Forces (IDF). Specifically, we argue for an anthropological perspective that highlights the modes through which rituals serve efficacious – as opposed to semiotic – ends. We demonstrate how amidst the low-level and long-term style of contemporary asymmetrical warfare, ritual practices function less as the matrix for broader meaning making systems, but are rather mobilized in ways that are meant to support certain practical and pragmatic goals.[8] In this way, we seek to push back against some of the academic scholarship on religion within military contexts that focus on what we term the 'faith in a foxhole' paradigm. Here religion is primarily seen as a meaning-making system whose nearly sole function is to aid soldiers in coping with the chaos and uncertainty of combat.[9]

We argue that religion as a lived experience within military units can transcend this rather limited role. Within the context of low level and long-term asymmetrical warfare, the majority of IDF combat soldiers in most theaters of operation rarely encounter the kinds of repetitive life and death experiences for which faith as a meaning-making system has been traditionally called upon to address in more conventional conflicts. This contemporary paradigm can highlight a broad range of instrumental functions that religious practices and experiences may serve, including morale boosting, unit solidarity, and more talismanic functions that can be defined as the use of ritual practices and accoutrements to achieve practical goals.

This is important for two reasons. Firstly, alarmist discourse within both the Israeli popular media as well as the academy warn of the growing influence religion plays within the combat units of the IDF as well as within Israeli society more broadly. These voices claim that the once secular and politically neutral IDF is being slowly 'theocratized' by the growing presence of religious nationalist soldiers within the officer corps and other command levels of the IDF.[10] This article offers a more sober ethnographically grounded argument that demonstrates how ritual practices within military contexts may not necessarily imply larger ideological beliefs or political identities. That is, there is a level of popular religious experience within the IDF which has not been properly understood by academics who have primarily focused on the political or ideological tenors of ritual practices within the military. Secondly, scholars have often noted how religion can act as a general motivating factor within military units – by either cultivating combat motivation,[11] or shaping unit cohesion.[12] Yet there is very little understanding of how specific ritual practices operate in the broader everyday moments of contemporary warfare. In this way, it is imperative that scholars have an empirically based grounding in how the rank-and-file combatant experiences popular religious ideas and practices in a very contemporary kind of warfare that is more often than not asymmetrical in nature.

Religion in the IDF

The IDF is currently experiencing conflict surrounding the proper place of religion within its ranks. The past several decades have seen a marked increase in the number of combat soldiers and commanders who emerge out of what is known as the 'national religious' sector (also known as 'religious Zionists') of Israeli society.[13] This sector places a primacy on messianic religious piety on the one hand while at the same time sanctifying the secular governmental institutions of the State of Israel on the other.[14] This view stands in contrast to Israel's ultra-orthodox population who largely fail to see any religious value in military service. In this way for the national religious, military service plays a central role both in their vision of ultimate redemptive as well as in how they engage with broader civil society.

The Israel Defense Forces itself accommodates the pietistic and ritual standards of all its soldiers through its own Chaplaincy Corp, which is officially known as the 'Military Rabbinate.'[15] The 'Chief Rabbi' of the IDF serves on the General Staff with the rank of brigadier general. While the rabbinate was originally tasked with the role of securing the religious and ritual standards of all IDF personnel, it has of late taken on a more motivational and educational role. For example during Operation Cast Lead[16] in the Gaza Strip, the Chief Rabbi of the IDF, Avichai Rontzki– a former combat commander himself – and his rabbinic officers, regularly visited the front lines speaking with soldiers, giving religious sermons, and otherwise motivating the soldiers. As he wrote in a popular religious nationalist publication in 2017, the role of the military rabbinate is to 'aid the commander in strengthening the combat spirit from the sources of Torah and the rabbinic sages.'[17]

The rabbinate's expanded role in combat operations has garnered a good deal of criticism from academics and lay observers alike who note that it introduces a politically right-wing discourse into a military structure that ought to be both secular and apolitical.[18] Rontzi himself responded to this criticism by arguing that the soldiers themselves were experiencing a kind of religious revivalism that was unrelated to the activities of the Rabbinate. 'It is important to highlight' he wrote in the Rabbinate newsletter shortly after Operation Cast Lead,

> that we are talking about a widespread populist phenomenon that emerges from the field itself, which the military rabbinate is responding to and not organizing. We don't deal with religious penitents nor with religious coercion. Rather we are attentive to the needs of the combatants themselves who yearn for faith and meaning.[19]

For Rontzki, this religious revivalism emerges organically from within the combat ranks of the IDF. For him the average combat soldier wants to find faith, a deeper moral significance, and historical meaning in the daily sacrifices that service entails. This paper takes seriously the Rabbinate's claim of a bottom up religious revivalism but traces its characteristics to the various vernacular expressions of religious and ritual experience that rest just beneath the surface of Israeli society more generally.

Beyond the Military Rabbinate, there are also other more quasi-official modes through which religion and state interact with one another in military frameworks. Political scientists have keenly noted the ways in which the IDF interacts with the various religious Zionist communities within Israel. Rosman Stollman[20] and Stuart Cohen,[21] for example, look to the many premilitary rabbinic academies common within Israel as providing the institutional framework for this interaction. These seminaries are officially recognized by the IDF, which allows these students to defer military service for specified periods of time, during which they both spiritually and physically fortify themselves for meaningful and mostly combat service within the military. In practical terms, however, these rabbinic/military institutions act as 'culture brokers' between the pietistic needs of individual soldiers and the operational needs of the military itself.[22] While this argument is certainly compelling in its scope and macro-analytical framework, it also elides the more nuanced ways in which Jewish soldiers of all stripes within the IDF practice religion and experience ritual in ways that transcend official institutional, rabbinic, ormilitary frameworks.

Methodology

To analyze this phenomenon both authors -along with advanced undergraduate students – conducted approximately 30 unstructured interviews with enlisted soldiers, non-commissioned officers, and junior officers who all served in combat infantry units between the start of the Second Palestinian Intifada in 2000 to the present. Most interviewees self-identified as 'secular' or 'traditional'.[23] This was important for the research because it demonstrates how the discussed religious practices are enacted by a wide variety of Israeli combat soldiers and not just by those who might self-identify as 'religious'. This interview material was supplemented by data gleaned from current news sources, and crucially from content posted on social media sites such as Facebook and YouTube by currently serving soldiers. This content is not censored by the IDF command and offers a near real-time window into the lives and worldviews of IDF soldiers. The research was further supplemented by the combat military experiences of the first author. In this way, we follow the research methodology of several Israeli anthropologists who have used their own military service as opportunities to gather ethnographic data on the military system itself.[24]

Faith and war

Both scholars and lay observers have long noted the seemingly close association that exists between religion and warfare. Much of this literature has focused on what may be termed the 'no atheists in a foxhole' paradigm.[25] Here faith in a divine order, along with the rituals and symbols that attend that faith, offer soldiers a means of overcoming the chaos and stress of combat.[26] This perspective – heavily centered on religious (usually

Protestant) strategies of meaning-making – focuses on the ways in which religious convictions give combatants a sense of 'equanimity when contemplating the risks of combat.'[27]

In the World Wars of the 20th century for example, religious practices such as individual and organized prayer were seen as being a primary factor that provided the necessary psychological resources to endure the grueling stresses of combat.[28] Some British military chaplains during the First and Second World Wars were quite skeptical of this sudden religious fervor, calling it pejoratively 'funk religion'.[29] American Protestant commentators on the other hand often expressed an instinctive sympathy towards the sentiment.[30] More recent psychological research has also demonstrated a relationship between a belief in a supernatural being and a holistic sense of meaning and purpose that assists individuals to better bear their suffering in times of adversity.[31] The connection between suffering and religious meaning is one that is deeply indebted to particular Protestant theological notions of theodicy (the defense of God's Goodness and omnipotence in view of the existence of evil).[32] In this Weberian and modern system of meaning-making, individual and isolated experiences of suffering are transformed into something more communal by offering a shared sense of hope and confidence in a better future.[33] The combat experience has largely been viewed through this prism of 'meaning-making.' There are considerably fewer social scientific, psychological, or theological studies which attempt to map 'the plethora of very un-modern superstitions, talismans, wonders, miracles, relics, legends and rumors' which are part and parcel of contemporary warfare but which may not be easily subsumed under the modern rubrics of locating meaning in suffering.[34] The majority of academic studies treat religious experience among military personnel as a means of finding existential meaning in the chaos and uncertainty of combat. This paradigm however, may not accurately reflect many of the efficacious ways in which religion is utilized in the protracted post heroic conflicts of asymmetrical warfare.

This article marshals classic anthropological literature on ritual instrumentality to analyze these very experiences. Socio-cultural anthropology has historically been very interested in examining the differences between practices that may be classified as 'religious' and those that are 'magical'. In the process, ethnographers have offered some keen and useful observations concerning the relationship between stress, uncertainty, and religious behaviour that is pertinent to the issue of religious practices and experiences in post-heroic warfare. For the Polish born British anthropologist Bronislaw Malinowski, a magical rite signified 'a definite practical purpose' and was meant to achieve an immediate specified goal when all other practical means of achieving that goal have been utilized.[35] He called this instrumental use of religion to effect an immediate change in the world 'magic'.

Sosis and Handwerker have extended Malinowki's theoretical insight regarding the instrumental uses of ritual towards the analysis of civilian populations respond to asymmetrical warfare.[36] This research has demonstrated how Jewish Israeli women during both the Second Intifada as well as the Second Lebanon War used the ritualized recitation of psalms not so much as a way of strengthening or demonstrating personal faith in a situation of suffering but rather as a practical means of warding off the effects of war and violence.

The differentiation between 'magic' and 'religion' may be arbitrary and was indeed sharply criticized by subsequent anthropological research.[37] Most famously E. E. Evans-Pritchard was quick to note the very rational and even philosophical ways in which 'magical' practices are made to make sense precisely in their moments of failure.[38] That is, ritual practices that serve instrumental ends are always subsumed in wider contexts of meaning that make them coherent to practitioners. Although they may have disagreed on the epistemological differences between religious 'rationalism' and 'magic', both Evans-Pritchard and Malinowski saw in the latter a means of highlighting aspects of the religious experience that have traditionally been overlooked by sociological and theological observers.[39] Most notably their ideas offer a means of viewing spiritual experiences in ways that transcend classic protestant theodicy by highlighting the instrumental functions of ritual practices.

In the active moments of asymmetrical warfare IDF combat soldiers often turn to rituals (wearing skullcaps, putting on phylacteries, or reciting psalms) to produce certain practical outcomes, such as creating a sense of order out of a chaotic situation, building morale, creating unit cohesion, and other esoteric forms of experiences. In this sense soldiers operating on contemporary asymmetrical battlefields are inspired less by notions of faith or meaningful suffering than they are by the very pragmatic and instrumental functions of ritual or talismanic practices.

Asymmetrical warfare and the post-heroic moment

Indeed, paradigms of faith and theodicy are uniquely suited to address the kinds of traumatic combat experiences that typify the kind of warfare prevalent throughout much of modernity, in which large regimented armies meet each other on fields of battle.[40] These militaries were backed by well-organized political structures, and enjoyed the moral, financial (and later industrial) support of their constituted polities. This kind of combat often entailed high-casualty rates and the political leadership along with their civilian constituencies had to accept this (likely) possibility.

Since the end of WWII, the nature and style of warfare has changed dramatically.[41] Large political entities rarely mobilize their industry, economies, and general society to war against each other. Instead many low-level and asymmetrical conflicts occur involving non-state actors, characterized by long term and low-level engagements (policing activities, foot and vehicular patrols, border control, and management of checkpoints, etc.) interspersed with short-term and high intensity combat operations. These activities are usually conducted in close proximity to, or even amidst, civilian populations in predominantly urban environments.

Scholars term the socio-cultural and political reaction to these kinds of conflicts as 'post-heroic'.[42] In post-heroic warfare (usually) democratic polities express a persistent aversion to the high casualty rates that have been so much a part of violent conflicts against state actors.[43] In this sense western militaries that engage in asymmetrical warfare have been reticent to accept high casualty rates both within their own armies and among the enemy.[44] Militaries have increasingly turned to advanced technological weapons systems whose tactical goal is to lessen the need to risk the lives of regular combat troops.

Currently Israel engages in military conflicts through a distinct post-heroic paradigm.[45] As of the summer of 2018 the Israeli military maintains a constant military presence in the West Bank and is currently standing off against Hamas in the Gaza Strip, Hezbollah in Lebanon, as well as Iranian and Hezbollah forces on the Syrian Golan Heights. The IDF is also preparing for confrontations with other Islamist paramilitary organizations both in Syria as well in the Sinai Peninsula. These 'protracted intractable conflicts' include brief periods of intense combat, coupled with longer periods watchful (though stressful) calm.[46]

The Israeli Army's involvement in these conflicts underscores the fact that asymmetrical warfare is characterized just as much by the long months (and even years) of routine watchfulness as it is by the periodic moments of violent engagements. It is within this more expansive understanding of the wider routines of post heroic warfare that the role of religion diversifies. With the IDF's increasing reliance on technological superiority and its tendency to avoid direct skirmishes with enemy fighters, most soldiers in the IDF have very little direct combat experience.[47] For the rank and file combat soldier, service is not characterized by the repeated chaotic and violent engagements with the enemy against which the theodicies of classical warfare are particularly capable of addressing.

In this context, the functions of religious practices and experiences will increasingly come to transcend meaning-making paradigms to include more instrumental and even talismanic roles. In what follows we will explore the diverse ways religion is utilized by IDF combat soldiers in post heroic warfare to include: faith, talismanic magic, social cohesion, cultivating a sense of spiritual strength, and negotiating between sacred and secular ideals.

Between faith and ritual instrumentality
Faith

'Faith' certainly plays a role in and around the brief moments of intense combat that characterize asymmetrical warfare within the IDF. The loss of close comrades was a common trigger for expressions of faith. As Eyal, a sergeant who participated in combat in Operation Protective Edge[48] in the Gaza Strip remarked,

> I certainly have more faith now. I saw miracles and other things, although it didn't come to the level of actually repenting [becoming an orthodox and practicing Jew]. It was more internal. My faith has been strengthened but not in an external way [i.e. through ritual practices and obligations]. It simply happens ....when you lose a friend or a soldier under your command then ... I think it just automatically happens.

Other triggers were the actual experience of being under fire. As Rotem, a reservist in the Second Lebanon War, noted,

> We went into Lebanon at four in the afternoon. I mean who goes into Lebanon during the day time? Anyways, at some point Hezbollah must have seen us. As we were passing through a valley we suddenly hear the screaming shrieks of mortar fire. We all throw ourselves down to the ground. And I said to myself [tightly closing his eyes -ed.] please God just let me come home safely. A soldier 400 meters behind me was killed by a direct hit.

Prayer and the rituals surrounding prayer were common themes that emerged in interviews with combat veterans of Israel's many recent conflicts in the Gaza Strip and Southern Lebanon. David, a reserve soldier, commented on the relationship between faith and fear in the divisional staging areas as he prepared to enter the Gaza Strip in 2014.

> In these staging areas many prayed by themselves, personal prayers. This is the time you have with God. There is no doubt that I felt much closer [to God]. I don't know whether to term this faith or rather fear, but you start to pray a lot; that we will go out [to war] successfully, that everything will pass peacefully, and many times we prayed that the attack on Gaza would be cancelled.

Naveh, a combat officer, related the kinds of personal faith and self-discovery that is found in war to larger ethnic and national claims,

> My faith has been greatly strengthened, very much so. At a certain point – and thank God I haven't since been in such extreme circumstances like in that war – but there I really connected to my innermost self and a very deep level. There [in the war] I also came to understand the real purpose of one Jew set against [in relation to] his entire nation.

While faith is certainly an element of the Jewish religion, the term 'religious' within Israel primarily denotes the observance of a series of rituals and commandments. Neither David, Eyal, Rotem, nor Naveh identified themselves as 'national religious,' or were particularly observant of Jewish law (known in Hebrew as *halacha*) in general. For them, faith was neither equated (as it classically is in Israel) with religious practice, nor with the more Protestant understandings of belief, dogma nor in the search for meaning in moments of stress. Rather, faith was mobilized in ways that underscored personal development, ethnic or national loyalties, or the harrowing desire to survive combat.[49]

Other soldiers related to ritual practices in more instrumental ways that move beyond the dogmas of faith or the search for meaning in moments of suffering. For IDF combat soldiers facing the specter of asymmetrical warfare, rituals, acts of prayer, or other religious practices bear a certain practical efficacy that combine talismanic or magical elements with a need to produce social cohesion. Judaism itself has often been seen as a practice-based religion. At the same time there exists a wide and long-standing spectrum of philosophical inquiry regarding the role of dogma within Judaism along with the purpose, meaning, and function of ritual observances.[50] While practical efficacy and even talismanic power have been one part of that historic dialogue, in the modern period they have given way to more rational theological discourses.[51] As the IDF, however, engages in long-term asymmetrical warfare along multiple fronts, ritual instrumentality, efficacy, and talismanic power are becoming ever more central in everyday expressions of religion in the military.

Ritual instrumentality

Morale

The instrumental power of ritual practices may often be used in a pragmatic sense, specifically as a means of relieving stress in the tense moments of preparation that occur in the operational gathering areas before combat operations commence. These gathering areas – usually situated a few kilometres outside of the combat zone – are used to review overall strategy, decide on tactics and navigational routes, organize or replenish supplies, and generally offer soldiers some final moments of rest. While the military makes an attempt to restrict access to these areas, they have traditionally been relatively open to the public. Friends, family members and general well-wishers visit the units and generously pass out food or distribute religious items.

Among the groups that tend to visit the soldiers are individuals who are loosely affiliated with the Breslov Hasidic sect. Breslov Hasidism was one stream of the larger pietisitic and mystical Hasidic movement that swept through Eastern Europe in the 18th and 19th centuries.[52] One contemporary branch of the movement in Israel is broadly penitential and conducts religious – though informal – outreach towards the wider Israeli society through the distribution of self-help manuals and religious amulets. They are also known for their distinctive dress that includes a shaved head, long side locks and large white knitted skullcaps that are embossed with a mystical rendition of the name of their central rabbinic figure, Rabbi Nachman of Bratzlav. These individuals can often be found dancing to techno trance music along Israel's roads and in city centers. They are also commonly congregate within the gathering areas before combat operations, and soldiers often referenced them and their activities.

As one sergeant noted,

> There were Breslov Hasidim in the operational gathering areas with vehicles. They began to dance and distribute tzitzit,[53] psalms, and all sorts of books related to faith. There were guys that I would never believe would take psalms and place in their pockets.

These activities are often seen as lifting the morale of servicemen about to begin combat operations. As one officer said in an interview,

It was the night before we went in [to Gaza]. People came to the operational gathering area and handed out all sorts of things related to religion, books of psalms, and hats of Rabbi Nachman. They sang with the soldiers, made them happy and lifted morale.

Other servicemen documented similar instances during the more recent engagements in the Gaza Strip. One national religious company commander of a combat infantry unit noted how while the activities of this sect and the ecstatic dancing might lift the spirits of soldiers and create a greater sense of solidarity between combatants, the effects would only be temporary. In general, he claimed that these activities added an element of chaos to the staging areas.

> As an officer I don't like chaos, especially in the staging areas where we are preparing for war. I like to control things, a controlled environment. I don't want soldiers who are ecstatic, I don't want soldiers who are wildly dancing, only to hit a 'down' when the ecstasy wears off. I want soldiers who are professional, trained and preparing.

When asked why he did not forbid the entry of this sect into his staging area, he looked quite surprised and responded, 'I can't give an order no one would follow. This is what soldiers expect, and I have to walk between the raindrops.' This officer's experiences and frustrations are indicative of how powerful vernacular religious revivalism can be among enlisted combat soldiers. Even when a national religious officer would have liked to have limited certain phenomena, he simply was unable to do so.

Social solidarity

Alongside morale, ritual practices are also strongly linked to unit cohesion and social solidarity. The social sciences have long expressed a keen interest in understanding if and how unit cohesion is linked to combat motivation.[54] In the Second World War, for example, it was shown how soldiers endured the rigors and deprivations of combat primarily for each other, and less so for larger political or ideological structures.[55] Currently, scholars have amply examined the role of religious and political ideologies in cultivating a unique fighting spirit within the IDF.[56] Little attention has been given, however, to the ways in which distinct rituals such as evening prayers or sabbath meals may influence unit cohesion in the midst of asymmetrical warfare.

One platoon commander described a Friday night Sabbath scene during the 2014 conflict in the Gaza Strip as follows:

> We entered into one of the houses [in Gaza] and we found some time in the midst of combat to say *kiddush*.[57] We brought wine especially to pray, and we also brought *kippot*[58] and bread. We really said *kiddush*, and this also strengthened us. It gave us a good feeling, a feeling of togetherness. It helped us understand a little of what we were doing [in combat] and for whom we are doing it – in order to protect the State and everything that we have.

Another combat officer also noted the efficacy of prayer/ritual in strengthening unit solidarity in the midst of battle.

> I wasn't able to don phylacteries during battle. Once however we spent the Sabbath inside [Gaza] in a house. It was crazy, we recited the Sabbath prayers, and after that we had the ritual meal. It was a Sabbath atmosphere that I can't describe in words. It was spiritual like, we all sang Lecha Dodi[59] together. It was like people were singing with a kind of strength that I've never seen before.

These excerpts broadly demonstrate how Sabbath rituals can be efficacious in multiple ways in the midst of combat. Firstly, wine for the ritual of *kiddush* ('*we brought wine especially to pray*') is equated with 'prayer.' The Sabbath meal more generally is transformed into a ritual that entails both spiritual and ideological functions. For these two combat officers a personal sense of 'spirituality' seemed to emerge out of the feelings of solidarity (or what one called 'togetherness') that was created through singing the Sabbath prayers, and partaking together in the ritual meal. In the second quote specifically, the Sabbath atmosphere in the Gazan house which could not be 'described in words' produced a communal feeling of strength that emerged through the prayer of *Lecha Dodi*. That prayer is commonly sung on Friday nights in synagogues. It too produces a sense of solidarity when in the last stanza congregations rise together, and symbolically greet the Sabbath by turning to face the door.[60]

The rituals surrounding prayer create certain operational dilemmas for soldiers in the midst of combat as well as for the military more broadly. The classic ritualized form of Jewish prayer is both time consuming and (depending on the specific prayer) requires certain ritual accoutrements. The length of the morning prayers along with its associated practices can be a source of stress for IDF combat soldiers who observe the ritual commandments as well as for the military more broadly.

For example one corporal who participated in combat operations in Ramallah during the Second Intifada cited the difficulty in deciding when was the right moment to don one's phylacteries. In one instance he chose to wear the phylacteries and recite a hasty version of his morning prayers while inside a school during a lull in combat. As he reported 'as I just finished putting my tefillin back in my pack the shooting started again.'

An officer in Gaza in 2014 reported how he considered a similar set of practical concerns regarding the practice of prayer in the midst of combat.

The problem was when to put on phylacteries[61] ... .Sometimes people prayed with great excitement, but to put on phylacteries, that's already more problematic, it depends on the situation that you're in. They [military command] can suddenly call you to an emergency, you'll have to move quickly, and you don't know if you'll have time to fold your tefillin properly so they aren't destroyed.

Talismanic

Of course, beyond building morale, vernacular ritual practices also serve more esoteric or talismanic functions. We use the term 'talismanic function' to refer to the wearing or the recitation of specific sacred texts or amulets to achieve specific practical goals. In this sense, a text may be recited not so much for its hermeneutic or cognitive value but as a practical means to produce good luck or other worldly outcome.[62] A company commander during the Second Lebanon War for example directly signaled how the recitation of prayers can have distinct talismanic value. 'My father used to send me certain psalms. He also sent me biblical verses [related to] my name and I used to recite them all the time.' In Jewish tradition the recitation of biblical verses that relate to the letters of an individual name is an instrumental Kabbalistic practice that is utilized as a means of acquiring God's grace and good fortune.

The recitation of psalms and the practical aspects of rituals was also a common theme for other combat soldiers. As one reserve combat support soldier stated, 'I saw people reciting a lot of psalms. There were moments of strength. People let's say who didn't wear *kippot* or didn't wear phylacteries all the time, suddenly carefully observed these practices.' Indeed, the biblical book of psalms is often used as a kind of talisman or amulet to ward away violence. For example one soldier who participated in combat missions during Operation Defensive Shield[63] stated that his mother had given him a pocket sized book of psalms as a talisman to keep him safe during his service. Combat solders who identify as traditional or even secular carrying psalms given to them by mothers is indeed quite common in interviews. Nir, a combat soldier noted, 'when I was drafted my mother gave me a [small] book of psalms. Something silly. It's not that I believe in it ... it's just that sometimes ... .I keep it because it can't hurt. I always keep it with me.' Or as Rotem, a secular veteran of Defensive Shield and the Second Lebanon War noted,

> My parents gave me a small book of psalms that I kept wrapped up in plastic in my front pocket. Whenever I changed shirts I would be sure to take the psalms. I kept it throughout my whole service.

One combat soldier said that he kept a prayer his parents gave him inside his dog tag as a talisman.[64] 'I believe other soldiers also quietly carried prayers in their pockets' he stated.

Another combat soldier also noted how common these ritual practices were. 'I always carry around phylacteries and I'm not always religiously observant. Suddenly, my friends who are also not religious borrowed my phylacteries and put them on.' This focus on the talismanic function of religious practices (reciting psalms or donning phylacteries) demonstrates how rituals can be mobilized by soldiers coming from a broad range of backgrounds as a kind of instrument of spiritual power to provide a sense of protection during combat (or even to prevent combat entirely).

This is not an attempt to reduce the function of ritual practices to mere social concerns. As Hildred Geertz noted, 'The force behind faith in astrological predictions or in curing by spells lies not in the severity of danger in the situation, nor in an anxious need to believe in an illusory solution to it, but in a conviction of their truth.'[65] Rituals may indeed function to produce certain social outcomes that may be seen as beneficial by military command. Yet for the combatants themselves, these practices often indicate more talismanic and esoteric experiences.

Miracle tales

A related kind of instrumental and talismanic perspective is perhaps most apparent in the various miracle tales that have emerged out of the IDF's conflicts in Gaza and Lebanon. One particular story revolves around the appearance of the biblical figure of Rachel to IDF combat soldiers operating within the alleyways of the Gaza Strip during Operation Cast Lead. The tale became quite popular in Israel at the time of the operation and can still (as of 2018) be heard recounted on various social media networks.[66]

It was reported that an elderly Palestinian woman who identified herself as 'Mother Rachel' had forewarned IDF combat forces of booby trapped homes in Gaza.[67] 'Mother Rachel' is a direct reference to the Biblical figure of 'Rachel' who, as Jacob's wife, was the mother of Joseph who died while giving birth to Benjamin. She reappears in the prophetic Book of Jeremiah as a motherly figure who sheds tears over the exile of her children.[68] In 2009 the Rabbi of the Safed Shmuel Eliyahu gave a series lectures where he claimed that his father Mordechai Eliyahu, the former Sephardic chief Rabbi of Israel, had a quasi-prophetic encounter with Rachel and beseeched her to protect IDF soldiers in Gaza.[69]

Miraculous tales of Rachel's apparition to combat soldiers in Gaza have been so widely disseminated that leading rabbinic figures within Israel's religious Zionist elite have taken note and offered somewhat skeptical opinions regarding their veracity or the impact they ought to have on faith. Rabbi Dov Lior for example, a leading Rabbinic figure in the West Bank Jewish settlements of Hebron-Kiryat Arba and beyond, expressed skepticism as to the veracity of the story by writing, 'One has to be very careful and not blindly believe every story, we don't [automatically] reject or approve of the tale.'[70] A more centrist rabbinic figure Yuval Cherlow offered a similar skeptical take on the tale. He claimed that even if the story has a positive effect on one's faith, if it is not true the tale ought to be discarded. As a result, 'The only question is whether we have the tools to determine if the story is true.'[71] Shlomo Aviner, a religious Zionist rabbinic figure widely known for his brief yet insightful answers to Jewish legal and philosophical questions offered a different take on the matter. He looks to the value that lies beneath the miraculous tale regardless of its veracity.

There were soldiers that died in combat who did not see Rachel, and there were soldiers who acted courageously with great sacrifice and heroism who likewise did not see Rachel. But definitely Rachel was there in the sense of an inner force that strengthens us, the People of Israel, and that returns us to our land.[72]

The gap between the popular experience of miracle tales and the elite rabbinic opinions regarding their veracity and usefulness only highlights how popular these tales are becoming among combat soldiers as well as within the wider Israeli society.[73]

Claims of miraculous apparitions are certainly not unique to asymmetrical warfare. Miraculous tales were common among British soldiers in both the First and Second World Wars (and were received with similar kinds of clerical skepticism),[74] and the same can be said for Canadian soldiers in the First World War.[75] One might be tempted to relegate these tales to the context of fear and the mass casualties that were associated with these wars. Yet even in a post heroic era, where combat risk and its associated casualties are discouraged, soldiers (as well as the Israeli public) are greatly influenced by talismanic power and miraculous tales of biblical figures. Indeed, the speed with which the tale of Rachel's appearance and its unique staying power within the Israeli popular mindset is instructive for how vernacular religious conceptions of the supernatural have been underappreciated in the study of post-heroic warfare.

Conclusion

Whether in the chaotic moments during combat, or in the tense period before the onset of combat operations, religion and religious practices in the IDF move beyond the purely 'faith in a foxhole' paradigm common in previous conflicts. By looking at specific aspects of ritual efficacy – or the ways in which religious practices serve instrumental ends – scholars can gain a wider sense of how religion becomes enmeshed in the day to day lives of combat soldiers. In this way religion can serve a variety of instrumental functions within asymmetrical warfare.

Social scientists who focus on issues of asymmetrical warfare in the Middle East would do well to take careful note of the modes through which vernacular religious ideas and ritual practices are mobilized on the ground by combat forces. This is certainly not to say that asymmetrical warfare provides a sole or even unique moment through which these vernacular and revivalist practices emerge. Rather, these generally long-term military conflicts, coupled with their sporadic yet intensely violent moments of combat call upon qualitative researchers of the military to reconsider the broader role of religion within military life. This anthropological observation speaks to wider debates current within Israeli society regarding the growing impact and importance that religious ideas and practices seem to be playing within the critical institutions of Israeli public life, such as the military.

In 2014 on the eve of commencing combat operations in the Gaza Strip as part of Operation Protective Edge, the national religious commander of the Givati Brigade, Colonel Ofer Winter offered a morale boosting prayer to his soldiers. The prayer included the line,

> I raise my eyes to the heavens and call out with you *Hear O Israel the Lord is our God the Lord is one*. God, the Lord of Israel make our path a successful one, as we are moving into battle for your name against an enemy who blasphemes you. [Emphasis in original]

When publicized the prayer generated some controversy. Pundits noted Winter's national religious credentials,[76] and either criticized or supported his use of religious terminology.[77]

Lost in the discussion however was an appreciation for the ways in which the soldiers who participate in asymmetrical operations understand and relate to religious concepts and ritual precepts. As Tomer, a combat veteran of the Second Intifada and the Second Lebanon War, noted in an interview, 'It's not that atheists suddenly discover faith during combat, it's just that within the IDF there are very few atheists who join combat units.'[78] Colonel Winter's remarks were not geared towards soldiers desperately in search of religious meaning as a fortification against the chaos of combat. Rather, he was speaking towards both secular, traditional, and religious soldiers who join combat units with their own deeply felt vernacular understandings of ritual and belief. Within the combat units of the IDF religion tends to function on a level that is decidedly revivalist, efficacious and with an uneasy relationship to the 'official' practices of the IDF command or to the larger philosophical interpretations of Judaism.

Too be sure, religious practices have always been deeply embedded in the institutional framework of the Israel Defense Forces. Nearly all military bases include a synagogue (many with Torah scrolls). All military bases observe (to varying degrees) strictures of Kashruth,[79] and religious soldiers regularly receive official exemptions for anything from shaving to physical activities on ritual fast-days. Out of this institutional framework, increased religious fervor in the IDF has often been viewed as the outcome of these top-down forces.

In this regard, scholars have noted the increasing resonance that religion plays within both the public sphere as well as the personal lives of Israeli citizens, and have explored the future impact that this phenomena may have on Israeli political life.[80] Others have also argued that the increased emphasis that Israelis place on religion is rooted more in ethnic, national, and political identities than in any overtly theological or spiritual paradigm.[81] Yet if one takes an anthropological look at the vernacular and efficacious forms of ritual expression, this picture of religionization becomes much more complicated. The typical academic focus on the institutional forces and political consequences of 'religionization' within Israeli society often elides the very vernacular ways in which Israelis mobilize and instrumentalize their use of ritual and religious practices.

If we think of Israeli society as Ben-Ari and Lomsky-Feder argue, as one 'that maintains democracy under conditions of protracted war' then the military itself becomes a reflection of some of the wider stresses and tensions within society itself.[82] In this way, an analysis of vernacular religious practices within the military context of protracted asymmetrical conflict offers scholars a unique ethnographic means to better contextualize the social and political issues at stake in the sometimes heated conversations surrounding the supposed rising tide of 'religionization' within Israel.

Notes

1. The complete recording can be found at: https://www.youtube.com/watch?v=RcapUKiSTFs Accessed June 6, 2018.
2. Levy, "The Clash Between Feminism And Religion In The Israeli Military"; Levy, "The Israeli Military: Imprisoned By The Religious Community"; and Levy, "The Theocratization Of The Israeli Military."
3. Kipa News Site, "Have You Gone Mad?"; and Tawil, "Shock: IDF Apologizes."
4. The modern version of the *Ani Maamin* is loosely based on Maimonides' thirteen principles of faith which are enumerated in his commentary on the Mishna. See Kellner, "Heresy And The Nature Of Faith."

5. Young, "The Moral Function Of Remembering"; Milhaud And Wiesel, "Ani Maamin"; and Adler, "No Raisins, No Almonds."
6. Flueckiger, *In Amma's healing room*, 2.
7. For an overview of the concept of vernacular religion see Primiano, "Vernacular Religion and the Search for Method in Religious Folklife," 44; and Bowman, "Vernacular Religion and Nature," 286.
8. For a discussion of anthropological approaches towards "ritual efficacy" see Quack and Töbelmann, "Questioning Ritual Efficacy."
9. For a discussion of meaning making systems as a way of coping with chaos see: Snape, "Foxhole Faith And Funk Religion"; Park, "Religion As A Meaning-Making Framework"; and Geertz, *The Interpretation Of Cultures*.
10. See: Levy, "The Israeli Military," 69; Levy, "The Theocratization Of The Israeli Military"; Harel, "Is The IDF Becoming An Orthodox Army?"; and Lubell, "Israeli Military Struggles With Rising Influence Of Religious-Zionist."
11. Kellett, *Combat Motivation*, 194; and Watson, "Religion And Combat Motivation In The Confederate Armies."
12. Røislien, "Religion and Military Conscription."
13. For a review of the national religious participation in the IDF see Cohen, "Dilemmas of Military Service in Israel"; Cohen, "Relationships Between Religiously Observant and Other Troops in the IDF."
14. For a theological overview of the national religious community in Israel see, Ravitzky, *Messianism, Zionism, and Jewish religious radicalism*; For an anthropological overview, see Stern, *First Flowering of Redemption*.
15. Cohen, Kampinsky, and Rosman-Stollman, "Swimming Against the Tide."
16. A major IDF incursion into the Gaza Strip lasting some three weeks.
17. Rontzki, "Sits in Tents."
18. Levy, "The Theocratization of the Israeli Military," 281; and Harel, "IDF Rabbinate Publication During Gaza War."
19. Rontzki, "The Military Rabbinate in Operation Cast Lead," Unnumbered.
20. Rosman-Stollman, "Mediating Structures and the Military"; and Rosman-Stollman, *For God and Country?*
21. Cohen, "The Hesder Yeshivot in Israel"; and Cohen, "From Integration to Segregation."
22. For more on cultural mediation between the military and other "greedy institutions" see Segal, "The Military And The Family As Greedy Institutions."
23. *Masortim* in Hebrew. Jews mainly of Middle Eastern descent who refrain from making sharp distinctions either in philosophy or practice between the 'religious' and the 'secular'. These individuals practice Judaism in what is seen by the dominant hegemonic Orthodox Jewish standards in Israel, in an eclectic and inconsistent fashion. For an ethnographic typology of the *Masortim*, see Goldberg, "The Ethnographic Challenge of Masorti Religiosity"; For a critique of the term, see Yadgar, "Jewish Secularism And Ethno-National Identity In Israel."
24. See for example, Ben-Ari, *Mastering Soldiers*; and Aran, "Parachuting."
25. For the origins of the phrase itself see Steckel, "Morale and Men," 339.
26. Kuehne, *Faith and the Soldier*.
27. Linderman, *Embattled Courage*, 102.
28. Stouffer et al., *The American Soldier*, 75.
29. Snape, *Foxhole Faith and Funk Religion*; and Richardson, *Fighting Spirit*, 44.
30. Snape, *Foxhole Faith and Funk Religion*, 230–1.

31. Levav, Kohn, and Billig, "The Protective Effect Of Religiosity Under Terrorism," 48; Ellison, "Religious Involvement And Subjective Well-Being"; and Ano and Vasconcelles, "Religious Coping And Psychological Adjustment To Stress."
32. Seeman, "Otherwise than Meaning," 58.
33. Das, "Sufferings, Theodicies, Disciplinary Practices," 564.
34. Fussell, *The Great War and modern memory*, 124; Judaic Studies in the 19th and early 20th centuries exhibited a similar paradigm with its emphasis on rationality and reason and elision of Jewish mysticism. See Biale, *Gershom Scholem*.
35. Malinowski, *Magic, Science and Religion*.
36. Sosis and Handwerker, "Psalms and Coping With Uncertainty"; and Sosis, "Psalms for Safety."
37. Homans, "Anxiety and Ritual"; Radcliffe-Brown, *Taboo*; and Hammond, "Magic."
38. Evans-Pritchard, *Theories of primitive religion*, 27.
39. Segal, "The Myth-Ritualist Theory of Religion."
40. McPherson, *For Cause and Comrades*, 56; Becker, *War and Faith*; and Doubler, "American Soldiers."
41. Coker, *Waging War Without Warriors?*
42. Luttwak, "Toward Post-Heroic Warfare"; and Ben-Shalom, "Introduction: Israel's Post-Heroic Condition," 2.
43. Levy, "An Unbearable Price."
44. Kober, "The Israel Defense Forces in The Second Lebanon War," 7.
45. Kober, "The Israel Defense Forces in the Second Lebanon War"; Kober, "From Heroic to Post-Heroic Warfare"; and Lebel and Ben-Shalom, "Military Leadership."
46. Inbar and Shamir, "Mowing the Grass."
47. Ben-Shalom, "Introduction: Israel's Post Heroic Condition."
48. A military conflict between Israel and Hamas in the Gaza Strip lasting some 50 days.
49. These implicit understandings of faith among soldiers who may not self-identify as 'religious' echoes the complicated relationship that exists within Israeli society between 'traditional' and 'secular' conceptions of faith and belief. See Yadgar, "Jewish Secularism and Ethno-National Identity in Israel."
50. On Jewish philosophical traditions regarding practice and belief, see Nadler, *Spinoza's Heresy*; and Shapiro, *The Limits of Orthodox Theology*.
51. On the rationalist trend within Judaism, see Biale, *Gershom Scholem*; and Huss and Linsider, "Ask No Questions."
52. For a broad theological overview of Breslov Hasidism, see Magid, *God's Voice from the Void*.
53. Ritual fringes worn under one's clothing.
54. Spiegel, "Preventive Psychiatry With Combat Troops"; Kirke, "Military Cohesion, Culture And Social Psychology"; Manning, "Morale, Cohesion, And Esprit De Corps."
55. Shils and Janowitz, "Cohesion and Disintegration in the Wehrmacht in World War II," 281.
56. Lebel, "Settling the Military"; Mashiach, "Going on the Offensive"; and Leon, "Heroic Texts in a Post-Heroic Environment."
57. A blessing over wine or grape juice recited before the ritual meal that ushers in the weekly Jewish Sabbath on Friday nights.

58. *Kippot* – Jewish Skullcaps. Bread is used for the second ritual element of the Friday night meal.
59. A poem welcoming in the 'Sabbath Bride' composed by Solomon Alkabetz in the 16th century.
60. Adler, "Kabbalas Shabbos."
61. Leather boxes containing biblical passages which are strapped to the head and arm and are generally worn during morning prayers.
62. Robson, "Signs of Power"; and Schaverien, "Gifts, Talismans and Tokens in Analysis."
63. A 2002 IDF military operation in the West Bank meant to halt the spate of deadly Palestinian terror attacks into Israel.
64. IDF soldiers are instructed to slip their metal dog tags and chains into a dark piece of cloth. This creates a small space in which one can carry keepsakes such as small pictures or prayers.
65. Geertz, "An anthropology of religion and magic."
66. See for example, "Ask the Rabbi – Mother Rachel." https://www.kipa.co.il/%D7%A9%D7%90%D7%9C-%D7%90%D7%AA-%D7%94%D7%A8%D7%91/%d7%a8%d7%97%d7%9c-%d7%90%d7%99%d7%9e%d7%a0%d7%95 [Hebrew] Accessed March 7, 2018.
67. Cohen, "I asked her, Who are you? She said, Mother Rachel." Arutz 7. https://www.inn.co.il/News/News.aspx/189655 [Hebrew] Accessed March 7, 2018.
68. Jeremiah 31: 14–16.
69. See for example "Mother Rachel appears in the Gaza War" https://www.youtube.com/watch?v=UrHAx9vn6Xo&t=323s [Hebrew] Accessed March 7, 2018; Rabbi Shmuel Eliyahu, Parshat Vayeira 5778 https://www.youtube.com/watch?v=b8n3BK9i9o4 [Hebrew] Accessed March 7, 2018.
70. Lior, "A soldier that saw Mother Rachel."
71. The implication here is that the story is false. Cherlow, "More on Mother Rachel."
72. Aviner, "Rumors of Mother Rachel's Appearance in the Gaza War Against Hamas." Emphasis in original.
73. For a wider typology of miracle tales in combat, see Rosman, "Towards a Typology of Battlefield Miracles."
74. Finlay, *Angels in the Trenches*; and Snape and Parker, "Keeping Faith and Coping."
75. Cook, "Grave Beliefs."
76. Winter was a graduate of the Or Etzion military high school as well as the pre-military seminary, Bnei David, in the West Bank Settlement of Eli. Both are well known national religious educational institutions within Israel.
77. Sharon, "Religious Overtones in Letter From IDF Commander."
78. For another expression of this idea, see Revivi, "The Givati Colonel is the Real Army."
79. Jewish dietary laws.
80. Fischer, "Yes, Israel Is Becoming More Religious."
81. Yadgar, "The Need for an Epistemological Turn."
82. Lomsky-Feder and Ben-Ari, *Military and Militarism in Israeli Society*, 2.

Acknowledgments

We would like to thank Montgomery McFate and our colleagues at the Anthropology of Small Wars and Insurgencies Workshop at the Naval War College, for their comments on previous drafts of this article. For Daniel and Eitan, may you know peace and strength.

Disclosure statement

No potential conflict of interest was reported by the authors.

ORCID

Nehemia Stern http://orcid.org/0000-0002-4842-0544
Uzi Ben Shalom http://orcid.org/0000-0002-1988-0744

Bibliography

Adler, Elchanan. "Kabbalas Shabbos: Welcoming the Sabbath in Body and Spirit." *Journal of Jewish Music and Liturgy* 33 (2015): 1–12.
Adler, Eliyana R. "No Raisins, No Almonds: Singing as Spiritual Resistance to the Holocaust." *Shofar: an Interdisciplinary Journal of Jewish Studies* 24, no. 4 (2006): 50–66. doi:10.1353/sho.2006.0078.
Ano, Gene G., and Erin B. Vasconcelles. "Religious Coping and Psychological Adjustment to Stress: A Meta-analysis." *Journal of Clinical Psychology* 61, no. 4 (2005): 461–480. doi:10.1002/jclp.20049.
Aran, Gideon. "Parachuting." *American Journal of Sociology* 80, no. 1 (1974): 124–152. doi:10.1086/225764.
Aviner, Shlomo. 2011. "Rumors of Mother Rachel's Appearance in the Gaza War against Hamas." [Hebrew]. Accessed October 7, 2018. http://www.havabooks.co.il/article_ID.asp?id=1030.
Becker, Annette. *War and Faith: The Religious Imagination in France, 1914–1930*. London: Bloomsbury Academic, 1998.
Ben-Ari, Eyal. *Mastering Soldiers: Conflict, Emotions, and the Enemy in an Israeli Military Unit*. Vol. 10. New York and Oxford: Berghahn Books, 1998.
Ben-Shalom, Uzi. "Introduction: Israel's Post-Heroic Condition." *Israel Affairs* 24, no. 4 (2018): 569–571. doi:10.1080/13537121.2018.1478783.
Biale, David. *Gershom Scholem: Kabbalah and Counter-History*. Cambridge, MA: Harvard University Press, 1982.

Bowman, Marion. "Vernacular Religion and Nature: The "Bible of the Folk" Tradition in Newfoundland." *Folklore* 114, no. 3 (2003): 285–295. doi:10.1080/0015587032000145333.

Cherlow, Yuval. "More on Mother Rachel and the Miracle of Gaza." [Hebrew]. Accessed October 7, 2018. https://www.ypt.co.il/beit-hamidrash/view.asp?id=5530

Cohen, Shimon. 2009. "I Asked Her, Who are You? She Said, Mother Rachel." Arutz 7. [Hebrew]. Accessed March 7, 2018. https://www.inn.co.il/News/News.aspx/189655

Cohen, Stuart, Aaron Kampinsky, and Elisheva Rosman-Stollman. "Swimming against the Tide: The Changing Functions and Status of Chaplains in the Israel Defense Force." *Religion, State and Society* 44, no. 1 (2016): 65–74. doi:10.1080/09637494.2015.1122881.

Cohen, Stuart A. "The Hesder Yeshivot in Israel: A Church-State Military Arrangement." *Journal of Church and State* 35, no. 1 (1993): 113–130. doi:10.1093/jcs/35.1.113.

Cohen, Stuart A. "From Integration to Segregation: The Role of Religion in the IDF." *Armed Forces & Society* 25, no. 3 (1999): 387–405. doi:10.1177/0095327X9902500303.

Cohen, Stuart A. "Dilemmas of Military Service in Israel: The Religious Dimension." *The Torah u-Madda Journal* 12 (2004): 1–23.

Cohen, Stuart A. "Relationships between Religiously Observant and Other Troops in the IDF: Vision versus Reality." In *The Relationship of Orthodox Jews with Believing Jews of Other Religious Ideologies and Non-Believing Jews*, edited by Adam Mints, 279–312. New York, NY: The Michael Scharf Publication Trust, Yeshiva University Press, 2010.

Coker, Christopher. *Waging War without Warriors?: The Changing Culture of Military Conflict*. Boulder Colorado: Lynne Rienner Publishers, 2002.

Cook, Tim. "Grave Beliefs: Stories of the Supernatural and the Uncanny among Canada's Great War Trench Soldiers." *The Journal of Military History* 77, no. 2 (2013): 521–542.

Das, Veena. "Sufferings, Theodicies, Disciplinary Practices, Appropriations." *International Social Science Journal* 49, no. 154 (1997): 563–572. doi:10.1111/j.1468-2451.1997.tb00045.x.

Doubler, Michael D. "American Soldiers: Ground Combat in the World Wars, Korea, and Vietnam." *The Journal of Military History* 67, no. 4 (2003): 1343–1344. doi:10.1353/jmh.2003.0291.

Dov, Lior. "Question regarding 'A Soldier that Saw Mother Rachel'." [Hebrew]. Accessed October 7, 2018. https://www.yeshiva.org.il/ask/43492

Ellison, Christopher G. "Religious Involvement and Subjective Well-being." *Journal of Health and Social Behavior* 32 (1991): 80–99. doi:10.2307/2136801.

Evans-Pritchard, Edward Evan. *Theories of Primitive Religion*. London: Oxford University Press, 1965.

Fischer, Shlomo. "Yes, Israel Is Becoming More Religious." *Israel Studies Review* 27, no. 1 (2012): 10–15.

Flueckiger, Joyce Burkhalter. *In Amma's Healing Room: Gender and Vernacular Islam in South India*. Bloomington, IN: Indiana University Press, 2006.

Geertz, Clifford. *The Interpretation of Cultures*. New York: Basic books, 1973.

Geertz, Hildred. "An Anthropology of Religion and Magic, I." *The Journal of Interdisciplinary History* 6, no. 1 (1975): 71–89. doi:10.2307/202825.

Goldberg, Harvey E. "The Ethnographic Challenge of Masorti Religiosity among Israeli Jews." *Ethnologie française* 43, no. 4 (2013): 583–590. doi:10.3917/ethn.134.0583.

Hammond, Dorothy. "Magic: A Problem in Semantics." *American Anthropologist* 72, no. 6 (1970): 1349–1356. doi:10.1525/aa.1970.72.issue-6.

Harel, Amos. 2009. "IDF Rabbinate Publication during Gaza War: We Will Show No Mercy on the Cruel." *Ha'aretz* 26. Accessed March 2, 2019. https://www.haaretz.com/1.5067403

Harel, Amos. 2011. "Is the IDF Becoming an Orthodox Army?" *Haaretz. com* 22. Accessed April 26, 2018. https://www.haaretz.com/1.5032934

Homans, George C. "Anxiety and Ritual: The Theories of Malinowski and Radcliffe-Brown." *American Anthropologist* 43, no. 2 (1941): 164–172. doi:10.1525/aa.1941.43.2.02a00020.

Inbar, E., and E. Shamir. "'Mowing the Grass': Israel's Strategy for Protracted Intractable Conflict." *Journal of Strategic Studies* 37, no. 1 (2014): 65–90. doi:10.1080/01402390.2013.830972.

Kellett, Anthony. *Combat Motivation: The Behaviour of Soldiers in Battle.* Boston, MA: Springer Science & Business Media, 2013.

Kellner, Menachem. "Heresy and the Nature of Faith in Medieval Jewish Philosophy." *The Jewish Quarterly Review* 77, no. 4 (1987): 299–318. doi:10.2307/1454369.

Kipa News Site. 2018. "'Have You Gone Mad?' Singing of Ani Maamin Leads to Angry Responses. *Kipa News Site*. [Hebrew]. Accessed July 28, 2018. https://www.kipa.co.il/חדשות/נפלתם-על-השכל-שירת-אני-מאמין-גררה-תגובות-נזעמות

Kirke, Charles. "Military Cohesion, Culture and Social Psychology." *Defence & Security Analysis* 26, no. 2 (2010): 143–159. doi:10.1080/14751798.2010.488856.

Kober, Avi. "The Israel Defense Forces in the Second Lebanon War: Why the Poor Performance?" *Journal of Strategic Studies* 31, no. 1 (2008): 3–40. doi:10.1080/01402390701785211.

Kober, Avi. "From Heroic to Post-Heroic Warfare: Israel's Way of War in Asymmetrical Conflicts." *Armed Forces & Society* 41, no. 1 (2015): 96–122. doi:10.1177/0095327X13498224.

Kuehne, Wayne E. *Faith and the Soldier: Religious Support on the Airland Battlefield.* Army War Coll Carlisle Barracks Pa, 1988.

Lebel, Udi. "Settling the Military: The Pre-Military Academies Revolution and the Creation of a New Security Epistemic Community–The Militarization of Judea and Samaria." *Israel Affairs* 21, no. 3 (2015): 361–390. doi:10.1080/13537121.2015.1036556.

Lebel, Udi, and Uzi Ben-Shalom. "Military Leadership in Heroic and Post-heroic Conditions." In *Handbook of the Sociology of the Military*, 463–475. Cham: Springer, 2018.

Leon, Nissim. "Heroic Text in a Post-heroic Environment: National Liturgy in Mizrahi ultra-Orthodox Prayer Books." *Israel Affairs* 24, no. 4 (2018): 634–647. doi:10.1080/13537121.2018.1478785.

Levav, Itzhak, Robert Kohn, and Miriam Billig. "The Protective Effect of Religiosity under Terrorism." *Psychiatry: Interpersonal and Biological Processes* 71, no. 1 (2008): 46–58. doi:10.1521/psyc.2008.71.1.46.

Levy, Yagil. "An Unbearable Price: War Casualties and Warring Democracies." *International Journal of Politics, Culture, and Society* 22, no. 1 (2009): 69–82. doi:10.1007/s10767-009-9048-x.

Levy, Yagil. "The Clash between Feminism and Religion in the Israeli Military: A Multilayered Analysis." *Social Politics* 17, no. 2 (2010): 185–209. doi:10.1093/sp/jxq002.

Levy, Yagil. "The Israeli Military: Imprisoned by the Religious Community." *Middle East Policy* 18, no. 2 (2011): 67–83. doi:10.1111/j.1475-4967.2011.00486.x.

Levy, Yagil. "The Theocratization of the Israeli Military." *Armed Forces & Society* 40, no. 2 (2014): 269–294. doi:10.1177/0095327X12466071.
Liddle, Peter, John Michael Bourne, and Ian R. Whitehead, eds. *The Great World War, 1914–45: The Peoples' Experience.* Vol. 2. HarperCollins (UK), 2001.
Linderman, Gerald. *Embattled Courage: The Experience of Combat in the American Civil War.* Simon and Schuster, 2008.
Lomsky-Feder, Edna, and Eyal Ben-Ari, eds. *The Military and Militarism in Israeli Society.* SUNY Press, 1999.
Lubell, Maayan. 2016. "Israeli Military Struggles with Rising Influence of Religious-Zionists." Accessed April 26, 2018. https://www.reuters.com/investigates/special-report/israel-military-religion/
Luttwak, Edward N. "Toward Post-Heroic Warfare." *Foreign Affairs* 74 (1995): 109–122. doi:10.2307/20047127.
Magid, Shaul, ed. *God's Voice from the Void: Old and New Studies in Bratslav Hasidism.* SUNY Press, 2012.
Malinowski, Bronisław, and Robert Redfield. *Magic, Science and Religion: And Other Essays, by Bronislaw Malinowski.* Selected, and with an Introduction by Robert Redfield. Beacon Press, 1948.
Manning, Frederick J. "Morale, Cohesion, and Esprit De Corps." In *Handbook of Military Psychology*, edited by Reuven Gal and David A Mangelsdorf, 453–470. New York: John Wiley & Sons, 1991.
Mashiach, Amir. "Going on the Offensive: The Religious Zionist Rabbinic Ethos in Judea and Samaria as a Response to Post-Heroism." *Israel Affairs* 24, no. 4 (2018): 648–663. doi:10.1080/13537121.2018.1478787.
McPherson, James M. *For Cause and Comrades: Why Men Fought in the Civil War.* New York: Oxford University Press, 1997.
Milhaud, Darius, and Élie Wiesel. *Ani Maamin: A Song Lost and Found Again.* New York: Random House Trade, 1974.
Nadler, Steven M. *Spinoza's Heresy: Immortality and the Jewish Mind.* Oxford: Oxford University Press, 2001.
Park, Crystal L. "Religion as a Meaning-Making Framework in Coping with Life Stress." *Journal of Social Issues* 61, no. 4 (2005): 707–729. doi:10.1111/j.1540-4560.2005.00428.x.
Primiano, Leonard Norman. "Vernacular Religion and the Search for Method in Religious Folklife." *Western Folklore* 54, no. 1 (1995): 37–56. doi:10.2307/1499910.
Quack, Johannes, and Töbelmann. Paul. "Questioning Ritual Efficacy." *Journal of Ritual Studies* 24, no. 1 (2010): 13–28.
Radcliffe-Brown, Alfred Reginald. *Taboo.* Cambridge, UK: Cambridge University Press, 2014.
Ravitzky, Aviezer. *Messianism, Zionism, and Jewish Religious Radicalism.* Chicago, IL: University of Chicago Press, 1996.
Revivi, Oded. 2014. "The Givati Colonel Is the Real Army." [Hebrew]. Accessed July 26, 2018. https://news.walla.co.il/item/2765460
Richardson, Frank M. *Fighting Spirit: A Study of Psychological Factors in War.* New York: Crane, Russak & Company, 1978.
Robson, James. "Signs of Power: Talismanic Writing in Chinese Buddhism." *History of Religions* 48, no. 2 (2008): 130–169. doi:10.1086/596569.
Røislien, Hanne Eggen. "Religion and Military Conscription: The Case of the Israel Defense Forces (IDF)." *Armed Forces & Society* 39, no. 2 (2013): 213–232. doi:10.1177/0095327X12449429.

Rontzki, Avichai. 2017. "Sits in Tents." *Olam Katan.* [Hebrew]. Accessed May 6, 2019. https://www.olam-katan.co.il/מאמרים/item/2869
Rontzki, Avichai. "The Military Rabbinate in Operation Cast Lead." Lehalacha U'leMaase: The Military Rabbinate Newsletter March 2009. Unnumbered.
Rosman, Elisheva. "Towards a Typology of Battlefield Miracles: The Case of Operation "Cast Lead" in the Israel Defense Forces." *Religions* 9, no. 10 (2018): 311. doi:10.3390/rel9100311.
Rosman-Stollman, Elisheva. "Mediating Structures and the Military: The Case of Religious Soldiers." *Armed Forces & Society* 34, no. 4 (2008): 615–638. doi:10.1177/0095327X07308629.
Rosman-Stollman, Elisheva. *For God and Country?: Religious Student-Soldiers in the Israel Defense Forces.* Austin, TX: University of Texas Press, 2014.
Schaverien, Joy. "Gifts, Talismans and Tokens in Analysis: Symbolic Enactments or Sinister Acts?" *Journal of Analytical Psychology* 56, no. 2 (2011): 160–183. doi:10.1111/j.1468-5922.2010.01900.x.
Seeman, Don. "Otherwise than Meaning: On the Generosity of Ritual." *Social Analysis* 48, no. 2 (2004): 55–72. doi:10.3167/015597704782352500.
Segal, Mady Wechsler. "The Military and the Family as Greedy Institutions." *Armed Forces and Society* 13, no. 1 (1986): 9–38. doi:10.1177/0095327X8601300101.
Segal, Robert A. "The Myth-Ritualist Theory of Religion." *Journal for the Scientific Study of Religion* 19, no. 2 (1980): 173–185. doi:10.2307/1386251.
Shapiro, Marc B. *The Limits of Orthodox Theology: Maimonides' Thirteen Principles Reappraised.* Oxford, UK: Littman Library of Jewish Civilization, 2004.
Sharon, Jeremy. 2014. "Religious Overtones in Letter from IDF Commander." *JPost.* Accessed February 27, 2018. https://www.jpost.com/Jewish-World/Jewish-News/Religious-overtones-in-letter-from-IDF-commander-to-his-soldiers-draws-criticism-support-3626%E2%80%A6
Shils, Edward A., and Morris Janowitz. "Cohesion and Disintegration in the Wehrmacht in World War II." *Public Opinion Quarterly* 12, no. 2 (1948): 280–315. doi:10.1086/265951.
Snape, Michael. "Foxhole Faith and Funk Religion: Anglo-American Perspectives from Two World Wars." *New Blackfriars* 96, no. 1062 (2015): 223–238. doi:10.1111/nbfr.12122.
Sosis, Richard. "Psalms for Safety: Magico-Religious Responses to Threats of Terror." *Current Anthropology* 48, no. 6 (2007): 903–911. doi:10.1086/523015.
Sosis, Richard, and W. Penn Handwerker. "Psalms and Coping with Uncertainty: Religious Israeli Women's Responses to the 2006 Lebanon War." *American Anthropologist* 113, no. 1 (2011): 40–55. doi:10.1111/aman.2011.113.issue-1.
Spiegel, Herbert X. "Preventive Psychiatry with Combat Troops." *American Journal of Psychiatry* 101, no. 3 (1944): 310–315. doi:10.1176/ajp.101.3.310.
Steckel, Francis C. "Morale and Men: A Study of the American Soldier in World War II." PhD diss., Temple University, 1990.
Stern, Nehemia. "First Flowering of Redemption: An Ethnographic Account of Contemporary Religious Zionism in Israel." PhD diss., Emory University, 2014.
Stouffer, Sauel A., Arthur A. Lumsdaine, Marion Harper Lumsdaine, Robin M. Williams Jr., M. Brewster Smith, Irving L. Janis, Shirley A. Star, and Leonard S. Cottrell Jr. "Volume I. Princeton. "The American Soldier: Combat and Its Aftermath." *Psychoanalytic Quarterly* 19 (1950): 275–276.

Tawil, Hayim. 2008. "Shock: IDF Apologizes for Soldiers Singing Ani Maamin at Official Ceremony." Channel 10 News. [Hebrew]. Accessed July 28, 2018. http://www.ch10.co.il/news/423056/#.WzSRtSBRXIU

Watson, Samuel J. "Religion and Combat Motivation in the Confederate Armies." *The Journal of Military History* 58, no. 1 (1994): 29–52. doi:10.2307/2944178.

Yadgar, Yaacov. "Jewish Secularism and Ethno-National Identity in Israel: The Traditionist Critique." *Journal of Contemporary Religion* 26, no. 3 (2011): 467–481. doi:10.1080/13537903.2011.616041.

Yadgar, Yaacov. "The Need for an Epistemological Turn." *Israel Studies Review* 27, no. 1 (2012): 27–30.

Young, Gloria L. "The Moral Function of Remembering: American Holocaust Poetry." *Studies in American Jewish Literature (1981-)* 9, no. 1 (1990): 61–72.

Doing one's job: translating politics into military practice in the Norwegian mentoring mission to Iraq

Kjetil Enstad

ABSTRACT
This article investigates how political ambitions are translated into military practice in the small Norwegian contribution to the International Coalition against ISIL in Iraq from 2017 to 2019. The most important Norwegian political aims do not correspond clearly to a military objective, and thus military practice must take on a symbolic function. Understanding the processes of translation that this requires and the social complexity of operating with such aims with partners and Coalition forces is not straight-forward. The analysis of my interviews with commanders and seconds-in-command concludes by suggesting that such missions may require small-state militaries like the Norwegian to reconceive what constitutes core military practices, and that practice theory or the wider disciplines of sociology and anthropology may inform such a reconception.

Carl von Clausewitz famously stated that 'war is not merely an act of policy but a true political instrument, a continuation of political intercourse, carried on with other means.'[1] In the wars of his time, viz. the campaigns of Frederick the Great and Napoleon in particular, the political interests at stake were quite different from those of our present-day international coalition operations. Modern-day stabilization operations are carried out by coalitions from a range of different countries with varying degrees of commitment and a host of motives and caveats. They have another kind of complexity from the military operations with which Clausewitz was concerned. They are, in the words of Emile Simpson, 'highly politicised, kaleidoscopic conflict environments.'[2]

Yet, Clausewitz had a keen eye for the nuances of the 'political intercourse' of war. While he maintains, in line with his famous maxim, quoted above, that '[t]he political object will [...] determine both the military objective to be reached and the amount of effort it requires,' he recognizes that '[t]he political object cannot [...] *in itself* provide the standard of measurement.'[3] To determine the appropriate military action, military leaders need to interpret what the political object means in military terms. Clausewitz continues:

> Sometimes the *political and military objective is the same* – for example, the conquest of a province. In other cases the political object will not provide a suitable military objective. In that event, another military objective must be adopted that will serve the political purpose and symbolize it in the peace negotiations.[4]

The international military intervention against the Islamic State of Iraq and the Levant (ISIL) has an overarching political objective that corresponds to a military objective: to defeat ISIL. The statement by the Coalition partners, of whom Norway is one, issued on 3 December 2014, identified wider political aims, such as delegitimization through exposure of ISIL's 'true nature' and 'addressing associated humanitarian relief and crises.'[5] However, on the face of it the military objective seems clear.

Norway may, in the greater scheme of things, play an insignificant role through its small advise-and-assist mission under US command to the Anbar region in Iraq. However, the Norwegian political interests are far-reaching. For Norway, the contribution to the US-led Coalition is first and foremost part of a central defense and foreign-affairs strategy aimed at bolstering transatlantic and NATO relations to ensure US and NATO support should there ever be a threat to Norwegian territory. There is only a symbolic and somewhat tenuous relation between such a political aim and the military practice that is meant to achieve it.

This article examines how such Norwegian political aims are translated into military practice. Understanding these processes of translation is key for military professionals and politicians alike. However, for small countries especially, who deploy with small units under the command of relatively junior officers, understanding the social dynamics in the Coalition and partner settings and how the conditions on the ground affect the interpretation and implementation of the political ambitions, is paramount. This article provides a brief overview of Norwegian policy concerning participation in international operations. Second, some of the challenges which small countries face in security-force assistance missions are highlighted. This will constitute the backdrop for the third part, which investigates how political aims are operationalized as military practice by military professionals. The complexity of the political aims for small-state contributions like the Norwegian one, challenges the notions of what constitutes military practice, and I argue in conclusion that this insight will have implications for planning, training, and the range of practices recognized as 'military practices.' My analyses in the final part are based on qualitative interviews with the commanders and the seconds-in-command from two contingents to Anbar from September 2017 to August 2018.

Bolstering the alliance through participation

Norway was one of the founding members of NATO and its NATO membership has been a key factor shaping security policy ever since. Numerous other factors contribute to policy, of course, including the policies of the EU, Nordic cooperation, and Russian politics, but NATO has been the cornerstone for Norwegian territorial defense. The fear that the US may no longer see NATO as an important element in its foreign and security policy since the first phase of the war in Afghanistan has been tangible. Norwegian participation in coalitions has therefore been a key priority so that, in the words of former Minister of Defense Kristin Krohn Devold, 'the US still benefits from European allied cooperation through NATO.'[6] In fact, a driving force behind the largest Norwegian military engagement in recent years, the 2001–2014 engagement in Afghanistan, was participation to bolster the alliance. The official report, entitled *A Good Ally: Norway in Afghanistan 2001–2014*, states it quite clearly.[7] The Norwegian government had

> three overarching objectives for its engagement in Afghanistan, presenting it as a battle fought together *with* the US and NATO, *against* international terror and *for* a better Afghanistan. The first and most important objective throughout was the Alliance dimension: to support the US and safeguard NATO's continued relevance.[8]

The report continues by observing that the Norwegian military contribution 'did not influence the big picture in Afghanistan. The most important objective for Norway, however, was to maintain good relations with the US and help to ensure NATO's relevance.'[9]

The latest policy statement from the Norwegian government, the white paper entitled 'Veivalg i norsk utenriks- og sikkerhetspolitikk'[10] ('Choice of Path in Norwegian Foreign and Security Policy'), restates the importance of transatlantic ties in Norwegian security policy. It identifies three paths, the first of which is to develop the 'long lines in Norwegian security policy.' "Long lines" means that Norway will 'seek to maintain the strong transatlantic ties and further develop the long-term security policy cooperation with the USA.'[11] The second path is to 'strengthen the European and Nordic dimension in Norwegian security policy,'[12] and the third path is to increase 'the efforts in the unstable regions near Europe' partly by 'implementing a strategy for Norwegian efforts in vulnerable states and regions.'[13] This strategy is currently being developed, but the white paper identifies specifically capacity building and military contributions as possible components of such a strategy, in addition to for instance humanitarian efforts and peace and reconciliation diplomacy.[14]

The current advise-and-assist mission to Iraq is thus clearly in line with the stated policy of participating to strengthen the ties across the Atlantic and contributing to efforts in vulnerable states and regions. The Norwegian contribution to the fight against ISIL is quite small in military terms (around 110 troops, most of whom are there for force protection, and a surgical unit of around 20).[15] It might, therefore, be tempting to see the contribution as merely symbolic. In fact, former Chief of Defense Sverre Diesen and researcher A. W. Beadle from the Norwegian Defence Research Establishment (FFI) claim that the Norwegian Defense cannot influence the outcome of an international operation.[16] Such a categorical claim does not hold in light of evidence for example from the air campaign in Libya in 2011,[17] nor, in fact, in light of the events in the initial phases of the Norwegian training-and-mentoring mission in Iraq, to which we return below.

At the political level and especially at the practitioner level Norway desires to make a substantive contribution in the missions to which it deploys troops. However, the policy aim of strengthening transatlantic ties leads to some vagueness regarding the appropriate military practices in a mission. In some respects, Norway had already achieved its most important objective in Iraq when Defense Secretary Ash Carter in 2016 was photographed with the Norwegian Minister of Defense Ine Eriksen Søreide on his visit to Norway and the website DoDLive.mil published an article stating that 'Norway has become a valuable contributor in combatting terrorism worldwide, especially recently in the campaign to deliver ISIL a lasting defeat.'[18] A news bulletin from the Norwegian government on 12 September 2016 covers the same visit, and in it Søreide says

> The USA is our most important ally, and Carter and I have discussed topics that are of great significance to both the USA and Norway. The strategic significance of the oceans around Norway increases, and it is important for us that our allies see the challenges in the North. I have also emphasized showing that Norway takes responsibility for our own security and is a credible ally.[19]

The bulletin continues with Carter's statement that 'Norway is a strong and invaluable security partner for us in many areas, and they are a valuable contributor in the fight against ISIL.'[20] Despite such successes at the political level, however, the Norwegian officers and soldiers still have to determine what 'being a good ally' means in terms of military practices on the ground.

The training-and-mentoring mission to Iraq is also an element in the third main path in the current Norwegian security policy, which is to increase the efforts in vulnerable states close to Europe. This type of mission under the broader category of capacity building is commonly referred to as Security Force Assistance.[21] There is a general drive in NATO countries towards SFA initiatives rather than direct military operations in unstable areas, as evidenced for instance by the decision to establish six SFA brigades in the USA.[22] The motivation for this shift in emphasis is, for the US, that it is 'tired of large land wars,'[23] and the US hopes that it can instead achieve its strategic goals with a much smaller footprint. Biddle et al. have offered the most substantial critique of this assumption, arguing that there is little empirical evidence to support that such missions are successful.[24] Furthermore, using principal-actor (PA) theory as a framework for their analyses, they argue that SFA missions suffer from 'interest misalignment between the provider (the principal) and the recipient (the agent), difficult monitoring challenges and difficult conditions for enforcement – a combination that typically leaves principals with limited real leverage and that promotes inefficiency in aid provision.'[25] These challenges are not impossible to overcome, they argue, but that requires 'a larger [...] footprint than many would prefer.'[26]

The concerns of a small state such as Norway in an SFA mission are quite different from the situations analyzed by Biddle et al. Small countries usually only deploy smaller units at the tactical level, and so what size the overall footprint has can only be very marginally determined by Norway. Nor is Norway in a position to influence the interest alignment of the principal and the actor, which Biddle et al. identify as one prerequisite for success in SFA missions.[27] The restrictions following from the limited Norwegian military capacities are obvious to policy makers, which is why emphasis is put on participation as a policy goal. Beadle and Diesen argue, however, that contrary to Norwegian policy, participation alone may not continue to engender the goodwill of Norwegian allies in the future. Qualitative contributions will come to be expected.[28] For small-state contributions like the Norwegian deployment to the Anbar region, the PA framework for understanding and gauging successes and failures, is less relevant. The main strategic objectives are in a completely different realm from the objectives that the services, in the vocabulary of PA theory, provided by the Iraqi army are intended to achieve. To understand the nature of small-state contributions to larger military operations and the conditions for achieving qualitative contributions, one must therefore investigate the particular dynamics of these operations and how the political aims can be and are translated into military practice. The beginning of such an analysis is what the remainder of this article offers.

95 key leader engagements

To understand how a qualitative contribution can be achieved (and through that the defense and security policy goals), it is necessary to understand the dynamics of such operations as they play out at the tactical and operational levels, and as they are managed and interpreted by the military professionals. Insight into how the professional military practitioners translate political aims and ambitions into military practice, what challenges they encounter in doing so, and how these challenges are met, is essential. Yet, despite the significant policy aims attached to the deployment of small units at the tactical level commanded by officers with relatively low military ranks, very little research has been done into the tactical and operational realities of such missions.

The advise-and-assist mission to Ain-al-Assad in the Anbar region of Iraq is part of the Norwegian contribution to the International Coalition against ISIL. The overarching goals are to contribute in the fight against ISIL, to make the Iraqi military better, and to be a good ally. The contingents consist of around 110 troops, most of whom are primarily concerned with force protection. The mentoring team consists of five officers. Specialists – medics, engineering and artillery troops in particular – offer training to their Iraqi counterparts. The first contingent, which consisted of soldiers and officers from the Telemark Battalion, had a small pre-deployment team in Iraq from May 2017, followed by the full advise-and-assist team and their force-protection troops from mid-August 2017. The second contingent, which came mainly from the Armoured Battalion, deployed in February 2018 and returned in August the same year.

The following analysis is based on semi-structured and explorative qualitative interviews with the commanders and their seconds-in-command. The interview subjects were encouraged to bring up whatever they thought was important to say about the mission, since understanding how political aims are translated into practice entails noting not only what is emphasized, but also how it is presented and articulated. However, I wanted to touch on five areas in the course of the interviews: 1) specific practices and important events; 2) challenges, successes, and failures; 3) reflections on important and other potentially relevant competencies; 4) general training and pre-deployment training; and 5) motivation.

Two interesting points emerged from the interviews. First, due to some level of indifference on the part of the Iraqi forces, the Norwegian forces had to recast the idea of *offering* advice and assistance to the Iraqi forces, into an idea that advice and assistance was something they had to achieve in order to meet other political aims. Second, complex challenges, such as the lack of access to Iraqi forces and the vague goal of being a good ally, were met with emphasis on simple, military basics, such as attention to dress, equipment maintenance, etc.

Admittedly, further research is required to validate the findings from these interviews. However, in light of the long-standing Norwegian policy and aims relating to participation in international operations, and in light of the particular challenges small-state armed forces such as the Norwegian Defense face when it comes to specialization for its range of tasks, I draw two tentative conclusions from these findings: First, such missions cannot rely exclusively on traditional military planning, but require a vocabulary for and understanding of social dynamics from mission design, through pre-deployment training, to execution. Second, to the extent that missions like these become staple parts of a military's duties, as Beadle and Diesen suggest,[29] key competencies, such as the ability to analyze social dynamics must become part of what is considered core military practices.

When the first contingent arrived in the Anbar region, the final campaign against ISIL was already under way. The Norwegian commander had deployed early and had managed to establish very good relations with his Iraqi counterparts, primarily in the Iraqi Army's 28th Brigade, but filled an important role in this last major campaign as advisory team to the 9th Armoured Division, to which I return below. After that, the Norwegian troops accompanied Iraqi forces on a few operations, such as various desert and *wadi* (dried river bed) clearance operations, but by the time the second contingent arrived, ISIL had been driven out of the area, and focus shifted to stabilization operations, minor desert-clearance operations, and potential threats of violence in connection with the May 2018 parliamentary elections.

Although an allied field exercise in northern Norway is clearly beneficial to the allied defense of Norway, it is less clear what kinds of military activities in an advise-and-assist operation in Iraq will bolster the alliance. The interviewees all recognized that bolstering the alliance was an important element of the mission, and perhaps even the most important one. In a casual aside, one interviewee said that, 'of course we were there to keep the Americans happy.' Expanding on what that would mean in practical terms, the interviewee mentioned always behaving professionally, being punctual, keeping all equipment in perfect condition, and having frequent meetings with their US superiors. Such professional behavior is important in a military unit. The importance, however, usually relates to how these practices increase the chances of winning a military conflict. In an advise-and-assist mission in Iraq, these practices lose their moorings in what Clausewitz termed the realities on the ground and become symbolic gestures to show that one is a reliable and credible ally. Somehow, the act of buttoning your shirt properly in the Iraqi heat constitutes defense of the cold Norwegian North.

One interviewee from the second contingent responded to my question about what they had achieved by saying that they had had '95 key leader engagements.' This quantitative measure of success was a direct result of their experience: a significant level of indifference to what the Norwegian forces had to offer in terms of advice and assistance. This interviewee recognized, however, the symbolic significance of interacting with Iraqi forces and the importance of achieving such interaction, as did the other interviewees. The Norwegian forces understood, in other words, that the act of mentoring fulfills several political goals. Another interviewee conceded that this quantitative measure is rather vacuous, saying that 'when what is important cannot be measured, the measurable becomes important.'

Norwegian experiences in Iraq are not challenges of a traditional military nature, but rather concern dynamics of social interaction and domestic and international politics. Norwegian doctrinal approaches to military planning and decision-making emphasize the importance of situational awareness and of understanding, and one interviewee emphasized the Norwegian military's skills in military planning as a key competence in the mission. The NATO Comprehensive Operations Planning Directive (COPD) has, for instance, a chapter on *knowledge development*, where it states that the 'KD process converts basic data to more usable information, information to awareness [...] and awareness to understanding [...]'.[30] Considering all actors, their individual capacities, the terrain – including time, the weather, the human terrain, etc., is one aspect of such knowledge development. *Capacities* in military planning, however, primarily concern military capacities such as armored units, artillery, air support, logistics etc. Given that the Norwegian forces were to engage in combat only in self-defense, capacities of this kind only play a limited role. To achieve the political aims, other capacities turned out to be more important or entirely lacking, as the case may be. Having access to aerial surveillance, for example, was a military capacity which the Norwegian forces could use to attain situational awareness and reduce risk in operations. On the other hand, it was also a capacity they could exploit to gain access to Iraqi leaders so that mentoring could be achieved. In the latter case aerial surveillance is not just a military capacity, but also an element that plays a role in social interaction. It was *capital in a social field* in Bourdieu's sense.[31] The Norwegian forces also exploited the Iraqi interest in the artillery and engineering expertise that the Norwegians could offer to achieve access to 'key leaders.' Furthermore, Iraqi indifference to Norwegian mentoring was also in part determined by the relative lack of combat experience in the Norwegian mentors as compared to the significant experience of their Iraqi counterparts.

The first contingent reported positive social interactions with their Iraqi counterparts. The first goal of the Norwegian battle plan was to be accepted by the Iraqi brigade commanders and the division commander. Courage and the display of courage were identified as an essential factor in attaining acceptance, and so they made a conscious decision to accept risks as their Iraqi counterparts did, which often meant accompanying commanders very close to the frontlines. Having been accepted by the Iraqis through courage and display of courage, the Norwegians could then use other assets to achieve the mission goals. The very flexible Norwegian mandate enabled the first contingent to relocate quickly to the 9th Armored Division in the final campaign, where there was no Coalition mentoring team, and provide invaluable satellite imagery and precise enough map coordinates for the 9th division to receive US close air support. In other words, the Norwegian commander and his men used a range of assets, military and personal, in a social game to achieve the Norwegian mission goals of being a credible ally.

Access to technology was thus important capital. So was the international legitimacy that the Norwegian and allied presence lent to the Iraqi operations. These were among the capacities that gave Norwegians access to the Iraqi forces and which enabled the Norwegian forces to achieve their aim of being a good ally. High military rank is important capital in this social field, also in interaction with allies, especially the French, as one interviewee pointed out. One interviewee experienced that being bookish, and being able to have conversations about military history, general history, and politics was of great importance in interacting with the Iraqi generals, who were well-read. Asked about his past as a battalion commander fighting the Americans and about changing sides, one Iraqi general pointed out that Norwegians have done the same: Norway was taken from Denmark and donated to Sweden after the Napoleonic Wars, which is an observation that few Norwegians could have made. Another interviewee observed that 'in the Iraqi culture, age and a few gray hairs matter,' and so the second contingent advised that the Norwegian government send officers with higher military rank. Military planning for such missions must therefore reconceptualize notions of what constitutes key capacities for achieving the political aims. Considering one's capacities is not simply a question of management of military force and violence. The mission could benefit, it seems, from a fundamental understanding of social dynamics in all stages of mission planning from force composition, through pre-deployment training, to execution.

'Softer' aspects of military missions, such as cultural understanding, gender issues, and many of the elements of what has been termed comprehensive approach, are often tasked to specialists or to civilian organizations. These specialists are often, but not always, civilians (e.g. gender advisors and legal advisors). In other words, the answer to unfamiliar challenges in military operations very often seems to be hiring specialist to advise the military.

The first Norwegian contingent to the Anbar region expected to train and mentor their Iraqi counterparts in the planning processes, and so they were prepared to assign mentors to the Iraqi commander and all the key staff functions, such as intelligence/security, operations, communication, logistics, etc. These staff functions are key in Norwegian and NATO planning processes. However, the Iraqi forces' planning processes did not resemble the ones with which the Norwegian forces were familiar. Usually everything was decided quite quickly by the force commander alone. While the Norwegian mentors seemed to adapt quickly to the realities of the Iraqi operational culture, the interesting aspect that emerged from the interviews concerned how they responded to frustrations and partial achievements.

To address the soldiers' disappointment over not being taken out on operations alongside the Iraqis, the force commander impressed upon them the importance of being professional, of diligently maintaining the equipment, and of always going through the checks and inspections thoroughly in preparation for operations, even if they would never get past the camp gate. Maintenance tasks were also assigned to combat boredom. The response to the lack of participation actual warfighting was to focus attention on military basics. Mentors, with a small exception of the Norwegian force commander, experienced related issues due to the lack of access and even relevance of their planned effort.

While admitting that they had not emphasized specific training for interaction with the Iraqi counterparts enough in pre-deployment training, the interviewees emphasized for example 'general officer competence' and 'experience and competence in military problem solving' as the key competencies for the mission. When asked what competencies had been *useful*, one interviewee pointed to his MA in history, which helped to understand phenomena in their context, and his experience from military intelligence, which helped to understand statements in terms of their motives and not just their superficial meaning. However, he maintained nonetheless that 'core military leadership' was quite sufficient to lead the mission successfully. To the extent that the limited data allows generalizations, unfamiliar situations during military operations (such as being ignored and left out, having vague and difficult-to-assess mission objectives) spurred emphasis on core competencies and military basics.

This is not the whole picture, of course, since the Norwegian forces also responded in creative and resourceful ways to these challenges by maximizing the opportunities they had. The first contingent managed to establish very good working relationships with Iraqi forces and, with some exceptions, allied forces as well. The Iraqi corps commander observed to the first contingent, that he had never experienced a foreign unit that worked so well with the Iraqi forces. However, this interesting attention to and emphasis on military basics in the interviews indicate an aspect of social practices in general and of professional practices in particular which must be understood to optimize the efforts of such complex missions: practices depend on what it makes sense to do in a specific setting.

Military practices

Practices constitute according to Theodore Schatzki 'the central phenomenon in the tangle that is human sociality.'[32] Schatzki emphasizes precisely the *meaning* of practices. Rather than spelling out the conditions under which practices are shaped and developed, Schatzki builds on Wittgenstein's concept of *family resemblance* and conceptualizes two realms of practices, *dispersed practices* and *integrative practices*.

Dispersed practices are practices, which are 'widely dispersed among different sectors of social life.'[33] For the sake of simplicity, we can call these everyday practices. One interviewee, for example, mentioned how 'younger mentors should have been better at indirection and not stating things directly. Mentioning things, for example, was perceived [by the Iraqis] as a promise.' Such misunderstandings concern dispersed practices. These problems belong to the realm of cultural differences and cultural understanding, and such questions have been prominent in much literature on international operations.[34] The ability to communicate efficiently and to recognize spatio-temporal practices as elements of communication are important preconditions for a successful mission, and the interviewees all recognized this and wished that there had been more time to address cultural understanding in pre-deployment training.

The emphasis placed on military basics in the face of the complexity of achieving one of the primary mission objectives, concerns the other category of practices in Schatki's practice theory: *integrative practices*. Integrative practices are 'in and constitutive of particular domains of social life.'[35] Examples Schatzki gives include 'farming practices, business practices, voting practices, teaching practices, celebration practices, cooking practices, recreational practices, industrial practices, religious practices, and banking practices.'[36] For our present purposes, we will add *military practices* as a case of integrative practices. What sets integrative practices apart from dispersed practices and constitute them as a category, is that integrative practices are joined by

> (1) understandings of Q-ing and R-ing (etc.) [i.e. the domain-specific practices of social life], along with "sensitized" understandings of X-ing and Y-ing (etc.), the latter carried by the transfigured forms that the dispersed practices of X-ing and Y-ing adopt within integrative practices; (2) explicit rules, principles, precepts, and instructions; and (3) teleoaffective structures comprising hierarchies of ends, tasks, projects, beliefs, emotions, moods, and the like.[37]

Schatzki's concept of integrative practices allows us to see the practices of military operations as doings and sayings that attain meaning and are transfigured by belonging to and happening within the special domain of social life that is military practices. Distinct practices within the military, e.g. 'flanking' or 'fire and movement' (Q-ing and R-ing), as well as practices that also belong to social life generally, e.g. 'greeting' or 'questioning,' become intelligible against the explicit rules of the domain. Thus, the emphasis the interviewees placed on military basics – discipline, punctuality, equipment maintenance – is indicative of these specific rules of professional military practices. These practices hold prime position within the hierarchies that characterize the military domain. In the setting of a military mission and as part of a military profession it *makes sense* to emphasize them.

While Norway has sent individual officers on training and mentoring missions for a long time, the prevailing experience of Norwegian officers in international operations is to plan and lead military operations. Admittedly, there is a very wide range of military operations, not just seizing and holding terrain. There are cordon-and-search operations, patrolling, vehicle check points, escorting, information gathering, in addition to operations that utilize the full range of the standardized NATO mission task verbs, verbs such as HOLD, TAKE, BREACH, SECURE, DESTROY. Practices related to missions and operations throughout this spectrum are clearly recognized as belonging to the realm of the armed forces. These practices are often offhandedly referred to as *doing military things* in every-day conversation in the Norwegian army, and in military culture *doing military things* is related to conceptions of *what it's really about*. As with any concept, its meaning is never fixed, and in the Military Academy reference to 'what it's really about' is often made in order to disqualify perspectives on what an officer should know and learn ('sociology or IR theory is irrelevant because that is not *what it's really about*'). Such rhetorical uses of the language of military culture signal notions about a core of practices, ideas and ideals that belong to the military, that characterize the military profession and its representatives, which is what the regress to military basics in the advise-and-assist mission in Iraq signals, too.

The crucial and unresolved question is, however, how apt these military basics are as means to achieving the range of political goals for the mission. As I discussed above, they seem not to provide all the solutions and may not even address the crucial problems. Understanding how to use military capacities as capital in social interaction (e.g. aerial surveillance employed to get access to Iraqi leaders) is not recognizable as *doing military things*. While the interview subjects recognized that 'we should have spent more time [in pre-deployment training] on practicing mentoring,'[38] military planning lacks a vocabulary and a framework for understanding social dynamics. Therefore, the regress to military basics, which seems to have been one response to complex and unfamiliar challenges, seems to indicate that new conceptions of what constitutes military practices must be developed.

In integrative practices, the meaning of practices along with notions of hierarchies of doings and sayings, in short what it makes sense to do in that domain, takes on 'transfigured forms.' That is not to say that focusing on military basics is somehow wrong. As a translation of the complex political aims it may be insufficient, and that the domain of military practices needs a greater repertoire. The complex range of political aims in such missions cannot readily be translated into traditional conceptions of military practices, and therefore new practices must be developed and become integral parts of the profession as integrative practices. Recognizing that accepting risk was crucial to gaining the trust and acceptance of the Iraqi commander, as the Norwegian commanders did, is not an element of integrative military practices. Risk reduction is a central concern of military planners. In fact, one second-in-command mentioned resistance and opposition to such risk-taking in the unit. While that is understandable, as force protection was their responsibility, it indicates that a key to success in this mission lay in changing common practices. Less important, perhaps, but even more dependent on chance qualities in the Norwegian commander, was the connection established through one commander's personal interest in history and in broad reading. The nature of this mission and its goals seems to challenge core conceptions of what *doing military things* entails and what the integrative practices of the military are.

One interview subject summed up his deployment and responded to my question of motivation for his participation in the mission towards the end of the interview by stating that, at the end of the day, 'it is my job.' The statement is interesting because it reduces the difficulties and disparate and intricately interlocking set of interests, aims, and ambitions to a matter of loyalty to a decision at the political level. It simultaneously appeals to responsibility, (particularly loyalty, obedience and conscientious performance of duty) while at the same time possibly sidestepping the difficult question of the responsibility to achieve any material progress towards the less measurable mission aims.

Educating for the future

The FFI report on the Norwegian Armed Forces towards 2040 identifies several crucial choices that need to be taken concerning priorities. Two demands seem inevitable: first, the need for a credible threshold defense to deter potential aggressors at home, and second, the need for participation in international operations.[39] Professional military education (PME) in Norway, as in many small countries, is uniform. There are different campuses and different educational programs for the different branches of the armed forces, but there is no specialization in officer training beyond a few electives in the higher officer training program. The PME programs are designed for the first of the two demands, viz. for threshold defense of Norwegian territory, and that often means focus on core military competencies as a matter of *what it's really about*.

SFA is, admittedly, normally a task associated with special operations forces. However, regular forces are often deployed as well, as the mission to Iraq shows. Yet, there is no regular SFA unit. If participation in SFA missions is to be an element of Norwegian policy in the future, and there is good reason to believe that it will be, a much broader analysis of the particular demands put on small contingents from smaller NATO countries is required. Furthermore, PME and pre-deployment training may need to be adapted to develop the best possible military practices for such missions.

War is not an abstraction, Clausewitz says, it concerns realities.[40] The political aims and ambitions, particularly the international 'political intercourse' that informs the use of military force in security-force-assistance operations, are in many respects far removed from the realities faced by an individual officer or soldier on the ground. Furthermore, what the officer or soldier does is not a matter of simple rational choice in a situation open to structured theoretical analysis, nor is it a mechanistic response arising from the historical, natural, social, personal and other conditions of the situation equally open to objective analysis. What they do – what anyone does – is a matter of life lived in the world, and making sense of what that means is never a simple matter. Understanding of and responses to the realities one encounters emerge from the complex interplay of historically and socially determined dispositions, rational reflection, external conditions, expectations, hopes, and a multitude of other factors. However, there has been a long tradition, and some identify the beginning of that tradition with Clausewitz, of trying to structure available knowledge and develop tools to aid analysis, planning, and execution of military operations to increase the chances of success. The experiences from the first two contingents who have returned from the Norwegian advise-and-assist mission in Iraq may seem to indicate that NATO military planning procedures and the notions of what constitutes military practices are only partially suited to the particular challenges of SFA missions.

Part of the present analysis relies on practice theory. Practice theory has found resonance in a wide range of areas, and one explanation could be that it has the 'capacity to resonate with the contemporary experience that our world is increasingly in flux and interconnected, a world where social entities appear as the result of ongoing work and complex machinations, and in which boundaries around social entities are increasingly difficult to draw.'[41] Practice theory adds to our understanding of the specific challenges faced by small states in SFA missions by focusing attention on experiences beyond the reflective and rational mental processes in social interaction and in the individual's sensemaking. Second, practice theory provides a vocabulary for understanding the particular challenges encountered in the complex social settings of the operation and for understanding how certain practices are arrived upon. These perspectives are not just tools for the outside academic-observer position, but they can be operationalized for better-informed professional military practice.

What this article has shown is, tentatively, that military planning needs a vocabulary for understanding social dynamics and that core military practices must be adapted to meet the exigencies of such missions. Practice theory may provide parts of such a vocabulary and constitute a starting point for developing military practices for such missions. However, the standardized approach to planning and mission execution, which is essential to achieving the efficiency, speed and coordination required in military operations generally, is fundamentally challenged at least in small-state contributions to advise-and-assist missions. Standardized approaches, which the military professionals refer to as methods, must give way to profound sensitivity to the unique specificities of the social realities in the situation. The 'ground truth' demands that the officers can appreciate, in the words of Paul Feyerabend, that '[t]he worlds in which cultures unfold not only contain different events, they also contain them in different ways.'[42] There is no general military planning framework suited to discerning the ways in which differences are different. Thus, practice theory and the related and more established disciplines of sociology and anthropology may not just provide a vocabulary for analysis, but can more profoundly and in essential ways inform the military professionals' capacity for understanding.

Notes

1. Clausewitz, *On War*, 99.
2. Simpson, *War from the Ground*, 5.
3. Clausewitz, *On War*, 90.
4. Ibid., 91.
5. United States Department of State, "Joint Statement Counter-ISIL Coalition."
6. Quoted in Græger, "Norway between NATO," 91.
7. The Norwegian Ministry of Foreign Affairs and Minstry of Defence, *A Good Ally*.
8. Ibid., 11.
9. Ibid.
10. The Norwegian Ministry of Foreign Affairs, *Veivalg norsk sikkerhet- og utenrikspolitikk*.
11. Ibid., 6.
12. Ibid.
13. Ibid., 7.
14. Ibid., 36.
15. The Ministry of Defence, "Militære bidrag i kampen."
16. Beadle and Diesen, *Globale trender mot 2040*, 157.
17. Beadle and Diesen are not entirely clear on this point. On the one hand, they state that the ability of the Norwegian Defence "to affect the outcome of the conflicts in question, can be counted as close to zero" (157). On the other hand, they acknowledge that Norway made a substantial contribution in Libya and with the special forces in Afghanistan, and that Norway thereby gains military recognition and credibility among our allies (*ibid.*).
18. Lange, "How Norway is helping the U.S."
19. The Norwegian Ministry of Defence, "USAs forsvarsminister besøkte Norge." My translation.
20. Ibid.
21. There is a plethora of terminology related to activities aimed at stabilizing a host nation (HN) and enabling it to deal adequately with internal and/or external threats to its security. In the USA the umbrella term Security Sector Assistance covers a range of programs, including building partner capacity (BPC), security cooperation (SC) and security sector reform (SSF). Such programs, in turn, comprise efforts along different lines, civilian as well as military, that are broadly aimed at improving safety, security and justice in the HN. The term Security Force Assistance (SFA) refers, in the NATO context, to "all NATO activities that develop and improve, or directly support, the development of local forces and their associated institutions in

crisis zones". NATO, *Allied Joint Publication 3.16*, 1. SFA concerns activities by special operations forces (SOF) or regular forces at the military strategic, operational, and tactical levels aimed at improving the HN's capability to deal with threats against its stability and security. SFA falls under the broader general term military aid, but in NATO terminology does not include military assistance, which concerns SOF operations that "support and influence critical friendly assets". Ibid., VIII.
22. Lopez, "Security Force Assistance Brigades."
23. Biddle, Macdonald and Baker, "Small Footprint, Small Pay-off," 89.
24. Ibid., 92.
25. Ibid., 94.
26. Ibid.
27. Biddle, Macdonald and Baker, "Small Footprint, Small Pay-off," 94.
28. See note 16 above.
29. Ibid.
30. NATO, *Allied Command Operations*, 2-2.
31. Bourdieu, *The Logic of Practice*.
32. Schatzki, *Social Practices*, 12.
33. Ibid., 91.
34. See for example Luft, *Beer, Bacon and Bullets*; Ruffa, *Military Cultures*; and Soeters and Manigart, *Military Cooperation*.
35. Schatzki, *Social Practices*, 98.
36. Ibid.
37. Ibid., 98–9.
38. By necessity, the main element of pre-deployment training consists in practicing such things as "action on IED", i.e. what to do if one encounters an improvised explosive device, and preparing for potential biological or chemical attacks.
39. Beadle and Diesen, *Globale trender mot 2040*.
40. Clausewitz, *On War*, 91.
41. Nicolini, *Practice theory*, 2.
42. Feyerabend, *Farewell to Reason*, 105.

Acknowledgments

The author acknowledges funding from the Research Council of Norway under the Peace Research Institute Oslo project *SFAssist* (project number 274645).

Disclosure statement

No potential conflict of interest was reported by the author.

Funding

This work was supported by the Research Council of Norway under the Peace Research Institute Oslo project SFAssist [project number 274645].

Bibliography

Beadle, Alexander William, and Sverre Diesen. *Globale Trender Mot 2040 - Implikasjoner for Forsvarets Rolle Og Relevans*. Oslo: The Norwegian Defence Research Establishment, 2015.

Biddle, S., J. Macdonald, and R. Baker. "Small Footprint, Small Pay-off: The Military Effectiveness of Security Force Assistance." *Journal of Strategic Studies* 41 (2018): 89–142. doi:10.1080/01402390.2017.1307745.

Bourdieu, Pierre. *The Logic of Practice*. Stanford: Stanford University Press, 1990.

Clausewitz, Carl von. *On War*. London: Everyman's Library, 1993.

Emmott, R. 2017. "NATO Agrees New Military Commands to Protect Europe." *Reuters*, November 8. https://www.reuters.com/article/us-nato-defence/nato-agrees-new-military-commands-to-protect-europe-idUSKBN1D82RK

Feyerabend, Paul. *Farewell to Reason*. London: Verso, 1987.

Græger, Nina. 2005. "Norway between NATO, the EU, and the US: A Case Study of Post-Cold War Security and Defence Discourse." *Cambridge Review of International Affairs*, April, 85–103.

Lange, Katie. 2016. "How Norway Is Helping U.S. Fight ISIL, Protect NATO Territory." September 9. Accessed February 12, 2019. http://www.dodlive.mil/2016/09/09/how-norway-is-helping-u-s-fight-isil-protect-nato-territory/

Lopez, C. Todd. 2017. "Security Force Assistance Brigades to Free Brigade Combat Teams from Advise, Assist Mission." May 18. Accessed February 13, 2019. https://www.army.mil/article/188004/security_force_assistance_brigades_to_free_brigade_combat_teams_from_advise_assist_mission

Luft, Gal. *Beer, Bacon and Bullets: Culture in Coalition Warfare from Gallipoli to Iraq*. Charleston, SC: BookSurge Publishing, 2010.

The Ministry of Defence. *Kampkraft Og Bærekraft: Langtidsplan for Forsvaret*. Oslo: Ministry of Defence, 2016.

The Ministry of Defence. 2018. "Militære Bidrag I Kampen Mot ISIL I 2018." *regjeringen.no*. February 28. https://www.regjeringen.no/no/aktuelt/militare-bidrag-i-kampen-mot-isil-i-2018/id2592092/

NATO. *Allied Command Operations Comprehensive Operations Planning Directive COPD V2*. Mons: Supreme Headquarters Allied Powers Europe, 2013.

NATO. *Allied Joint Publication 3.16: Allied Joint Doctrine for Security Force Assistance (Edition A Version 1)*. Brussels: NATO, 2016.
Nicolini, Davide. *Practice Theory, Work, and Organization: An Introduction*. Oxford: Oxford University Press, 2012.
The Norwegian Ministry of Defence. 2016. "USAs Forsvarsminister Besøkte Norge." *regjeringen.no*. September 12. https://www.regjeringen.no/no/aktuelt/carterbesok/id2510910/
The Norwegian Ministry of Foreign Affairs. *Veivalg I Norsk Utenriks- Og Sikkerhetspolitikk*. Oslo: The Norwegian Ministry of Foreign Affairs, 2017.
The Norwegian Ministry of Foreign Affairs and Minstry of Defence. *A Good Ally: Norway in Afghanistan 2001–2014*. Oslo: The Norwegian Ministry of Foreign Affairs and Ministry of Defence, 2016.
Ruffa, Chiara. *Military Cultures in Peace and Stability Operations: Afghanistan and Lebanon*. Philadelphia, PA: University of Pennsylvania Press, 2018.
Schatzki, Theodore R. *Social Practices: A Wittgensteinian Approach to Human Activity and the Social*. Cambridge: Cambridge University Press, 1996.
Simpson, E. *War from the Ground Up: Twenty-first-century Combat as Politics*. London: Hurst & Co, 2012.
Soeters, Joseph L., and Philippe Manigart. *Military Cooperation in Multinational Peace Operations: Managing Cultural Diversity and Crisis Response*. Abingdon on Thames: Routledge, 2008.
United States Department of State. 2014. "Joint Statement Issued by Partners at the Counter-ISIL Coalition Ministerial Meeting." *U.S. Department of State*. December 3. https://2009-2017.state.gov/r/pa/prs/ps/2014/12/234627.htm

'The perfect counterinsurgent': reconsidering the case of Major Jim Gant

David B. Edwards

ABSTRACT
In 2009, Major Jim Gant published a treatise online entitled *One Tribe at a Time*, outlining a strategy for victory in Afghanistan based on the still untested counterinsurgency doctrine developed by General David Petraeus. Gant was given the opportunity to put theory to the test by returning to the village of Mangwal in eastern Kunar Province. Evaluation of Gant's mission has been overshadowed by the scandal that led to his resignation from the US Special Forces. This essay provides a re-examination of Gant's time in Mangwal based on interviews with residents of Mangwal and an appraisal of the lessons that can be learned from Gant's attempt to put counterinsurgency principles into practice.

The rush to forget

With the drawdown of US combat operations in Afghanistan, there has been a rush not only to the exits but to forgetting, never mind that US troops are still engaged in that country and that casualties, while fewer in number, continue to occur. As the Afghan conflict recedes in the distance for most Americans, issues that seemed of considerable importance just a few years ago have also been pushed out of mind by the onrush of new crises and the day-to-day concerns of paying bills and keeping up with celebrities. Some of the major personalities associated with the war in Afghanistan have also faded from view, perhaps foremost among them General David Petraeus, architect of the much heralded Surge that introduced large-scale reinforcements at critical moments in both the Iraq and Afghan campaigns and that – at least in the case of Iraq and at least at the time – was believed to have saved US efforts from ignominious failure. More fundamentally, Petraeus was also the principal proponent of a major redesign of US counterinsurgency (COIN) strategy, which sought to fundamentally overhaul how the US would allocate its funds, train its troops, and deploy its assets.

In the current atmosphere of forgetting, few people are talking about sending troops to foreign battlefields. That is an eventuality that is anathema to liberals and conservatives alike. Under President Trump, concern has centered on how to stay out of places like Afghanistan, but just a few years ago in 2009, as the theater of post-September 11th military operations shifted from Iraq back to Afghanistan, the atmosphere was very different. The Neo-Crusaderism that held sway during the Bush years had retreated, but there was still at least a minority sense, if not a consensus, that wars in places like Afghanistan were both necessary and 'winnable,' and one briefly ascendant view – shaped to a large extent by General Petraeus – was that the best way to achieve that end was by creating a military force skilled not only in killing, but also in demonstrating forms of cultural awareness more often associated with the social than the military sciences.

Petraeus's plan was to deploy troops that could win the hearts and minds of local people. It was a plan that he developed in consultation with a high-powered group of academics and military officers and enshrined in the *Counterinsurgency Field Manual (FM 3–24)*, which became an unexpected best-seller in 2007. The *Manual* was the bible for the conduct of counterinsurgency operations, but in order to demonstrate the utility and viability of the method laid out in that text, Petraeus needed field officers who could prove that his theories of culturally-sensitive military operations could work in the real world, which brings me to the principal subject of this essay, a once larger than life, but now largely forgotten figure of the Afghan War, Major Jim Gant.

When U.S. attention shifted from Iraq to the orphaned campaign in Afghanistan, Gant became Petraeus's Lancelot, who would carry the COIN standard into battle against the Taliban and thereby bring home to the President and Congress the utility of COIN as the best (and maybe only) way to win asymmetric wars of the kind we faced in Iraq and Afghanistan and that we were likely to face elsewhere in the future. Petraeus's own primary battlefield was in the bureaucratic and political jungle of Washington DC. However, in order for his campaign to convince the Congress and Pentagon to redeploy significant resources toward the creation of a new kind of culturally-aware fighting force capable of sorting out and separating hostile insurgents from compliant civilians, he needed someone like Gant who could look and play the part of warrior-anthropologist that Petraeus's COIN initiative required and thereby not only gain results in the Afghan battle space, but also sell those results to resistant Pentagon officials, congressmen, and the American public at large.

Ultimately, the plan didn't work. The Obama administration rejected the uncertain promise of a kinder, friendlier COIN in favor of more direct forms of military lethality, especially drones strikes and quick-strike kill missions of the sort that brought the long-sought death of Osama bin Laden. The causes for the collapse of COIN are multiple and include Pentagon preference for high-tech weaponry and cinema-worthy Delta 6-style combat teams, the draw-down of troops in Iraq, as well as the taint of scandal that brought Petraeus crashing to earth in a swarm of lurid tabloid reports about extramarital infidelity. With Petraeus's temporary retreat to private life, discussions of COIN went into cold storage, with little consideration of the merits and demerits of the policy that informed much of our effort in the Iraq and Afghanistan campaigns. The discrediting of the policy's architect at least in part led to the abandonment of the tactical insights and instruments through which his policy and strategy were implemented.

Despite his obvious loathing of foreign entanglements, President Trump has found himself bogged down not only in the foreign commitments he inherited, but in new trouble spots as well, especially in Syria and sub-Saharan Africa. The Islamic State remains the primary challenge, but there are states on nearly every continent that could fail in the near future, creating the conditions with which new insurgencies are likely to spring up. That being the case, and given the possibility, if not likelihood, that the United States will find itself engaged in further counterinsurgency operations in the not-too distant future, it is worthwhile reconsidering the merits of COIN, and specifically, reopening the casebook on Major Gant, who more than any one individual came to represent – for however brief a period – the promise of that policy.

One tribe at a time

Major Jim Gant first came to General Petraeus's attention through the online publication in October 2009 of an extended treatise entitled *One Tribe at a Time* which Gant wrote based on experiences during a four-month deployment as a U.S. Army Special Forces officer in eastern Kunar Province in 2003. Following that tour of duty, Gant served with distinction in urban combat operations in Baghdad, but memories of Afghanistan had never left him, particularly encounters he had in the village of Mangwal in southern Kunar Province near the border with Pakistan. When the focus of attention began shifting back to Afghanistan in 2009 and he was given a new assignment in that country, Gant decided to put on paper some of the lessons he had learned from his earlier tour, lessons he believed would be critical if America was to be successful in defeating the Taliban.

The gist of Gant's argument was that in order to work effectively with the Afghan people the military had to understand the importance of tribes. 'We must support the tribal system,' Gant wrote, 'because it is the single, unchanging political, social and cultural reality in Afghan society and the one system that all Afghans understand, even if we don't.'[1] To create trust with the local people, soldiers first had to gain their respect, and the way to do that was by abandoning the usual way of carrying out operations, with troops living in armed fortresses separated from the people they were supposed to be assisting, launching periodic patrols from the security of their bases, interacting with local people from inside armored vehicles, invading homes in the middle of the night in search of 'bad guys,' but otherwise keeping to themselves as much as possible.

Gant's plan was to locate his base of operations within the village itself and not out on some neighboring hilltop and to have his troops living among allied Afghan troops recruited from the local population. In place of the tactic of sending out heavily armored patrols, Gant proposed maintaining a porous base, with locals being welcomed inside and he and his men making frequent hospitality visits to surrounding homes. Instead of wearing the usual uniforms, body armor and Oakley sunglasses, he and his men would don the same clothing worn by local men and grow out their beards, in conformity with native custom. They had to not only eat Afghan food when out on their visits, but also prepare the same kind of meals, resourced locally, for themselves. Instead of spending their free time pumping iron and playing video games inside their forward operating base (FOB), they would attend the informal gatherings in which the Pakhtun men from this part of the country spend much of their free time, drinking tea, discussing the issues that mattered most to them, and instead of always dictating, they would just listen.

All of these measures were proposed in response to the recognition that US military operations had fallen into a predictable and unproductive pattern, with uncomprehending and often hostile encounters that in turn produced new recruits for the Taliban from among those whose family members were in one way or another dishonored or killed by the Americans. The key to defeating the Taliban was convincing the tribes to join forces with the Coalition, and the only way to do that was by gaining their respect. The first step in this process was – as the title of his treatise indicated – to win them over 'one tribe at a time.' While the Taliban had the advantage of cultural and linguistic affinity, as well as kinship ties with the local people, Gant believed that the civilian population was unsympathetic to the Taliban's brand of Islam and tired of the prolonged civil war that had had such a devastating effect on their lives, their communities, and their economy.

Essential to Gant's thesis was the recognition that soldiers and tribesmen had much more in common than either realized. At their core, both were warriors and shared a common warrior's creed. *Pakhtunwali*, the tribal code of honor, was for Gant different from the soldier's code of honor only to the extent that it articulated specific practices related to the context of Afghan village life. In all other respects, the code that soldiers and Pakhtun tribesmen lived by was the same, and once that fact was recognized by both sides, they would see the merits of working together and finding common cause against the Taliban, whose rigid religious dictates – as the local tribes well knew – represented a threat to the principles of honor that were the bedrock of tribal society.

Prior to publishing his treatise, Gant had not spent a long time in Afghanistan; what informed the work more than anything else was a friendship forged during his 2003 tour in Kunar Province with an elder in the village of Mangwal. This meeting had become Gant's 'eureka' moment, on the basis of which he had developed his own, homespun counterinsurgency doctrine, which unlike the far more abstruse and labored *Counterinsurgency Manual* supervised by Petraeus, conveyed an immediate sense of lived experience: this is what happened to me; this is what it is like to be there; contrary to what you might think, these are not bad people; we can be friends with them; they share our values; they want for themselves and their families what we want for ourselves and our families; here are the steps we need to take in order to succeed.

One Tribe at a Time was originally published on the website of the novelist Stephen Pressfield, whose 1998 work of historical fiction, *Gates of Fire*, about the Spartan defense at Thermopylae has long been a favorite of US soldiers. From the Pressfield website, *One Tribe at a Time* was relocated to the *Small Wars Journal* website where it gained a wider readership and generated considerable comment and controversy. Fans of Gant's work included a number of former military men who had served in Afghanistan and were frustrated by what they saw as the ineffectiveness and inflexibility of the military's conduct of the war. Several dozen of these fans posted their comments on the SWJ website, of which the following is representative:

> Awesome article. Someone finally got it right and wrote about it. After spending time with my "Boots on the Ground" (Gardez, A-Stand 03-04) I must agree with Major Gant totally. He got it right. Afghanistan is not a conventional conflict. Surge troops are not going to win the conflict in the long run. We must link up with and bond with the local tribes in the building process ... Our nation was started from the ground up also, not top to bottom ... The mainstream Army must wake up and stop the "Feather in my Hat" & "No Risk is Good Risk" approach to management of forces on the ground. Get the footprint smaller ... Search high and low for the type of Men who already possess the skill set needed to not only do this, but make it a success. They are out there. I've worked with them, I've seen it firsthand.[2]

Critics were just as harsh as Gant's fans were enthusiastic:

> The paper is a collection of nativist mythologies that have run as a theme throughout the West's imperial age. Last of the Mohicans? Lawrence of Arabia? Dances with Wolves? They're in there. So is an element of Stockholm Syndrome, for that matter. The problem arises not with Lawrence, of course, but with his evil twin, Kurtz, who has already served as a symbol of colonial-era (Heart of Darkness) *and* modern American (Apocalypse Now) hubris.[3]

Reflecting the impact of the article closer to the epicenter of the conflict, a friend who was working with no NGO in Kabul offered the following comment on the stir raised by Gant's essay when it first appeared online:

For about three months in the winter of 2009–2010 and into the spring, it was difficult to sit through a meeting with either ISAF [International Security Assistance Force] or State Department officials without them bringing up Gant's piece, even if the agenda was on something completely different ... Even after several pieces came out criticizing *One Tribe at a Time*, it was still implied in many conversations that while the details in the paper might not have been exactly accurate, the international community needed to move towards this type of bottom-up approach.[4]

In the end, the audience that mattered most was General Petraeus, who was then serving as the commander of the U.S. Central Command and would return to Afghanistan midway through 2010 as commanding officer of ISAF overseeing military operations in the country. Not only was Gant saying the right things at the right time in terms of what Petraeus wanted communicated, he had the 'street cred' of a battle-tested soldier who had won a Silver Star for his conduct in the maelstrom of urban street fighting in Baghdad, while also winning kudos during his earlier Afghan tour for engaging Taliban in firefights in the rugged hills of eastern Afghanistan. He was, in General Petraeus's own words, 'the perfect counterinsurgent,'[5] and with Petraeus's assistance, Gant got what he wanted most: the opportunity to return to Mangwal, to revive his friendship with the tribe and tribal elder he had first met seven years earlier and, through the renewal of those earlier contacts, begin to put into practice the lessons he had declared so boldly in *One Tribe at a Time*.

Gant in Mangwal

Beginning in August 2010 and for most of the next two years, Mangwal was the base from which Gant launched his campaign to win over the tribes and prove the merits of COIN. If the people of Mangwal could be persuaded to cooperate with the United States, then neighboring villages would see the success and prosperity that had come to this village through the association with Americans and would want the same for themselves. Gant set the gears in motion by first arranging a meeting with his old friend, Nur Afzal, and securing his support to situate the FOB within the confines of the village itself. Once a house had been rented and occupied, Gant began to live the dictates he had written about in *One Tribe at a Time*, and he endeavored to instill in his men, who were new to all of this, an understanding that the only effective way they could be secure while serving in Mangwal was, counter-intuitively, by relinquishing responsibility for their security and placing it in the hands of their hosts.

Gant also set out to recruit, train and deploy local tribesmen as a police force to supplement the small band of US soldiers who served with him. Afghans refer to such local police as *arbaki* or, in the parlance of the central government and its acronym-loving military advisors, ALPs (Afghan Local Police). There were two obvious incentives for local villagers to join the *arbaki*: access to weapons and a regular paycheck. However, Gant knew that he needed to appeal to more than opportunism. He had to make the local police a partner in defending the village and its people, and he tried to affect this outcome by sharing their meals and living side-by-side with them, in a way that stood in stark contrast to the behavior of other American forces that kept their distance and communicated their condescension in ways great and small.

As Gant was filling the role of counterinsurgent in Afghanistan, he was also assuming the role of insurgent vis à vis the entrenched Pentagon bureaucracy that viewed Petraeus's reforms as disruptive of the status quo. At Petraeus's behest, Mangwal became a showcase for numerous high-level Congressional and Pentagon delegations that included, among others, Senators Lindsay Graham and John McCain, Admiral Eric Olson, then Commander of the United States Special Operations Command (USSOCOM), and Petraeus himself. Photos from the time show the bearded Gant striding through the village with his clean-shaven visitors in tow: civilian guests in button-down blue oxford cloth shirts and khaki pants, military guests in their regulation camo uniforms, and Gant, walking confidently beside them, playing the role of tour guide-in-chief in his Afghan *shalwar-kamez* clothes, a shawl around his neck, and a prayer cap or woolen *pakol* perched on his scruffy head.[6]

The plan worked for a while. Gant seemed to have achieved a level of understanding and engagement with the Afghans that had previously been absent. That at least was the perception, and whether it was true or not, it was the case that what he was doing he was doing cheaply and he was doing it without incurring American casualties. Also, on some level, he seems to have been fulfilling not only his fantasies, but those of his guests as well. Not everyone bought into the program, but at least for some, Gant invoked images of that most venerated and charismatic of counterinsurgents, T.E. Lawrence, and more than one of those officers sympathetic to Gant's mission and impressed by the audacity and fearlessness of the man began to refer to him as 'Lawrence of Afghanistan.'[7]

Despite the support of powerful allies, however, Gant never overcame entrenched opposition from some quarters in the U.S. military command up to and including the upper echelons of the Pentagon itself. Those forces appeared not only to have feared the repercussions of a successful COIN operation for the funding of programs closer to their hearts, but also took personal umbrage at Gant's disregard for established military protocols, his long hair and beard, his preference for Afghan clothing over proper military attire. Petraeus kept that opposition at bay for a time, but Gant's great experiment ended abruptly after, Lieutenant Thomas Roberts, a recent West Point graduate who had been assigned to a neighboring base, submitted a confidential report in March 2011 accusing Gant of various breaches of military regulations beyond the more trivial breaches of military decorum for which he was already well-known. These included drug and alcohol use while stationed in theater and, most damning of all, the accusation that Gant had been living in Mangwal with his civilian lover, Ann Scott Tyson, a journalist, who in January 2010 had penned an article in *The Washington Post* headlined 'Jim Gant, the Green Beret Who Could Win the War in Afghanistan.'[8] Roberts' report was Gant's undoing. In short order, a military investigation found him guilty of the alleged infractions, which led in turn to his demotion in rank from major to captain, the removal of the Special Forces tab he had so long worn with pride, and his forced retirement from the military.[9]

In this way, a distinguished and controversial military career came to an end. Gant and Tyson retreated to the Pacific Northwest, Gant presumably to lick his wounds and Tyson to write *American Spartan: The Promise, Mission and Betrayal of Special Forces Major Jim Gant*, published in 2015. The highlight of the promotional efforts on behalf of the book was an episode of *ABC News Investigative Report* entitled *'Lawrence of Afghanistan' ... And His Woman*. The focus of the book and the television report were the same: that Gant was on to something important and that, while maybe he broke too many rules, the reason for his downfall was not his excesses, but the hidebound self-interest of Pentagon officials who could not countenance a maverick like Gant in their midst.[10] Regardless of the hype and whatever the truth of the assertion, the story gained little traction, and there it seems to have ended. Neither the television report nor Tyson's book could overcome the deep well of apathy, if not antipathy that Americans felt for all things associated with the benighted military campaigns initiated after September 11th.

Lessons from Mangwal

While it is fair to say that Gant was never as unique as he was represented to be, there are lessons to be learned from his time in Kunar, and these lessons are not merely of historical interest. Objects in the mirror are closer than they appear, and with the Islamic State still active in various countries, including Afghanistan, and other insurgencies bubbling in Africa, the Middle East and South Asia, there is a fair chance that the US will find itself enmeshed in future asymmetrical conflicts of the sort we ran afoul of in Iraq and Afghanistan. The lessons of COIN are consequently something we need to attend to and learn from, and Gant's time in Mangwal is not a bad place to start a reappraisal, in part because we have quite a bit of information on which to draw some larger conclusions.

Gant can be accused of having let vanity get in the way of the mission he set for himself, but it might also be the case that some of the actions for which he was punished – the drug use in particular – were evidence of a soldier who had suffered both psychological and physical damage from his years in the high-stress world of counterinsurgency and who had finally found that he had to self-medicate to keep himself going. These are matters that will never be entirely resolved, but Gant's personal travails should also not hinder us from trying to learn what we can from the experiment he conducted in Kunar, an experiment that might have enduring value if and when the United States decides what sort of superpower it wants to be in the future.

Allies, informants, friends

Before undertaking this assessment, however, some background is in order. In the first paragraph of *One Tribe at a Time*, Gant noted that anytime he received instruction from anyone, listened to someone speak, or read an article, his first question always was, 'Who are you? Why is what you are saying relevant? What is your background? What are your experiences? What are you getting out of what you are doing or saying or selling?'[11] While I have never served in the military, I have spent a considerable amount of time in Afghanistan and the better part of my now thirty-plus year career in academia studying the country, its people, and its problems. My experience with Afghans and Afghanistan began with a two-year stint as an English teacher in Kabul in the mid-1970s and continued in the early 1980s when I began a second two-year stretch conducting PhD dissertation fieldwork on the Afghan mujahidin parties operating in Peshawar, Pakistan. In 1984, I had the opportunity to travel in eastern Paktia Province with guerrilla fighters belonging to the party of Maulawi Jalaluddin Haqqani, who would later organize what became known as the Haqqani Network. Since that time, I have made numerous trips back to Afghanistan and have written three books and many articles on subjects related to Afghanistan, as well as directing a documentary film.

In the course of my initial fieldwork in Peshawar, I had the good fortune to meet a young refugee named Shahmahmood Miakhel who was living with his family in the Kacha Garhi refugee camp on the outskirts of Peshawar. Shahmahmood served as my research assistant throughout my time in Pakistan and has remained a close friend ever since.[12] A native of Mangwal, the village where Gant established his base of operations, Shahmahmood has provided me with background information on the village, most especially the position and history of Gant's mentor and friend, Nur Afzal, as well as information and insight on the nature of social relations in the area, which is central to Gant's treatise and the actions he undertook during his tenure in Kunar.[13]

I bring up my experiences in Afghanistan and my relationship with Shahmahmood, not only – per Gant's challenge – to demonstrate my *bona fides*, but also because of the importance Gant attached to his own friendship with the Mangwal elder, Nur Afzal. Gant's relationship with Nur Afzal was as significant an alliance for his work as a field commander as was my relationship with Shahmahmood for the conduct of my field research. Indeed, Gant's friendship with Nur Afzal was a great deal more important in the sense that life and death decisions were being made on the basis of that relationship. As in the case of my friendship with Shahmahmood, Gant's with Nur Afzal cannot be explained solely in utilitarian terms. Gant's descriptions of their first meeting and his subsequent interactions with Nur Afzal demonstrate that his feelings for the man were not just rooted in opportunism but derived from his intuition that the man in front of him was touched by greatness, and he signaled this impression by immediately referring to Nur Afzal as 'Sitting Bull,' in reference to the renowned nineteenth-century Lakota Sioux chief. As Anne Scott Tyson recounts,

> Jim felt that, like Sitting Bull, Noor Afzhal was a proven fighter, but he had chosen to lead primarily due to his strength of character, charisma, and concern for the safety of his people. From then on, Noor Afzhal would be known to many Americans and Afghans alike as Sitting Bull.[14]

According to Tyson, Nur Afzal was, for Gant, 'like my own father,' and he hoped that 'when they write the story of the war, Sitting Bull will be included, because he was a great man.'[15]

Gant's connection with Nur Afzal began in 2003, when he traveled to Mangwal after hearing that there was a volatile land dispute going on there between residents of the village and a neighboring, upland group. On his arrival in the village, Gant was introduced to Nur Afzal, who told him about the dispute. Despite the fact that he had only just arrived and had heard only Nur Afzal's side of the story, Gant announced to Nur Afzal that he would offer his assistance and that of his soldiers to help the elder reclaim the land:

> "Malik, I am with you. My men and I will go with you and speak with the highlanders again. If they do not turn the land back over to you, we will fight with you against them." Malik Noor Afzhal then told me he had only eight warriors on duty at the current time. I told him, "No, you have sixteen."[16]

Not surprisingly, Gant's intervention led to a speedy resolution of the dispute in favor of the Mangwalis. Gant himself recounts the story in *One Tribe at a Time*, and he does so unashamedly, even though he had no objective basis for backing one side over the other.[17] Gant offers no defense for his actions, other than his innate sense of Nur Afzal's extraordinary character.

Based on Shahmahmood's testimony, one can say that Nur Afzal was indeed an honorable and decent man; however, as good a man as he might have been, he was decidedly not Sitting Bull, or even any rough Afghan approximation of the Sioux chief. According to Nur Afzal's younger brother, Dost Muhammad, who was Shahmahmood's teacher in the village school when he was a boy and with whom he later spoke about his brother's life, Nur Afzal had little interest or involvement in village affairs until late in his life, the majority of his adult years having been spent laboring on the docks in Karachi. As for Nur Afzal's status as a 'warrior,' Dost Muhammad remembered that his brother had been conscripted into the Afghan Army when he was a young man. Then, as now, there were longstanding border disputes between Afghanistan and her neighbor to the east (India until 1947 and thereafter Pakistan). These disputes sometimes devolved into skirmishes between the two armies, but there is no record or memory of Nur Afzal having distinguished himself in these fights. Nor was he known to have participated in the fighting that overtook Mangwal after the Marxists took power in 1978. That fighting was intense but short-lived as the village was mostly destroyed and its residents forced to flee across the border, ultimately to refugee camps in Pakistan.[18] It was this fighting that led Shahmahmood to the Kacha Garhi camp, where I first met him, but Nur Afzal was not among those who fled the village because he was in Karachi when these events occurred. Nur Afzal apparently remained in the port city, far from Kunar throughout the decade of the Soviet occupation, and only returned permanently to Mangwal in 1995, after the death of his brother, Muhammad Afzal, who had assumed the position of *malik* after the death of the oldest brother, Sher Afzal.

It should be noted that Nur Afzal was one of many residents of Mangwal who found work in Karachi, which is why no one disparaged or thought less of him when he remained there during the jihad years of the 1980s. By Shahmahmood's estimate, there are more Mangwalis in Karachi than in Mangwal itself, and this has been the case for generations. This connection is not unusual. Many Pakhtun groups living on both sides of the Afghan/Pakistan border keep two homes – a pattern that in Pakhtu is referred to as *dwa kora*.[19] One of the homes is in their original homeland, and the second home is usually in an urban area where they can earn a better livelihood than they can in their natal villages, where most people scratch out a minimal living through subsistence farming and keeping small herds of sheep and goat.

Tribes

In Gant's view, Afghanistan was a tribal society, and recognizing the tribal constitution of Afghan society was the Rosetta Stone that would allow the U.S. to win the hearts and minds of the Afghan people and thereby win the war. This is a point he makes repeatedly and unreservedly:

> The central cultural fact about Afghanistan is that it is constituted of tribes. Not individuals, not Western-style citizens – but tribes and tribesmen.[20]
>
> When one says 'Afghan people' what I believe they are really saying is "tribal member."[21]

In supporting this thesis, Gant offers a number of characteristics that he sees as fundamental to tribal society:

- Tribes understand people and have a knack for seeing through incompetence and deception;
- Tribes understand protection and are organized to provide security for their people;
- Tribes understand honor and will stop at nothing to preserve their tribe's integrity and 'face;'
- Tribes understand power, (how many men can I put into the field, how many guns do we have?); and
- Tribes understand the importance of projecting power in relation to their adversaries.[22]

Though he refers to tribes throughout *One Tribe at a Time* and repeatedly insists on the importance of tribes in Afghanistan, he never defines what he means by the term, beyond these general 'understandings.' It probably should not be surprising that Gant chooses 'understandings' over 'definitions.' As a soldier, what mattered to him was gauging how people could be expected to behave and react in given situations. He was not interested in academic debates over what constituted a viable, general definition of tribe, state, or any other political unit. Nevertheless, the absence of a deeper consideration of the nature of Pakhtun society and the structure of the specific community he was engaged with led to his misunderstanding of the extent to which Pakhtuns (and Afghans more generally) could, in fact, be categorized as 'tribesmen' and, consequently, who these people really were, what motivated them, and how they were likely to respond in any given situation. In Afghanistan as elsewhere in the Middle East and South Asia, there is enormous variation in the constitution of 'tribes' and how they operate. Even in the relatively isolated context of Mangwal, it is not a straightforward matter to identify or delineate what is and is not a tribe, to determine how tribes differ from other resident groups, or to generalize regarding the relations of local people with the central government.[23]

If you were to ask men in Mangwal to what tribe they belonged, the majority would respond that they *are* Mohmand, but beyond identifying themselves as such, it is not at all clear what the nature of that identification is or what claiming that identity would entitle them to or entail of them. People who identify themselves as Mohmand live on both sides of the Afghan/Pakistan border. While no accurate census exists, the number of self-described Mohmands certainly is in the tens, if not hundreds, of thousands, and they are prominent enough in Pakistan that the administrative district adjacent to Kunar on the Pakistani side of the border is known as the Mohmand Agency. That, however, is about as far as it goes in terms of certainty.

While the majority of people in Mangwal would make the limited claim to being 'Mohmand,' and would be supported in doing so, it is not at all clear what the claim means in practice beyond the statement itself. What is clear is that, if saying of someone that he is 'a *member* of the Mohmand tribe' or that he '*belongs* to the Mohmand tribe' implies that the tribe exists as a corporate entity, then that description would be false and unsubstantiated by what people do in their everyday lives. Thus, even though the majority of residents of Mangwal will refer to themselves as Mohmand, and while 'being Mohmand' is an important part of how they conceive of their identity, their connection to anything like a 'Mohmand tribe' is without concrete foundation, at least if one expects that being a member of a tribe entails of that person a sense of obligation to the collective or of shared action with others who claim this identity as well.

One of the few times in which local people can remember the Mohmands acting in anything like a coordinated fashion was at the beginning of the uprising against the Communists in 1979. At that time, representatives of the 'tribe' met in the mountains near the Pakistan border and organized a tribal *lashkar*, or army, but that army, such as it was, was short-lived, in large part because the tribe was simply not capable of coordinating action or managing essential functions like procuring and distributing arms and feeding men in the field. Subsequently, as the conflict stabilized into a decade-long war of attrition, the role of the tribe further deteriorated as the Islamic political parties based in Peshawar, Pakistan, with the cooperation and assistance of both the Pakistan and U.S. governments, took control of arms and began separately and competitively recruiting manpower. The result was that in any given 'tribe,' from three to ten different political parties might have recruited men and assigned them to their separate fronts. After that time, the 'tribe' as a whole essentially ceased to function, except intermittently at a local level, for example in the case of land and personal disputes. Extended family networks and relations within and between tribal lineages still influence personal matters such as inheritance and the choice of marriage partners, but at a broader level, tribes have less role to play and are more or less inert.

Ironically, if Gant had wanted to support a group that was close to what he imagined a tribe to be, it would have been the Mitakhel branch of the 'Mohmand tribe' who were on the opposite side of the land dispute from Nur Afzal and his Mangwal kinsmen. The Mitakhel are sometimes referred to as 'Shade Mohmands' (*sori Mohmand*) because they live in the shadow of the mountains lying along the Afghan-Pakistan border. The Mitakhel, in comparison to the Mangwal Mohmand, are relatively free from entanglement with the government and consequently adhere more uniformly to what might be called traditional tribal custom. The Mohmands of Mangwal, however, do not have that freedom. They are enmeshed in other webs of social, economic, and political connection that mitigate in various ways their identity as Mohmands.[24] Comparing the Mohmands of Mangwal and the Mitakhel Mohmands, we might say that there are some groups that are *more* tribal and some groups that are *less* tribal in their constitution, customs, and actions. The fact that there is such disparity between more and less 'tribal' Mohmands is indicative of the fact that when we talk about tribes, we have to be prepared to account for a range of variations in the structure and practice of those who use tribal nomenclature in their self-identification.[25]

In his research study of the Mohmands on the Pakistan side of the frontier in the 1970s, the anthropologist Akbar S. Ahmed distinguished between *nang* and *qalang* tribes, which is to say those who live by the dictates of honor *(nang)* and those who are settled or pay taxes *(qalang)*.[26] While the terminology of *nang* and *qalang* is not systematically employed by Afghans, if it were to be adopted in the Afghan context, Mangwal would certainly fall into the *qalang* category, for in addition to the tribal frame of reference, the people of Mangwal also have been incorporated into the top-down governmental system, which operates at both the district and provincial level. In this context, Mangwal is first of all a part of the district of Khas Kunar, and it is through the district administration that matters such as taxation are handled.

The district administration is the first and most present representative of the central government, and it is generally referred to in many legal matters of note, including property disputes. In recent years, it has also been the framework of organization that has come in for the greatest criticism, because of the general perception that government officials – who often come from other parts of the country and sometimes are not even native speakers of the language spoken in the areas they administer – are corrupt and self-serving. This was Gant's view, and whether or not this is always or even often the case, the government still represents an important component in the social organization of Mangwal, and it is one with which *maliks* like Nur Afzal must constantly interact and in relation to which he and other *maliks* obtain a portion of their limited power and authority.

While Gant glorifies the tribe and denigrates the government, he seems to have been largely unaware of, or at least to have subsumed within his model of tribal organization, a third framework of association, which is what is locally referred to the *wand*, or section system. The section system overlaps with the tribal system, but is not synonymous with it, for while tribal lineages are scattered, the members of a *wand* all live together. In terms of the practical management of local affairs, the section system – rather than the tribal frame – is the center of gravity, in the sense that it is in relation to the section system that most problems arise and most collective decisions are made.[27] Mangwal is itself divided into seven sections, six of which 'belong' to the Atamarkhel branch of the Mohmand tribe.[28] The seventh section is comprised of members of other tribes who live in the village, along with families associated with hereditary occupations, including ferrymen, carpenters, weavers, and gleaners.[29] In addition to these groups, there is also one other significant descent group living in Mangwal that is likewise categorically distinct, which is the extended family that my friend Shahmahmood belongs to. In the past, this family enjoyed special status because of its descent from a well-known Sufi saint, Mia Ali Sahib, whose shrine in the village of Samarkhel, outside Jalalabad, is famous for curing people suffering from mental disorders.[30]

Of the three organizational frames – tribe, government, and section – the latter is the most relevant on a day-to-day basis and the organizational frame most often called on to resolve outstanding issues in the community. Apportionment of both responsibilities and profits within the section system is based not on tribal membership but rather on the number of families living in Mangwal, and it is in relation to this system that local people, Mohmand and non-Mohmand alike, sort out issues of representation (e.g. how many people from each family are entitled to vote in local assemblies), communal labor (e.g. how many people each group must produce to clean out irrigation canals), profit and loss (e.g. how proceeds from the sale of common stands of lumber should be divided), etc. For present purposes, the important point is that while the section system overlaps with that of the tribe, they are not the same thing. The section system includes people unconnected to the dominant Mohmand tribe, and it is often the section system that provides the context within which important matters such as marriage alliances and even gaining revenge for crimes committed against family members are organized and carried out.[31]

Honor

When trying to reconcile the more complex social organization that exists on the ground in Mangwal with Gant's vision of the tribal system as 'the single, unchanging political, social and cultural reality in Afghan society,' we need to go back to Gant's own account of this time in Mangwal, especially his transformative relationship with Nur Afzal, whom he tagged with the nickname of Sitting Bull. Gant's eagerness to make more of Nur Afzal than was really there might have been the result of his needing to substantiate the image he had of himself. Being a soldier for Gant was not simply a profession, or even a calling. It was his preordained destiny made inevitable by his belief that he had lived previous warrior lives, one of which, as the title of Tyson's book – *American Spartan* – indicates, was in ancient Sparta. The recognition of this particular earlier life had been kindled by Pressfield's novel, *Gates of Fire*, a book that 'spoke to me like the Bible ... I immediately knew those people. I knew that time. I was meant to be a Spartan, perhaps I was. Every single part of that touched me.'[32]

Gant's belief that he had lived past lives and that he had been a warrior in those earlier lives led him to the conviction that warriors were a species apart from other human beings, a conviction he tried to instill in the men who served under him, as demonstrated in a speech Gant made to his men:

> Who am I? I am a warrior. My physical, emotional, and spiritual self revolves around being a warrior. I believe war is a gift from God ... I am not a patriot or

mercenary. I fight to fight ... I believe if you want to kill, you must be willing to die. I am willing to do both, whichever the situation calls for. I am a student of war and warriors ... I believe in God but I do not ask for his protection in battle. I ask that I will be given the courage to die like a warrior. I pray for the safety of my men. And I pray for my enemies. I pray for a worthy enemy ... I believe in the wrathful god of combat.[33]

Gant was convinced that the ancient code of honor under which the Spartans lived and died was, at its core, no different from the one that underpinned Pashtun society. 'Jim fell hard for the desert civilization code and its ethos of Pashtunwali ... He related to their warrior creed as parallel to the life he'd embraced himself as a Green Beret and one he preached to lead his small band of men into battle.'[34] Gant further believed that the men of Mangwal intuitively recognized the kinship he felt for them because 'Honor, strength, and loyalty were not empty platitudes to Afghanistan's tribes; they were as important to tribal members as were water and wheat. As important as they were to Jim.'[35] Gant took the tribal code so much to heart that he had two Pakhtu words for honor (*ghairat* and *nang*) tattooed around his right wrist, and on his left wrist, he had the word *namoos* inscribed, 'referring to those things a man has – women, land, and guns – that he must protect.'[36]

This identification with Pakhtun honor informed all of Gant's actions, from the prosaic decisions to wear Afghan clothing and let his beard grow out, to eating Afghan food with his Afghan men, to reciting Pakhtu proverbs, to carrying prayer beads, to walking unarmed through the village, and even to riding on horseback in the manner of the Afghan champion he imagined himself to be. Gant appeared to believe that in adopting all of the manners, customs, and affectations of the Mangwalis he could become indistinguishable from them. In this, he did not endeavor merely to fit in. Rather, by adopting all aspects of their culture great and small, and continual imitation of the most elementary movements and expressions, he wanted to become even more Afghan than the Afghans themselves:

> ... To the casual observer Jim's interactions with Afghans might seem spontaneous and unscripted, but the opposite was true. He meticulously planned his words, gestures, and clothing based upon whom he was meeting and what he wanted to achieve. He weighed, for example, where to sit among a roomful of tribal elders, whose hand he should kiss, and whose he should refuse to touch. He decided when to pull out a string of prayer beads, conveying respect for Islam, or to clean his teeth with a wooden stick that he kept in his pocket in the Afghan style. He reflected on whether or not to drink *chai* or take a dip of opium-laced *naswar*, popular among Afghan men. Clothing also sent messages; he donned his finest Afghan *jami* suit in a show of respect, or wore a dirty, ragged one as an insult. Sometimes he dressed all in white, the preferred color of the Taliban, to subtly let people know that he understood the enemy.[37]

There were, of course, tactical advantages to adopting these affectations and Gant's willingness to assimilate as he did certainly made him stand out from the vast throng of American soldiers who kept their distance from the Afghans, feeling superior to them, and ultimately making little effort to understand their culture, their lives, or the hardships they had faced over the course of so many years. But, at the same time, it has to be recognized that however closely he tried to imitate Afghan customs, he never really understood them, at least as Afghans themselves understood them. This is especially true in relation to the so-called 'code of honor.'

Books on Afghanistan often bring up the subject of *pakhtunwali*, assuming that this code of honor is followed by all Pakhtuns, if not all Afghans, and that it constitutes a set of formal rules to be obeyed. The conceptual basis of Pakhtun tribal society is better described by the term *doing pakhtu* (*pakhtu kawal*), which conveys the idea that honor is founded in actions, not in rules, and in the evaluation of those actions according to principles that have been formulated through prior actions and the stories that are told and retold about those actions. Many of the provisions of *pakhtunwali*, in fact, relate not to the attainment of honor per se but to problems of maintaining relations in a society where personal reputation is paramount and where there is no central authority to impose its will on recalcitrant individuals.[38]

Rather than thinking of Pakhtun honor as governed by a code, it is better to think of it as a cultural conceptual space within which identity is negotiated. Referring to it as a code implies that it is straightforward in every instance to know what the proper action would be and to act accordingly. In fact, doing *Pakhtu* is highly complex and subject to contestation. It centers on a series of conceptual contradictions that have to be worked out in practice, not through any rule book. The most important of these contradictions centers on the contrary impulses toward self-determination and negotiated compromise. Thus, though much is made of the Pakhtun ethos of bravery and independence, there is a countervailing social pressure toward conformity and acceptance of social norms, as expressed especially in the *jirga*, which is the institution that punishes those who violate those norms. Too much self-determination, and the person is seen as arrogant (*badmash*) and is shunned; too much willingness to compromise, and a man is considered weak and effeminate (*daus*). Too much social control, and individuals are discouraged from acting independently, with the result that the tribe itself becomes vulnerable; too little social control, and the brakes against internal violence fail. Managing these negotiations is a delicate business that is constantly subject to disruption and abuse. All of this is to say that honor is less a transcendent and trans-historical warrior code (as Gant imagined it) than a means for allowing men (and through different forms, women) to maintain the pretense of autonomy while at the same time conforming to social norms and, when violence proves unavoidable channeling that violence in ways that mitigate its most damaging effects within the boundaries of the community.

Takeaways

When we assess Major Gant's actions in Mangwal, it is important to recognize the extent to which his understanding of the people with whom he was interacting was pre-determined by his conception of his military world and, most of all, himself. With regard to tribes, Gant saw them as essentially identical to his own team of soldiers, each bonded by its sense of honor and its adherence to a warrior ethos. Tribes, in his view, were 'self-contained fighting units who will fight to the death for their tribal family's honor and respect. Their intelligence and battlefield assessments are infallible. Their loyalty to family and friends is beyond question.'[39] He would have said the same thing about his own unit, which in the course of its time in Mangwal had demonstrated that it 'could unite with an Afghan tribe, becoming trusted and respected brothers-in-arms.'[40] We do not know the extent to which that feeling was shared by the people of Mangwal, but it became Gant's bedrock belief, just as he imagined that, more than simply allies of the Mangwalis, he and his men and the people of Mangwal were all 'family members.'[41]

Underwriting Gant's conception of the tribe was his friendship with Nur Afzal, and while it is unclear from what Gant has written how he came to the conclusion that Nur Afzal was a warrior chieftain comparable in greatness to Sitting Bull, the remoteness of this identification from any empirical evidence leads one to conclude either that Nur Afzal bamboozled Gant or that Gant saw in his interlocutor only what he needed to see. Based on Shahmahmood's description of Nur Afzal, I am inclined to believe the latter – that Gant, in assuming the role of 'the perfect counterinsurgent,' needed a local partner of equal stature, and knowing little about Afghanistan or tribal societies in general, landed in his imagination on the iconic figure of Sitting Bull. In so doing, Gant demonstrated the absence in himself of one of the key characteristics he discovered in Afghan tribes, namely their adeptness at 'understanding one another and others.' Gant noted in his treatise that he has 'preached and preached to the Special Forces officers headed to Afghanistan that I have trained in the unconventional warfare (UW) portion of their training, "You damn well better know yourself, because they know you." The Afghan people have a knack for looking straight through deception and incompetence.'[42] In his magnification of Nur Afzal to iconic stature, Gant showed how easy it is for someone trying to find his way in a foreign culture to deceive themselves, despite their own best intentions, and consequently to see in the other, not who they are, but who they want them to be.

With respect to Gant's understanding of tribal honor, we find the same problem in its most rarified and abstracted form, for it is here that we see Gant construct a mythic image of himself that transcends time and space. In seeing himself as a reincarnated Spartan warrior connected to the Afghan tribes through the mystical bond of the eternal warrior code, Gant demonstrates the extent to which he had disconnected from reality. Based on the evidence Tyson provides in her account of Gant's time in Afghanistan, it would be easy enough to conclude that he simply had 'lost it' and leave it at that. But it is important to learn a lesson here as well. Gant's magnification of Nur Afzal; his belief that Afghan tribes and US military units could be 'one family' his imagination of himself as a mythic warrior – all of these are symptoms, in extreme form, of a more general tendency to use foreign others as a mirror for envisioning our imagined selves and to see in those foreign others not who they are but who we need them to be.

While I spent a number of years around Afghans and Afghan mujahidin, including in combat situations, I have never been a soldier myself and cannot pretend to know or appreciate the kind of pressures that soldiers must endure. But I assume that the dangers associated with counterinsurgency must only exacerbate the tendency to see in those whom the soldier must trust for their survival the traits and characteristics he desperately needs those people to exhibit. But that is a danger and temptation that should be avoided, for soldiers as well as for anthropologists. Context matters, definitions matter, gaining an empathetic, but clearheaded and undramatized understanding of the people with whom we are interacting is the necessary foundation for trust, mutual respect, and an enduring relationship. Denigrating or looking down on our foreign counterparts leads more directly to distrust and animosity, but inflating who the other is can have even more disastrous effects, leading beyond disappointment and distrust to a profound sense of betrayal on both sides when the other fails to live up to our expectations, expectations that were from the start based on our own desires rather than on shared understandings earned through hard listening over long time.

Conclusion

Early in this essay, I quoted a critic who derided Gant as a grotesque Hollywood caricature that combined within himself a host of noble savage/Orientalist fantasies drawn from Hollywood cinema. These included both *Dances with Wolves*, with Gant in the Kevin Costner/John Dunbar role of the big-hearted soldier among the doomed savages, and *Apocalypse Now*, with Gant in the role of Brando/Kurtz, going native and gradually losing his grip. Personally, I think the Hollywood archetype that fits Gant best comes, in fact, from *Lawrence of Arabia*, not so much the T.E. Lawrence of history as the Lawrence of David Lean's classic film from 1962, with Gant in the role played so memorably by Peter O'Toole.

I make this comparison sympathetically, because of the respect I have for that film's nuanced portrait of a complicated and conflicted man who seeks to the best of his ability to reconcile incommensurate cultural worlds and to do so in the difficult circumstances of war. Lawrence as rendered by David Lean is a man shouldering the weight not only of a problematic and difficult military campaign, but also of his own substantial cultural and personal baggage. He is a man who finds temporary respite from his burdens by becoming someone set apart, speaking in an exotic language, performing customs not his own. However, speaking another language and donning different clothes cannot hide his foreignness from others and from himself. In the end, Lawrence discovers that the dream of melting into another culture and assuming another identity than the one into which he was born can never be more than a dream.

Gant, like the Lawrence we see in the film, is a man divided by his own contradictions and pulled down by the undertow of historical events and political actors who ultimately regard him as a liability to their own ambitions. To this extent, the two share a bond, but ultimately one must conclude that Gant was a poor imitation of Lawrence, who had spent years in the Middle East prior to his engagement in the war, spoke fluent Arabic, including tribal dialects, and had a far deeper understanding of Bedouin society and culture than Gant had of the Pakhtuns. Even accepting that Gant was no match for Lawrence, I am nevertheless inclined to give him credit for his willingness to view Afghans as equals who had much to teach him at a time when many of his peers in the military showed open disdain for the people they had been sent to help. It is undoubtedly difficult to operate as a maverick in the heavily routinized world of the modern U.S. military, and Gant deserves praise as well for recognizing that the way the Army was conducting the war was counter-productive and for trying something different.

All of this redounds to Gant's credit, but it still should be noted how much he got wrong, as well as how much more his mistakes could have cost him and his mission if Nur Afzal or those around him had been more inclined to take advantage of his support and largesse. Fortunately, for Gant and for Mangwal, Nur Afzal does not seem to have abused the power and resources vested in him by Gant. At least, I know of no incidents of the sort that happened elsewhere in which men favored by the Americans used their position to attack their rivals and gain power for themselves. Which is to say, it could have been a lot worse. But in terms of evaluating Gant's experiment, his association with a single political figure and his disregard for the complex system of social relations that existed in Mangwal deformed–at least for the duration of Gant's stay–the balance of power in the village and the surrounding region. Moreover, if perchance Nur Afzal had been of a mind to misuse the power given to him, Gant's experiment could have caused lasting and pernicious damage to social relations in the village.

In his belief that Afghanistan was essentially a tribal society and that the state was a cancer that corrupting tribal values, Gant failed to understand both the variety of non-tribal social formations that exist in the country and the fact that the tribes that do exist in the country have evolved over many generations in tandem with the state and not simply in opposition to it. By attributing singular nobility to the idealized tribe and endemic corruption to the ignoble state, Gant fundamentally misread the nature of the relationship and also reads out of the equation the role that foreign powers, the United States most recently, have played in fomenting the corruption that has long beset Afghanistan. Gant was not wrong in lamenting the corruption of the Afghan state, but what he underestimated was both the source of that corruption and the opportunism that is also endemic to tribes and the dynamics by which opportunism devolves into corruption. Coming after decades of war, deprivation, and resource scarcity, the sudden arrival of Westerners eager to find allies and quickly fix Afghanistan's problems through the trifecta of money, technology and democracy was bound to end badly. In this regard, Gant was not the solution. Rather, he was symptomatic of the problem as an overeager American, well-meaning but inexperienced, undoubtedly courageous and empathetic but also rash and naïve, and importantly the *mana* that flowed forth from Gant was not just any kind of bounty. It was primarily weapons, which in the hands of a younger and more ambitious man than Nur Afzal might have provoked precisely the sort of bloodbath that some critics wrongly accused Gant of producing.

Given the potential for tragedy that existed, it could be argued that what saved the situation Gant created from ending in a more tragic fashion was that Mangwal was not, in fact, a tribal society and that Nur Afzal was not, in fact, the powerful tribal chieftain Gant imagined him to be. Had Mangwal been the sort of society Gant envisioned, the rivalries to which Pakhtun tribes are prone might have produced bloodshed, particularly given the likelihood that Nur Afzal, as the primary recipient of Gant's largesse, would have been expected to hand over much of that lucre to his own relatives at the expense of his rivals. But Nur Afzal was a village *malik* rather than a tribal *khan*, and as such he was in the habit of meeting in assembly with other *maliks* and following established procedures for distributing goods. His role was not to act unilaterally, but to work in consort and by consensus with others, and he seems to have fulfilled that more modest responsibility as the people of Mangwal expected of him. Mangwal, it turns out, did not need a Sitting Bull. It just needed an ordinary man to fulfill the civic responsibility he had reluctantly taken on. That, in the end, made all the difference.

Notes

1. Gant, *One Tribe at a Time*, 14 (47). The first page number refers to the online version of the treatise that appears on Steven Pressfield's website. The second page number refers to the printed version of the text (see bibliography).
2. Costen, *Comment on One Tribe at a Time*.

3. Judah Grunstein, "The Horror, The Horror."
4. Noah Coburn, Personal communication.
5. The 'Perfect counterinsurgent' quote is taken from the front cover of the published edition of *One Tribe at a Time*.
6. Tyson, *American Spartan*, includes a number of photographs, including examples of Gant meeting with American dignitaries in Mangwal.
7. Tyson, *American Spartan*, 58.
8. It is worth noting that just a month before the charges against Gant were filed, Afghanistan had erupted in riots when accounts surfaced that soldiers at the Bagram military base had burned copies of the Qur'an. On the same day the complaint against Gant was filed, Sergeant Major Robert Bales was detained in Qandahar for the massacre of sixteen Afghan civilians. I am not aware of anyone connecting these three incidents, but it is not unreasonable to suspect that, under the circumstances, the military had reason to get Gant out of Afghanistan as quickly as possible, since Gant's actions would have brought further attention to a military already under fire.
9. In his formal letter of reprimand, the commanding officer wrote the following: You were entrusted to maintain the highest standards of discipline, operational deportment, and leadership in an environment of austere conditions and high risk; the very conditions in which Special Forces is intended to thrive. Instead, you indulged yourself in a self-created fantasy world, consciously stepping away from even the most basic standards of leadership and behavior accepted as norm for an officer in the U.S. Army. In the course of such self-indulgence, you exposed your command and the reputation of the Regiment to unnecessary and unacceptable risk. In short, your actions disgrace you as an officer and seriously compromised your character as a gentleman." Tyson, *American Spartan*, 346.
10. It should be noted that, while Tyson's book represents a defense of her husband's actions in Kunar, it is also the work of a serious reporter, who maintains standards of journalistic objectivity and provides a great deal of factual material in her book, including details that are not exculpatory to her husband.
11. Gant, *One Tribe at a Time*, 4 (5).
12. Following our two years working together and while still a refugee in Pakistan, Miakhel went on to work for a Belgian relief organization, the Voice of America, and the United Nations. After being given political asylum in the United States, he worked for a computer company and the VoA, as well as driving a a taxi in northern Virginia, while putting his children through school (all have gone on to gain college degrees). In 2003, he was asked to return to Afghanistan to serve as the Deputy Minister of Interior. Later, he became Country Director of the U.S. Institute of Peace in Kabul, and is currently the Governor of Ningrahar Province.
13. In addition to providing much of the information in this essay on Mangwal and its social organization, as well as background on Nur Afzal, Shahmahmood also contacted other residents of Mangwal on my behalf to answer the various questions I posed to him that he was unable to answer based on his own experience. Those he contacted included Dr. Akbar, whose photograph appears in *One Tribe at a Time* and whom Gant identifies in his treatise as the first person he met in Mangwal and who was an important interlocutor for him throughout his time in the village. Over the three decades I have been studying Afghanistan, I have interviewed a number of men myself from Mangwal and Kunar more generally.

My first trip to Kunar was in 1976 when I trekked with a group of Afghan and expatriate friends to the top of the Kamdesh Valley in northern Kunar. In 1986, I led a survey team for the United Nations investigating the conditions in Afghan refugee camps in Pakistan, and had the opportunity to visit camps in Bajaur and the Mohmand Agency which border Kunar. In 1995, I accompanied Shahmahmood on a trip to the Pech Valley in northern Kunar (where Gant briefly served many years later, prior to his deployment to Mangwal). During that trip, I joined Shahmahmood on a visit to his family home in Mangwal. On the Pech Valley, see Edwards, *Heroes of the Age* (Chapter 2); and *Before Taliban* (Part 2).
14. Tyson, *American Spartan*, 108.
15. Ibid, 66. It is not unusual for anthropologists to assert that in the course of their fieldwork they established such close relationships with their research subjects that they were essentially adopted into their families, a status symbolized by their being referred to thereafter by a kinship term such as brother, sister, uncle, aunt. Being awarded such a title is thought to indicate the closeness of the relationship between anthropologist and his or her informants. However, what is less often noted is that, whatever affection the people might have felt for the anthropologist (or the military officer), they are also exercising a form of social control, the expectation being that the individual in question might thereby act in accordance with the established norms and restraints associated with the kin position they have been awarded.
16. Gant, *One Tribe at a Time*, 17 (60).
17. One commentator accused Gant of 'genocide' in response to his actions supporting one side over another in a land dispute unrelated to the Taliban insurgency. To the best of my knowledge, that accusation is unfounded, and the dispute has not been revived to date.
18. See Edwards, "Origins of the Anti-Soviet Jihad."
19. Ahmed, *Pukhtun Economy and Society*, 220–1.
20. Gant, *One Tribe at a Time*, 8 (22).
21. Ibid., 10 (28).
22. Ibid., 13 (41–44).
23. On tribes and states in the Middle East generally, see Khoury and Kostiner, ed, *Tribes and State Formation in the Middle East*; on tribes and states in Afghanistan, see Richard Tapper, ed., *The Conflict of Tribe*.
24. Nur Afzal's own story demonstrates the ways in which tribal identity is interwoven with other connections and commitments. Both of Nur Afzal's brothers, who served as *maliks* before him, were employed by the government – Sher Afzal as a tax collector and Muhammad Afzal as an army nurse – and Nur Afzal's own heroics, if indeed there were any, would have come not while fighting the government but while serving as an army conscript.
25. In 1984, Shahmahmood and I conducted a survey of the social organizational units that had constituted themselves in the Kacha Garhi camp. Our goal in particular was to discover to what extent the social units established by refugees in the camp reflected their tribal kinship ties. Of the fifty-nine groups we surveyed in Kacha Garhi (each of which had built and supported its own mosque), the vast majority contained families from an assortment of tribes. Some had previously lived and worked together in Afghanistan; some had established marriage connections prior to becoming refugees; some were thrown together by circumstance. Only a small handful of units consisted exclusively or even primarily of families connected to one another by ties to a

common patrilineal ancestor, which is assumed to be the *sine qua non* of tribal organization in Afghanistan. See Edwards, "Marginality and Migration."
26. Ahmed, *Pukhtun Economy and Society*.
27. For purposes of identification within the local section system, the residents of Mangwal proper are divided into five groups, each of which is understood to include the descendants of five 'fathers': Maluk Baba, Wahdat Baba, Sadat Baba, Amir Baba, and Jangi Baba. Even though they come from different backgrounds and lines of descent, the members of the various occupational groups in Mangwal are clustered in two groups that are also named after a supposedly 'common' ancestor: Dendar Baba and Musa Baba.
28. The Mohmand tribe has four major subtribes (Bayzi, Khoyzi, Halemzi, and Tarakzi). The Atamarkhel is a sub-branch of the Bayzi.
29. Not all of the representatives of these families still practice these occupations, but these lines of descent are remembered and often preserved in the names by which these families are known, and they are considered of lower social status because of the perception of inferior ancestry.
30. The association with Sufism disappeared after his grandfather's death, but Shahmahmood's father, who served in government ministries in different parts of the country, was often called back to the village to help resolve disputes and for consultation regarding important community affairs, a role Shahmahmood is called on to perform as well, especially since his father's death.
31. I base this description both on personal conversations with Shahmahmood Miakhel and a paper he has written which includes a description of the social organization of Mangwal. See Miakhel, *The Importance of Tribal*.
32. Tyson, *American Spartan*, 134–5. According to Tyson, Gant read that the Spartans had affixed the Greek lambda to their shields, so he tattooed it on his own forearm and had it made it into a patch for his men's uniforms and affixed it as well to the sides of their vehicles in the field (Ibid., 100).
33. Tyson, *American Spartan*, 139.
34. Ibid., 72.
35. Ibid., 72.
36. Ibid., 82.
37. Tyson, *American Spartan*, 152–3. Two examples from Tyson's book stand out as exemplary of how Gant viewed himself as more Afghan than the Afghans themselves, the first of which involved a local man who Gant believed had disrespected one of his men. In response to this act of disrespect, Gant put on old clothes, rummaged around in the compound's trash heap to ensure that he smelled bad before meeting the man, then refused to shake his hand, declaring to him that he was 'more Pashtun than you are.' (195) The second involved an incident in which a vehicle that he and Tyson were riding in was struck by an IED, 'Jim's rage was all the more intense because he could not help but see the incident through the lens of Pashtunwali, as an unforgivable blow to his honor, to his namoos. They had attacked his family, his wife.' (249).
38. For a more complete description and analysis of the Pakhtun culture of honor, see Anderson, "Khan and Khel"; "Sentimental Ambivalence"; and Edwards, *Heroes of the Age*, especially Chapter 2.
39. Gant, *One Tribe at a Time*, 7–8 (4).
40. Ibid., 4 (9).
41. Ibid., 4 (8).
42. Ibid., 13 (41).

Disclosure statement

No potential conflict of interest was reported by the author.

Bibliography

Ahmed, Akbar S. *Pukhtun Economy and Society: Traditional Structure and Economic Development in a Tribal Society*. London: Routledge & Kegan Paul, 1980.

Anderson, J.W. "Sentimental Ambivalence and the Exegesis of 'Self' in Afghanistan." *Anthropological Quarterly* 58, no. 4 (1985): 203–211. doi:10.2307/3318150.

Anderson, Jon. "Khan and Khel: Dialectics of Pakhtun Tribalism." In *The Conflict of Tribe and State in Iran and Afghanistan*, edited by Richard Tapper, 119–149. New York: St. Martin's Press, 1983.

Costen, M. 2010. *Comment to One Tribe at a Time, in Small Wars Journal*, October 5. Accessed September 28, 2019. https://smallwarsjournal.com/blog/one-tribe-at-a-time-0

Edwards, David B. "Marginality and Migration: Cultural Dimensions of the Afghan Refugee Problem." *International Migration Review* 20 (1986): 313–328. doi:10.1177/019791838602000211.

Edwards, David B. "Origins of the Anti-Soviet Jihad." In *Afghan Resistance: The Politics of Survival*, edited by Farr, Grant M., and John G. Merriam, 21–50. Boulder: Westview Press, 1987.

Edwards, David B. *Heroes of the Age: Moral Fault Lines on the Afghan Frontier*. Berkeley: University of California Press, 1996.

Edwards, David B. *Before Taliban: Genealogies of the Afghan Jihad*. Berkeley: University of California Press, 2002.

Gant, Jim. *One Tribe at a Time*. Reprinted as *One Tribe at a Time: The Paper that Changed the War in Afghanistan*, New York: Black Irish Entertainment. 2014. https://stevenpressfield.com/2009/10/one-tribe-at-a-time-4-the-full-document-at-last/

Grunstein, Judah. 2009. "The Horror, the Horror: Afghanistan Edition." *World Politics Review*, November 6. Accessed September 19, 2019. https://www.worldpoliticsreview.com/trend-lines/4569/the-horror-the-horror-afghanistan-edition

Khoury, Philip S., and Joseph Kostiner, editors. *Tribes and State Formation in the Middle East*. Berkeley: University of California Press, 1990.

Miakhel, Shahmahmood. "The Importance of Tribal Structures and Pakhtunwali in Afghanistan: Their Role in Security and Governance." Conference on Challenges and Dilemmas of Reconstruction and Institution-building: social, economic and political factors, Organized by Maulana Abdul Kalam Azad Institute for Asian Studies, New Delhi, India, New Delhi, India, March 18–19, 2009.

Tapper, Richard, editor. *The Conflict of Tribe and State in Iran and Afghanistan*. New York: St. Martin's Press, 1983.

Francis FitzGerald's *Fire in the Lake*, state legitimacy and anthropological insights on a revolutionary war

Paul B. Rich

ABSTRACT

This paper examines Frances Fitzgerald's *Fire in the Lake* in the context of wider ethnological research in Vietnam stretching back to the Francophone era of Paul Mus in the 1930s and 1940s. It argues that Fitzgerald's heavily criticised book was important for raising uncomfortable issues of political legitimacy in the US military involvement in Vietnam as well as feeding into wider debates on social revolution in Vietnam and Indochina more generally. The paper concludes by arguing that *Fire in the Lake* has helped shift the focus in the study of Vietnam from a western-oriented, orientalist focus on American military and political mistakes towards an emphasis on the Vietnamese rebuilding of a postcolonial society anchored in Confucian precepts and values.

Fire in the Lake by Frances FitzGerald was first published in August 1972, too late to have any serious impact on the direction of US policy in Vietnam though in time for the heated discussion on what went wrong. The book won the Pulitzer Prize, the Bancroft Prize and the National Book Award and rapidly established itself as one of the major popular works to emerge from the war, given its thesis that the war essentially derived from a clash of vastly different states of mind and culture. The US had, FitzGerald argued, got involved in a war it did not properly understand and found itself, from the mid-1950s onwards, supporting a series of corrupt South Vietnamese regimes. Indeed, the absence of any serious legitimacy of the South Vietnamese state, conjured into existence after partition in 1954, ensured it lacked any serious claim to the ancient Chinese/Vietnamese Confucian concept of a 'Mandate of Heaven.' This mandate had effectively passed to the authoritarian Marxist regime of the North which had acquired the status of an official morality under its Marxist-Leninist-cum-Confucian leader Ho Chi Minh, suggesting that American strategy in the war had been misconceived right from the start.[1]

The thesis met a mixed reception in the US and perhaps touched a rather raw nerve. Stanley Hoffman wrote glowingly in *The New York Times* of the book's 'compassionate and penetrating account of the collision of two cultures that remain untranslatable to one another.'[2] But other critics attacked Fitzgerald for romanticising the National Liberation Front (NLF) and North Vietnamese Army (NVA). From the left, too, the Vietnamese dissident intellectual historian Nguyen Khac Vien dismissed the book on the grounds that Marxism came to Vietnam less as a doctrine than as an 'instrument of liberation after the Confucian scholars had failed to liberate the country and the efforts of bourgeois intellectuals against the colonial and feudal regimes had proved feeble and without compromise.'[3] Outside the US, the French insurgency expert Gerard Chaliand also criticised the book's emphasis on the Mandate of Heaven concept, arguing that that the impact of Confucianism should be seen in total while the political legitimacy of ruling regimes had also collapsed in non-Confucian colonial societies.[4]

Conservatives, unsurprisingly, displayed a remarkably hostile and dismissive attitude to the book that has seemed only to deepen with time. In 1999, the historian Michael Lind dismissed FitzGerald's book as 'undisguised admiration for the communists' while the re-issue of the book in 2002 brought an acerbic response from the right, perhaps indicating the growing willingness of the neo conservative right to attack any liberal writers who they could accused of undermining public morale during the war. The editor of *New Criterion* tartly suggested that the teachings of Confucianism 'resemble those of Marxism-Leninism about as closely as a hippopotamus resembles a sparrow.'[5] Stephen B. Young also suggested that Fitzgerald underplayed nationalist support for the South Vietnamese regime which, he maintained, represented a more 'real' nationalism than that of the North, which in any case lacked any Confucian mandate and was essentially 'western' given its emphasis on class warfare.[6]

Frances FitzGerald was a freelance reporter who first went to Vietnam in 1966 for sixteen months. She had graduated from the female liberal arts college Radcliffe in 1962, before going on to major in Middle Eastern History at Harvard.[7] In Vietnam she found herself amongst a remarkable range of characters in the news corps including editors, cub, and crime reporters and what she termed 'spaced out young photographers' and 'combat veterans from Korea.' All conceivable kinds of people in fact except, she later recalled, 'a determined opponent of the war.'[8] Returning to the US in 1967, FitzGerald was introduced by the former US Marine John McAlister to the French ethnologist and leading Buddhist scholar Paul Mus, with whom he was working on an English translation of Mus's classic text *Viet-Nam: sociologie d'une guerre* (part of which was published in 1969 as *The Vietnamese and Their Revolution*.)[9]

McAlister and Mus steered FitzGerald into a study of Vietnamese culture and religion, becoming in the process less a reporter than critical public intellectual. FitzGerald combined reportage with scholarly political and historical works on Indochina with some anthropological analysis, especially the work of Mus, who taught part time at Yale in the 1960s before his death in 1969.

FitzGerald wrote as a Washington political insider. Her mother, the socialite Marietta Tree, had been close friends with the historian and big government liberal Arthur Schlesinger and was also the lover of Adlai Stevenson and, sporadically, the film director John Huston.[10] Her father, Desmond FitzGerald, was part of the East Coast elite, coming from the same Irish-American background as the Kennedys, though the Fitzgeralds were Protestant rather than Catholic. Desmond FitzGerald had worked in a law firm before being selected by Frank Wisner to serve in the CIA as a Far East specialist in the CIA. Here he ran disastrous undercover operations into China in the early 1950s and became a strong exponent within the Agency of counter-guerrilla warfare until his early death in 1967.[11] Both parents embodied in microcosm many of the features of the Kennedy era; living in a mansion in Georgetown they combined a strong anti-communism with considerable glamour, with Jack Kennedy reputedly admiring Desmond's supposed James Bond image.[12]

In 1968, Arthur Schlesinger, he later claimed, took FitzGerald to the ill-fated Democratic Convention in Chicago; she has no recollection of ever going.[13] Whatever the case, the Convention signalled a crisis within establishment liberalism, increasingly accused by anti-war groups of being more concerned with distinguishing itself from the left rather than the Cold War anti- communist right.[14] Broadly sympathetic to the anti-war movement, FitzGerald attempted to speak truth to power by examining the apparent cultural blindness that was widely rooted in the class of foreign policy and intelligence bureaucrats that had guided US foreign policy since World War Two. This class had moved some distance from the Ivy League elite that had dominated policy-making in the post-war years.[15] By the mid to late 1960s it was fracturing under the impact of the war, especially at the middle level of non-career officials who started selective leaking to the media, less as a moral or political protest than to save their jobs and careers.[16]

Like several other critics, Fitzgerald set out to investigate the reasons for US military involvement. However, by focusing on the cultural dimensions of the US 'quagmire', she moved beyond the framework of strategic realism underpinning much US decision-making to construct an anthropologically-informed analytical framework to explain how the US had largely lost a vital strategic centre of gravity of the war. This was defined less in terms of the public mood in the US or even the fighting abilities of the South Vietnamese Army (ARVN) than the legitimacy of the South Vietnamese state the US was purportedly defending.

Some recent revelations suggest that not all the Washington policy-making elite were completely blind to the legitimacy issue by the mid to late 1960s. Henry Kissinger, for instance, visited Vietnam twice before entering the Nixon administration in 1969. '[M]erely physical security will not solve the problem,' he wrote in his diary during his first visit in 1965. 'The people of South Vietnam must develop a long-term commitment to their government if they wish to attain political and economic stability.'[17] Such observations, though, became largely lost as Kissinger became embroiled in the withdrawal policy of the Nixon administration which was driven more by domestic political considerations than strategic imperatives in Vietnam itself.[18]

The war in Vietnam was emerging as a revolutionary war, a type of conflict that the US political elite and military bureaucrats understood in only remote and abstract terms, never having actually fought a major war before Vietnam against a Marxist revolutionary enemy beyond the largely conventional war in Korea. This war had some similarities to what some French military experts termed a *guerre revolutionnaire* in the 1950s, though it was hardly seen as such in American military and strategic circles.[19] 'Revolution' emerged as a heady if poorly conceived concept in American political debate by the late 1960s and early 1970s, mainly through the anti-war movement and the Marxist-inspired new left. Both were attracted to a myth of rural guerrilla warfare waged by heroic black-clad peasants pitted against a faceless American military machine, though for many activists the real hero was Che Guevara fighting in Cuba rather than NLF guerrillas fighting in Indochinese jungles.[20] Most of the American radicals of the era tended to view revolutionary change through a Eurocentric prism centred on historical patterns derived from the American, French, and Bolshevik revolutions.[21] The idea that revolutionary forces might follow alternative paths drawing on ancient cultural roots and mentalities was rarely embraced at this time; it would, arguably, only begin to emerge on the intellectual landscape in the aftermath of the Islamic revolution in Iran in 1979.

FitzGerald's book can thus be re-examined as a work that contained significant insights into non-western cultural myths harnessed behind an agenda of revolutionary change. *Fire in the Lake* mobilised French ethnological insights, derived from the work of Paul Mus; psychological insights derived from the theoretical work on colonialism by Otare Mannoni and Frantz Fanon; and the work of a few American anthropologists working in Vietnam such as Gerald Hickey.

In this paper I will examine some of these influences on an important book about an unpopular war. Some of its insights of *Fire in the Lake* have certainly been bypassed by the emergence in academe of Vietnam Studies.[22] But I shall contend that *Fire* remains a remarkable single volume foray into explaining an Asian culture, shaped in part by Confucian values. I shall examine this in three sections: the first section looks at the dominant social science traditions in the US in the late 1960s and early 1970s; the second examines the tradition of French ethnology that helped shape Fitzgerald's approach, especially the work of Paul Mus, while the third section assesses the longer-term importance of *Fire* in relation to the historical re-examination of the US involvement in Vietnam as an unwitting colonial intrusion.

Post-war american social science and the idea of 'revolution' in Vietnam

FitzGerald's resort to ethnological explanations of Vietnamese culture derived from the general paucity of anthropological research in Indochina before the military escalation of the 1960s. The lurch by the US towards informal empire after 1945 largely avoided detailed anthropological knowledge that previous imperial powers like Britain and France had mobilised to understand their varied colonial terrains. The US military and policy-making elites tended to rely on a collection of economic, educational and aid packages that could be used to win over compliant post-colonial political elites, often formulated with little detailed knowledge of the people and cultures for which they were targeted.[23]

'Revolution' was an abstract if menacing concept for the vast Pacific region, riven as it was by Cold War ideological rivalries. The centrality of the 'domino theory' in strategic debate shaped much social science research, leading to what Ninkovich has termed a philosophically-inspired 'historical preunderstanding' rather than serious and informed historical and cultural insights.[24] Functioning alongside the domino theory was social science interest in modernisation theory, leading to many political scientists focusing, until at least the late 1960s, on Lockean-based models of political development and democratisation emerging out of economic and social modernisation.[25] These Cold War academic approaches tended to associate Marxist frameworks of analysis with the Soviet model of revolution, ignoring in the process how Vietnamese readings of Marxist texts might differ radically from those in Russia and Eastern Europe.[26]

There was some funding in the post war years for American anthropologists working in Asia and the Pacific, though Indochina remained marginalised until the early 1960s. Indochina had not featured in US grand strategy during World War Two, when it had formed the core of the Japanese-controlled empire in the southern Asian landmass. The region emerged after 1945 rather like an experiment waiting to be tested. There were a series of nationalist movements, though the strongest non-communist group had been decimated in an insurrection against the French in the early 1930s. The one group with the strongest claims to power, at least in the north, were the communist Viet Minh under the formal leadership of Ho Chi Minh, though far less was known about this group than Mao Zedong's communist Red

Army in Yenan. Declaring independence in August 1945 in Hanoi, Ho's Viet Minh seemed destined to form a new communist state on the Asian mainland when this did not, as yet, seem inevitable to many American Asian observers in China itself.

The obsession with the domino theory among the foreign policy-making elite focused attention on geopolitics. In the aftermath of the Chinese revolution in 1949, Indochina was increasingly viewed as a the 'gateway' to South East Asia, an image reinforced by feature films such as Ken Annakin's *The Planters Wife* (1952) and Sam Fuller's *China Gate* (1958) suggesting that Mao's China was seeking communist subversion into Indochina, then more widely into South East Asia and beyond. The region tended to be perceived therefore as a strategic rather than a cultural entity, marginalising serious anthropological attention.[27]

Nevertheless, there was a sense by the mid-1950s that the US had an opportunity to transform the political landscape in the South, securing a new compliant regime like those elsewhere in South East Asia. US military involvement occurred when policy-making was shaped, in part at least, by modernisation theory. This theory, especially as it became expounded by the scholar-bureaucrat Walt Rostow, appeared an all-embracing concept capable of matching the appeals of Marxism-Leninism by highlighting certain uniform patterns of political, economic and social modernisation in developing societies about to undergo 'take off' into sustained economic growth.[28] The theory supplied a language and sense of historical direction for US foreign policy-making and, more specifically, a rationale for supporting the Diem regime in Saigon, committed, in general terms at least after 1954, to modernisation, land reform, and an unspecified form of 'revolution.'[29] The theory paid scant regard to Vietnamese history and culture and entered into terminal crisis following the 1968 Tet Offensive, when evidence increasingly emerged of the corruption and paralysis within the South Vietnamese state.[30]

The limited interest by the Washington policy-making elite in the history and cultures of Vietnam was replicated by the US military. What can be termed, after Russell Weigley, as the 'American Way of Way' involved a strategy of frontal attack and the complete defeat of the enemy rather than more protracted political-type conflicts usually including various forms of guerrilla insurgency.[31] The outlook remained unchallenged in US military circles in the post-1945 years, despite the engagement with guerrilla war in the Philippines and Burma in the 1940s, and sporadically in Korea in the early 1950s. By the late 1950s the US military was pivoted towards waging possible future conflict with the Soviet Union; smaller-scale guerrilla conflicts were viewed as peripheral brushfire affairs that could be managed and contained through counter-insurgency (COIN) doctrine, a term that came into general use after 1958.

COIN was viewed by the Kennedy administration as a series of tactical methods that could borrowed or learned from other conflicts. This revealed, once again, the slender interest in the specifics of Vietnamese culture and history. Until the early 1960s the US role in South Vietnamese was, in public at last, a limited advisory one behind the Army of the Republic of Vietnam (ARVN) largely constructed through American expertise, hardware and doctrine. The expectation was that the Diem regime could be successfully entrenched on lines not so dissimilar to the Syngman Rhee regime in South Korea. Although there had been major US military assistance to the French in the last few years of their failing war against the Viet Minh before 1954, the involvement in South Vietnam could be technically viewed as a different enterprise given that it was now oriented towards building up an independent sovereign South Vietnamese state.

The US military did not support serious anthropological research in South Vietnam prior to the escalation of the mid-1960s. American anthropological interest in Vietnamese culture had been slow to get off the ground after 1954, though a more co-ordinated programme of anthropological research attached to the Military Assistance Advisory Group (MAAG) (originally created in 1950 to support the French army with military equipment) might have had some impact on the way the Diem regime was seen to be functioning so poorly at the local level.

American anthropology had traditionally veered towards China rather than Vietnam, given the scale of American missions in the country prior to 1949. The communist revolution had led to a massive exodus of Americans and by 1957 it was estimated a mere 23 Americans were resident in the country compared to 13,300 in 1937.[32] Mainland China became increasingly viewed as another totalitarian Marxist Leninist state hidden behind a bamboo rather than an iron curtain. By the middle 1950s the communist regime in North Vietnam was largely viewed as a replica of its northern neighbour. There were few to challenge this given both North and South Vietnam remained largely unknown in US intelligence circles and were ignored by the American press until the end of 1960.[33]

The Diem regime had six years at least of insulation from wider scrutiny in the either the US or Western Europe until the early 1960s. It first started with a civic action programme under the influence of the CIA adviser Edward Lansdale; this formed the centre of Diem's nation-building efforts in the late 1950s to establish structures to bind Vietnamese at the local level to the regime in Saigon. The programme ran into difficulties with the Eisenhower administration in Washington, which refused to support it financially. The renewal of communist insurgency in the South after 1959 was partly a reflection of the failure of the program, as the NLF exploited widespread disaffection among the peasantry in the South against a scheme that centralised power and control in Saigon. After 1961, the Diem regime turned to a scheme to create strategic hamlets, partly through the advice of the British counter-insurgency expert Robert Thompson. This also attempted to consolidate tighter top-down control of the peasantry and replace non-compliant village leaders with advisory 'councils of elders' composed mostly of the relatively wealthy.[34]

There was some sporadic criticism of these policies, though any serious review was hampered by the absence of serious anthropological research capable of querying what were, in effect, two ill-thought-out experiments in social engineering: first civic action and them the despised strategic hamlets that NLF found easy to subvert. Most social science research that did occur was performed under the auspices of the Michigan State University Group (MSUG), a body created out of a contract between Michigan State and the CIA between 1955 and 1959. The MSUG later came under attack in the 1960s by anti-war protesters, though it was initially involved in efforts to resettle refugees fleeing from the North, an issue highlighted in the US by the Vietnam Lobby and its (temporary) media celebrity Tom Dooley.[35]

One of the few anthropologists to attempt serious research in South Vietnam was Gerald Hickey. The Diem regime remained largely hostile to anthropologists working in the country and tried to steer what interest there was towards the so-called 'Montagnard' or Nung peoples in the Central Highlands, communities that had invited considerable interest from French ethnologists in the years prior to World War Two. In the early 1960s, Hickey published a RAND study of the strategic hamlet programme that did not completely oppose the hamlet programme, but pointed to encampments where freedom of movement was severely restricted and villagers cut off from their traditional farming areas.[36] In a critical re-assessment of Hickey's work David Price has acknowledged that the report was an 'impressive piece of anthropological work' covering as it did over twenty different ethnic groups in the Highlands.[37]

Alongside the Rand work, Hickey published in 1964 a study of the village of Khang Hau in the Mekong Delta south of Saigon. This was a detailed study of the family and kinship in a village that engaged in small trade and shop-keeping. Hickey pointed out that the villagers had a variety of religious beliefs, including some Catholics while others were Buddhist or followers of the Cao Dai sect, traditionally strong in this part of southern Vietnam. Almost all shared what he saw as a cosmological view strongly shaped by a Chinese philosophical tradition where destiny is shaped by a particular star as well as concepts of harmony closely linked to the use of folk medicine. 'Floods, droughts and other catastrophes are indicative of disharmony and the disapproval of heaven,' Hickey concluded. 'This is the time for a "change of mandate", the literal Vietnamese expression for revolution.'[38]

This was a building block at the local level for the thesis that Frances FitzGerald would expound in *Fire in the Lake*. Hickey's book suggested close links between beliefs held by peasant communities and the legitimacy of the central state. The thesis suggested a central role for local level anthropological research in developing a wider political anthropology, a sub-branch of the discipline of anthropology that developed extremely slowly in the post-war years. There was as yet no serious political anthropology of Vietnam examining, for example, how myth becomes transformed into political ideology as states became increasingly centralised or how far historical consciousness co-relates with the forms and degrees of political power.[39] Such projects remained remote in South East Asia in the 1950s and 1960s, though some advances would be made in anthropological research of this type in other regions such as the colonial terrains of Sub Saharan Africa.

Paul Mus and French ethnology in Vietnam before and after partition

By the 1960s there was a growing fascination in some quarters of Asian Studies in the US with French ethnology, especially as this was expounded by the patrician Francophone figure of Paul Mus. Looked at from a distance of over six decades, it is easy to conclude that Mus's ethnology was a product of belated French imperialism and anchored in a view of the colonised as one collective mass largely divorced from history. Such was the conclusion of Edward Said, who dismissed Mus as an exponent of French enlightened tutelage rather than traditional colonial rule over a population whose culture was always better understand by the Chinese, the rulers of the country for centuries, rather than the late-arriving French.[40] But Mus was not a straightforward example of European orientalism looking at powerless Asian others; his stress on Vietnamese agency and, to some degree, on historicity, locates him more in a longer tradition of Durkheimian-inspired sociology stressing the ability for cultures to adapt to rapidly changing currents of modernity, though one that lacked any clear theoretical insights into the political and economic dynamics of revolutionary change.[41]

Mus burst onto the academic scene in the United States in the late 1950s and early 1960s, imparting a more nuanced approach to the study of Asian cultures and their differing religious traditions signally different from the static orthodoxy of 'oriental despotism' espoused by Karl Wittfogel following the decimation of Asian Studies during the McCarthyite purges of the early 1950s.[42] He was a rather unusual figure within the French tradition of colonial ethnology. The French colonial enterprise had traditionally been moulded by a centralised Napoleonic state-class structure geared towards the ideal, in formal imperial doctrine at least, of 'civilising' its subjects and integrating them into a common centrally-managed framework. This might, in theory at least, provide less of a role for ethnologists than for the anthropologists in the British empire, where the doctrine of indirect rule ensured a degree of devolution to power to tribal authorities whose kinship systems, trading and economic networks and cosmological beliefs required detailed anthropological study. However, in the case of Indochina, French ethnologists had been extraordinarily busy from the late nineteenth century onwards studying the various local groups around the region, describing different tribal or village structures, dress styles, physical features, techniques of farming and hunting, as well as dance and marriage and funeral ceremonies. By the inter-war years there was a vast array of research and publication outlining the ethnic complexity of Indochina. This research attempted to dissolve the idea that the region was the land of the Viet as well as claim that all groups were bound towards the distant imperial power of Mother France as their ultimate imperial protector.[43]

Mus's early upbringing in Hanoi early in the twentieth century instilled a strong paternalistic devotion to Vietnamese culture in contrast to other ethnic groups. His education was partly shaped by the pacifist humanism of Alain (Emile Chartier 1868–1951) while preparing for university at the Lycee Henry IV in Paris. Alain emphasised experience, empathy, honesty, poetic writing style as well as the free play of intellectual enquiry, in a climate of benign liberalism that another of his pupils, Jean Paul Sartre, would later castigate.[44] Mus however, did not follow Alain's pacifism too seriously; he underwent officer training at St Cyr in 1926–27 before returning to Hanoi as a reservist in the French colonial army in 1927. But Alain's influence was important for restating the nineteenth century French obsession with the idea of a humanity reconciled after the fracturing endured during the French revolution, and one which he would later see embodied in the apparently cohesive cultures of Indochina.[45] This outlook steered him towards the wider French imperial project during the interwar-years of a benign colonial humanism that imagined a dissolution of any differences between a national republic in France and an imperial nation embracing its overseas colonies.[46]

Before the war Mus had been silent despite the resurgence of Vietnamese nationalism and the violent suppression by the French army of the communist supported peasant uprising in Nghe-Tinh in 1930–31.[47] It was the experience of war after 1940 that was the major turning point in Mus's thinking. After the French Army's collapse in June 1940, he left to join De Gaulle's Free French Forces in North Africa in 1942. He later undertook commando training in Ceylon (Sri Lanka) before parachuting into Indochina to contact the resistance to the Vichy regime. In Hanoi he witnessed the dramatic end of the French colonial state as the Japanese military overthrow of the Vichy regime in March 1945 and was in Tokyo to see the capitulation of Japan on 2 September, the same day Ho Chi Minh proclaimed an independent Vietnam in Hanoi.

By the end of the war Mus had abandoned the idea that France had any sort of serious civilising mission left in Indochina. In a report titled 'Note sur la crise morale franco-indochinoise' he stressed that France had forfeited its moral authority to rule in Indochina, though this did not chime well with decision-makers in Paris reluctant to go down a road of phased decolonisation.[48] Regaining Indochina was, for many political figures in France in the mid-1940s, a matter of regaining French honour lost at the time of the collapse in 1940. For Mus, by contrast, it was essential to develop a new form of humanism that broke with the colonial past through what he termed *la quete de l'humain* (the search for the human). French colonisers, he argued, needed to put themselves in the shoes of the colonised in a new post-colonial order in which all people were equal.[49] Few in post-war France were prepared to listen to such arguments, as a visionary project of restoring the French empire became a defensive response to the disaster of 1940.[50]

Mus left Vietnam permanently in 1947 to return to France to direct the *Ecole Nationale de la France d'Outre Mer*. Here he tried to get French politicians and administrators to take Vietnamese nationalism seriously, though between 1947 and 1949 the French government attempted a belated internal solution via the emperor Bao Dai. By 1949 Mus's position became untenable as he spoke out against the French Army's attacks on civilians. Withdrawing from the apparatus of French colonial administration, Mus was free to develop a wider critique of French colonialism as the French Army became effectively the last great champion of the nineteenth century European imperial civilising mission in its escalating war against the Viet Minh.[51]

This critique formed the basis the book *Viet-Nam: Sociologie d'une guerre* (1952), which applied an essentially Chinese-inspired theory of revolutionary change based on the notion of an imperial mandate of heaven. The French had lost the war in Vietnam, Mus argued, two years before Dien Bien Phu; the faith they had placed in the legitimacy of 'traditional' institutions surrounding the emperor in Hue was forfeited as the mandate of heaven had inextricably passed to Ho Chi Minh's communists after 1945. The 'consecration' of this new regime at the village level revealed, in the eyes of the Vietnamese masses at least, that there was no serious way that the French could rebuild the old colonial order.[52]

The mandate of heaven concept had been expounded by the philosopher Mengzi (or the Latinised variant 'Mencius' used by later Jesuit missionaries) between 372–279 BCE. Strictly speaking, his writings were an example of 'second stage' Confucianism emphasising the importance of ethical inspiration among rulers, drawing on ancient written texts. 'Virtue' in this context embraced specific virtues such as benevolence, courage and wisdom; it also became inked to the charismatic influence of a ruler through the concept of *de* or inner character, virtue and morality.[53] This formed, in effect, an early theory of political legitimacy which can still be seen to shape the understanding of legitimacy in modern 'Confucian' Asian societies.

The mandate concept formed a major component of western understanding of Chinese imperial authority. In the early 1830s, Hegel in his

Philosophy of History described the China as the land of the recurrent principle and Chinese emperor as a 'Lord of Nature' who alone was able to approach heaven to conduct religious rituals such as the divine blessing for the sowing of crops. The divine quality of the Chinese state expressed what Hegel viewed as the 'spirit of its people' that was likely to continue more or less indefinitely.[54] This static and orientalist conception of Chinese imperial power was increasingly challenged by the late nineteenth and early twentieth century as historians and sociologists began to examine the changing nature of imperial power as well as the bureaucratic class of mandarins that underpinned it. The mandarins were scholars educated in the classics and had arrived at their posts only after rigorous examinations. This Confucian-inspired education sustained a gentlemanly code of social etiquette that ensured that all mandarins would adhere to religiously-sanctioned custom when resolving disputes.[55]

But the mandarins after the year 1000 CE also began to gain increasing control of land and political power in their own right. They became in effect a feudal aristocracy managing large pools of serf labour, though largely avoiding slavery. This mandarin gentry created patrilineal domains that spread into south China as well as parts of Indochina. The historical anthropologist Eric Wolf has challenged the idea that the mandarinate represented a unique class of philosopher kings; while by the eighteenth century the Manchu dynasty weakened its autonomy as it attempted to destroy serfdom, leading to a resurgence of landholding by wealthy peasants.[56]

Mus argued that the Confucian-inspired concept of an imperial Mandate of Heaven had become instilled into Vietnamese culture during the long Chinese domination of the region, forming part of the dominant religion of the society along with Buddhism and Catholicism after the arrival of the French. His Vietnamisation of the Chinese concept of an imperial mandate led to an examination of forces being exerted upwards from the local level; these surfaced sporadically in the form of periodic rebellion over the century between the 1840s and the 1930s. In China, the most spectacular of these was the Taiping Rebellion from 1850–1864, the bloodiest conflict of the nineteenth century with between 20–30 million dead that seriously challenged the heavenly mandate of the Manchu dynasty in China.[57]

Contemporary China scholars have queried the cyclical theory of history contained in the mandate theory, which became fashionable among some analysts such as John Fairbank following the Communist revolution in 1949. Recent work on the Chinese state urges a focus on a combination of factors shaping state power, including internal evolutionary dynamics as well as the encounter with the west and forces of globalisation. In this context the Maoist period from 1949–1979 can be seen as standing as something of an historical aberration once the Deng Xiaoping reforms started picking up on earlier patterns of modernisation prior to 1949, though the violent revolutionary social transformation of the 1950s and 1960s had also created a fairly high degree of social cohesion by this time.[58]

Mus failed to explore this historical dimension in the case of Vietnam, though arguably a similar pattern of modernisation can be seen with the Doi Moi reforms of the middle 1980s, without quite the same transformation of the ruling regime as occurred in China after 1979. Much of Mus's work from the mid-1950s onwards was focused on Buddhist culture in Asia. The mandate theory propounded in *Viet-Nam: Sociologie d'une guerre* was heavily shaped by the communist brief seizure of power in Hanoi at the end of World War Two. The close linkage between the party's Marxism-Leninism with Vietnamese nationalism had considerably reduced the orthodox Marxist emphasis on the revolutionary potential of the bourgeoisie, though it did emphasise the centrality of the classes rather than families and villages. But many Vietnamese intellectuals were also fascinated with Social Darwinist ideas of struggle underpinning a rejuvenation of Vietnamese culture. As Ho Tai has pointed out, the triumph of the Marxist vision also pushed out many of the humanist concerns championed by Mus and the continuing war against the French and the Americans would continue to side-line these until well after the final reunification of 1975.[59]

Nevertheless, during the 1950s and 1960s Mus emerged as a major Asian Studies scholar using symbolic anthropology as part of the deep analytical penetration of cultures of the kind that that would later be associated with the deep penetration of culture by Clifford Geertz.[60] There were paths here too for later psychological research in Asian societies, especially at the village level, though this was in a rudimentary stage when Fitzgerald wrote *Fire in the Lake*.

Fire in the lake and the crisis of American liberalism

Fire in the Lake was by no means the first book on Vietnam to draw on Mus's analytical framework. However, it was particularly innovative in the way that it drew on both Francophone cultural ethnology as well as a theory of collective colonial psychology, shaped by Mannoni and Fanon, to explain the US inability to understand Vietnamese culture or the enemy they were up against. In this regard, the book was a signal departure from most previous attempts in the US to understand revolutionary transformation in Vietnam. The late 1960s was a period of mounting crisis among American liberals as many college and university campuses became locked down in student protests against the war and the formerly cohesive consensus among the policy-making elite in Washington began to fray at the seams, exemplified spectacularly by the leakage of the Pentagon Papers to *The New York Times* by the former RAND researcher Daniel Ellsberg in 1971. There was a sense of growing anxiety if not despair among some prominent observers of the war. Among the various authors Fitzgerald cited in *Fire in the Lake*, three names stand out: Robert Shaplen, David Halberstam and John T. McAlister. All three were influenced, in varying degrees, by the work of Mus as they tried to engage with the complexities of Vietnamese culture.

Shaplen, who wrote regularly for *The New Yorker*, was the most conventionally-oriented of the three, despite his recognition of Vietnam as a kind of laboratory of revolutionary change. In two books, *The Lost Revolution: Vietnam 1945-65* (1966) and *Time Out of Hand: Revolution & Reaction in Southeast Asia* (1969) he argued that the revolution occurring in Vietnam had been essentially 'lost' by the United States as early as the mid-1960s, with several lost opportunities to take 'a nationalist revolution away from the communists.'[61] Shaplen was mainly focused on American policy failings and there was a strong element of *deja vu* in his assumption that the revolution had been 'lost' just like China had been apparently 'lost' for right wing Republicans in the 1940s, though he acknowledged that the first real 'lost' opportunity had arisen with the initial French commitment to return to Vietnam in 1945-46. Shaplen was one of the first analysts to consider Ho Chi Minh as a major revolutionary leader in South East Asia. Quoting Mus's opinion of Ho as a 'great actor, – one cannot afford to be naïve with him,' Shaplen tried to alert American public opinion to the realities of the communist revolution in the North as well as the weaknesses of the regimes in the South, though his discussion was focused mainly on the nuances of politics and the failings of key individuals at particular moments in time, an approach later adopted by Halberstam.[62]

Shaplen saw 'revolution' as a general term that was broadly understandable within modernisation theory. It involved inexorable social and economic processes occurring in various ways throughout South East Asia. It was also something that the United States could, with sufficient political will, divert and modify for its own purposes at certain key historical moments before the opportunity was lost. His avoidance of any fatalistic view of history ensured that his books were directed as much at policy makers as the broader public, given their warning that bold decisions could not be avoided without the prospect of longer-term disaster.

A rather more pessimistic approach was Halberstam's, whose extensive writings on Vietnam became associated with a fatalistic view of US relations with Vietnam defined through the 'quagmire theory,' so called after his first book in 1965 titled *The Making of a Quagmire*.[63] Halberstam, who had covered the war in Vietnam between 1962-64, detected a pattern of ever-closer involvement in this Vietnamese 'quagmire' after decision-makers in successive administrations continued to make a serious of small steps that they thought would be just enough to keep the escalating conflict on the ground under control. In the process, they unwittingly drew the US ever more deeply into a conflict without any apparent exit. This historical theory gained some refinement in the influential essay by Arthur Schlesinger *The Bitter*

Heritage: Vietnam and American Democracy in 1967 arguing that the US had got itself into Vietnam though a combination of ignorance, misjudgement and muddle.[64]

The Halberstam/Schlesinger quagmire theory eventually received a strong rebuttal by Daniel Ellsberg, on the basis of the Pentagon Papers leaked to *The New York Times*. Ellsberg argued that the pattern since the 1940s was less one of US policy-makers becoming progressively mired in a quagmire but rather one of flight as they continually escalated the war in order to run away from hostile right-wing opinion in the US, rather (Ellsberg noted) like Eliza running to safety across the ice floes of the Ohio River in *Uncle Tom's Cabin*. Pointing to John F. Kennedy's comment that he would pull the troops out of South Vietnam, but only in 1965 after he had won the 1964 presidential election, Ellsberg suggested that the main driving force of US policy was domestic pressure from the right and fears of a repeat of the 'loss' of China, a view that did not, in the end, differ radically from Shaplen.[65]

None of these arguments paid that much attention to the dynamics of Vietnamese culture, about which all three authors displayed a remarkable estrangement, employing as they did metaphorical language involving geographical phenomena such as bogs, quagmires, and frozen rivers. The debate largely bypassed the issue of how far the US foreign policy elite had failed to understand the culture of the enemy the US military was fighting. Halberstam belatedly recognised this in 1971 in his short biography of Ho Chi Minh which argued that there was no credible nationalist alternative to Ho's communists by the time the French left Vietnam in 1954.[66] Halberstam did not tangle with any heavenly mandate theory to explain the apparent Communist popularity among the peasantry, only that Ho was one of a number of 'folk heroes who had always fought colonialists and who now stepped out of their mountain hideouts and walked into Hanoi as liberators.'[67]

This view seemed to accept, in part at least, the romantic image of peasant revolutionaries among the anti-war new left and Michael Lind later described Halberstam's account as 'perhaps the most sympathetic portrait of a Stalinist dictator ever penned by a reputable American journalist identified with the liberal rather than the radical left.'[68] Halberstam, influenced in part by a reading of Mus, saw Ho as a leader of Vietnamese agrarian revolution ensuring that the Diem regime in Saigon was doomed to go down in the face of 'revolutionary forces that left mandarin ways smashed in their wake,' though he failed to spell out what form this revolution would take.[69] As a reporter, Halberstam was, perhaps, attempting to understand radicalised local communities in Vietnam through the prism of the earlier civil rights movement in the South he had covered as a junior reporter in Tennessee. But the dominant ethos among the opposition to racial segregation in the South had been Gandhian non-violence; such a strategy was not on offer in the Vietnam of the 1960s, suggesting an inexorable path to more violent revolutionary change.[70]

The paths of analysis offered by Shaplen, Schlesinger, Halberstam and Ellsberg displayed serious limitations in their understanding of Vietnamese history and culture; indeed, Vietnamese actions were largely viewed as a result of mistaken American decision-making and strategic blindness. By contrast, the first real attempt to probe into the dynamics of the Vietnamese revolution was John T. McAlister, who, like FitzGerald, had studied under Mus and brought out *The Vietnamese and Their Revolution* in 1969.[71] McAlister's career had started with his being assigned to the Navy section of the US mission to Vietnam in 1959. He was soon sent into the Mekong Delta region not so far from where Gerald Hickey would pursue his anthropological research. Unlike Hickey, McAlister had rather less freedom to influence wider policy. A staff study on proposals for political action, for instance, was ignored given the constraints on criticising the Diem regime; instead his work was used to fortify a military response to the mounting guerrilla activity in the Delta region.[72] Even in this early period of the war, McAlister discovered a growing American uncertainty over what to do 'and an unwillingness to examine the full range of options open to us.'[73] Indeed, all the problems the US engaged with were all designed to secure greater physical surveillance and control from Saigon 'rather than to close the gap of political legitimacy through an identification with the villagers on their own terms.'[74]

In *Vietnam: The Origins of the Revolution* McAlister attempted to explain an indigenous revolution he saw emerging in Vietnam. Drawing on some of emerging sociology of revolutionary change, he recognised that the Vietnamese revolution was different to earlier revolutions in France and Russia since it amounted to a 'series of changes so convulsive and persuasive as to call into question conventional assumptions about revolution.'[75] The resulting revolutionary conflict in Vietnam had left the society divided against itself, though it displayed a pattern that could be compared to other societies in history, including the United States, which had experienced a 'democratic revolutions' in terms shaped by the classic study of R.R Palmer.[76]

McAlister's perfunctory account of revolution in Vietnam certainly highlighted the absence of a robust comparative sociology of revolutionary change that would, over time, become familiar from the work of scholars such as Theda Skocpol and Jack Goldstone. Fitzgerald had interestingly posed the question in cultural terms by linking Ho Chi Minh's apparent success in acquiring the Confucian mandate with the ancient Chinese sacred text known as the *I Ching* or Book of Changes dating back to 1000 to 750 BCE. Here the 'fire in the lake' occurs when 'the superior man/sets the calendar in order/and makes the seasons clear.'[77] The *I Ching* was not strictly speaking a 'Confucian' text since it was written before Confucius' time even though it had considerable impact on later Confucian thinking as well as Taoism and Buddhism. Consisting of a series of 64 hexagrams, it is Hexagram 49 that propounds the dramatic image of revolution being like a lake fire (presumably an image familiar to peasant communities living close to cases of spontaneous combustion in bog land and wetland areas), implying that for any revolution to be successful it had to be in accordance with laws of nature as well as good timing. The imagery is appropriate for a peasant-based society, though testing it requires detailed anthropological knowledge of Vietnamese rural communities, something almost impossible to substantiate with hard and reliable evidence in the middle of a war. At a broader level, though, the approach has some relevance to more recent postcolonial challenges to western social science concepts, suggesting the need for comparative research on the cultural understandings of revolution and revolutionary change on a global basis.

Here, FitzGerald introduced another body of Francophone cultural theory centred on Otare Mannoni's book on Madagascar/Malagasay *Prospero and Caliban: The Psychology of Colonization*, first published in 1950 and influential in the debate on the Algerian War.[78] Fitzgerald suggested that Mannoni's theory of colonial psychological dependency could help explain the eventual Vietnamese revolt in the 1920s and 1930s and their own self-mastery in the North by the time of partition in 1954. Judged by this standard, the nominally sovereign state of Ngo Dinh Diem attempted to legitimise itself in Confucian terms, though all it ended up doing was buttressing an increasingly unpopular structure of paternalistic rule in the villages, reproducing patterns of colonial dependency inherited from the French.[79]

Mannoni's model of colonial dependency underpinned by a white colonial 'Prospero complex' had run into criticism within a few years of its appearance. In 1952 Frantz Fanon, in *Black Skins, White Masks*, attacked the theory's failure to explain why colonialism had emerged in the first place, though Fitzgerald pointed out that Fanon corroborated many of Mannoni's observations from a rather different standpoint.[80] The theory at least provided some collective psychological basis for the progressive American involvement in Vietnam, as she pointed to the somewhat 'curious phenomenon' of an American military presence that had taken on a colonial form even though there was no obvious economic payoff for the Americans to stay in Vietnam, unlike the previous colonising French.[81] The huge amount of American 'aid' dispensed in Vietnam created a vast network of groups dependent on the US staying in the country: refugees, translators, secretaries, maids, prostitutes, shoeshine boys, and so on. The huge American military presence effectively transformed the country into a dependent state making it difficult to leave.

Fitzgerald's understanding of this in 1972 was borne out over the next three years. The formal US military departure in 1973 still left a lingering American presence on the ground as it was hoped a militarised South Vietnamese state could somehow survive on its own. The final catastrophic flight from Saigon in April 1975 belied the earlier false optimism and indicated a quasi-colonial mindset among some, at least, of the US personnel staying on in South Vietnam. One of the most extraordinary of these was the last US ambassador, Graham Anderson Martin, who refused until almost the very last to abandon the 'quagmire' and to acknowledge that the war was lost even when the North Vietnamese army was close to entering Saigon.[82] Like some other wars of decolonization, the Vietnam war was another example of an intra-indigenous civil war in which the ARVN increasingly found itself having to do the brunt of the fighting as the US progressively withdrew. Even when US forces were at their greatest in the country at over 500,000, the ARVN was fielding over a million men, though many of these often proved reluctant to fight the NVA and NLF.[83] The war was thus a late example of an imperial war fought in a poorly understood geographical periphery defending a weak client state with slender structures of political support in the countryside outside the major cities.

The US militarily establishment in South Vietnam acquired many of the features of a quasi- colonial society, even if the American quasi occupation became linked with brothels, bars and gambling dens rather than planters' clubs, colonial governors in pith helmets or planter interests such as those in the Philippines. Certainly, few Americans fighting in Vietnam thought of the US role in colonial-type terms, though some experienced observers detected an extraordinary cultural remoteness from the Vietnamese given the poor understanding of English by many Vietnamese translators, who in many cases simply told the Americans what they thought they wanted to hear.[84] *Fire in the Lake* suggested that the US, more or less by default, took over from the departing colonial French and never succeeded in breaking from the colonial past, even if official US political doctrine in the Cold War aligned itself behind newly-independent sovereign nations.

To this extent, Fitzgerald's thesis concerning unwitting American quasi or neo-colonialism in Vietnam dovetails with more recent work in postcolonial studies. Nicholas Thomas, for instance, has questioned the notion that colonial conquest necessarily implies the successful imposition of colonial cultural fantasies and myths. Colonial dominators often find it difficult to maintain a cohesive ideological uniformity; and this was all too evident in the case of French imperial rule in Indochina by the late 1940s. Colonizers, Thomas suggests, are frequently plagued by an inability to realise myths of total domination ending up 'frequently haunted by a sense of insecurity, terrified by the obscurity of the "native mentality" and overwhelmed by indigenous societies' apparent intractability in the face of government.'[85] The US military and political mission in South Vietnam inherited this haunting insecurity without any accompanying imperial ideology of *mission civilisatrice* beyond the fulfilment of the abstract strategic imperatives of the domino theory and various forms of 'modernisation.' The war was, in this sense, an example of 'colonialism without colonies,' one that spawned an anxiety that only grew as the legitimacy of the South Vietnamese state manifestly failed.[86]

The reluctance, therefore, to test this failing legitimacy by serious anthropological research proved to be – arguably – one of the major strategic blunders of the war, surpassing even the bitter debate on the calculus of American decision-making leading to progressive immersion in the 'quagmire.' *Fire in the Lake* moved some way beyond this by pointing to the cultural limitations of American bureaucratic decision-making. As one later survey by Anthony Marc Lewis for the CIA in 1996 acknowledged, the book represented a 'breakthrough' in efforts to understand 'the hidden psychological dimension' of the war in Vietnam.[87]

Concluding remarks

This paper has examined *Fire in the Lake* in the context of ongoing debates in the US on the nature of war, revolution and political legitimacy in Vietnam. For its time, the book was a major excursus into Vietnamese cultural history in an era when this was poorly understood. The book also offered insights into why the US foreign policy elite continued to misunderstand the conflict in Vietnam as well as the cultural barriers to any diplomatic resolution. Contrary to later accusations by conservatives, Fitzgerald did not hold to the view that a simple victory for the North was inevitable and argued, rather, that most Vietnamese probably wanted some form of coalition government. 'The Vietnamese way Is not that of balance of power,' she observed strongly echoing the arguments of Mus, 'but that of accommodation leading to unanimity.'[88] This might perhaps explain the absence of regime change in post-1975 Vietnam, unlike China in the late 1970s. The collapse of communism in Eastern Europe in the late 1980s though heightened demands for some form of political pluralism as the communist regime began to looked increasingly anchored in the past around certain basic documents such as Ho Chi Minh's last will and testimony. This brought though a resounding rebuff from the party elite; but the issue has rumbled on with more recent protest over issues such as bauxite mining, environmental issues and relations with China.[89]

Some of FitzGerald's political analysis of the Vietnam War might appear somewhat dated with the emergence of a vast array of archival collections and oral interviews. The chief importance of the book really lies in the way it attempted to tackle the issue of political legitimacy during military conflict and to pinpoint this as a crucial to the success or failure of any counter-insurgency campaign. Even now, there is a remarkably limited anthropological focus on issues of state legitimacy during COIN campaigns such as those in Iraq and Afghanistan.

Notes

1. FitzGerald, *Fire in the Lake*, 217–27.
2. Hoffman, "An Account of the Collision."
3. Vien, *Tradition and Revolution in Vietnam*, 46.
4. Chaliand, *Revolution in the Third World*, 90.
5. Lind, *Vietnam*, 176; and Kimble, "Deja-vu 1."
6. Young, "Who were the Real Nationalists in Vietnam?" Young served with the CORDS program in South Vietnam. One recent website review reflected some anger with the way *Fire in the Lake* was used in university courses. 'this book has been required reading in all "revisionist" undergraduate history seminars and lectures since its first publication in 1972,' wrote one critic, " … As I watch the people of Vietnam being pimped by their government to enrich its coffers and those of the Nike Corporation, I think of how stupid, ignorant and ultimately vile this book is and was." www, antoinedonline.com/Product.aspx?productCode = 0009780316159197. Accessed 9 September 2018.
7. Part of the last cohort of 300 women to do so with a Radcliffe diploma rather than a Harvard degree. Stanley, "The Way It Was at Radcliffe."
8. FitzGerald quoted in Bass, *The Spy Who Loved US*, 145.
9. McAlister and Mus, *The Vietnamese and Their Revolution*.
10. Meyers, *John Huston*, 305–11. Marietta Tree briefly appeared in Huston's 1961 film *The Misfits* in a scene with Clark Gable.
11. Ranelagh, *The Agency*, 223.
12. Weiner, *Legacy of Ashes*, 239. Desmond Fitzgerald's relationship with Bobby Kennedy was rather more fractious.
13. Personal communication from Frances FitzGerald.
14. Schlesinger Jr, *Journals, 1952–2000*, 290, 713; and Mailer, *Miami and the Siege of Chicago*.
15. See for example Barnett, *The Roots of War*, 48–9.
16. Morris, *Uncertain Greatness*31–2.
17. Cited in Ferguson, "Kissinger Diaries.'
18. Hughes, *Fatal Politics*.
19. The authority of this school declined markedly in France itself after the independence of Algeria in 1962 and mainly ended up influencing authoritarian right-wing regimes in Latin America in the 1970s. See Paret, *French Revolutionary Warfare*; and Robin, *Escadrons de la Mort, I-ecole Francaise*.
20. Hellman, *American Myth and the Legacy of Vietnam*, 75.
21. For one recent study of the new left in the US at this time, including the terrorist weather underground see Burrough, *Days of Rage*.
22. In contrast to earlier sub-branch of research known as Vietnam War Studies looking to explain why the US lost the war.
23. Reflecting to some degree a mindset shaped by what Amy Kaplan has identified as 'ambiguous spaces that were not quite foreign nor domestic' in which it also created 'vast de-territorialized arenas in which to exercise military, economic and cultural powers divorced from political annexation.' Kaplan, *The Anarchy of Empire*, 15.
24. Ninkovich, *Modernity and Power*.
25. See in particular Packenham, *Liberal America and the Third World*. In a pioneering book in 1970 addressed mainly to political science colleagues, the British scholar Peter Calvert wrote that defining 'revolution' was a problem given that it was such a 'mystical concept', though he urged fellow scholars to at least

retain the word as a 'political term.' Calvert, *Revolution*, 140–141. M.J. Heale notes that by the 1960s many politicians were becoming increasingly wary of being tagged as 'McCarthyite' while the anti-communism of right-wing televangelists was subsumed by a broader attack on 'secular humanism', Heale, *American Anticommunism*, 199.

26. FitzGerald, *Fire in the Lake*, 209. On this point, Fitzgerald was influenced by Susan Sontag's essay *Trip to Hanoi*.
27. Hallin, *Uncensored War*, 58.
28. Tyrrell, "American Exceptionalism"; and Fisher, "The Illusion of Progress."
29. Kuklick, *Blind Oracles*.
30. Latham, "Redirecting the Revolution?"
31. Weigley, *The American Way of War*.
32. Isaacs, *Scratches on Our Minds*, 212.
33. Knightley, *The First Casualty*, 410.
34. Stewart, *Vietnam's Lost Revolution*.
35. Several other organisations were working on the resettlement programme ensuring that the exact role of the MSUG was hard to assess. Price, *Cold War Anthropology*, 302–303. See also Fisher, "'A World Made Safe for Diversity'".
36. Price, *Cold War Anthropology*, 304.
37. Ibid 311. Though Price criticised Hickey's apparent involvement with military and political strategy when he advocated the South Vietnamese regime end its opposition to the political group championing the Highlanders' interests, the *Front Unifie de Lutte les Races Oppresses* (FULRO).
38. Hickey, *Village in Vietnam*, 57.
39. Balandier, *Political Anthropology*, 20.
40. Said, *Culture and Imperialism*, 252.
41. Bayly, "French Anthropology and the Durkheimians" and "Conceptualizing Resistance and Revolution in Vietnam." Bayly's emphasis on Durkheim has been challenged by Laurent Dartigues, who has suggested that ethnologists such as Levy-Bruhl were more significant in French colonial ethnology and the work of colonial administrators and missionaries. Dartigues, "La Sociologie de Paul Mus, entre theory et sens sur l'alterite vietnamme."
42. Cummings, "American Orientalism," 53–55; and Newman, *Owen Lattimore and the 'Loss' of China*.
43. Pelley, *Postcolonial Vietnam*, 73.
44. Chandler, "Paul Mus (1902–1969)," 153.
45. Dartigues, "La Sociologie de Paul Mus."
46. The project was most developed in Francophone West African with small groups of black intellectuals espousing negritude; it would only unravel in the aftermath of World War Two with the demise of French imperial authority. Wilder, *The French Imperial Nation-State*.
47. Goscha, "'So what did you learn from war?'" 574.
48. Logeval, *Embers of War*, 191; Clayton, *The Wars of French Decolonization*, 186–187; and Sheppard, *The Invention of Decolonization*.
49. Goscha, "'So What Did You Learn from the War?'" 579.
50. Mus was sent away empty handed from a meeting with De Gaulle in 1945, on the grounds, the general explained, that the French were 'stronger.' Ibid., 592. See also Porch, *Wars of Empire*, 206–7.
51. Thornton, *Doctrines of Imperialism*, 185.
52. Mus, *Viet-Nam: Sociologie d'une Guerre*.

53. Van Norden, "Mencius."
54. Hegel, *The Philosophy of History*.
55. Wolf, *Europe and the People Without History*, 53-4.
56. Ibid., 55.
57. Spence, *God's Chosen Son*.
58. Fairbank, "The Peoples Middle Kingdom"; and Miller, "The Late Imperial Chinese State," 1.
59. Tai, *Radicalism and the Origins of the Vietnamese Revolution*, 258-263 and passim.
60. Bayly, "French Anthropology and the Durkheimians."
61. Shaplen, *The Lost Revolution*, 352; and Shaplen, *Time out of Hand*, 3.
62. *The Lost Revolution*, 49.
63. Halberstam, *The Making of a Quagmire*.
64. Schlesinger, *The Bitter Heritage*
65. Ellsberg, "The Quagmire Myth."
66. Halberstam, *Ho*, 49, 60.
67. Ibid., 77.
68. Lind, *Vietnam the Necessary War*, 176.
69. *Ho*, 107.
70. Halberstam, *The Children*.
71. See note 9 above.
72. McAlister Jr, *Vietnam*, ix.
73. Ibid., x.
74. Ibid., xi.
75. Ibid, xi.
76. Ibid, 336-7; Goscha, *The Penguin History of Vietnam*, 397; and Palmer, *The Age of Democratic Revolution*. A similar Eurocentric view of revolution emerged in the 1968 documentary *In The Year of the Pig*, directed by Emile de Antonio, in which Mus briefly appeared talking about the cohesion and resilience of Vietnamese villages. *The Year of the Pig* ostensibly focused on Vietnam but ended up not in Indochina but the landscape of American revolutionary myth. Hellman, *American Myth*, 94.
77. Fitzgerald, *Fire in the Lake*, 27.
78. The shift of French debate towards colonialism in the 1950s was impelled by the strong emphasis placed by many French intellectuals on moral choice, an approach that seemed racially constrained by the ideological orthodoxies of the French Communist Party. Judt, *Past Imperfect*, 283-4.
79. FitzGerald, *Fire in the Lake*, 118.
80. Fanon, *Black Skin, White Masks,* 67; and FitzGerald, *Fire in the Lake*, 470, n.1.
81. FitzGerald, *Fire in the Lake*, 433-4.
82. Michaels, "Delusions of Survival."
83. Walter, *Colonial Violence*, 102.
84. See the observations of the military expert William Lederer after a ninth visit to Vietnam. Lederer, *Our Own Worst Enemy*, 21-2.
85. Thomas, *Colonialism's Culture*, 15.
86. Luthi and Purtschert, "Colonialism without Colonies."
87. Lewis, "Re-Examining Our Perceptions on Vietnam," CIA Historical Review Program, released 2 July 1996.
88. FitzGerald, *Fire in the Lake*, 449.

89. Hiebert, "Vietnam Says No to Pluralism"; and Vasavakul, "Vietnam"; Thayer, "Political Legitimacy of Vietnam's One-Party State."

Acknowledgments

I would like to thank Christopher Goscha and Nathaniel Moir for comments on an earlier version of this paper

Disclosure statement

No potential conflict of interest was reported by the author.

Bibliography

Balandier, Georges. *Political Anthropology*. Harmondsworth: Penguin Books, 1972. (1 ed 1967).
Barnett, Richard J. *The Roots of War: The Men and Institutions behind US Foreign Policy*. Baltimore, MD: Penguin Books, 1972.
Bass, Thomas A. *The Spy Who Loved US: The Vietnam War and Pham Xuan An's Dangerous Game*. New York: Pubic Affairs, 2009.
Bayly, Susan. "French Anthropology and the Durkheimians in Colonial Indochina." *Modern Asian Studies* 34, no. 3, July (2000): 581–622. doi:10.1017/S0026749X00003954.
Bayly, Susan. "Conceptualizing Resistance and Revolution in Vietnam: Paul Muss Understanding of Colonialism in Crisis." *Journal of Vietnamese Studies* 4, no. 1 (Winter 2009): 192–205. doi:10.1525/vs.2009.4.1.192.
Benedict, Ruth. *The Chrysanthemum and the Sword*. London: Routledge and Kegan Paul, 1967. (1 ed 1946).
Burrough, Bryan. *Days of Rage: America's Radical Underground, the FBI Ans the Forgotten Age of Revolutionary Violence*. New York: Penguin Press, 2015.
Calvert, Peter. *Revolution*. London: Pall Mall, 1970.
Chaliand, Gerard. *Revolution in the Third World*. New York: Penguin Books, 1989. (1 ed 1977).
Chandler, David. "Paul Mus (1902–1969): A Biographical Sketch." *Journal of Vietnamese Studies* 4, no. 1 (Winter 2003): 149–191.
Clayton, Anthony. *The Wars of French Decolonization*. London: Longman, 1994.
Cummings, Bruce. "American Orientalism at War in Korea and the United State: A Hegemony of Racism, Repression, and Amnesia." In *Orientalism and War*, edited by Tarak Barkawi and Keith Stanski. London: Hurst, 2012.

Dartigues, Laurent. 2107. "La Sociologie de Paul Mus, entre theory et sens sur l'alterite vietnamme." December 19, n.4. Accessed August 30, 2018. https://halshs.archives-ouvertues.fr./halsh0000207575
Ellsberg, Daniel. "The Quagmire Myth and the Stalemate Machine," *Public Policy* (Spring 1971 and repr). Accessed September 18, 2018. http://tseanray.com/documents/ellsbergstalematemachine.pdfln
Fairbank, John King "The Peoples Middle Kingdom." *Foreign Affairs* 44, 4 July (1966): 574–586. doi:10.2307/20039192.
Fanon, Frantz. *Black Skin, White Masks*. London: Paladin, 1972.
Ferguson, Niall. 2015. "Kissinger Diaries; What He Truly Thought about Vietnam," *POLITICO*, November 10, 2. Accessed September 8, 2018. www.politico.eu/article/the-kissinger-diaries-vietnam-unuted-states-military-vietcong
Fisher, Christopher T. "The Illusion of Progress: CORDS and the Crisis of Modernization in South Vietnam, 1965-1968." *Pacific Historical Review* 75, no. 1 (2006): 25–51. doi:10.1525/phr.2006.75.1.25.
Fisher, James T. "A World Made Safe for Diversity': The Vietnam Lobby and the Politics of Pluralism, 1945–1963." In *Cold War Constructions: The Political Culture of United States Imperialism 1945–1966*, edited by Christian G. Appy, 217–237. Amherst: The University of Massachusetts Press, 2000.
Fitzgerald, Frances. *The Evangelicals: The Struggle to Shape America*. London: Simon and Schuster, 2018.
FitzGerald, Frances. *Fire in the Lake: The Vietnamese and the Americans in Vietnam*. New York: Little Brown and Co, 2002.
Gilman, Nils. *Mandarins of the Future: Modernization Theory in Cold War America*. Baltimore: The Johns Hopkins University Press, 2003.
Goscha, Christopher E. "'So What Did You Learn from War?' Violent Decolonization and Paul Mus's Search for Humanity." *South East Asia Research* 20 (December 2012): 4. doi:10.5367/sear.2012.0124.
Goscha, Christopher. *The Penguin History of Vietnam*. London: Penguin Books, 2016.
Halberstam, David. *The Making of a Quagmire*. New York: Random House, 1965.
Halberstam, David. *Ho*. Lanham, MD: Rowman and Littlefield, 1971.
Halberstam, David. *The Children*. London: Fawcett, 1999.
Hallin, Daniel, C. *Uncensored War: The Media and Vietnam*. Berkeley: University of California Press, 1989.
Hansen, Victor Davis. *Carnage and Culture: Landmark Battles in the Rise of Western Power*. New York: Random House, 2001.
Heale, M.J. *American Anticommunism: Combatting the Enemy Within, 1830–1970*. Baltimore: The Johns Hopkins University Press, 1990.
Hegel, Georg Wilhelm Friedrich. *The Philosophy of History*. New York: Dover Pub, 1956.
Hellman, John. *American Myth and the Legacy of Vietnam*. New York: Columbia University Press, 1986.
Hickey, Gerald Cannon. *Village in Vietnam*. New Haven and London: Yale University Press, 1964.
Hiebert, Murray. 1989. "Vietnamsays No to Pluralism." *The Washington Post*, September 15
Hoffman, Stanley. 1972. "An Account of the Collision of Two Societies." *New York Times*, August 27.
Hughes, Ken. *Fatal Politics: The Nixon Tapes, the Vietnam War and the Casualties of Reelection*. Charlottesville: University of Virginia Press, 2015.
Isaacs, Harold R. *Scratches on Our Minds: American Images of China and India*. New York: John Day, 1958.

Judt, Tony. *Past Imperfect: French Intellectuals, 1944–1956*. New York: New York University Press, 2011.
Kaplan, Amy. *The Anarchy of Empire in the Making of US Culture*. Cambridge, MA: Harvard University Press, 2002.
Kimble, Roger 2002. "Deja-vu 1: On the Recent Re-issue of Francis FitzGerald's Fire in the Lake." *The New Criterion*, September.
Knightley, Philip. *The First Casualty: The War Correspondent as Hero and Myth Maker from Crimea to Kosovo*. London: Prion Books, 2000.
Kuklick, Bruce. *Blind Oracles: Intellectuals and War from Kennan to Kissinger*. Princeton: Princeton University Press, 2006.
Latham, Michael E. "Redirecting the Revolution? the USA and the Failure of Nation=building in South Vietnam." *The Third World Quarterly* 27, no. 1 (2006): 27–41. doi:10.1080/01436590500368743.
Lederer, William J. *Our Own Worst Enemy*. New York: Norton, 1968.
Lewis, Anthony Marc. 1996. "Re-Examining Our Perceptions on Vietnam," *CIA Historical Review Program*, July 2.
Lind, Michael. *Vietnam: The Necessary War*. New York: The Free Press, 1999.
Logeval, Fredrik. *Embers of War: The Fall of an Empire and the Making of America's Vietnam*. New York: Random House, 2013.
Luthi, Barbara. "Francesca Falk and Patricia Purtschert, "Colonialism without Colonies: Examining Blank Spaces in Colonial Studies,"." *National Identities* 18, no. 1 (2016): 1–9. doi:10.1080/14608944.2016.1107178.
Mailer, Norman. *Miami and the Siege of Chicago*. London: Penguin Books, 1971.
Mander, Mary S. *Pen and Sword: American War Correspondents, 1898–1975*. Chicago: University of Illinois Press, 2010.
Mannoni, O. *Prospero and Caliban*. Ann Arbor: University of Michigan Press, 1990. (1 ed 1950).
McAlister, John T. *Vietnam: The Origins of Revolution*. New York: Knopf, 1971.
McAlister John, T, and Paul Mus. *The Vietnamese and Their Revolution*. New York: Harper and Row, 1969.
McFate, Montgomery McFate. *Military Anthropology: Soldiers, Scholars and Subjects at the Margins of Empire*. London: Hurst, 2018.
Meyers, Jeffrey. *John Huston: Courage and Art*. New York: Crown Pub, 2001.
Michaels, Jeffrey. "Delusions of Survival: US Deliberations on Support for South Vietnam during the 1975 'Final Offensive'." *Small Wars and Insurgencies* 26, no. 6 (2015): 957–975. doi:10.1080/09592318.2015.1095838.
Miller, H. Lymann. "The Late Imperial Chinese State." In *The Modern Chinese State*, edited by David Shambaugh, 15–41. Cambridge: Cambridge University Press, 2000.
Modell, Judith. *Ruth Benedict*. London: Chatto and Windus/The Hogarth Press, 1984.
Morris, Roger. *Uncertain Greatness: Henry Kissinger and American Foreign Policy*. London: Quartet Books, 1977.
Mus, Paul. *Viet-Nam: Sociologie d'une Guerre*. Editions du Seul: Paris, 1952.
Newman, Robert P. *Owen Lattimore and the "Loss" of China*. Berkeley: University of California Press, 1992.
Ninkovich, Frank. *Modernity and Power: A History of the Domino Theory in the Twentieth Century*. Chicago: University of Chicago Press, 1994.
Packenham, Robert A. *Liberal America and the Third World: Political Development and Ideas on Foreign Aid and Social Science*. Princeton: Princeton University Press, 1973.
Palmer, R. R. *The Age of Democratic Revolution: A Political History of Europe and America, 1760–188*. Princeton: Princeton University Press, 2014. (1 ed 1960).

Paret, Peter. *French Revolutionary Warfare from Indochina to Algeria*. London: Pall Mall Press, 1964.
Pelley, Patricia M. *Postcolonial Vietnam: New Histories of the National Past*. Durham: Duke University Press, 2002.
Porch, Douglas. *Wars of Empire*. London: Cassell, 2001.
Price, David H. *Cold War Anthropology: The CIA, the Pentagon and the Growth of Dual Use Anthropology*. Durham: Duke University Press, 2016.
Pye, Lucien W. *The Spirit of Chinese Politics*. Cambridge MA: Harvard University Press, 1968.
Ranelagh, John. *The Agency: The Rise & Decline of the CIA*. London: Hodder and Stoughton, 1988.
Robin, RobinMarie-Monique. *Escadrons de la Mort, l-ecole Francaise*. Paris: La Decouverte/Poche, 2004.
Said, Edward. *Culture and Imperialism*. London: Vintage, 1994.
Said, Edward. *Representations of the Intellectual*. New York: Pantheon, 1994.
Schlesinger, Arthur. *The Bitter Heritage: Vietnam and American Democracy*. Boston: Houghton Mifflin, 1967.
Schlesinger, Arthur, Jr. *Journals, 1952–2000*. London: Atlantic Books, 2000.
Shaplen, Robert. *The Lost Revolution: The US in Vietnam 1946–1966*. New York: Harper Torchbooks, 1965. (1 ed 1955).
Shaplen, Robert. *Time Out of Hand: Revolution and Reaction in Southeast Asia*. London: Andre Deutsch, 1969.
Sheppard, Todd. *The Invention of Decolonization: The Algerian War and the Remaking of France*. Ithaca: Cornell University Press, 2006.
Sontag, Susan. *Trip to Hanoi*. New York: Farrar, Strauss and Ciroux, 1968.
Spence, Jonathan D. *God's Chosen Son: The Taiping Heavenly Kingdom of Hong Xiuquan*. New York: Norton, 1996.
Stanley, Alessandra. 1992. "The Way It Was at Radcliffe." *The New York Times*, June 7
Stewart, Geoffrey C. *Vietnam's Lost Revolution: Ngo Dinh Diem's Failure to Build an Independent Nation, 1955–1963*. Cambridge: Cambridge University Press, 2017.
Tai, Hue-Tam Ho. *Radicalism and the Origins of the Vietnamese Revolution*. Cambridge: Harvard University Press, 1992.
Thayer, Carlyle A. "Political Legitimacy of Vietnam's One-Party State: Challenges and Responses." *Journal of Current Southeast Asian Affairs* 4 (2000): 47–70.
Thomas, Nicholas. *Colonialism's Culture: Anthropology, Travel and Government*. Cambridge: Polity Press, 1994.
Thornton, A.P. *Doctrines of Imperialism*. London: John Wiley, 1965.
Tyrrell, Ian. "American Exceptionalism in an Age of International History." *The American Historical Review* 96, no. 4, October (1991): 1031–1055. doi:10.2307/2164993.
Van Norden, Bryan. 2014. "Mencius." December 3. Accessed September 8, 2018. www.plato.stanford.edu
Vasayavakul, Thaveeeporn. "Vietnam: The Changing Models of Legitimation." In *Political Legitimacy in Southeast Asia*, edited by Muthiah Alagappa, 276–289. Stanford: Stanford University Press, 1995.
Vien, Nguyen Khac. *Tradition and Revolution in Vietnam*. Translated by David Marr. Washington: Indochina Resource Center, 1974.
Walter, Dierk. *Colonial Violence: European Empires and the Use of Force*. London: Hurst, 2017.
Weigley, Russell F. *The American Way of War: A History of United States Military Strategy and Policy*. Bloomington: Indiana University Press, 1973.

Weiner, Tim. *Legacy of Ashes: The History of the CIA*. London: Penguin Books, 2007.

Wilder, Gary. *The French Imperial Nation-State: Negritude and Colonial Humanism in between the Two World Wars*. Chicago: University of Chicago Press, 2005.

Wolf, Eric. *Europe and the People without History*. Berkeley: University of California Press, 1982.

Young, Stephen B. 2018. "Who Were the Real Nationalists in Vietnam?" *The New York Times*, March 9.

Accidental ethnographers: the Islamic State's tribal engagement experiment

Craig Whiteside [ID] and Anas Elallame

ABSTRACT
The disillusionment with U.S.-led counter insurgent efforts to gain a deeper understanding of social dynamics in countries with extensive tribal structures has led to a rejection of programs aimed to improve cultural competency. The Islamic State movement does not share this perception, and its strategists blamed its early failures during the U.S. occupation on a flawed understanding of tribal dynamics. This paper traces the political, ideological, and structural changes the leaders of the Islamic State movement made to adapt its approach toward the Sunni tribes of Iraq and later Syria, in order to develop a deeper base of popular support for its caliphate project. The group's study of the tribes was done by a new tribal engagement office that put into motion an ethnographic study of tribal networks in key areas. There is evidence that the inspiration for this change came from its opponents. The Islamic State movement used these new insights to win a greater level of influence in rural areas, which in turn influenced its success in 2014. This research supports the idea that insurgency and counterinsurgency success often depend on which side is best at the incorporation of cultural and societal knowledge into policy and strategy.

Introduction

Failure can be a tremendous catalyst for learning. According to an October 2018 opinion piece in the Islamic State's weekly newsletter *Al-Naba*, the early incarnation of the group – the Islamic State of Iraq – foundered in 2007 because of an "American malicious project' that enlisted 'apostate insurgent groups, parties, and tribes' to fight against the mujahidin. This conspiracy had driven 'the mujahidin [into] the deserts and desolation' before they were able to turn their fortunes around.[1] The idea that the Islamic State learned from this negative experience is underexplored, despite many books and articles written about the period referred to as the Sunni Awakening (or *Sahwa* in Arabic). Most accounts view this period from the tribal or U.S. perspective, and ignore the perspective of the Islamic State of Iraq.[2]

The tribal-led backlash to the nascent Islamic State stunned the group, and forced the insurgents to process a public and painful betrayal by a population it strongly identified with. A subsequent period of introspection inspired the leaders to alter its original approach to the Iraqi tribes, and make fundamental changes in their shadow governance of Sunni populations in Iraq after the *Sahwa* uprising. To accomplish this, the leaders chose to rely on a technique from applied anthropology and conduct an amateur ethnography of local tribes in strategic locations, in order to determine the failures that led to the *Sahwa* uprising and how to best co-opt tribal structure into the group's political project of establishing an Islamic State.

In our research, we reconstructed this process by examining primary documents – both captured and publically released – written by the Islamic State between 2006 and 2010 to identify the process by which the group adjusted its basic approach to the tribes. We found that the Islamic State's leadership attributed their failures to a central misunderstanding of the tribes and its role in rural Iraqi society, and how the group's political project could co-exist with the tribes. This acknowledgement was bitter medicine to take for a group dominated by rural Iraqis with a tribal background, considering their 'American' opponents had successfully implemented a tribal engagement program that the group blamed for its 2007 defeat. The group's imitation of the tribal engagement effort, to better map out the tribe's social and political structure using an applied anthropological approach, informed a new approach to relations with the tribes that set the foundation for the creation of a proto-state/caliphate in Iraq and Syria in 2014.

Background

Recent U.S. experience in counterinsurgency has imparted on military leaders an appreciation for 'understanding the social, political, and cultural environment and how this environment may enhance or preclude desired policy outcomes.'[3] The wars in Afghanistan and Iraq have taken place in an extensive tribal setting that are incomprehensible to modern militaries drawn from much different societies. Nonetheless, NATO forces in Afghanistan and the U.S. and its partners in Iraq made progress in adjusting to these environments. Many point to the efforts to recruit local tribal partners as adjunct counterinsurgents as bright spots in otherwise muddled campaigns, despite ephemeral gains at the tactical level.[4] Unfortunately, frustration with the larger geo-strategic and military outcomes of the conflicts in Iraq and Afghanistan has resulted in a pessimistic attitude towards engagement with population in general, and specifically the co-option of local auxiliaries, which Kalyvas notes has historically been an 'essential part of counterinsurgent efforts.'[5] Based on these perceptions of failure, analysts have largely dismissed associated experiments in cultural engagement and understanding of indigenous tribal elements, and U.S. efforts to institutionalize a new military approach to learning about local social dynamics, known as the Human Terrain System, have failed to institutionalize.[6] What should we make of this disconnect between theory and recent praxis?

Counterinsurgency is a bundle of tactics used by intervening powers to bolster weak states, whose poor performance in governance and limited power invites internal challengers who have different ideas on how to administer and govern the society. In these situations, tribes function well in the undergoverned spaces of these weak states, as they provide structure, stability, and social meaning for eligible members. In fact, countries like Iraq – which went from stability to relative anarchy in short period of time – have seen large-scale re-adoption of tribal identities, corresponding with an increase in the power of tribal leaders.[7]

Anthropologist Kenneth Brown defined tribes as 'autonomous, genealogically structured groups' made up of those who are eligible for membership based on verified lineage.[8] In Iraq, the term 'tribe' is used loosely to address the basic unit – the house (*bayt*), several of which make a clan. Multiple clans form a tribe, and associated tribes of shared lineage make up a tribal federation.[9] These associations are voluntary, and tribal leaders (sheikhs) have a legitimacy based on social customs and the provision of benefits for the group.[10] While tribes have been the predominant organizing social construct in the region for several millennia, the effects of modernity has diluted the cohesion of tribes and the corresponding power of the sheikh.

Tribes largely exist to protect its members from aggression, and tribal warfare is a pragmatic affair that largely consists of defending against transgressions of personal honor (blood feuds), raiding, and collective self-defense.[11] This style of limited conflict and preference for guerrilla warfare leaves significant room for misinterpretation and misperception on the part of outsiders. When the United States invaded Iraq in 2003, its military commanders administered large areas with active tribal units that frequently had other economic interests and tribal feuds that preoccupied their time; the occupiers often found the micro-dynamics of conflict confusing.

In the early occupation of Iraq, one U.S. commander, Colonel Greg Reilly, who had experience in NATO's Kosovo intervention and its complex local power dynamics, recognized that the tribes in Anbar province played an important role in the informal governance of the populated and rural areas in Anbar province. The tribes were influential in the evolving black market economy, which replaced much of the regime patronage system that existed prior to 2003, as well as handled much of the legal and criminal disputes through reliance on tribal mediation and long-standing tribal law. By the summer of 2003, Colonel Reilly was having regular tribal engagements to learn the social structure and gain information about problems the tribal leaders wanted to bring to his attention. Upon the commander's return to Anbar in mid-2004, sources reported to him the growing influence of the network that would soon become al-Qaeda in Iraq, and its growing conflict with some of the tribes.[12]

If some officers immediately understood how to read and incorporate local tribes into the attempts at pacification of a growing insurgency, the majority of the early U.S. military units in Iraq handled relations with the tribes poorly.[13] Fortunately, their jihadist opponents were struggling as well, and attempts to dominate Sunni areas of Iraq forced tribal leaders to act against a growing threat to tribal autonomy and financial viability.[14] In a strange twist, both the outsiders and the jihadist insiders had read the tribes wrong, and the actor that changed attitudes quickest would gain an important advantage in the Iraqi civil war.

This interaction of a triad of actors – the tribes, the U.S., and al-Qaeda in Iraq – all working for the first time in the same political space, resulted in something unusual. Anbari tribal sheikhs who participated in the Awakening, according to Cottam and Huseby, at first had a largely negative view of the U.S. military officers who seemed to know little about their culture or region and were uninvited guests. On the other hand, they held neutral to positive views of the al-Qaeda figures operating in their communities. Attacks against the Americans were not a concern of the tribes.[15] This same research documents that by 2006, a growing number of tribal leaders had radically shifted their view of the Americans, largely because of changes in U.S. views on working with the tribes and a growing threat of an arrogant and violent al-Qaeda.[16] This cognitive shift by both the Americans and the Sunni tribal leaders allowed them to join together to fight against al-Qaeda in Iraq (soon to be the Islamic State of Iraq) in the 2006–7 period.[17] Political worldview, or images of the imagined collective self and the other, is normally difficult to change because it consists of the inherent bias and thought patterns one group has about another group in regards to perceptions of cultural congruity, level of threat to the in-group, and opportunities for collaboration.[18] This sea change in relations, a rarity for group dynamics, facilitated and fueled the growth of the Awakening movement during the U.S. 'Surge' in Iraq.[19] The combination of these two events was enough to defeat the early Islamic State of Iraq in 2007–8 and end what was essentially a multi-sided Iraqi civil war.[20]

Missing in the analysis, due to the clandestine nature of the Islamic State, is the remaining leg of the triad consisting of the tribes, the U.S. (and to a lesser extent its Iraqi partners), and the jihadists. Did the Islamic State change its view of the tribes in response to their shift toward working with the U.S.? If so, how and why did they change? As events developed after 2008, how did the tribes respond to the departure of the U.S. and corresponding loss of sponsorship in a dynamic political environment? To answer these questions, the next section delves into the early relationship between the Islamic State movement and the tribes for clues to what went wrong.

The jihadists and the tribes

In the early period of the occupation of Iraq, the tribes and the small but influential Salafi-jihad movement led by Abu Musab al-Zarqawi coexisted with each other, with some minor exceptions. The unabated growth of the movement, which became al-Qaeda in Iraq and later the Islamic State of Iraq, soon became a problem for the independent tribes. Efforts by tribal leaders to play all sides, working with the Coalition for monetary gain while at the same time green lighting attacks in their areas by various resistance groups, eventually conflicted with the movement's ideological principles. After a series of skirmishes with unruly tribes in Western Anbar, Zarqawi made the following statement in September 2005, a full year before the official announcement of the Awakening movement[21]:

> The tribesmen are among the most important mainstays of the Jihad. These tribes have been very supportive of the Jihad and its men. Be that as it may, we warn the tribes that any tribe, party, or association that has been proven to collaborate with the Crusaders and their apostate lackeys – by God, we will target them just like we target the Crusaders, we will eradicate them and disperse them to the winds. There are only two camps – the camp of truth and its followers, and the camp of falsehood and its Shi'ites. You must choose in which of the two trenches you lie. What befell some of the traitors at al-Qaim is the best proof of this.[22]

This quote by the founder perfectly distilled al-Qaeda in Iraq's early attitude toward the tribes.[23] Like a growing parasite does to its host, the foreign jihadist guests made deep inroads among the young and combative elements of the tribes, and began to increasingly direct how the tribes would relate to the occupation and the new Iraqi government. Importantly, the import of Zarqawi's remarks are clear; the Islamic State would use brutal force against tribal elements that failed to adhere to its takfirist doctrine – meaning the imposition of mandatory sanctions (excommunication) for Muslims who associate with the 'Crusader' Coalition and the 'apostate' Iraqi Government. During Zarqawi's leadership, this black and white determination led the Islamic State movement into conflict, not only with many tribal elements, but also with other resistance groups who were flirting with political participation in the government either through the Iraqi Islamic Party (Muslim Brotherhood) or their own nascent political parties.[24] This group attitude, rigidly held during the rise of Zarqawi's group, would soon be tested.

Zarqawi's quote also highlights a fundamental problem that bedeviled the Islamic State movement's early members: the difficulty of making generalizations about the tribes, historically a diverse and shifting social structure. While tribal leaders can signal allegiance to either government or insurgents, in reality each tribe, clan, and family is often working in their own best interests and has different ideas of loyalty, patriotism, and religious convictions. Making matters even more difficult, local tribes/clans/families often picked sides in the early days of post-invasion Iraq based on long-standing tribal rivalries, leaving open to question any claims of permanence in allegiance to any side.[25]

The collision course between a highly ideological jihadist group and the pragmatic tribes led to a drastic shift in relations between the Islamic State of Iraq, which by October 2006 had subsumed al-Qaeda in Iraq and a handful of smaller groups, and the recently formed Awakening movement made up of select tribes and fragments of resistance groups. The catalyst (for this round of tribal rebellion) seems to have been the jihadists' beheading of an influential tribal sheikh, whose severed head was prominently placed in the center of the regional capital of Anbar province, Ramadi.[26] The usually fragmented tribes surprisingly united around a small group of tribal leaders, and fought the jihadists with vigor. In contrast, the Islamic State leadership was stunned by the betrayal. It would take the group over a year to re-chart a course to deal with the tribes, a milestone marked by the successful assassination of Awakening founder Abu Risha al-Sittar in September 2007.[27]

After years of dealing with problematic tribes leading up to the Awakening, the Islamic State had failed to ask a simple question: what is the nature of the tribes? The Awakening crisis – which embarrassingly had Sunni tribes siding with infidel occupiers over fellow Muslims – made it difficult for leaders to honestly address the root cause of the problem. They had misjudged the the tribes, despite their own tribal backgrounds. Cottam, who interviewed the tribal leaders of the Awakening, attributes this to the Islamic State's ideological nature, and its belief that the tribes were an outdated social institution in need of drastic reform. There would be no room for tribal affiliations in a future caliphate where allegiance was to the caliph, and his substructure of provincial *wali* (governors). According to social anthropologist Ernest Gellner, 'characteristically the tribe is both an alternative to the state and also its image, its limitation and the seed of a new state.'[28] Since ideologues and revolutionaries frequently see the world as they want to see it, and not how it really is, to succeed the group would have to find an answer to how the tribes fit into their future caliphate.[29]

This cognitive dissonance about the tribal backlash is manifested in a captured document written by a high-level Islamic State leader in 2007 and titled *Analysis of the Islamic State of Iraq*. Despite the centrality of the

Awakening movement during the period when the document was composed, the author awkwardly talks around the conflict with the tribes. The only mention was of the tribes' 'changing position.'[30] The document, a fifty page hand-written work that was captured by U.S. forces in al-Anbar province, instead discussed at length the American experiment in working with the tribes in an unabashedly positive, even envious tone. Without explaining how this happened, the anonymous author complained that the 'enemy Crusaders exploited the opportunity to segregate the united Mujahidin from interacting with the general population by recruiting some of the general population against them and encouraging them to spy against them (the Mujahidin) in the name of national interest.' By stirring up trouble between tribes, and buying the loyalty of others, the U.S. was applying a 'carrot and sticks' method of 'conducting random arrests and raiding civilians' houses, then compensating them with money and condemning the terrorists, bad sheikhs, and outlawing tribal leaders for causing the damage.'[31]

This initial assessment of the Islamic State's defeat in Iraq displays an unwillingness to discuss the real problem: that many tribes chose to work with the U.S. and Iraqi government rather than acting out of loyalty to fellow Muslims in the Islamic State of Iraq. As Hafez insightfully explained it at the time, 'the tribes were looking for a pretext to benefit from coalition money without appearing as illegitimate collaborators with the occupation.'[32]

The lack of truthfulness in the internal document is not the only interesting thing to be noted. The author, almost as an afterthought, attached to this cogent strategic analysis a rather cryptic request to eliminate three Iraqis by name. This macabre postscript to the strategy is revealing, partly due to the deliberate omission of any justification for the recommended killings, but also for the tribal affiliation of one of the names listed: Muhammad Shufair al-Jughayfi. The Jughayfi tribe, much like the Albu Mahal tribe that rose up against the early Islamic State elements in al-Qaim, is very influential in Haditha, Iraq, and one of the rare tribes that was largely anti-Islamic State from the beginning.[33] The tribe rallied to the government and filled governance roles as early as 2005. Without mentioning the role of this particular tribe in pushing the Islamic State of Iraq out of Haditha in 2007, the author of the analysis was asking permission to eliminate an important member of the anti-Islamic State coalition. This reliance on coercive means to cow the tribes would survive whatever revision of the role of tribes in future Islamic State strategy, and exemplifies the group's endemic culture of violence to solve its problems. Five years later, the Islamic State released a video depicting the killing of Muhammad Shufair al-Jughayfi during a large-scale raid of Haditha in 2012. They never forgot.[34]

It might have taken until 2012 before the Islamic State of Iraq could reach its enemies in Haditha, but the larger assassination campaign targeting tribal leaders was already put into motion when the author of *Analysis of the Islamic*

State of Iraq wrote his paper. In September 2007 the Islamic State of Iraq announced the killing of Abu Risha al-Sittar by a member of his own tribe, which was described by the group as a tribal honor killing.[35] With the head of the Awakening dead, Zarqawi's successor Abu Umar al-Baghdadi felt secure offering repentance for tribes that had fought the Islamic State or collaborated with the government.[36] The only condition was that the repentance seekers had to present themselves to the Islamic State. If the security squads reached the apostates first, they would be killed. The Islamic State had formed its own 'carrot and stick' approach, mirroring what it saw as a successful American approach to the tribes.[37]

Dissent and decision

Norm Cigar once observed that how the Islamic State of Iraq 'views and manages the tribal system within its individual areas of operation in many cases can mean the difference between success and failure, and the jihadist movement cannot ignore this issue, which has been a major factor affecting its prospects, especially in Iraq.'[38]

Our knowledge of the Islamic State's predilection for violence sometimes blinds us to an important point: that despite an operational code that relies on coercion as a reflexive tool to achieve results, the Islamic State made an important exception for the Sunni tribes of Iraq after 2006. This is not to say that they did not employ violence against them, only that the group learned to employ it in a very careful manner. This discrimination would require exquisite knowledge of social dynamics of the tribes, in order to determine which elements could be co-opted and which had to be eliminated for the group to achieve its goals. They did not reach this decision easily, and a dispute at the highest level of the Islamic State leadership would speak to how difficult it was to change course.

The decision to offer repentance to tribes and resistance members who had worked against the group sparked an important dissent that could have torn the Islamic State apart in its infancy. The *Analysis of the Islamic State of Iraq* had urged commanders to 'avoid brutality; brutality is darkness.'[39] However, this shift created a split between the top leadership, with Abu Umar al-Baghdadi, Abu Hamza al-Muhajir, and spokesman Muharib al-Jubouri on one side, and Chief Sharia judge Abu Sulayman al-Utaybi on the other.[40] Although both groups admitted that the Mujahidin committed mistakes, the two sides saw the cause of the failure very differently. Following the general slide in the Islamic State's strategic position thanks to the Awakening's tribal forces in al-Anbar, the group was already adapting. Just a few months into his appointment, al-Utaybi sent a letter to al-Qaeda leadership in Afghanistan castigating his group's leadership for making many mistakes – none worse than their decision to offer repentance to certain Sunni tribes. According to Brian Fishman, the Utaybi letters were an early sign of both dissension and a lack of communication and control between the erstwhile Iraq affiliate and Al Qaeda Central, long before the split became public in 2011.[41]

Al-Utaybi's dissent was explosive in more than one way; that summer he ordered the burning of three Awakening fighters from a Saladin tribe that had skirmished with Islamic State fighters in the late spring of 2007. He also videotaped the killings, possibly as a demonstration of his sincerity, and this video found its way onto the internet.[42] This egregious and public act against Sunni tribesmen, by a foreigner in a time of increased strife with the Iraqi tribes, led to his public dismissal. Al-Utaybi fled to Pakistan and al-Qaeda Central, where he was killed in a drone strike.[43] The leadership, up to this point hesitant to commit to a new tribal strategy, began offering reconciliation to the rebellious tribes, adding a carrot to the well-used stick. The dismissal of their former Sharia chief paved the way for this decision, as reconciliation was something al-Utaybi was not amenable to.

The decision to remake relations with tribal elements, taken shortly before the plan to assassinate Abu Risha came to fruition, belies much of the analysis about the intransigence of ideological groups like the Islamic State. Hafez, writing in 2007, called 'the errors of AQI [meaning the Islamic State of Iraq] are not incidental: they are hardwired in the genetic code of global jihadis.'[44] The Islamic State's contemporary problem (circa 2017–8) with extremists trying to push the organization even more in a takfiri direction supports Hafez's claim here.[45] Nonetheless, it is wrong to say that the jihadists cannot moderate and restrain their worst instincts. Just as the current caliph Ibrahim (Abu Bakr al-Baghdadi) has moved to replace extremist elements in the Delegated Committee and repeal takfiri fatwas, the early Islamic State demonstrated a capability to learn from its mistakes in 2007 in its comeback in Iraq and its later conquests in Syria.[46]

The decision to move forward with a reconciliation program inspired Abu Umar and Abu Hamza to learn more about the tribes, what drove their behavior, and how to enlist their support, all the while staying true to the political vision and ideology of the group.

Determining the roots of betrayal

The rest of 2007 and 2008 were largely transition years for an Islamic State that was chased into remote areas of Iraq, thanks to a hostile Sunni tribal-former resistance group alliance that knew its adversary well and could prevent its members from operating freely. Abu Hamza al-Muhajir, the second in command of the Islamic State of Iraq, put forth a theory on what happened with the tribes in a 2009 speech:

> The tribes in Iraq are divided into parts. One part stood by and supported the Islamic State, whether visibly or in a concealed manner, employing its youth and

old men. In the case of this group, we would never be able to re-pay or thank them in this lifetime ... Another part worked on their farming, tilling, and trade, and did not show enmity toward the mujahidin or cooperate with the occupier. Even though they have forsaken one of their duties and a religious duty, we still give them the benefit of the doubt. God willing, they will join the good group. Another part cooperated with the occupier and fought the mujahidin. They were victims of the deviating fatwas and the lies and deceit of the Islamic Party and the traitors of jihad. Even though we fight them, we hate doing so. We hope for the coming of the day in which they would repent to God and return to their senses, especially after they have witnessed the Crusader violence and the hate of the rejectionists and how they want to enslave Sunnis.[47]

This account favors a version of the past where tribes were manipulated by bad actors, and had little agency in fighting the group. It conveniently removes any fault from the Islamic State, and influences a possible strategy where if the group could eliminate these bad actors, there might be a chance to reconcile with many of the tribes who were against collaboration with the government and had been misled. Abu Hamza was not Iraqi and had an outsider view of Iraqi tribal dynamics, while his partner Abu Umar al-Baghdadi, the amir of the group and a member of the Zawi tribe from Haditha, was deeply familiar with this dynamic. In fact, Abu Umar regularly discussed the topic of tribal relations in his audiotaped speeches.[48] What changed by early 2009 was the Islamic State's acknowledgment that its troubles centered on tribal relations, and the group's growing understanding of the reasons why fellow Muslims betrayed them. However, there was still no viable strategy on how to engage the tribes in anything other than a coercive manner.

The year 2009 was a pivotal year in this regard, as key leaders in the Islamic State wrote a fifty-page strategy document known as the *Fallujah Memorandum* – officially titled the *Strategy to Improve the Political Position of the Islamic State of Iraq*. This document reflected their new approach to operating in a contested politicized environment, one that included important actors like the tribes. The critical goal was unification: 'It should be their [jihadists'] priority and primary concern because if it happens, it will with no doubt disturb the crusaders plans.'[49] While the Islamic State was facing severe losses to the Awakening and Iraqi forces, it saw in unification with other groups an achievable goal. Accordingly, it invited other groups to put the small differences aside and work together against their common foe.

This document reveals the beginning of a sociological approach to understanding the tribal problem. The anonymous author(s) of the *Fallujah Memorandum* used Islamic history to illustrate the dilemma of the day, referring to the how the Rightly Guided Caliphs (*Rashidun*) dealt with rebellious tribes to promote an evolution in dealing with the *Sahwa*. Citing historian Ibn Khaldun, the authors wrote that tribes are an omnipresent social condition in the region, and that 'kinship is a natural desire among humans, it bonds the close ones and relatives together during catastrophe.'[50] Ibn

Khaldun's thoughts on balancing the paradoxical aspects of tribal inclusion in any political enterprise were also helpful to the authors: 'A state is stronger if it creates ties with its citizens through religion rather than clannishness. This is because religion, unlike clannishness, does not evolve around competition and envy.'[51]

In the Wars of Apostasy, Muhammad's successor Abu Bakr had to deal with a tribal uprising after the Prophet's death. This was not due to any injustice committed by the Caliph, but to the fickle nature of the tribes.[52] Using this logic, the Islamic State should not be blamed for the tribal Awakening since it is the very nature of tribes to defy attempts at unification. While this narrative was a self-serving one, it allowed the leaders of the Islamic State to process the tribal betrayal.

The tactic going forward would blatantly steal a page from the American's playbook, and establish what the strategy document described as 'Awakening Jihadist Councils, similar to the ones the prophet – peace be upon him – convened at the Medina delegations.'[53] In a complete reverse of what had happened to the group in 2006–8, the authors advocated enlisting 'honorable' tribal leaders to form militias out of tribal members in order to protect them from government 'traitor' security forces. Tribal leaders could be influential in this regard, as the population lived in these rural areas according to 'tribal traditions.' Funding, unlike in the American project, would be done in 'collaboration' with the Islamic State.[54] This most likely meant cutting the tribes into a share of the Islamic State's lucrative economic smuggling, extortion, contract padding, and the expropriation of property of pro-government figures.[55] This would not be easy according to the authors, clearly understanding the differences between a powerful state and a defeated insurgency trying to recover."We saw how the crusaders were able to remove many obstacles they had to achieving their apostate councils in all regions by paying money. Therefore, the difficulty of achieving this project does not mean we should give it up."[56]

Learning from the enemy

The leaders in the Islamic State displayed no qualms about adopting U.S. methods and even terminology in its plan to turn things around after 2009. There is precedence for this; during the period between world wars, the Germans studied the British and Soviet use of tanks to help formulate its future doctrine of armored warfare, due to the restrictions of the Treaty of Versailles.[57] In addition to a willingness to learn from others, the German military developed a culture of honest self-assessment, a habit that is rarely found even among the world's most professional armies.[58] If the Islamic State was reluctant to discuss its problems directly in 2007, at the very moment of its defeat, by late 2009 it seems that a level of frankness had prevailed which facilitated the creation of a viable strategy for dissemination to the ranks.

The new attitude toward dealing with the tribes was incorporated into a larger phased strategy that deemphasized targeting U.S. forces and focused on dismantling of the Awakening councils. The Islamic State communicated this strategy, called the Strategy to Improve the Political Position of the Islamic State of Iraq, also known colloquially as the 'Fallujah Memorandum,' in late 2009. By then, the author(s)' assessed the Awakening councils in the past tense, noting 'this is a great achievement [the demolishing of the councils] that shows that the Islamic State now has enough military and political power to allow it to be able to deal with internal conflicts.'[59] By internal conflicts, it is thought that the author is referring to jihadist rivals that were lingering in the post-Surge period in Iraq. These rivals did not survive the pre-caliphate period in any meaningful way and were largely disbanded or defunct by the end of 2014.[60]

The key to implementing the ideas contained in the *Fallujah Memorandum* would follow Abu Hamza's earlier advice to distinguish the good from the bad from the fence sitters. Much like the Human Terrain System would try to assist counterinsurgents in learning how to operate in complex socio-political environments, the Islamic State would create its own ethnographic teams of ambassadors to move among the tribes and develop a better understanding for the purpose of increasing its political coalition. Failing that, this knowledge would inform the implementation of the coercive tools of its tribal engagement strategy.

The accidental ethnographers

The Tribal Engagement office was created sometime in 2009 to manage all aspects of the relationship between the Islamic State of Iraq and the Sunni tribes in Babil, Anbar, Saladin, and Diyala provinces. It was not mentioned in the official announcement of the second slate of cabinet positions in the Islamic State, but there is captured correspondence that indicates the leader of this office worked directly for the amir Abu Omar al-Baghdadi and his deputy, Abu Hamza al-Muhajir.[61]

The operatives working in the Tribal Engagement Office served as socio-cultural political outreach agents, tasked with gaining detailed information about the Sunni tribal structure in their assigned areas, any political affiliations, and assessing political support for the Islamic State. Key information found in a series of 2009 post-engagement reports had detailed names, possible replacements for eliminated Awakening leaders, and pointers from tribal members on how best to 'dismantle' the local 'Sahwa of apostasy and hypocrisy.'[62] As Cigar described it in 2012,

> Al-Qaida's new approach was characterized by an easing in of the implementation of strict Islamic practices, a reduced reliance on foreign personnel in leadership positions, a greater willingness to work with tribal leaders and to accept neutral tribes, and a more focused targeting to avoid collateral damage.[63]

These policies were informed by the Engagement office's amateur efforts to conduct a superficial version of political ethnography, which Rattelle describes as 'immersion in a community ... long enough ... to be able to grasp and take seriously local actor's self-understanding of a political phenomenon.'[64] The office's study was politically motivated, to assess areas within the tribes of support for and opposition to the Islamic State, and influence undecided blocs. Despite the Islamic State's roving ambassadors' high level of cultural fluency in tribal networks, the operators had no observable training in ethnographic study and an ad-hoc process.[65] Accordingly, this method differed greatly from efforts like the Human Terrain Teams employed by the group's opponents.

According to captured reports from the raid that killed Abu Umar and Abu Hamza in 2010, the Islamic State's Tribal Engagement Office had multiple operatives working the tribes, including someone named Abu Khaldun, who worked the 'southern belt' of Sunni farmland south of Baghdad in what reporter Anthony Shadid called the 'Triangle of Death.'[66] Abu Khaldun used his social connections from prison, and access to Sunni mosques in influential Sunni areas like the Euphrates River town of Jurf ah-Sakhr, to approach tribal figures for an audience. He asked for their advice and dutifully relayed it to his superiors in his reports, while flagging political actors who were obviously playing both sides.[67] By making the effort to map out the political attitudes of tribes and clans in dozens of critical areas, the Islamic State proved itself serious to the task of understanding a critical base of future support.

The Islamic State movement made inroads into the tribal networks by 2010, aided by a disengaging U.S. military and a wary Iraqi government that viewed the post-2003 resistance pedigree of the *Sahwa* with great suspicion. Although the U.S. was in an advising role at this point, it did have a capable special operation task force working to eliminate Islamic State targets in support of the Iraqi government.[68] It is unlikely that the U.S. were targeting the tribal engagement teams, nor is there evidence that they were even aware of their existence (despite the captured documents). In fact, the Special Investigator General for Iraq Reconstruction once blamed Prime Minister Maliki for killing off the *Sahwa*, a remarkable misattribution that demonstrates how quickly the U.S. lost its situational awareness of critical events in Iraq after 2008.[69] The Iraqi government might have tried to derail the *Sahwa* for misguided political purposes, but they were not responsible for the 2300 leaders and tribal members the Islamic State killed since 2008. U.S. officials neglected the *Sahwa* once its emergency was over; this was not the case for the Islamic State, who proudly claimed these killings in their focus on shaping tribal dynamics for the future.[70]

The Iraqi government's dismissive attitude toward the tribal Awakening served the Islamic State's ends in the very way that the *Fallujah Memorandum* predicted. Benraad, who conducted field research on the *Sahwa* movement in Iraq, predicted its eventual demise in 2010:

> Reliable sources have reported that the organization [Islamic State of Iraq] currently exploits the Sahwa's grievances to approach and recruit many of its members, bribing them to carry out paid attacks or act as accomplices ... Combined with the political chaos brought about by the 7 March 2010, legislative elections, the government's anti-Sahwa attitude has obviously given space to the insurgency, more particularly al-Qaeda [Islamic State] affiliates, to escalate their attacks on tribal mobilization and capitalize on the Sahwa's numerous socioeconomic and political frustrations to lure its members back into the armed struggle and radicalize their animosity towards the government. In several instances, Sahwa fighters have even expressed regret for having applied for public jobs.[71]

The Islamic State's new public spokesman in 2011, Abu Muhammad al-Adnani, spent time in his first speech warning the tribes about the change in political dynamics: 'but these days we can see you while you can see us not ... your masters [the Americans] have turned their back and left you alone, while the Rafida [Shi'a] do not differentiate between you and us.'[72] Repentance was the only way out, Adnani argued, and it is hard not to assume that many of the pragmatic tribes heeded this advice during the rise of the Islamic State's caliphate project. Videos of mass tribal allegiance ceremonies organized by the tribal engagement office after the declaration of the caliphate offer somber evidence of this sustained effort.[73]

Conclusion

The Islamic State's tribal engagement entity still exists in the Office for Public and Tribal Relations, surviving the group's transformation to a dual-state insurgency (ISIS) in 2013, the establishment of the caliphate in 2014, and its demise in 2019.[74] It remains an advisory office to the Delegated Committee, the highest advisory council in the group and the men who run the day-to-day policy decisions to protect the caliph from exposure.[75] The importance and care of tribal relations have been put to use in the Islamic State's expansion into Syria, Sinai, and other areas where tribes and clans are important social structures – such as the Philippines.[76]

The inspiration to learn as much as they could about the tribes cannot be ascribed to any benevolent trait of the men who ran the Islamic State. They used this information in many cases to kill and destroy, much as others use technology to pinpoint and eliminate key leaders in terrorist organizations. The Islamic State's purpose of 'mapping the human terrain' was to produce knowledge derived for the careful use of violence or threat of violence in the pursuit of policy goals, and reliant on a shared cognitive faith in the utility of violence to instill fear into their enemies.

This research provides some much needed detail to our understanding of how the group uses violence within their own identity in-group of Sunni Muslims. The evidence from their counter-Awakening campaign demonstrates that violence was only used by permission of the highest authority, and only after the tribal engagement teams had identified key nodes and tried multiple times to persuade these specific tribal leaders to join, or at least accommodate, the group's political agenda. Norman Cigar described the evolution of the group's thinking this way in 2012:

> despite its past failures with Iraq's tribes, al-Qaida [Islamic State of Iraq] is an adaptive organization and has exhibited the ability to learn from experience. It has modified its approach at least sufficiently to place it in a position to try to take advantage of an evolving political situation and the emerging critical vulnerabilities that the situation present.[77]

The learning that took place was motivated by a tremendous failure of the Islamic State of Iraq, at the hands of infidel occupiers who leveraged their own kin against them. This injury seemed to inspire them, and they spared no effort to seek a better understanding of the tribes. Rubin's study of Islamist exploitation of tribalism among the Bedouins of Israel's Negev Desert demonstrates that others have learned this tactic long before the Islamic State.[78] The spread of violent Islamist movements in Africa demonstrate that this topic is worthy of additional study to understand the global proliferation of the jihadist ideology.

Cultural knowledge is not just a requirement of the militaries of foreign interventionists. This case study demonstrates that a highly ideological revolutionary movement could drastically misunderstand the culture of a very important actor in its political universe. Unfortunately, the Islamic State movement adjusted and avoided a total collapse, returning to prominence in disenfranchised and disillusioned Sunni areas of Iraq and later Syria. This turn of events was not an accident, but the result of intensive study of the object of their attention – the Sunni tribes of Iraq. Today's advanced militaries have soured on the necessity of this idea, which had driven experimentation on Human Terrain System from 2006 to 2012. The intellectual force behind the Human Terrain System, Montgomery McFate, later argued that contrary to criticism, a 'COIN doctrine that stresses limited use of force, minimization of collateral damage, and cultural understanding is very well suited to the social complexities of conflict in Iraq.'[79] The irony might be that having successfully adjusted in Iraq, in a manner complimented by its enemies, armies like the American military have discarded the idea of making a careful study of the population it fights for – to the advantage of its opponent in the forever war.

Notes

1. The translation from *al-Naba* can be found in Orton, "The Islamic State's Lessons-Learned."
2. One recent account revises some of the legends of the tribal Awakening, including a better inclusion of the Islamic State's perspective, see Malkasian, *Illusions of Victory*.

3. Gvosdev and Alvi, "Seeing the World."
4. Petraeus, "How We Won in Iraq."
5. Kalyvas, *The Logic of Violence in Civil War*, 107.
6. Green and Mullen, *Fallujah Redux*; Silverman, *Awakening Victory*; Gentile, *Wrong Turn*; and McFate and Fondacaro, "Reflections on the Human Terrain System."
7. Cigar, *Al-Qaida, the Tribes, and the Government*, 3–4.
8. As cited in McFate, "The 'Memory of War'," 317.
9. Ibid.
10. Ibid., 318.
11. Ibid., 321–6.
12. Interview with Colonel (retired) Greg Reilly, U.S. Army, Monterey, CA, 22 February 2019. Reilly commanded a cavalry squadron in Anbar province in 2003–4 and related how difficult it was to gain a deep understanding of the place tribes had in the complex social fabric of rural Sunni Iraq. According to Reilly, the other two legs of the governance of Anbar prior to the invasion were the Ba'ath party – including professionals and retired Army officers – and the clerics. After the de-Ba'athification policy began to be enforced, Colonel Reilly felt the tribes held the real power of the remaining two legs in the post-Saddam era in places like Anbar Province. Reilly learned 'mapping the human terrain' from the British in Kosovo, who had applied similar techniques in Northern Ireland in decades before.
13. Ricks, *Fiasco*, 149–250; and Cottam and Huseby, *Confronting al-Qaeda*. For an account on how the military innovation and learning did occur in Anbar between 2005–2007, see Russell, *Innovation, Transformation, and War*, 192. One such officer was Captain Travis Patriquin, who was killed in Ramadi in late 2006. He famously constructed a PowerPoint on how to work with the Sheikhs called 'How to win in Anbar.' For an example of his understanding of local power dynamics in general in Tel Afar, see 'Using Occam's Razor to Connect the Dots.'
14. Montgomery and McWilliams, *Al-Anbar Awakening, Volume II*, 133, 140, 196, and 254.
15. Cottam and Huseby, *Confronting al-Qaeda*, 47–67.
16. Ibid., 69–96.
17. In October 2006, about the time the Tribal Awakening (Sahwa) was founded, the Islamic State of Iraq was formed and al-Qaeda in Iraq dissolved into the larger front. Analysts who downplayed this merger continued to call the group al-Qaeda in Iraq for many years, until the expansion into Syria and the establishment of the Islamic State caliphate made the old moniker completely outdated.
18. Cottam and Huseby, *Confronting al-Qaeda*, 11–21.
19. Ibid., 97–113.
20. It is likely that some of the impetus for the dramatic shift was also a sense that the civil war between Sunni and Shi'a in Iraq was largely over and accommodations with the stronger party had to be made (allowing for considerations of honor), much in accordance with tribal warfare norms. See Douglas Ollivant, 'Countering the New Orthodoxy.'
21. al-Rishawi, "Interview 3," 46.
22. al-Zarqawi, "Leader of Al-Qa'ida in Iraq Al-Zarqawi Declares 'Total War' on Shi'ites."
23. Not all tribes joined the Awakening; in fact, it was probably a minority of tribes and only around 100,000 tribal fighters and former resistance members ever joined the

official Awakening rolls according to Iraqi government figures. This number immediately began dropping for a variety of reasons, including disillusionment, distrust of between the Sahwa and the government, and pressure from the Islamic State.
24. Milne, "Out of the Shadows."
25. Simon, "Tribal Transition."
26. Montgomery and McWilliams, 55.
27. Whiteside, "Nine Bullets for the Traitor," 11–14.
28. As cited in Irwin, "Ibn Khaldun, an Intellectual biography," 47.
29. Telephonic interview with Dr. Martha Cottam, January 2019.
30. Anonymous, "Analysis of the ISI," 22 (original 17).
31. Ibid., 25.
32. Hafez, "Al-Qa'ida Losing Ground in Iraq," 1.
33. For the Albu Mahal tribe, see Knarr, "Al-Sahawa: An Awakening in Al Qaim;" for the Jughayfi tribe, see Knarr, *Al Sahawa – The Awakening, Volume III-B*, 52, 93, 143, as well as Hejab, "The Defiant Iraqi Tribe of Haditha."
34. Anonymous, "Analysis of the ISI," 52 (original page 38). Shufair had been an Awakening leader who successfully ousted Islamic State members from Haditha and later allegedly killed returning Islamic State fighters being released from Camp Bucca. For more on the 2012 special operation targeting Shufair, see Whiteside, Rice, and Raineri, "Black Ops."
35. Ministry of Information, Islamic State of Iraq, "The Petraeus-Crocker Report and the American Defeat."
36. al-Baghdadi, "They Plan and Allah Plans."
37. Islamic State of Iraq, "Strategy to Improve the Political Position of the Islamic State," Chapter 3.
38. Cigar, *Al-Qaida, the Tribes, and the Government*, 5.
39. Anonymous, "Analysis of State of ISI," (original p.27), 36.
40. Abu Sulayman al-Utaybi, "Letter to al-Qaeda Leadership."
41. Fishman, "The First Defector."
42. Scholar Fanar Haddad verified this video existed in 2007 and watched it, and @Mr0rangetracker made us aware of its existence.
43. See note 41 above.
44. Hafez, "Al-Qa'ida Losing Ground in Iraq," 1. For a longer discussion about the Islamic State's errors in Iraq, including a wider discussion of the Analysis of the ISI document, see Fishman, *Dysfunction and Decline*.
45. Bunzel, "The Islamic State's Mufti on Trial;" al-Tamimi, "An Extremist Commentary"; and Hamming, "The Extremist Wing of the Islamic State."
46. See Bunzel, "Caliphate in Disarray," Jihadica, 3 October 2017 http://www.jihadica.com/caliphate-in-disarray/
47. al-Muhajir. "The Second Audio Interview."
48. al-Iraqi, "Stages of the Jihad of Amir Abu Umar al-Baghdadi."
49. Islamic State of Iraq, "Strategy to Improve the Political Position of the Islamic State," 21.
50. Ibid., 6.
51. Ibid., 31.
52. Ibid., 6. Ironically, McFate pointed out the same parallel in her 2008 article cited in this piece, a year before the Islamic State used it in its 2009 strategy document, the *Fallujah Memorandum*. The same thing can be said for the Ibn Khaldun quotes in both her article and the strategy document, a strong affirmation for the academic piece.

53. Islamic State of Iraq, "Strategy to Improve the Political Position of the Islamic State," 26.
54. Ibid.
55. Johnston, et al., *Foundations of the Islamic State*.
56. See note 53 above.
57. Murray, "Armored Warfare," 39–42.
58. Murray, "Innovation: Past and Future," 314; Watts and Murray contrast this German habit of honest assessment with U.S. failure to frankly examine its own performance in the 1991 Gulf War in their chapter on "Military Innovation in Peacetime," 411.
59. Islamic State of Iraq, "Strategy to Improve the Political Position of the Islamic State," 22.
60. al-Tamimi, "Rise Of The Islamic State And the Fading Away of the Rest of the Iraqi Insurgency."
61. al-Baghdadi, "Declaration of the Second Cabinet Reshuffle;" documents housed at the Captured Records Research Center describe the office's function well as detailed by an Islamic State operative: see Khaldun, "Synopsis of the Relations Committee in Baghdad's Southern Belt;" and Khaldun, "OPSuM from Abu Mustafa of Southern Belt trying to overturn Sahwa."
62. Khaldun, "OPSUM from Abu Mustafa."
63. Cigar, *Al-Qaida, the Tribes, and the Government*, 5.
64. Ratelle, "Making Sense of Violence in Civil War," 159.
65. The collection of tribal engagement reports we researched are detailed and informative, but basic and lack any observable methodology or rigor. They were amateur, but effective.
66. Shadid, "Iraq's Forbidding 'Triangle of Death'," A1.
67. Khaldun, "OPSum from Abu Mustafa."
68. Arango, "Top Qaeda Leaders Reported Killed."
69. Bowen and Hamid, "Discussion About Islamism, Perilous Situation in Iraq".
70. Whiteside, "The Islamic State and the Return of Revolutionary Warfare," 754.
71. Benraad, "Iraq's Tribal 'Sahwa'," 121.
72. Al-Adnani, "The State of Islam Will Remain Safe." His reference to seeing can be interpreted from an intelligence perspective, but also that the group understands the tribes better, while the converse was not true anymore. Adnani was a Syrian and a movement veteran since 2002, who sat out the tribal backlash in Camp Bucca from 2005–9. He was killed in 2016 in Syria.
73. Simon, Islamic State video can be found at https://www.alwatanvoice.com/arabic/news/2015/04/01/689957.html
74. Islamic State, "The Structure of the Caliphate."
75. Ingram, Whiteside, and Winter, "The ISIS Reader," Chapter 11.
76. Whiteside, "Nine Bullets," 23–24.
77. Cigar, *Al-Qaida, the Tribes, and the Government*, 124.
78. Rubin, Islamic Political Activism among Israel's Negev Bedouin Population," 430.
79. McFate, "The Memory of War," 326.

Acknowledgments

Much thanks to Martha Cottam, Todd Greentree, Hassan Hassan, Mohammad Hafez, Montgomery McFate, Liam Murphy, and Paul Rich for material support and improvements to this manuscript.

Disclaimer

This reflects the authors' opinions and do not reflect the views of the U.S. Naval War College or the U.S. Government.

Disclosure statement

No potential conflict of interest was reported by the authors.

ORCID

Craig Whiteside http://orcid.org/0000-0002-4094-7173

Bibliography

al-Adnani, Abu Muhammad. 2011. "The State of Islam Will Remain Safe." *al-Fajr Media*, August 7.
al-Baghdadi, Abu Umar. 2007. "They Plan and Allah Plans." Audio message posted online, *Al-Furqan Media*, September.
al-Baghdadi, Abu Umar. 2009. "Declaration of the Second Cabinet Reshuffle for the Islamic State of Iraq." *al-Furqan*, September 21.
al-Iraqi, Abu Usama. 2012. "Stages of the Jihad of Amir Abu Umar al-Baghdadi." posted on Global Jihad Network, May 12. https://drive.google.com/file/d/13MVVBKGLsTynxRtm8W8dTCLTKsyTjH-7/view
al-Muhajir, Abu Hamza. 2009. "The Second Audio Interview with Shaykh Abu Hamzah al-Muhajir, May God Protect Him." *Audio Message, al-Furqan Media*, April 20.
al-Rishawi, Sheikh Ahmad Bezia Fteikhan. "Interview 3." In *Al-Anbar Awakening, Vol II: Iraqi Perspectives*, edited by Gary Montgomery and McWilliams Timothy, 44–51. Quantico: Marine Corps University Press, 2009.
al-Tamimi, Aymenn. 2015. "Rise of the Islamic State and the Fag Away of the Rest of the Iraqi Insurgency Interview with Aymenn Jawad al-Tamimi." Interview by Joel Wing, Musings on Iraq, May 4. http://musingsoniraq.blogspot.com/2015/05/rise-of-islamic-state-and-fading-away.html
al-Tamimi, Aymenn. 2018. "An Extremist Commentary on the Islamic State's Current Situation." Online blog. December 26. http://www.aymennjawad.org/2018/12/an-extremist-commentary-on-the-islamic-state
al-Utaybi, Abu Sulayman. 2013. "Letter to al-Qaeda Leadership." Originally written April/May 2007, posted on *Ana al-Muslim* network on November 24.

al-Zarqawi, Abu Musab. 2005. "Leader of Al-Qa'ida in Iraq Al-Zarqawi Declares 'Total War' on Shi'ites, States that the Sunni Women of Tel'afar Had 'Their Wombs Filled with the Sperm of the Crusaders'." *al-Qa'ida in Iraq Media Battalion*, September 14. Downloaded by MEMRI, Available from the Haverford al-Qa'ida statements collection.

Anonymous. 2007. "Analysis of State of ISI." Document NMEC-2007-612449. CTC at West Point. https://ctc.usma.edu/harmony-program/analysis-of-the-state-of-isiorigi nal-language-2/

Arango, Tim. 2010. "Top Qaeda Leaders Reported Killed in Raid." *The New York Times*, April 19.

Benraad, Myriam. "Iraq's Tribal" Sahwa": Its Rise and Fall." *Middle East Policy* 18, no. 1 (2011). doi:10.1111/j.1475-4967.2011.00477.x.

Bowen, Stuart, Jr., and Shadi Hamid. 2015. "Stuart Bowen Jr. And Dr. Shadi Hamid in Discussion About Islamism. Perilous Situation in Iraq". *Video*, Chautauqua Institution. August 19. https://www.youtube.com/watch?v=jwgPtCuelz0

Bunzel, Cole. 2017. "Caliphate in Disarray: Theological Turmoil in the Islamic State." *Jihadica*, October 3. http://www.jihadica.com/caliphate-in-disarray/

Bunzel, Cole. "The Islamic State's Mufti on Trial: The Saga of the Silsila Ilmiyya." *CTC Sentinel* 11, no. 9 Oct (2018). https://ctc.usma.edu/islamic-states-mufti-trial-saga-silsila-ilmiyya/.

Cigar, Norman. *Al-Qaida, the Tribes, and the Government: Lessons and Prospects for Iraq's Unstable Triangle*. No. 2. Washington DC: Government Printing Office, 2012.

Cottam, Martha, and Joe Huseby. *Confronting al-Qaeda: The Sunni Awakening and American Strategy in Iraq*. Lanham, MD: Rowman & Littlefield, 2016.

Fishman, Brian. *Dysfunction and Decline*. West Point, NY: CTC, 2009. Mar 16.

Fishman, Brian. 2015. "The First Defector: Abu Sulayman al-Utaybi, the Islamic State, and al-Qa`ida." *CTC Sentinel*. https://ctc.usma.edu/the-first-defector-abu-sulayman-al-utaybi-the-islamic-state-and-al-qaida/

Gentile, Gian. *Wrong Turn: America's Deadly Embrace of Counterinsurgency*. New York: The New Press, 2013.

Green, Daniel, and William Mullen. *Fallujah Redux: The Anbar Awakening and the Struggle with Al Qaeda*. Annapolis, MD: Naval Institute Press, 2014.

Gvosdev, Nikolas, and Hayat Alvi. "Seeing the World the Lens of Culture, Religion, Ideology, and Nationalism." *Theater Security Decision Making Lesson 6/7-1*, Newport: Naval War College Curriculum, April 2016.

Hafez, Mohammad M. "Al-Qa'ida Losing Ground in Iraq." *CTC Sentinel* 1, no. 1, (December 2007): 6–8.

Hamming, Tore. 2016. "The Extremist Wing of the Islamic State." *Jihadica*, June 9. http://www.jihadica.com/the-extremist-wing-of-the-islamic-state/

Hejab, Omar. 2015. "The Defiant Iraqi Tribe of Haditha." *Arab Weekly*, March 7. https://thearabweekly.com/defiant-iraqi-tribe-haditha

Ingram, Haroro, Craig Whiteside, and Charlie Winter. *The ISIS Reader: Milestone Texts of the Islamic State Movement*. London: Hurst Publications, 2019.

Irwin, Robert. *Ibn Khaldun, an Intellectual Biography*. Princeton, NJ: Princeton University Press, 2018.

Islamic State. 2016. "The Structure of the Caliphate". *al-Furqan Media*, July 6. Jihadology. https://jihadology.net/2016/07/06/new-video-message-from-the-isla mic-state-the-structure-of-the-caliphate/

Islamic State of Iraq. 2018. "Strategy to Improve the Political Position of the Islamic State." *Posted online in late 2009, translated by Anas Elallame from the Middlebury Institute for International Studies,* Monterey, CA, April.
Johnston, Patrick, Jacob Shapiro, Howard Shatz, Benjamin Bahney, Danielle Jung, Patrick Ryan, and Jonathan Wallace. *Foundations of the Islamic State: Management, Money, and Terror in Iraq, 2005–2010.* Santa Monica, CA: RAND Corporation, 2016. https://www.rand.org/pubs/research_reports/RR1192.html
Kalyvas, Stathis. *The Logic of Violence in Civil War.* Cambridge: Cambridge University Press, 2006.
Khaldun, Abu. 2009. "OPSUM from Abu Mustafa of Southern Belt Trying to Overturn Sahwa." *CRRC document AQ-POAK-d-001–695,* September 9.
Khaldun, Abu. "Synopsis of the Relations Committee in Baghdad's Southern Belt." *CRRC document AQ PMPR-d-001–717* (sometime in 2009).
Knarr, William. "Al-Sahawa: An Awakening in Al Qaim." *CTX* 3, no. 2 May (2013). https://globalecco.org/al-sahawa-an-awakening-in-al-qaim
Knarr, William, Dale Alford, David Graves, Tracy King, Thomas Jones, Mary Hawkins, Jennifer Goodman, et al. 2016. *Al Sahawa—The Awakening, Volume III-B: Al Anbar Province, Area of Operations Denver, Haditha–Hit Corridor.* Institute for Defense Analysis, May. https://apps.dtic.mil/dtic/tr/fulltext/u2/1015541.pdf
Malkasian, Carter. *Illusions of Victory: The Anbar Awakening and the Rise of the Islamic State.* Oxford: Oxford University Press, 2017.
McFate, Montgomery. "Memory of War': Tribes and the Legitimate Use of Force in Iraq." In *Armed Groups: Studies in National Security, Counterterrorism, and Counterinsurgency,* edited by Jeffrey Norwich, 187–202. Newport, RI: Naval Institute Press, 2008.
McFate, Montgomery, and Steven Fondacaro. "Reflections on the Human Terrain System in the First Four Years." *PRISM* 2, no. 4 (2011): 63–82.
Milne, Seamus. 2007. "Out of the Shadows." *The Guardian,* July 19. https://www.theguardian.com/world/2007/jul/19/iraq.features11
Ministry of Information, Islamic State of Iraq. 2007. "The Petraeus-Crocker Report and the American Defeat." *al-Fajr Media,* September 18.
Montgomery, Gary W, and Timothy S. McWilliams. *Al-Anbar Awakening, Volume II: Iraqi Perspectives, from Insurgency to Counterinsurgency in Iraq, 2004–2009.* Quantico: Marine Corps University Press, 2009.
Murray, Williamson. "Armored Warfare: The British, French, and German Experiences." In *Military Innovation in the Interwar Period,* edited by Williamson Murray and Allan Millett, 6–49. Cambridge: Cambridge University Press, 1996.
Murray, Williamson. "Innovation: Past and Future." In *Military Innovation in the Interwar Period,* edited by Williamson Murray and Allan Millett, 300–328. Cambridge: Cambridge University Press, 1996.
Ollivant, Douglas. 2011 "Countering the New Orthodoxy: Reinterpreting Counterinsurgency in Iraq," *New America Foundation,* June.
Orton, Kyle. 2018. "The Islamic State's Lessons-Learned About Insurgency." Online blog, October 5. https://kyleorton1991.wordpress.com/2018/10/05/the-islamic-states-lessons-learned-about-insurgency/#more-5801
Patriquin, Travis. 2006. "How to Win in Anbar." *PowerPoint presentation.* https://abcnews.go.com/images/us/how_to_win_in_anbar_v4.pdf
Patriquin, Travis. 2007. "Using Occam's Razor to Connect the Dots: The Ba'ath Party and the Insurgency in Tel Afar." *Military Review,* January–February. doi:10.1094/PDIS-91-4-0467B.

Petraeus, David. 2013. "How We Won in Iraq: And Why All the Hard-won Gains of the Surge are in Grave Danger of Being Lost Today." *Foreign Policy*, October 29. https://foreignpolicy.com/2013/10/29/how-we-won-in-iraq/

Ratelle, Jean-Francois. "Making Sense of Violence in Civil War: Challenging Academic Narratives through Political Ethnography." *Critical Studies on Security* 1, no. 2 (2013): 159–173. doi:10.1080/21624887.2013.824654.

Ricks, Tom. *Fiasco: The American Military Adventure in Iraq, 2003 to 2005*. New York: Penguin Press, 2006.

Rubin, Lawrence. "Islamic Political Activism among Israel's Negev Bedouin Population." *British Journal of Middle East Studies* 44, no. 3 (2017): 429–446. doi:10.1080/13530194.2016.1207503.

Russell, James. *Innovation, Transformation, and War: Counterinsurgency Operations in Anbar and Ninewa, Iraq, 2005–7*. Palo Alto, CA: Stanford University Press, 2011.

Shadid, Anthony. 2004. "Iraq's Forbidding 'Triangle of Death,'." *Washington Post*, November 23, A1.

Silverman, Michael. *Awakening Victory: How Iraqi Tribes and American Troops Reclaimed Al-Anbar and Defeated al-Qaeda in Iraq*. Philadelphia: Casemate, 2011.

Simon, Alex. 2016. "Tribalism in Transition: Iraq's Sunni Tribes Before, during and after the Islamic State – Part I." *SAIS Review*, November 5. https://www.saisreview.org/2016/11/05/tribalism-in-transition-parti/

Whiteside, Craig. "The Islamic State and the Return of Revolutionary Warfare." *Small Wars & Insurgencies* 27, no. 5 (2016). doi:10.1080/09592318.2016.1208287.

Whiteside, Craig. 2018. "Nine Bullets for the Traitor, One for the Enemy: The Slogans and Strategy of the Islamic State's CounterSahwa Campaign." *The Hague: ICCT-The Hague*, September.

Whiteside, Craig, Ian Rice, and Daniele Raineri. 2019. "Black Ops: The Islamic State's Innovation in Irregular Warfare." *Studies in Conflict and Terrorism*, June. doi:10.1080/1057610X.2019.1628623.

The anthropology of Al-Shabaab: the salient factors for the insurgency movement's recruitment project

Mohamed Haji Ingiriis

ABSTRACT

Harakaat Al-Shabaab Al-Mujaahiduun (henceforth Al-Shabaab) is an active insurgent group in southern Somalia battling against the foreign forces and foreign-backed Somali forces. Despite recruiting both in Somalia and in the diaspora, this insurgency movement continues to increasingly recruit more local Somali youth than diaspora Somalis or non-Somalis. This article suggests that Al-Shabaab solicits support from diverse youth who – due to a confluence of factors – join the insurgency movement in various ways. The article reveals how the movement's methods are flexible insofar as it skilfully recruits both powerful clans and marginalised clans. This pattern tests the limits of the Somali federal government in Mogadishu who have yet to develop innovative approaches to challenge and contain Al-Shabaab. The government failure not only allows Al-Shabaab to successfully carry out its operations but also to sustain itself in the midst of local communities. Through interviews with former Al-Shabaab youth, the article explores youth recruiting efforts and finds that the militant movement pursues various sophisticated means to lure numerous youth into its ranks.

Introduction

Two former Al-Shabaab defectors were sitting in a spacious house very close to the Villa Somalia (the Presidential Palace). There was a cool breeze outside the house during a humid evening in Mogadishu in early May 2016 and the two young men were reflecting on their days with Al-Shabaab. One was a young man in his late twenties who once lived in the United Kingdom, the other young man of his late thirties from Hargeysa, northern Somalia (present-day Somaliland). When they separately defected from Al-Shabaab between 2014 and 2015, they joined the security service of the Federal Government of Somalia. Both were now friends who would regularly visit Mogadishu hotels where most of those who worked for the government came to converse over a tea about a myriad of intricate everyday issues, most notably politics. The two young men noted the oddity of the Al-Shabaab recruitment project, one of the least understood aspects of the insurgent movement. They said they were often asked during their government security debriefing how they had managed to defect from Al-Shabaab.[1] But nobody ever asked them: how did they initially come to join Al-Shabaab? This remains one of the critical questions for those seeking to study and fully understand the insurgent movement. In his 2013 study on Al-Shabaab (the first book on the movement), Stig Jarle Hansen detailed the advent of the insurgent movement, the historical dynamics from which it emerged, and how it operated initially.[2] Al-Shabaab is not an easily understood organisation, but it is an incredibly secretive one. Even though Al-Shabaab has been historicised, it has not been anthropologised.

Recent research has addressed the systems and structures of Al-Shabaab, yet there is little in-depth study specifically exploring the youth recruitment project of the insurgent movement. The literature on Al-Shabaab tends to emphasise the number of non-Somali recruits on the grounds of global security concerns, lest they return to their home countries and use the military experience gained from the Al-Shabaab training centres.[3] However, much more critical aspects of their local recruitment project are often overlooked. The majority of the academic literature continues to concentrate on the external recruitment of Al-Shabaab, notably in Canada and Kenya, identifying different methodologies of recruitment in specific contexts.[4] These young men are presented as having no alternative other than joining various armed groups. They are characterized as being motivated by the spoils found through looting, banditry and robbery in war-torn societies, what David Keen calls 'economics by other means.'[5] The most salient and significant factors that explain recruitment – political marginalisation, economic exclusion and religious ideology – are less explored. The existing literature has not sufficiently explained how and why Al-Shabaab has been successful in recruitment in contrast with the government in Mogadishu's recruiting for security forces. While Hansen and other authors have analysed Al-Shabaab's success in political and religious radicalisation, an all-inclusive framework is needed to go beyond one or two aspects in the Al-Shabaab recruitment project.[6] In-depth nuanced studies are necessary for understanding Al-Shabaab from various cultural, economic and political aspects.

Framed within the broader questions of radicalisation and recruitment, this article examines one of the least understood aspects of Al-Shabaab: the multi-faceted recruitment process of the organization. The article discusses how Al-Shabaab recruits young men who join to fight for the insurgent movement and why many who join decide to become *jihadists*. It also looks at the extent to which the push and pull factors of youth recruitment in Al-Shabaab have reinforced radicalisation in Somalia. Whereas the push factors are facilitated by negative dynamics, such as the hostile environment and indoctrination, the pull factors are reinforced by issues of identity, cultural dimensions and economic exclusion. The article also assesses the extent to which the clan system assists Al-Shabaab in the recruitment project. Those writing about Al-Shabaab sometimes approach and interview current (and former) major figures of the movement over the phone, but they tend to overlook the voices of defectors of Al-Shabaab who could provide valuable insights into the insurgent movement.[7]

The difficulty conducting research in an Al-Shabaab-controlled area is well-known to those who study the insurgent movement. Thus, gathering empirically-grounded oral data on how youth join Al-Shabaab and why they are attracted to the movement are important for two reasons: this approach adds unique insights into the contemporary attempts to tackle the threats posed by insurgency and it contributes to the efforts of creating peace and stability in southern Somalia.

Methodologically, this article is based on intensive one-on-one and group interviews with former Al-Shabaab defectors. Most of those interviewed were male former members of Al-Shabaab between the ages of 25–35 years. They were either commanders or foot soldiers of the movement before defecting to the government in Mogadishu.[8] Interviews were conducted in government-controlled areas in Mogadishu or the relatively small farming town of Afgooye, an area very close to Al-Shabaab-controlled areas. When the research for this article was carried out, Al-Shabaab was few kilometres away from Afgooye. The article was also informed by field-based qualitative ethnographic research carried out between May-September 2015, April-August 2016, September-October 2017 and February-June 2018, except for brief intervals in Nairobi, Kenya. Supplemented by other data, the combination of all these sources provides a unique perspective of the pervasiveness of Al-Shabaab. In the following sections, the main reasons why many young Somalis join Al-Shabaab are identified by examining four clusters: (1) religion and ideology, (2) economic vulnerability and social injustice, (3) environment and demography, and (4) political exclusion. The first section focuses on the conditions under which young men seek to join the insurgent movement. The second section discusses various strategies and tactics adopted by the movement to attract local and diasporic youth. The third section seeks to evaluate how the movement utilises the local culture during the projection of recruitment strategies. The fourth section continues to assess how the movement exploits inter-clan conflicts and grievances within and between the Somali clans.

Perspectives on youth recruitment

Since the beginning of the Civil War in Somalia (the date is disputed), young people have been the backbone for the warring factions. The armed Islamic courts that emerged in Mogadishu and some parts of southern Somalia in the 1990s to provide security and justice for the local population under state collapse recruited many young men (as was also the case with the clan-based factions). When the Islamic court authorities felt threatened by warlords financed by the United States, they came together to form the Union of Islamic Courts (UIC) to fend off the warlords. The UIC defeated the warlords in early 2006. The Somali capital city of Mogadishu fell under the rule of the UIC for six months (between June and December 2006), resulting in a peaceful environment in Mogadishu.[9] The UIC victory was nonetheless a painful headache for both the United States and Ethiopia; the latter defeating the UIC in a subsequent conflict. Al-Shabaab (which was hitherto hidden under the UIC) arose as a powerful jihadist movement as a consequence of the Ethiopian invasion of southern Somalia between December 2006 and January 2009. During and after the Ethiopian invasion, Al-Shabaab presented itself as a nationalist/Islamist insurgency capable of liberating the Ethiopian invaders from Somalia.[10] Many young people from Somalia and beyond joined Al-Shabaab to fight in this jihad. More than ten years later, Al-Shabaab still attracts young people for their insurgent activities.

Why do many youths decide to join Al-Shabaab? Where do they go to join? How and when do they join? Why are young men more prone to radicalisation in southern Somalia than in other areas? Neither ideological nor economic deprivation is the only (or most important reason) why people join Al-Shabaab. Local political and security concerns are much more salient motivations for young men to become members of Al-Shabaab. The conditions that encourage joining Al-Shabaab are not different from other social movements globally. Social movements have tended to formulate a set of agendas for their radicalisation project and recruit individuals to implement their goals.[11] Generally, there is a principle ideology driving social movements, which affect their forms of radicalisation and recruitment.[12] In the Somali case, Al-Shabaab's recruiting of both Somalis living in Somalia and in the diaspora began during the fall of the Islamic Courts in 2007-2009, when the Ethiopian forces invaded southern Somalia. Many young men travelled to Somalia to fight alongside the UIC remnants, including Al-Shabaab, against the Ethiopians in the name of nationalism.[13]

The scant literature on Al-Shabaab recruitment strategies shows that young men are vulnerable to being recruited because of the desperately impoverished situation in southern Somalia.[14] This area of Somalia has been in a perpetual armed conflict since the collapse of the state in 1991. Many people lost their lives, while others fled from war and insecurity. Somalia is ranked as one of the poorest countries in the world.[15] Every year, many young men and women risk their lives on the high seas to reach Europe as refugees. It is thus assumed that recruits of Al-Shabaab are poor, impoverished, unemployed, orphaned youth acting as 'fortune-seekers' in opportunistic banditry who have been recruited from marginalised communities.[16] From this perspective, unemployment pushes many young men to join Al-Shabaab and, as such, many youths found no alternative other than joining various armed groups competing for economic resources. Admittedly, many ranks and files of Al-Shabaab are unemployed, impoverished youth – or, much worse, orphans lacking families or relatives able to take care of them – who found opportunities within the movement to improve their lives. Yet, this is not a sufficient explanation of why many young men involve themselves in violent conflict and insurgency. There are other more crucial factors pushing many young men to join Al-Shabaab on their own.

Whilst the level of youth immigration to Europe has recently been higher in northwest Somalia (present-day Somaliland) than in southern Somalia (Mogadishu and its environs), many other young men continue to navigate other ways of creating jobs at home.[17] In spite of unemployment and impoverishment, unemployed youths in Akaara, Isha Boorame, and so-called Kandahar (the poorest neighbourhoods in Hargeysa in Somaliland, where many youths live in poorer conditions but in a more peaceful environment than in southern Somalia), would not dare to travel to southern Somalia to join Al-Shabaab.[18] This is an indication of the existence of other salient factors pushing youths to join the insurgency. It is worthy of note, nevertheless, that Al-Shabaab has attempted to recruit from Somaliland youth on several occasions in the past years, as well as sending a whole armed brigade mostly comprising of teenagers and children to northeast Somalia (present-day Puntland) in 2015. A prominent case in point was the late powerful leader of Al-Shabaab, Abdi Ahmed Godane, known as Abu Zubeyr, himself a young man in his mid-thirties, who hailed from Somaliland. Godane left his mid-level banking job prior to travelling to southern Somalia to participate in the formation of Al-Shabaab in 2003, subsequently becoming one of the most committed jihadists within Al-Shabaab.[19] His motivation, as well as many of his fellows in Al-Shabaab, forces us to probe into other critical factors of radicalisation and recruitment of the insurgent movement.

A strong correlation has always been made between recruitment for armed violence and poverty. For example, the material interests of recruitment has occupied a prominent place in the early literature on the Somali civil war. With the benefit of hindsight, at the height of the Somali civil war in the 1990s, when security was generally privatised, many private businessmen hired armed youths to provide protection to foreign international aid agencies and generate money from them. This resulted in the deadly case of the 'banana wars' between the American-owned Dole-Sombana banana company versus the Italian-owned Somali Fruit company in southern Somalia in 1995.[20] Apart from the deadly competition between these foreign companies, local Somali armed factions and businessmen profiting from the war economy also used youth militia in the 2000s to fight each other. Roland Marchal, who did some of the first field-based research in southern Somalia during the early 1990s, has published extensive reports describing the emergence of freelance armed youth being drawn into the war economy by politico-war entrepreneurs monopolising the informal economy – basically the only available resource in the country.[21] Other scholars have summarised the main reasons for joining the insurgency in Somalia as being about protest, revenge and material interests.[22]

Beyond economics and individual interest

Al-Shabaab recruiters search for recruits, but potential recruits also search for the recruiters. This can be considered as a pull-and-push phenomenon. In this sense, Al-Shabaab recruiters individualise their recruitment techniques, approaching foreign elements differently than local recruits. Local – rather than external – recruitment is less costly for Al-Shabaab and can take the form of forced recruitment, although this happens rarely.[23] Forced recruitment is also conducted when the Al-Shabaab leadership feels increasingly threatened by external forces, such as the 2011 retreat from Mogadishu.[24] In March 2016, the case of Al-Shabaab attack in Puntland, where the militant movement dispatched fighters including children, was a prominent case in point of successful recruitment to boost the number of fighters. To save themselves from the government wrath, young and elderly fighters who were captured on the battlefront asserted on Somali television that they were either indoctrinated by their friends or conscripted by force by Al-Shabaab.[25] Aside from these statements, there are other reasons, such as the prospects of paradise after martyrdom in the jihad that are used during the recruitment procedure.

Youth radicalisation also plays a decisive role in Al-Shabaab recruitment. Some theories identify ways in which youth can be radicalised around deprivation and economic exclusion.[26] More importantly, during the recruitment process, young Somalis are reminded of their responsibility to fight for their religion, their Muslim *ummah* (Muslim religious community) and their country, which had been invaded from far afield by external infidel powers who desire to divide their people and country for their benefit. Al-Shabaab employs the promising jihad discourse more than any other to attract the minds and hearts of young people. Many young men are vulnerable to believing in the calls that Al-Shabaab fights for the Islamic existence against the crusading infidels. One Al-Shabaab defector simply said that 'Al-Shabaab hate foreigners' for religious purposes.[27] Indeed, the main military strength of

Al-Shabaab is not the fiercest of their force or their forms of fighting tactics, but the strict application of *Sharia*, which allows discipline and direction among their rank and file as well as hasty recruits during peace and war. In London, a young man who lived with his large family (mother, father and seven siblings), was recruited into Al-Shabaab. He was told by his Al-Shabaab recruiters he should join 'to defend his country from the timid Kenyans.'[28]. The young man who was born and bred outside Somalia decided to participate in the jihad to resist the Kenyan invasion of southern Somalia in October 2011. While he was preparing himself, his mother found out about his trip to southern Somalia and called the police who arrested him at home. She re-indoctrinated him for a while by lecturing on the precarious situation of Somalia and finally persuaded him to stay, thus preventing her son from joining Al-Shabaab. This case was not necessarily motivated by economic exclusion, although his family lived in deprivation in the UK.

Recruits driven by jihadi ideology can hardly be distinguished from those who are motivated by profit or looking for power, because almost all justify joining Al-Shabaab for religious reasons while suppressing other reasons including their political grievances against the government. Among the interviews I conducted, many young men joined Al-Shabaab for their own individual reasons, including grievances, personal gain or better economic prospects. The most powerful reasons for young, dispossessed men to join Al-Shabaab are grievance-based motivations, especially areas around Mogadishu. Al-Shabaab exploits the growing grievances against the government's lack of ability to distribute power and resources equally among the Somali clans.[29] The young men joining the insurgency movement consider the Mogadishu government and other clan-based federal states in the country as externally-imposed predatory power machines based on patrimonial political cronyism. In interviews these young men justified potential suicide attacks on the grounds that the government was 'living off the public asset,' a political metaphor which refers to government personnel siphoning off public assets through collapsed state institutions to serve personal interests.[30] Drawing from a political economy perspective, Marchal maintains that joining Al-Shabaab 'was a matter of necessity not ideology.'[31] Whilst necessity is an important factor, other factors should not be underestimated in explaining the recruitment process.[32]

There are two types of such recruits within Al-Shabaab: the *qurbojoog* (diaspora) youth, who while they mostly lived in poor conditions in the West, are considered 'privileged' and the *qorraxjoog* youth (literally meaning Somali people who live under the sun), who are regarded as 'poor' because of their local background. The two youth groups differ in their aims and objectives for joining Al-Shabaab, yet their motivations have often been misunderstood. The youths from poor backgrounds have long been perceived as easy prey for recruiters from Al-Shabaab, whereas the youths from the diaspora background are labelled as innocent 'brainwashed' youth remote from their 'unbroken' families. Quite the contrary; evidence gathered from former Al-Shabaab defectors suggest that the *qorraxjoog* boys are not less susceptible to being brainwashed and recruited into the movement than the *qurbajoog* boys, given the supposed privileged background in the diaspora.[33] As witnessed by one local resident living in Afgooye town, just less than 30km away from Mogadishu:

> There are no educated men among these youths in the middle of Al-Shabaab. You find a child whose parents could not afford to pay their education, who came to the town from the rural areas; those from rural areas are eager to have a name; urbanites are small in number and very few are educated. There are also others who want revenge because they have been displaced from their land, so a difficult life forced them to join [Al-Shabaab]. There are also others who want power and to become famous; [still] others also who want money; you would see someone [from Al-Shabaab] say to you 'I was given US$200 dollars to carry out controlled bomb explosion.'[34]

This testimony was also echoed by a senior Somali member of a 'moderate' Islamist group opposing Al-Shabaab who argued that there is a well known Al-Shabaab member who had been a 'well-attended religious person' before the emergence of Al-Shabaab.[35] Most of those who have been influenced by Islamic awakening were attached to specific mosques in Mogadishu and other towns in pre-civil war Somalia. However, such an observation overlooks the fact that the bulk of Al-Shabaab's membership was born after 1990.

The desire of some young men to lead an adventurous life also plays a role in the Al-Shabaab recruitment project. Viewed from this perspective, Al-Shabaab appears to be the 'anti-politics machine'[36] where teenage males could enact their manhood to make a change in an uncertain situation. Many young men in Mogadishu complain about their perceived powerless position and talk about the possibility of changing the status quo through violence. This resentment discourse is invariably powerful among younger elements of the Al-Shabaab fighting force.[37]

During the early stages of the civil war, many young men subscribed to the Islamist discourse that the solution to the Somali conflict could only be gleaned from the Islamic religion.[38] They did not join the pre-Al-Shabaab movements like Al-Itihaad Al-Islaami focused on local politics, but rather pursued a wider jihadi attachment to the Muslim world such as Afghanistan. The most powerful instrument used by Al-Shabaab for recruitment and justification is its religious discourse, which claims to oppose infidels who divided up Somalia into mini-states. The religious discourse discards the secular nationalist position, which pushes the religion element aside by attaching itself to the international community. Secular nationalism, in the Somali setting, can hardly work against the religious nationalism of Al-Shabaab. Indeed, the Ugandan leader Yoweri Museveni berated the Somali government in Mogadishu for the lack of a clear nationalist ideology to counter Al-Shabaab.[39] In fact, the government does not lack a nationalist ideology, but it lacks a clear religious nationalist ideology, even when counter-ideological religious messages against the insurgent movement are broadcast regularly on the government radio.

To confront the predominant Al-Shabaab religious discourse, the federal government enlisted higher *uluma* (religious scholars). However it could not chart a common and convincing – let alone an alternative and authentic discourse – that could successfully destroy Al-Shabaab's powerful call for jihad against the West and its Somali partners. Some Somalis continue to support Al-Shabaab purely for nationalist purposes because the activities of the insurgent movement appear to them as a national liberation. In Do'oleey, central Somalia, dozens of old men cheered in my presence when they heard on the radio that morning that Al-Shabaab had ambushed a convoy of Ethiopian forces, killing 19 of them at Leego, southern Somalia.[40] The attraction of Al-Shabaab's achievement to average elderly Somalis is illustrative of the combination of the nationalist cause and grievances against the neighbouring countries. The use of asymmetric attacks (suicide-bomb attacks and improvised explosive devices) is a prime, consistent war strategy for Al-Shabaab after hit-and-run tactics. Strikingly, when there is a political crisis in Mogadishu, Al-Shabaab puts its suicide attacks on hold to let the government and its opposition engage in political squabbles.[41] This invisible act directly connects Al-Shabaab to the national politics of Somalia.

Many Somali young men in Europe and America believe external powers have caused and continue to perpetuate the condition of Somalia as the most failed state on earth. They lament that their country has been captured by war profiteers who think of their own self-interest rather than that of the Somali people. As a result, many young men join Al-Shabaab to change the situation in southern Somalia by punishing those Somalis and non-Somalis they hold accountable for contributing to the collapsed state. Often young men talk about how they could change such an unnerving image of a failed state of Somalia, which wounds their personal pride and national belonging.[42] In one of her speeches in 2016, the former president of the Somali Central Bank Yusur Abraar has made an apt observation on the reality of what is currently happening in southern Somalia.[43] Despite her resignation (for some, a 'defection') from the government, Abraar raised a crucial point that the maladies of maladministration, corruption and the collapsed state condition feed into the grievances of the Somali youth in the West, urging them to have faith in the resurrection of their home country.[44] (Her reflections conform to the conclusion of the Fund for Peace's *Fragile States Index 2016* which has repeatedly ranked Somalia as the most failed and fragile state in the world for the eighth year in a row.[45]) This narrative is also crucial in the recruitment project of Al-Shabaab, because it provides youth and others joining Al-Shabaab with concrete evidence that an insurgency is the only alternative way to help the collapsed country. Harding observed that Al-Shabaab's 'ranks were soon swelled by earnest young men convinced the militants were, for all their faults, the only group prepared to defend the integrity of Somalia's borders and its honour'.[46]

The relationship between Al-Shabaab recruiters and recruits is based on top-down and bottom-up approaches. Hardcore Al-Shabaab members recruit their families and relatives using two important incentives: by persuading them to fight an Islamic *jihad* and by promising financial rewards. Al-Shabaab recruiters not only aim at recruiting unemployed and disposed youth, they also target orphaned children for recruitment. An Al-Shabaab defector pointed out that the insurgency movement resorted to recruiting local children because of the reduction of non-Somali fighters joining Al-Shabaab.[47] The most crucial moment for Al-Shabaab recruitment project occurred recently when hundreds of Somali youth (between 25- and 35-year-old) were deported forcefully from European countries, Saudi Arabia and the United States and returned to their communities in deep southern Somali towns and villages, especially the Jubbada Dhexe (Lower Jubba) and Shabeellaha Hoose (Lower Shabelle) regions. Feeling aggrieved, economically excluded and politically powerless, many of those repatriated young men fell under the sway of Al-Shabaab who used their Arabic and English language skills to advance their day to day intelligence gathering.[48] Critically, the government in Mogadishu had no plan to tackle such an exodus.

Al-Shabaab and the exploitation of clan

Many young men feel less discrimination from Al-Shabaab for their age or for their clan background than they do from the government.[49] Ambitious young recruits are granted political power to join the high command administrative leadership and military power structures of the movement. In contrast with the government's strategy which is based on a clan formula, Al-Shabaab abhors the notion of clan representation and within its institutional structure no clan group is side-lined in favour of another. Each clan is given consideration in the recruitment process. In this regard, Al-Shabaab distributes power and resources not through the normalised clan-based system in Somali politics, which has been loosely adopted by the government in Mogadishu, but through the support it receives. This is similar to a give-and-take mutual push/pull approach. By contrast, to join the government service, many young men need clan elders or political brokers to bring them to the government authorities to secure a minor position in the government. As one former Al-Shabaab defector simply put it, 'the government is clan-based, whereas Al-Shabaab is religion-based, not clan-based or even region-based.'[50] This does not mean that the insurgent movement avoids using the clan system for its own advantage.

Al-Shabaab exploits the grievances expressed by clans and communities who feel marginalised by the federal government (and by regional clan-based states). Many, if not most, local Al-Shabaab young members belong to those marginalised clans or communities. The former Mayor of Mogadishu Mohamoud 'Tarzan' Ahmed Nuur recounted publicly the story of a young Somali man from an unarmed clan who defected from the government to Al-Shabaab after suffering from clan discrimination and injustice.[51] The exclusion from power and resources is the main reason why many aggrieved young men adhere to Al-Shabaab's calls that the federal government authorities are *gaalo* (infidels) and *murtidiin* (apostles). Markus Hoehne has aptly observed that 'as long as any regime in Somalia will continue to be inimical to its own people – a life-and-death situation that will persist unless the governance system is renegotiated – insurgency groups like Al-Shabaab will easily find grounds for potential recruitment.'[52]

The existing literature has not explored the question of clan and other related cultural and political dynamics. Yet, one of the most significant aspects through which one can assess the Al-Shabaab recruitment project is the clan system, which is one of the most important parameters in Somali politics.[53] Understanding Al-Shabaab's membership poses a challenge to those who believe Somali politics and conflict can be explained through clan or class. Many Al-Shabaab fighters hail from regions to which they do not belong in terms of clan identification, a phenomenon suggesting the local communities in southern Somalia are not differentiating the insurgency from the foreign-supported government. What makes the Al-Shabaab recruitment project successful is also the lack of clan division among its cadres. Since the Somali Youth League (SYL), Al-Shabaab has been the first Somali organisation that effectively suppressed the divisive nature of the clan system. This also explains why no single Somali clan has defeated Al-Shabaab, including clan-based mini-state entities in southern Somalia which rely on Ethiopian or Kenyan support. By exploiting the clan system for their own benefit, Al-Shabaab tactically operationalises the clan card when it deems it necessary but avoids when the system leads to a destructive outcome.[54] The main reason why Ahlu-sunna wal Jame'a in central Somalia and other militias throughout the country are unable to effectively defeat Al-Shabaab can be found in the composition of clan mobilisation. While Al-Shabaab mobilises all Somali clans, Ahlu-sunna draws from specific clans, notably the Dir, the Habar Gidir and the Mareehaan clans.[55] Hizbul Islam, a defunct parallel movement, was also a cross-clan movement, but not as all-inclusive as Al-Shabaab. By contrast, recruits are trained to follow the strict Al-Shabaab position on the clan, which is to side with the movement in case one's clan poses a challenge to insurgency activities. Only when did they defect from the movement they can reunite their families and clansmen.[56]

The strategic exploitation of clan by Al-Shabaab is an essential element of survival, explaining why the movement rules vast areas inhabited by various clans. Interestingly, the Al-Shabaab insurgency is very weak in areas inhabited by one single clan, but remains powerful and strong in areas populated by diverse contesting clans.[57] Even though Al-Shabaab attempts to ignore clan politics, it reignites the long-held grievances among clans. Clan genealogies and clan grievances are exploited by Al-Shabaab as a way of maintaining its rule. Under Al-Shabaab territory, clans are given the possibility of adopting customary clan laws (*Xeer*) among themselves, but paradoxically Al-Shabaab authorities do not allow the same customary laws to judge between the clans.[58] This does not mean that Al-Shabaab depends on clans and their traditional leaders as a judiciary, but rather Al-Shabaab's avoidance of clan politics helps the militant movement to effectively administer and conduct its operations in Mogadishu and elsewhere. The clan dynamics frustrates the ideological goals of Al-Shabaab and, even when repressed or exploited, the clan card is not often useful for the continuation of the jihad.[59] Yet, one elder who lives in the midst of Al-Shabaab insisted that 'clannism exists in Al-Shabaab.'[60] Al-Shabaab uses the clan card when it suits for specific purposes. At times, Al-Shabaab leaders deliver well-crafted speeches and poems composed to praise those clan militias who have supported insurgency activities or to affront those clans who have resisted the jihadi cause.[61] At all times, Al-Shabaab deliberately displays the clan names of suicide bombers to encourage other clans to follow suit.

Apart from the Digil-Mirifle clan, the bulk of the Al-Shabaab rank and file in Shabeellaha Dhexe (Middle Shabelle) region comes from the historically marginalised communities such as the Bantu/Jareer, who are traditionally impermissible to intermarry with the Somali clans. A former Al-Shabaab defector disdainfully remarked that 'most of the people whom they [Al-Shabaab authorities] exploit are people who do not have power in the country.'[62] He pointed out that Al-Shabaab provides 'those who do not have power in the country' more political emancipation than they expect, socially empowering to marry to such "proud "Somali clans as the Hawiye and the Daarood. The Al-Shabaab defector reported how he witnessed the 'forced' marriage between a Bantu/Jareer young man and a young pretty Ogaadeen girl.[63] A young woman living in an Al-Shabaab-controlled area also recounted about her friend who was an Ogaadeen girl married by a Kenyan from the coastal area.[64] Al-Shabaab's marriage arrangements demonstrate that the insurgent movement discards the cultural Somali pastoralist notion of *'isma guursanno'* (we do not inter-marry) which defines the socio-economic relations between 'pure' Somalis and 'impure' Somalis. To counter the socio-political dominance of certain groups, it is Al-Shabaab's strategy to back up the less powerful actors of the Somali armed conflict who were often inclined to endorse extremism.[65]

Al-Shabaab's exploitation of clan is situational; whereas 'big' clans are suppressed to have a dominant role within Al-Shabaab's top leadership ladder, marginalised clans are given power in the sense that those who had oppressed them are punished to their satisfaction.[66] According to an Al-Shabaab defector, when Al-Shabaab is directly empowering the traditionally alienated and oppressed 'minority' clans and communities (the so-called 'Others'), it is indirectly alienating those 'powerful' and 'big' clans who perceive themselves as predominant and political actors, thus attracting more recruitment.[67] Whilst some clans were rewarded, others were beaten or punished, depending on a measurement of their stance on Al-Shabaab. When two clan militias clashed in Shabeellaha Hoose (Lower Shabelle) region in 2015, Al-Shabaab was quick to intervene and instruct its fighters to side with one of the fighting clan militia.[68] Joining Al-Shabaab is thus a way of reasserting power and privilege outside of the clan system but also helping one's clans against their rivals. This makes any attempt to attack Al-Shabaab on a clan basis impossible. In 2015, for example, clan leaders along with their clan militia attempted to flush out the movement in parts of Shabeellaha Dhexe (Lower Shabelle) and Galguduud regions. The clan leaders were beaten and their militias ran away and abandoned the army vehicles given to them by the Mogadishu authorities. The federal government continues to be powerless to resolve conflicts among clans under its orbit.[69] As a female officer in the government army pointed out:

> You may see captured Al-Shabaab [individual] who is said he hailed from *reer hebel* (clan so and so). People do not have confidence in the government, because it is lineage-based, clan-based, women are raped, people are robbed or extorted. [Al-]Shabaab has a place to complain against [any crimes] but the government has no place to complain, there is no [real] government, if somebody who is a soldier dies that is it, the dead among [Al-]Shabaab is compensated, I conversed with [Al-]Shabaab defectors, there is a rule of law among them, [on the other hand] the government army is divided along clan brigades and it is difficult to unite them, they operate as clan units, there is no real chain of command, the rule of law is so weak that order is taken from any officer from the presidential palace.[70]

Al-Shabaab has instrumentalized the Somali clan structure much better than the government. Most of the Al-Shabaab-controlled areas are populated by inter-riverine communities, who although known for their peaceful inclinations, feel grievances against the government, in contrast with pastoral nomadic clans who constitute the bulk of the governments' fighting force. Taking advantage of clan marginalisation to advance its insurgency activities, Al-Shabaab encourages government defectors to join in order to resist political marginalisation by using its calls for jihad against aggressors and oppressors. For example, two government officers, with their military vehicles, defected to Al-Shabaab from their army stations in Afgooye.[71]

A key question is what prevents young men recruited by Al-Shabaab defecting to the Mogadishu government? The federal government describe recruited Al-Shabaab fighters as *'kuwa la qalday'* (those who were indoctrinated).[72] According to one former Al-Shabaab defector, many recruits are wary of defecting to the government side for fear of reprisals for the crimes they committed while fighting for Al-Shabaab.[73] As a result, they have no choice other than to stay in Al-Shabaab and wait for their final fate, or to flee and migrate to the Middle East (mainly Saudi Arabia and Yemen) or Europe. Conversely, a small number of individuals with the Mogadishu government join Al-Shabaab because they have been involved in criminal activities within the army or security apparatus. Between 2009 and 2012 many officers trained in Djibouti or Uganda by American, French, German and other trainers joined Al-Shabaab in senior positions after being discovered committing crimes like selling army equipment to Al-Shabaab.[74]

Conclusion

The scholarship on Al-Shabaab has tended to emphasise the role of identity and economics in the Al-Shabaab recruitment project. Recent studies, for example, have mentioned the significance of the Al-Shabaab recruitment project, but rarely discussed the various methods of this recruitment.[75] The article has assessed the cultural, economic and religious aspects of Al-Shabaab's recruitment project. In so doing, it has examined the many ways in which the militant movement succeeds in recruiting fighters from various Somali communities inhabiting the areas of war-torn southern Somalia that are broadly under its control. The article has identified various ways through which Al-Shabaab recruits fighters, noting that recruitment varies, depending on the desires and determinations of those who join the insurgent movement as well as the needs of the insurgent movement itself. Other structural factors like economic insecurity also create conditions for young men to join Al-Shabaab.

The evidence presented here suggests that it is not necessarily unemployment or impoverishment, but other enduring underlying factors which are more prominent in southern Somalia. While the youths who joined and fought for Al-Shabaab as a militia have been driven by various factors, the most important factors in southern Somalia are political marginalisation and religious indoctrination, which contribute to personal or communal grievances, leading to successful recruitment for Al-Shabaab. This uncertain situation is exacerbated by clan politics, resulting in inclusion or exclusion. The existence of unequal political power and socio-economic status has made young local Somali men prone to extremist ideologies of empowering marginalised clans and communities and punishing those who accumulated wealth through the government's patronage system. This delineation is not clear cut, though, because there are some within the 'powerful' clans who are marginalised within the government system. But the lack of political and socio-economic justice assists the Al-Shabaab's various strategies to attract recruits. This does not mean that the clan identity is weak in Al-Shabaab as suggested by some studies. Clans are crucial within Al-Shabaab, which both activates and deactivates depending on its needs. Unlike the government, Al-Shabaab pursues a recruitment process based on both personal and clan interests, and this undoubtedly deserves further empirical research. The defection between the government and Al-Shabaab also warrants further investigation.

Notes

1. Interviews with A. G. and M. M., Al-Shabaab defectors, Mogadishu, Somalia, 6 May 2016.
2. Hansen, *Al-Shabaab in Somalia*.
3. Hellsten, "Radicalisation and Terrorist Recruitment"; and Meleagrou-Hitchens, "ICSR Insight – Al-Shabaab." One exception is Botha, and Abdile, "Radicalisation and al-Shabaab Recruitment."
4. Botha, "Political Socialization"; and Joosse, Bucerius, and Thompson, "Narratives and Counternarratives."
5. Keen, "The Economic Functions."
6. Hansen, *Al-Shabaab in Somalia*; and Marchal, "A Tentative Assessment."
7. Ibid.
8. It should be cautious that stories often provided by Al-Shabaab defectors can be reliable on a research study or other purposes unless employed with critical analysis or used other sources for triangulation.
9. Focus group discussions, Mogadishu, April and July 2016.
10. Ingiriis, "From Al-Itihaad to Al-Shabaab," 2033–52; and Ingiriis, "The Invention of Al-Shabaab in Somalia," 217–37.
11. Almeida, *Social Movements*, 9.
12. Higazi, "Social Mobilization and Collective Violence," 107–35.
13. See note 10 above.
14. Hellsten, "Radicalisation and Terrorist Recruitment"; Meleagrou-Hitchens, "ICSR Insight – Al-Shabaab"; and *Sunday Nation*, "How Poverty and Search for Identity."
15. Fund for Peace, "Fragile States Index."
16. Hansen, *Al-Shabaab in Somalia*, 2, 9, 19, 28, 45.
17. *Waxsansheeg*, "Halkan Ka Daawo."
18. Fieldwork ethnographic observations in Hargeysa (Somaliland), July–August 2016 and April–May 2018.
19. *YouTube*, "Daawo warbixin cajiib ah."
20. Anonymous, "Banana Wars in Somalia." See Little, *Somalia: Economy without State*; Marchal, "Monetary Illegalism and Civil War"; and Mubarak, "The 'Hidden Hand'."
21. "La Guerre à Mogadiscio," 120–5. For the background of the 1990s clanised conflicts, see Caddow, *Somalia*. For the radicalisation of Islam in Somalia, see Adam, "Islam and Politics in Somalia"; Menkhaus, "Political Islam in Somalia."

22. Bakonyi, "Between Protest, Revenge and Material Interests."
23. Interview with Al-Shabaab defectors, Mogadishu, Somalia, 4 May 2016.
24. Interview with Al-Shabaab defectors, Mogadishu, Somalia, April-May 2016. Markus Hoehne noted that there are "many young people who have been lured into joining the group based on religious rhetoric as well as forcibly recruited ones and others who joined for the sake of getting a regular salary. There is also a core of more dedicated fighters, some of who[m] are Somali, others are foreigners." Hoehne, "No Intervention!" 8. As Marchal noted, forced recruitment is the exception, not the norm. Marchal, "The Rise of a Jihadi Movement," 40.
25. *Jariiban News*, "Wiil Ka Mid ah Maxaabiistii Deegaanka Garacad."
26. Check, "Radical Movements and their Recruitment Strategies"; Gurr, *Why Men Rebel*.
27. Interview with A. A. M., Mogadishu, Somalia, 6 May 2016.
28. Conversations with family members, including the mother, March 2012 and again May 2019.
29. ICG, "The Islamic State Threat in Somalia's Puntland State."
30. Interview with Al-Shabaab defectors, Mogadishu, Somalia, 4 May 2016; interview with Al-Shabaab defectors, Mogadishu, Somalia, 6 May 2016. For a theoretical understanding of the will to die for a cause, see Bloom, *Dying to Kill*.
31. Marchal, "A Tentative Assessment," 394. See also Bryden, "The Reinvention of Al-Shabaab."
32. Hansen, "Somalia – Grievance, Religion, Clan, and Profit," 127–38. See also Duckitt and Sibley, "Personality, Ideology, Prejudice, and Politics," 1869.
33. Interview with Al-Shabaab defectors, Mogadishu, Somalia, 4 May 2016; and interview with Al-Shabaab defectors, Mogadishu, Somalia, 6 May 2016; *ENCA*, "Somali Street Kids Lured into Al-Shabaab."
34. Interview with C. A. H., Afgooye, via IMO from Afgooye, Somalia, 8 March 2017. In neighbouring Kenya, one study found that 71.5% of Al-Shabaab did not complete secondary level of education, chapter three and none of the returnees (156 in total) interviewed in the study had university level of education. *Working with the National Government and Coastal Counties*.
35. Interview with A. T., London, 18 June 2017.
36. Ferguson, *The Anti-Politics of Machine*.
37. Interview with Al-Shabaab defectors, Mogadishu, Somalia, 4 May 2016; interview with Al-Shabaab defectors, Mogadishu, Somalia, 6 May 2016.
38. Ingiriis, "The Invention of Al-Shabaab in Somalia."
39. *New Vision*, "Lack of Ideology is Somalia's Problem." On counter-ideological attempts, see Abdullah, "Merits and Limits of Counter-ideological Work."
40. Fieldwork ethnographic observations, Do'oleey, central Somalia, 1 June 2015.
41. Fieldwork ethnographic observations, Mogadishu, May-September 2015, April-August 2016, September-October 2017 and February-June 2018.
42. *Madasha Barbaarta TV*, "Deg deg waano cajiib ah."
43. *YouTube*, "yusra abraar oo cadeeysey."
44. Ibid.
45. See also Fund for Peace, "Fragile States Index."
46. Harding, *The Mayor of Mogadishu*, 164. As Harding recorded: "One of the Al Shabab fighters was a slim, soft-spoken twenty-one year old called Hanad. He'd joined four years earlier, tempted by the prospect of a job and an income. To

begin with, he was told he could have no contact with his family, but, in the chaos of Mogadishu, the rules about mobile phones were harder to enforce, and Hanad had finally called his brother Mohamed. It turned out that Mohamed had joined Somalia's new national army, and was now fighting in the very same sector in Mogadishu," 179.
47. Ibid. It is estimated that 'over half its force are children'. The UN Secretary-General Antonio Guterres said he was 'alarmed at reports that children may constitute a large part of the force recruited and used by al-Shabaab'. Drawing from a UN report, Guterres added that Al-Shabaab 'used children in combat, with nine-year-olds reportedly taught to use weapons and sent to front lines. Children were also used to transport explosives, work as spies, carry ammunition or perform domestic chores'. The report mentioned that, even though Al-Shabaab 'was the main perpetrator... the Somali National Army (SNA) and other groups also recruited and used children'. See *Africa Research Bulletin*, "SOMALIA: Al-Shabaab Forces Target Youth." Compare Human Rights Watch, "'It's like We're Always in Prison.'".
48. Interview with A. A. M., IMO interview from Mogadishu, Somalia, 16 December 2016.
49. Interview with Al-Shabaab defectors, Mogadishu, Somalia, April-May 2016.
50. Interview with A. A. M., Mogadishu, Somalia, 10 May 2016. On how the clan structure and the political system in Mogadishu intersect and often overlap, see Ingiriis, 'Politics as a Profitable Business'.
51. *YouTube*, "Tarsan oo sheegay in musuq-maasuqa dalka ka jira uu ka khatarsan yahay Al-Shabaab."
52. Hoehne, "No Intervention!" 8.
53. Laitin and Samatar, *Somalia*; and Lewis, *Blood and Bone*.
54. Interview with A. A. H., an Al-Shabaab defector, Mogadishu, Somalia, 4 May 2016.
55. Di Domenicantonio, "'With God on Our Side'"; and Marchal and Sheikh, "Ahlu Sunna wa l-Jama'a in Somalia."
56. During the parliamentary election preparations in mid-2016, I observed a meeting between members of the Udeejeen clan, the clan of the first Somali president, where a defector of Al-Shabaab had attended to support the candidacy for the parliament of the former mayor of Mogadishu Mohamoud Ahmed Nur "Tarzan." I met the defector who was among my former interviewees as soon as he came out of the conference. Observations, Hotel Afrik, Mogadishu, 13 May 2016.
57. Interview with A. A. H., an Al-Shabaab defector, Mogadishu, Somalia, 6 May 2016. For overviews on how Al-Shabaab uses religious and clan ideologies simultaneously, see Anderson and McKnight, "Understanding al-Shabaab"; Solomon, "Somalia's Al Shabaab." Marchal seems to surprise that the Jareer received equal representation under Al-Shabaab, so much so in comparison to one dominant Hawiye sub-clan in Jowhar. Cited in Hansen, *Al-Shabaab in Somalia*, 80.
58. There are reports from Al-Shabaab-held areas that clan elders are issued identification cards. See *Caasimada.net*, "Kaararka Aqoonsiga."
59. Focus group discussions held with Afgooye residents in Somalia between 18 and 21 May 2010 and 11 September 2015. For a review, see Ingiriis, 'Review '*Al-Shabaab in Somalia*'. For Al-Shabaab and clannism, see Anderson and McKnight, 'Understanding al-Shabaab'. On the politicisation of clan and clanship, see

Barnes, "*U dhashay, Ku Dhashay*"; Luling, "Genealogy as Theory"; and Mohamed, "Kinship and Contract in Somali Politics."
60. Interview with H. S., Mogadishu, Somalia, 27 February 2018. Hansen has contended that clannism is very weak, quite expectedly, among Al-Shabaab. Hansen, *Al-Shabaab in Somalia*, 45.
61. *Voice of Somalia*, "Gabay. Hawiye Ganato Weeyaane."
62. Interview with A. A. M., Mogadishu, Somalia, 4 May 2016.
63. Ibid.
64. Telephone conversations with F. A. D., 2 July 2015.
65. Marchal, "Joining al-Shabaab in Somalia."
66. Interview with Al-Shabaab defectors, Mogadishu, Somalia, 5 May 2016; and *Caasimada.net*, "Al Shabaab oo caana[-]shubtay."
67. See note 54 above.
68. Focus group discussions held with Afgooye residents in Somalia between 18 and 21 May 2010 and 11 September 2015.
69. Human Rights Watch, "Clashes in Galkayo, Somalia Harm Civilians"; UNSOM, "Press Release"; and *Villa Somalia*, "Press Statement."
70. Interview with F. I. E., female army officer, Mogadishu, Somalia, 3 and 5 July 2016.
71. *Caasimada.net*, "Sawir: Ciidamo ka tirsan."
72. Interview with government authorities, Mogadishu, May-September 2015 and April-July 2016.
73. See note 62 above.
74. *WARSOM*, "Ciidamo lyo Gaadiid Ka Soo Baxsaday Dowlad TFG-da."
75. Hassan, "Understanding Drivers of Violent Extremism"; Ingiriis, "Al-Shabaab's Youth Recruitment Project"; and Marchal, "Joining al-Shabaab in Somalia."

Disclosure statement

No potential conflict of interest was reported by the author.

Bibliography

Abdullah, Walid Jumblatt. "Merits and Limits of Counter-ideological Work against Terrorism: A Critical Appraisal." *Small Wars & Insurgencies* 28, no. 2 (2017): 291–308. doi:10.1080/09592318.2017.1288401.

Adam, Hussein M. "Islam and Politics in Somalia." *Journal of Islamic Studies* 6, no. 2 (1995): 189–221. doi:10.1093/jis/6.2.189.

Almeida, Paul. *Social Movements: The Structure of Collective Mobilization*. Oakland, CA: University of California Press, 2019.

Anderson, David M., and Jacob McKnight. "Understanding al-Shabaab: Clan, Islam and Insurgency in Kenya." *Journal of Eastern African Studies* 9, no. 3 (2015): 536–557. doi:10.1080/17531055.2015.1082254.

Anonymous. "Banana Wars in Somalia." *Review of African Political Economy* 22, no. 64 (1995): 274–275. doi:10.1080/03056249508704133.

Bakonyi, Jutta. "Between Protest, Revenge and Material Interests: A Phenomenological Analysis of Looting in the Somali War." *Disasters* 34, no. 2 (2010): 238–255. doi:10.1111/j.1467-7717.2010.01156.x.

Barnes, Cedric. "*U Dhashay, Ku Dhashay*: Genealogical and Territorial Discourse in Somali History." *Social Identities* 12, no. 4 (2006): 487–498. doi:10.1080/13504630600823718.

Bloom, Mia. *Dying to Kill: The Allure of Suicide Terror*. New York: Columbia University Press, 2005.

Botha, Anneli. "Political Socialization and Terrorist Radicalization among Individuals Who Joined Al-Shabaab in Kenya." *Studies in Conflict & Terrorism* 37, no. 11 (2014): 895–919. doi:10.1080/1057610X.2014.952511.

Botha, Anneli, and Mahdi. Abdile. "Radicalisation and al-Shabaab Recruitment in Somalia." *Institute for Security Studies* no. 265 (2014). September 28.

BRICS East Africa Project. 2016. Working with the National Government and Coastal Counties to counter violent extremism in the Coast Region of Kenya, Taita Taveta University College.

Bryden, Matt. 2014. "The Reinvention of Al-Shabaab: A Strategy of Choice or Necessity?" Washington, DC: CSIS, February.

Caasimada.net. 2017. "Sawir: Ciidamo ka tirsan Dowlada FS oo isku dhiibay Kooxda al-Shabaab." April 13. http://www.caasimada.net/ciidamo-ka-tirsan-dowlada-fs-oo-isku-dhiibay-kooxda-al-shabaab/

Caasimada.net. 2017. "Al Shabaab oo caana[-]shubtay Imaamka beesha Mudullood ee deegaanada ay maamulaan." July 6. https://www.caasimada.net/al-shabaab-oo-caana-shubtay-imaamka-beesha-mudullood-ee-deegaanada-ay-maamulaan/

Caasimada.net. "Kaararka Aqoonsiga ee odayaasha taageera [Al-] Shabaab oo la soo bandhigay." Accessed September 3, 2018. https://www.caasimada.net/shabaab-oo-bilaabay-inay-diiwaan-geliyaan-magacyada-qabiilada-iyo-deegaanada-ay-kasoo-jeedaan-odayaasha-shabeelada-hoose/

Caddow, Axmed Jilao. *Somalia: Gelbiskii geerida*. N.P., N.P., 2001.

Check, Nicasius Achu. "Radical Movements and Their Recruitment Strategies in Africa Some Theoretical Assumptions." *Africa Insight* 46, no. 3 (2016): 67–82.

Di Domenicantonio, Giulio. "'With God on Our Side': A Focus on Ahlu Sunna Waljama'A, A Sufi Somali Paramilitary Group." *The Annual Review of Islam in Africa*, no. 12/13 (2015–2016): 64–69.

Duckitt, John, and Chris G. Sibley. "Personality, Ideology, Prejudice, and Politics: A Dual-Process Motivational Model." *Journal of Personality* 78, no. 6 (2010): 1861–1894. doi:10.1111/j.1467-6494.2010.00672.x.

Editors. "Somalia: Al-Shabaab Forces Target Youth." *Africa Research Bulletin* 54, no. 1 (2017): 21298B–21300A. doi:10.1111/j.1467-825X.2017.07476.x.

ENCA. 2017. "Somali Street Kids Lured into Al-Shabaab." June 19.

Ferguson, James. *The Anti-Politics of Machine: "Development', Depoliticization, and Bureaucratic Power in Lesotho*. Cambridge: Cambridge University Press, 1990.

Fund for Peace. 2016. "Fragile States Index." Washington, DC.

Gurr, Tedd R. *Why Men Rebel*. Princeton: Princeton University Press, 1970.

Hansen, Stig Jarle. "Somalia – Grievance, Religion, Clan, and Profit." In *The Borders of Islam: Exploring Samuel Hunting's Faultlines, from Al-Andalus to the Virtual Ummah*, edited by Stig Jarle Hansen, Atle Messoy, and Tuncay Kardas, 127–138. London: Hurst, 2009.

Hansen, Stig Jarle. "Somalia – Grievance, Religion, Clan, and Profit." In *The Borders of Islam: Exploring Samuel Hunting's Faultlines, from Al-Andalus to the Virtual Ummah*, edited by Stig Jarle Hansen, Atle Messoy, and Tuncay Kardas, 127–138. London: Hurst, 2009.

Hansen, Stig Jarle. *Al-Shabaab in Somalia: The History and Ideology of a Militant Islamist Group, 2005–2012*. London: Hurst, 2013.

Harding, Andrew. *The Mayor of Mogadishu: A Story of Chaos and Redemption in the Ruins of Somalia*. London: Hurst, 2016.

Hassan, Muhsin. "Understanding Drivers of Violent Extremism: The Case of al-Shabab and Somali Youth." *CT Sentinel* 5, no. 8 (2012): 18–20.

Hellsten, Sirkku. 2016. "Radicalisation and Terrorist Recruitment among Kenya's Youth." The Nordic Africa Institute, February.

Higazi, Adam. "Social Mobilization and Collective Violence: Vigilantes and Militias in the Lowlands of Plateau State, Central Nigeria." *Africa* 78, no. 1 (2011): 107–135. doi:10.3366/E0001972008000077.

Hoehne, Markus Virgil. "No Intervention! the Way Forward in Somalia." *Horn of Africa Bulletin* 24, no. 2 (2012): 8–11.

Human Rights Watch. 2016. "Clashes in Galkayo, Somalia Harm Civilians – Tens of Thousands Displaced by Three Weeks of Fighting." Nairobi, October 25.

Human Rights Watch. 2018. "'It's like We're Always in Prison': Abuses against Boys Accused of National Security Offences in Somalia." February 21.

Ingiriis, Mohamed Haji. "Review '*Al-shabaab in Somalia: The History and Ideology of a Militant Islamist Group, 2005–2012*, by Stig Jarle Hansen." *African Affairs* 113, no. 451 (2014): 327–329. doi:10.1093/afraf/adu007.

Ingiriis, Mohamed Haji. "Politics as a Profitable Business: Patronage, Patrimony, Predation, and Primordial Power in Contemporary Somalia." *Journal of Somali Studies* 2, no. 1–3 (2015): 67–97.

Ingiriis, Mohamed Haji. "Al-Shabaab's Youth Recruitment Project." In *War and Peace in Somalia: National Grievances, Local Conflict and Al-Shabaab*, edited by Michael Keating and Matt Waldman, 339–348. London: Hurst, 2018.

Ingiriis, Mohamed Haji. "From Al-Itihaad to Al-Shabaab: How the Ethiopian Intervention and the 'War on Terror' Exacerbated the Conflict in Somalia." *Third World Quarterly* 39, no. 11 (2018): 2033–2052. doi:10.1080/01436597.2018.1479186.

Ingiriis, Mohamed Haji. "The Invention of Al-Shabaab in Somalia: Emulating the Anti-Colonial the Dervish Movement." *African Affairs* 117, no. 467 (2018): 217–237. doi:10.1093/afraf/ady001.

International Crisis Group. 2016. "The Islamic State Threat in Somalia's Puntland State." *Africa Briefing*, October 26. https://www.crisisgroup.org/africa/horn-africa/somalia/islamic-state-threat-somalias-puntland-state

Jariiban News. 2016. "Wiil Ka Mid ah Maxaabiistii Deegaanka Garacad." https://www.youtube.com/watch?v=DTbMRCDXTCQ

Joosse, Paul, Sandra M. Bucerius, and Sara K. Thompson. "Narratives and Counternarratives: Somali-Canadians on Recruitment as Foreign Fighters to Al-Shabaab." *British Journal of Criminology* 55 (2015): 811–832. doi:10.1093/bjc/azu103.

Keen, David. 1998. "The Economic Functions of Violence in Civil Wars." *Adelphi Paper* 320. London: Oxford University Press for the International Institute for Strategic Studies.

Laitin, David D., and Said S. Samatar. *Somalia: Nation in Search of a State*. London: Gower, 1987.

Lewis, I. M. *Blood and Bone: The Call of Kinship in Somali Society*. Trenton, N.J.: The Red Sea Press, 1994.

Little, Peter D. *Somalia: Economy without State*. Oxford: James Currey, 2003.

Luling, Virginia. "Genealogy as Theory, Genealogy as Tool: Aspects of Somali 'Clanship'." *Social Identities* 12, no. 4 (2006): 471–485. doi:10.1080/13504630600823692.

Madasha Barbaarta TV. 2017. "Deg deg waano cajiib ah oo ka timi dhalinyaro kuna socota dhalinyarada." https://www.youtube.com/watch?v=Xb7xAIwuWPQ

Marchal, Roland. "La Guerre à Mogadiscio." *Politique Africaine* 46 (1992): 120–125.

Marchal, Roland. "A Tentative Assessment of the Somali *Harakat Al-Shabaab*." *Journal of Eastern African Studies* 3, no. 3 (2009): 381–404. doi:10.1080/17531050903273701.

Marchal, Roland. "Monetary Illegalism and Civil War: The Case of Somalia." In *Organized Crimes and States: The Hidden Faces of Politics*, edited by Jean-Louis Briquet and Gilles Favarel-Garrrigues, 221–246. New York: Palgrave Macmillan, 2010.

Marchal, Roland. 2011. "The Rise of a Jihadi Movement in a Country at War: Harakat Al Shabaab Al Mujaheddin in Somalia." CERI Research Paper, Sciences Bo, Paris, March.

Marchal, Roland. "Joining al-Shabaab in Somalia." In *Contextualising Jihadi Thought*, edited by Jeevan Deol and Zaheer Kazmi, 259–274. London: Hurst, 2012.

Marchal, Roland, and Zakaria M. Sheikh. "Ahlu Sunna Wa l-Jama'a in Somalia." In *Muslim Ethiopia: The Christian Legacy, Identity Politics and Islamic Reformism*, edited by Patrick Desplat and Terje Østebø, 215–239. New York: Palgrave, 2013.

Meleagrou-Hitchens, Alexander. 2014. "ICSR Insight – Al-Shabaab: Recruitment and Radicalisation in Kenya." International Centre for the Study of Radicalisation, King's College London.

Menkhaus, Ken. "Political Islam in Somalia." *Middle East Policy* 9, no. 1 (2002): 109–123. doi:10.1111/mepo.2002.9.issue-1.

Mohamed, Jama. "Kinship and Contract in Somali Politics." *Africa* 77, no. 2 (2007): 226–249. doi:10.3366/afr.2007.77.2.226.

Mubarak, Jamil A. "The 'Hidden Hand' behind the Resilience of the Stateless Economy of Somalia." *World Development* 25, no. 12 (1997): 2027–2041. doi:10.1016/S0305-750X(97)00104-6.

New Vision. 2016. "Lack of Ideology Is Somalia's Problem." November 3.

Solomon, Hussein. "Somalia's Al Shabaab: Clans vs Islamist Nationalism." *South African Journal of International Affairs* 21, no. 3 (2014): 351–366. doi:10.1080/10220461.2014.967286.

Sunday Nation. 2014. "How Poverty and Search for Identity Drive Youth into Terrorism." August 10.

UNSOM. 2016. "Press Release: SRSG Keating Welcomes Agreement Reached in Abu Dhabi to Defuse Crisis in Gaalkacyo." November 3.
Villa Somalia. 2016. "Press Statement: Somali President Welcomes the Abu Dhabi Peace Agreement Signed by Puntland and Mudug over Galkayo Conflict." November 3.
Voice of Somalia. 2016. "Gabay. Hawiye Ganato Weeyaane." https://www.youtube.com/watch?v=5f6aTICQNRg
WARSOM. 2011. "Ciidamo Iyo Gaadiid Ka Soo Baxsaday Dowlad TFG-da Oo U Goostay Xarakada Al-shabaab." September 17. http://warsom.com/wararka/2011/09/ciidamo-iyo-gaadiid-ka-soo-baxsaday-dowlad-tfg-da-oo-u-goostay-xarakada-al-shabaab/
Waxsansheeg. 2016. "Halkan Ka Daawo: WasaaradaDhalinyarada SOMALILAND oo Ka Hadashay Tahriibka Dhalinta." April 20. http://waxsansheeg.com/?p=66214
YouTube. 2014. "Daawo warbixin cajiib ah: Taariikhda Axmed Godane iyo mustaqbalka Al-Shabaab dilkiisa kadib." https://www.youtube.com/watch?v=YQsGz-ReQA4 (between min. 13:00 and 13:27).
YouTube. 2016. "Yusra Abraar Oo Cadeeysey Lacagta Somali Loogu Talagaley Meelaha Ay Ku Baxdo Q 1aad." https://www.youtube.com/watch?v=sP1bl6l16z8
YouTube. 2016. "Tarsan oo sheegay in musuq-maasuqa dalka ka jira uu ka khatarsan yahay Al-Shabaab." https://www.youtube.com/watch?v=k8Lo4A16siM

Index

Note: Footnotes are indicated by an "n" and the footnote number after the page number e.g., 47n66 refers to footnote 66 on page 47.

95 key leader engagements 125–130

AAA (American Anthropological Association) 37, 84
Abraar, Yusur 221
acceptance 58, 128, 132, 155
Accidental Guerilla, The 61
advise-and-assist missions 4, 5, 122, 124, 126, 127, 132, 134–135
Afghanistan 2, 4, 5–6, 9, 38, 76–93, 123; and archaeology 35, 37, 38, 40, 42, 43, 47n66; Major Jim Gant in 139–162, 160n8
Afzal, Nur 144, 147–149, 151, 152, 153, 156, 157, 158, 159, 161n24
agency 172, 200
Alain (Emile Chartier) 173
al-Anbar *see* Anbar province, of Iraq
al-Baghdadi, Abu Umar 65, 198, 199, 200, 202, 203
Albu Mahal tribe 197, 207n33
al-Muhajir, Abu Hamza 198, 199–200, 202
Al-Qaeda in Iraq (AQI) 6, 64, 65–66, 68, 199
Al-Shabaab 7, 213–230
al-Utaybi, Abu Sulayman 198–199
al-Zarqawi, Abu Mus'ab 65, 195
American anthropology 37, 55, 84, 167, 168–169, 170
American liberalism 176–182
American neo-colonialism 181
American social science 168–172
'American Way of War' 9, 169
Analysis of the Islamic State of Iraq 196–197, 197–198
Anbar province 64, 65–66; Islamic State tribal engagement 193–194, 195, 196, 197, 198, 202, 206n12, 206n13;

Norwegian mentoring mission 122, 123, 125, 126, 127, 129
Angkor Wat 41
Ani Maamin liturgy incident 95, 96, 111n4
anthropology: American 37, 55, 84, 167, 168–169, 170; applied 192; combat 9–25; cultural 84, 100; military 1, 2, 3–4, 5, 7, 91; professional 10, 32, 36, 42; of war 1, 5–6, 7
anti-Huk campaign 17, 19
anting-anting 15, 17
anti-politics machine, Al Shabaab as 220
antiquities 35, 36, 45; acquisition of 31, 33, 36; damage to/destruction of 39; expropriation of 3, 34, 44, 201; looting/ trafficking of 29, 31, 40, 43, 44
anti-Shia identity 65
applied anthropology 192
AQI (Al-Qaeda in Iraq) 6, 64, 65–66, 68, 199
archaeology 28, 29, 31, 37, 38, 40, 44, 45, 91; battlefield 31, 42–43, 45; forensic 41; and heritage tourism 40–41; military relationship with 29–30, 31, 32, 35, 36, 37, 38, 44; rehabilitation 42; traditional 41–42
archival research 2
armed violence 217–218
Army of the Republic of Vietnam (ARVN) 19, 166, 170, 181
assassination campaign, of Islamic State of Iraq 197–198
asymmetrical warfare 43, 140, 221; and Israel Defense Forces 95–114
Atran, Scott 55, 56, 58, 60, 68

Awakening, Sunni 6, 64, 66, 220; Islamic State tribal engagement 192, 194, 195, 196, 197, 198, 199, 200, 201, 202, 203, 206–207n23, 207n34; Jihadist Councils 7, 201

Balkan conflicts 38
Bamian Buddhas 3, 38
Barney-style communication 89–91
battlefield archaeology 31, 42–43, 45
battlespace 29, 30, 44, 83, 84, 85, 86–87
belonging 55–56, 58, 60, 61, 67, 221
betrayal 157, 192, 196, 199–201
bifurcation, of archaeology-military relationship 29–30, 38–44
Black Skins, White Masks 180
Bohannan, Lieutenant-Colonel Charles Ted Routledge (Charles T. R.) 2–3, 9–11, 20–25; academic work of 14–15; education of 11–13; expeditions of 13–14; mentors of 13–14; in Philippines 15–18; in Second World War 14–15; in Vietnam 19–20
bonding 83
Book of Changes (I Ching) 179–180
Bourdieu, Pierre 128
Breslov Hasidism 104–105
Byman, Daniel 60

caliphate 65–66, 191, 192, 196, 202, 204, 206n17
camaraderie 42, 55, 58
Cambodia 38, 41
CAOCL (Marine Corps Culture Center) 77–78, 79, 80, 81, 82
capacities 125, 128, 129, 132
capital in a social field 128, 129, 132
capitalism 58
'carrot and stick' approach 197, 198, 199
Carter, Defense Secretary Ash 124
chaos, of combat 95, 97, 99–100, 105, 111
Chartier, Emile (Alain) 173
China 15, 35, 37, 40, 44; in *Fire in the Lake* 166, 169, 170, 175–176, 177, 178, 182
Choice of Path in Norwegian Foreign and Security Policy 123
Cigar, Norman 198, 202, 205
clan system 215, 222, 223, 225
Clausewitz, Carl von 121–122, 127, 133–134
Coalition, against Islamic State of Iraq and the Levant 4, 6, 28, 142, 195, 197; and collective identity building 62, 63–64, 65, 66, 68, 69; and Norwegian mentoring mission 121, 122, 126, 128–129; Provisional Authority (CPA) of 62, 63

cognitive dissonance 196–197
cohesion 4, 60, 97, 101, 102, 104, 106, 176, 193
COIN *see* counterinsurgency (COIN)
Cold War 10, 37, 38, 41, 166, 168, 181
collaboration 194, 200, 201
collateral damage 202, 205
collective identity 3, 55–71
colonialism 31, 34, 36; in *Fire in the Lake* 167, 174, 180, 181, 182, 185n78
combat anthropology 9–25
combat assets 84, 91
combat operations 14, 21, 139, 141; of Israeli Defense Force 96, 98, 102, 104, 105, 107, 110
combat risk 109–110
common destiny 67, 69
Communist revolution 170, 175, 177
comparative sociology, of revolutionary change 179
competencies 32, 126, 127, 128, 130, 133
Confucianism 6, 164–165, 167–168, 174, 175, 179, 180
constitution (governance) 63, 68
contractors 80–81, 83
conventional warfare 10, 62, 64, 167
Counter Guerrilla Operations: the Philippines Experience 10, 20
counter-Awakening campaign 204–205
counter-guerrilla warfare 16, 166
counterinsurgency (COIN): campaigns 6, 182; collective identity building in 55–71; strategy 56; *see also* Afghanistan; Iraq
Counterinsurgency Field Manual (FM 3–24) 60, 61, 140, 143
CPA (Coalition Provisional Authority) 62, 63
cross-cultural issues 4, 76, 77, 83
Crusader violence 200
culture 166, 167, 191, 194, 215; Afghan 38, 47n66, 78, 82–83; analysis of 85–87; anthropology of 84, 100; differences 59, 76, 77, 79, 83, 91, 131; expertise in 76, 77, 79, 80, 83–85, 87, 89, 90, 91, 92; heritage 3, 28, 30, 31, 37, 38, 39, 42, 43, 44, 45; of honest self-assessment 201; Iraqi 129; knowledge of 77, 78, 80, 83, 84, 129, 131, 191, 205; subject matter experts (SMEs) 76, 77, 79, 80, 83–85, 87, 89, 90, 91, 92; terrain of 86–87; tourism 37, 39; training in 76, 77, 80, 90, 91; understanding of 77, 78, 80, 83, 84, 129, 131, 191, 205; Vietnamese *see* Vietnamese culture

DDR (disarmament, demobilization, and reintegration) programs 40–41
decolonization 31, 181
defectors 7, 213, 215, 218–219, 220, 222, 224, 225, 226, 227n8
defensive jihad 65
Delegated Committee 199, 204
demography 79, 90, 215
destruction, of material cultural heritage 3, 28, 29, 30, 31, 37, 38–39, 44, 45
development projects 67
diaspora youth 219
Diệm, President Ngô Đình 19, 20
Diem regime 169, 170–171, 178, 179
disarmament, demobilization, and reintegration (DDR) programs 40–41
dispersed practices 130–131
dissent 198–199
divisive identity 3, 62
DoD (U.S. Department of Defense) 45, 62, 63, 76, 78, 81
dogma 104
'doing military things' 5, 132, 133
doing pakhtu (pakhtu kawal) 155
'domino theory' 168, 169, 181–182
Dupree, Louis 37, 47n66

Economic Development Corps (EDCOR/EDUCOR) 18
economics 214, 215, 218, 219, 226
EDCOR (Economic Development Corps) 18
education 57, 173, 175, 220, 228n34; of Charles T. R. Bohannan 10, 11–12; military 43, 45, 68, 78, 133
EDUCOR (Economic Development Corps) 18
ego-identity 56–57
Ellsberg, Daniel 20, 176, 178, 179
emotional resources 55, 56
environment 11, 62, 105, 192, 195, 200; Al-Shabaab 215, 216, 217; contrasting worldviews of anthropologists and US marines 78, 83, 86
Erikson, Erik 56–57
ethics 18, 43, 45, 82, 84, 91, 92n5, 174
ethnic conflict 58–59
ethnic small wars 41
ethnicity 58–59, 62, 63, 87, 88, 171, 173; in Israeli Defense Force 103, 104, 111
ethnology 6, 164, 168, 172–173; French 167, 168, 171, 172–176, 184n41; see also Mus, Paul
Evans-Pritchard, E. E. 101
expropriation, of antiquities 3, 34, 44, 201

extremism 7, 55, 57, 66, 199, 224, 226

failed states 7, 221
faith (religious) 4, 65; in Israeli Defense Force 95–114, 113n49
'faith in a foxhole' paradigm 95, 97, 110
Fallujah Memorandum 7, 200, 202, 203, 207n52
Fanon, Frantz 167, 176, 180
fear 103, 109, 204, 226
fieldwork 5, 6, 32, 42, 58, 79, 147, 161n15, 215, 218
financial rewards 222
Fire in the Lake 6, 164–186
First World War 32–33, 36, 109
FitzGerald, Francis 6, 164–186
FM101-5-1 (Operational terms and Graphics) 88
FM 3–24 (Counterinsurgency Field Manual) 60, 61, 140, 143
forced recruitment 218, 228n24
foreign policy 1, 65, 166, 169, 178, 182
forensic archaeology 41
French colonialism 174, 185n78
French ethnology 167, 168, 171, 172–176, 184n41

Galula, David 59–60, 61, 64
Gant, Major Jim 5–6, 139–141, 156–162; counterinsurgency doctrine of 143; honor 153–155; in Mangwal 139, 141, 143, 144–147; Nur Afzal 147–149; One Tribe at a Time 141–144, 147; tribes 149–153
Gaza Strip 98, 102, 103, 105, 106, 108, 110
Geertz, Clifford 57, 58, 69, 176
Geertz, Hildred 108
good ally, goal of being a 124, 126, 129
Good Ally: Norway in Afghanistan 2001–2014, A 123
Great Game 34, 35, 40
grievance-based motivations 219
grievances 7, 59, 64, 204; and Al-Shabaab 215, 219, 221, 223, 224, 225, 226
group identities 58–59, 60
guerrilla war/warfare 167, 169, 193; Charles T. R. Bohannan on 9, 11, 12–13, 16, 17, 19
Gulf War 40, 208n58

Hague Convention on the Protection of Cultural Property in the Event of Armed Conflict 37, 44, 45
Halberstam, David 177, 178, 179

INDEX

Harakaat Al-Shabaab Al-Mujaahiduun 7, 213–230
heritage tourism, archaeological-based 40
Hickey, Gerald 167, 171, 179
hit-and-run tactics 221
Ho Chi Minh 6, 164–165, 168, 169, 173, 174, 177, 178, 179, 182
honest self-assessment, culture of 201
honor 6, 142, 150, 152, 153–155, 156, 162n38, 193, 198
hostile environment 215
Hrdlička, Aleš 13
HTTs (Human Terrain Teams) 43, 76, 77, 83–85, 91, 203
Huk rebellion 2, 10, 15, 16, 17–18, 19, 21
human behavior 55, 56, 87
human terrain 85–87, 128, 204
Human Terrain System 2, 83, 193, 202, 205
Human Terrain Teams (HTTs) 43, 76, 77, 83–85, 91, 203
Hussein, Saddam 62
hybrid conflicts 28, 39, 46

I Ching (Book of Changes) 179–180
Ibn Khaldun 200–201
identity 3, 55–71
ideology 7, 39–40, 58, 65, 66, 97, 106; of Al-Shabaab 214, 215, 216, 219, 221, 224, 226–227, 229n57; in *Fire in the Lake* 168, 172, 181–182, 185n78; of Islamic State 191, 195, 196, 199, 205
IDF (Israel Defense Force) 4, 95–114
'imagined communities' 58
impact avoidance 44
imperialism 31, 32, 34, 36, 37, 172
impoverishment 55, 88, 216, 217, 226
individual radicalization 57
individualism 58
Indochina 164, 166, 168–169, 173–174, 175, 181
indoctrination 17, 57, 215, 218, 219, 226
industrialism 31
instructors 78, 80, 81, 82–83
insurgency: collective identity building in 55–71; movement 213, 219, 222; and Al-Shabaab's recruitment project 213–230
integrative practices 130, 131, 132, 133
intelligence, battlefield 44, 84, 86, 91
internal violence 155
international legitimacy 129
interpreters 43, 76, 77, 79–83
interviews 2, 4–5, 139, 182; of former Al-Shabaab youth 213, 215, 219; of Israeli Defense Force personnel 99, 103, 108; of Norwegian mentoring mission personnel 121, 123, 126, 129, 130; of US Marines 76, 77, 78, 79, 82, 88, 92n5
IPB (intelligence preparation of the battlefield) 44, 86
Iraq, Norwegian mentoring mission to 4–5, 121–136
irregular forces 28, 44, 59, 102
irregular warfare 10, 16, 32, 36, 39, 59, 78
IS (Islamic State) *see* Islamic State (IS)
ISIL (Islamic State of Iraq and the Levant) 4, 121, 122, 124, 126, 127
ISIS (Islamic State in Iraq and Syria) 40, 63, 64, 65–67, 68, 204
Islamic State (IS) 4, 6–7, 28, 66–67; and Major Jim Gant 141, 146; tribal engagement experiment of 191–208, 206n17
Islamic State in Iraq and Syria (ISIS) 40, 63, 64, 65–67, 68, 204
Islamic State of Iraq *see* Islamic State (IS)
Islamic State of Iraq and the Levant (ISIL) 4, 121, 122, 124, 126, 127
Islamism 3, 41, 55, 56, 61, 62–67, 69, 102, 205, 216, 220
Israel Defense Force (IDF) 4, 95–114

jihad 7, 38, 64, 65, 66, 149; of Al-Shabaab 214, 216, 217, 218, 219, 221, 222, 224, 225; of Islamic State 194, 195–198, 199, 200
Joint US Military Assistance Group (JUSMAG) 2, 16
Judaism 104, 111, 112n23, 113n51
Jughayfi tribe 197, 207n33
JUSMAG (Joint US Military Assistance Group) 2, 16

Keep It Simple Stupid (KISS) communication 89–91
Kilcullen, David 60, 61
kinship 58, 60, 171, 173, 200–201; and Major Jim Gant 142, 154, 161n15, 161–162n25
kippot 106, 107, 114n58
KISS (Keep It Simple Stupid) communication 89–91
knowledge development 128

lake fire, revolution like a 6, 164–186
language skills 79, 222
Lansdale, General Edward 2, 170; and Charles T. R Bohannan 9, 10, 16, 17, 18, 19, 20, 21, 24n62, 24n79, 25n91, 25n92
Lawrence, T. E. 33, 36, 143, 145, 157–158

leader engagements 81, 125–130
learning from the enemy 201–202
Lecha Dodi 106
legitimacy 6, 15, 38, 129, 164–186, 193
liberal individualism 58
liberalism 65, 166, 173, 176–182
limited use of force 205
liturgy 95, 96, 111n4
looting, of material cultural heritage 29, 30, 31, 34, 37, 38, 40, 44, 214
low-intensity conflict 38
Lucas, George 1, 2, 3

MAAG (Military Assistance Advisory Group) 170
McAlister, John T. 165–166, 177, 179
McFate, Montgomery 91, 205, 207n52
magic 100, 101, 102
Magsaysay, Ramon 10, 16, 17, 18, 19, 25n91
Malinowski, Bronislaw 100, 101
mandarins 175, 178
'Mandate of Heaven' 6, 164–165, 174–175, 176, 178, 179
Mangwal, Afghanistan 6, 139, 141, 144–147, 148, 150–153, 154, 156, 158, 159, 160n13, 162n27
manipulation, of material cultural heritage 28, 31
Mannoni, Otare 167, 176, 180
Marine Corps (US), in Iraq and Afghanistan 4, 60, 76–93
Marxism-Leninism 165, 169, 176
material heritage 28, 30, 39
MCU (Marine Corps University) 78, 86, 87
Mead, Margaret 57
meaning-making 95, 97, 100, 102
methodology 7, 66, 92n9, 99, 208n65, 214, 215
MFAA (Monuments, Fine Arts, and Archives) sections 37
Miakhel, Shahmahmood 147–148, 149, 152–153, 160n12, 160–161n13, 161n25, 162n30, 162n31
Michigan State University Group (MSUG) 171, 184n35
military anthropology 1, 2, 3–4, 5, 7, 91
Military Anthropology: Soldiers, Scholars and Subjects at the Margins of Empire 1
military assistance 170
military conflicts 6, 102, 110, 127, 182
military culture 78, 87, 132
military effectiveness 1, 5
military operations, 79, 81, 91, 140, 142, 144; of Norwegian mentoring mission 121, 125, 129, 130, 131, 132, 134

military practice, translating politics into 4, 5, 121–136
Military Rabbinate, of Israeli Defense Force 98–99
military strategy 17, 18
military-archaeology relationship 29–30, 31, 32, 35, 36, 37, 38, 44
miracle tales 108–110, 114n73
mission civilisatrice 181
Mitakhel Mohmands 151–152
modernisation theory 168, 169, 177
Mohmand tribe 150–151, 151–152, 153, 162n28
Monuments, Fine Arts, and Archives (MFAA) sections 37
morale 4, 97, 101, 104–105, 107, 110, 165
'Mother Rachel' incident 108–109
motivations 7, 97, 98, 106, 125, 126, 133, 216, 217, 219
MSUG (Michigan State University Group) 171, 184n35
Mus, Paul 6, 164, 165–166, 167, 168, 172–176, 177, 178, 179, 182, 185n76
myths 167, 181, 185n76

Napoleonic Wars 11, 31, 32, 129
nation building 61, 170
national entrepreneurs 67, 68–69
national identity 61, 62, 67
National Liberation Front (NLF) 165, 167, 170, 171, 181
national religious community, of Israeli society 97–98, 104, 105, 110, 112n13, 112n14
national security policy 1, 5
National Solidarity Program (NSP) 67
national unity 3, 40, 62
nationalism 216, 220–221; and archaeology 31–32, 37, 39; and collective identity building 58, 64, 65; in *Fire in the Lake* 165, 168, 173, 174, 176, 177, 178; and Israeli Defense Force 95, 97, 98
Native Americans 2, 9, 10, 12, 13, 21, 23n27
NATO (North Atlantic Treaty Organization) 4, 6, 41, 192; and Norwegian mentoring mission 122, 123, 124–125, 128, 129, 132, 133, 134, 135–136n21
need to belong 55–56, 58, 60, 61, 67, 221
neo-colonialism 181
'Nine Innings' wargame 87, 88, 90
NLF (National Liberation Front) 165, 167, 170, 171, 181

'no atheists in a foxhole' paradigm 99–100
non-state actors 28, 44, 59, 102
'noodle' slide 76, 77, 88
North Atlantic Treaty Organization see NATO (North Atlantic Treaty Organization)
North Vietnamese Army (NVA) 165, 181
Norwegian mentoring mission, to Iraq 4–5, 121–136
'no-strike' lists 44
NSP (National Solidarity Program) 67
NVA (North Vietnamese Army) 165, 181

oath, for Iraqi military fighting alongside US forces 68
Office for Public and Tribal Relations 204
Office of Strategic Services (OSS) 16, 36
officer professionalism 22n4
One Tribe at a Time 139, 141–144, 147, 148, 150
online survey, on attitudes towards culture and language learning 79
Operation Iraqi freedom 62–64
Operational Terms and Graphics (FM101-5-1) 88
OSS (Office of Strategic Services) 16, 36

PA (principal-actor) theory 125
pakhtunwali 82, 142, 154, 155, 162n37
Palestinian Exploration Fund (PEF) 33
Palmyra 28, 29, 30
participation: of anthropologists in war 42, 43; Norwegian 123–125, 126, 130, 133
Pashtunwali 82, 142, 154, 155, 162n37
PEF (Palestinian Exploration Fund) 33
personality 20, 56–57
Petraeus, General David 5, 63, 139, 140, 141, 143, 144, 145
Petrovsky, Nikolai 35–36
Philippines 2, 9, 10, 12, 14, 15–18, 20, 21, 23n50, 37, 40, 87, 88, 169, 181, 204
phylacteries 4, 101, 106, 107, 108
Pitt-Rivers, Lieutenant-General Augustus 32
PME (professional military education) 43, 133
policy making 166, 167, 168, 169, 176
political aims 4–5, 121, 122–123, 125–126, 128, 129, 132, 133–134
political exclusion 215
political ideology 172
political imagination 58
political legitimacy 6

political marginalisation 214, 225, 226
political strategy 17, 18, 184n37
politics 5, 16, 177; Somali 214, 220, 221, 222, 223, 224, 226; translated into military practice 121–136
post-Cold War era 3, 38, 44
postcolonial society 164, 168, 174, 180
post-conflict issues 29, 38, 41
post-heroic warfare 100, 101–102, 110
post-war American social science 168–172
poverty 55, 88, 216, 217, 226
power point presentations 76–77, 85–87, 88, 89, 90
practice theory 121, 131, 134, 135
prayer 96, 100, 103, 104, 106–107, 108, 110, 145, 154
principal-actor (PA) theory 125
professional anthropology 10, 32, 36, 42
professional military education (PME) 43, 133
professional military practice 5, 10, 22n4, 43, 105; and Norwegian mentoring mission 125–126, 127, 130, 131, 134
profiteers 221
Prophet Muhammed 65, 66, 201
Prospero and Caliban: The Psychology of Colonization 180
'Prospero complex' 180
protection, of material cultural heritage 28, 29, 30, 31, 37, 38–39, 40, 41, 43, 44, 45
'protoinsurgencies' 60
protracted conflicts 100, 102, 111, 169
Przhevalsky, Nikolai 35
psychology 10, 16, 17, 18, 20–21
Putin, President Vladimir 28, 39

qorraxjoog youth 219, 220
'quagmire' theory 166, 177–178, 181, 182
qualitative research 110, 125–126, 215; *see also* interviews
qurbojoog youth 219

radicalization 57, 214–215, 216, 217, 218
Rashidun (Rightly Guided Caliphs) 200
recruitment, in Al-Shabaab 213–230
regime change 182
rehabilitation archaeology 42
religion 30, 57, 60; within Israeli Defense Force combat units 95–114
religionization 95, 111
religious ideology 214
religious meaning 100, 110–111

religious practices 4, 131; of Israeli Defense Force 95, 96–97, 99, 100, 102, 104, 108, 110, 111
religious revivalism, in Israeli Defense Force 98, 105
religious Zionists 97–98, 104, 105, 110, 112n13, 112n14
repentance 198–199, 204
reprisals 226
reversal, of archaeology-military relationship 29–30, 38–44
revolutionary warfare 6, 164–186
Rightly Guided Caliphs (*Rashidun*) 200
ritual practices, in Israeli Defense Force 95–97, 98, 99, 100–101, 103–108
Rontzki, Avichai 98
rule of law 3, 61, 62, 63, 225
Russia 28, 29, 35, 39, 44, 168, 179

Sabbath 106, 113n57
Sahwa (Sunni Awakening) 192, 200, 202, 203–204, 206n17, 206–207n23
Saigon Military Mission (SMM) 19
Schatzki, Theodore 130, 131
Schlesinger, Arthur 166, 177–178, 179
Second World War 14–15, 36–37, 91, 100, 109
section system, of tribal organization (*wand*) 152, 153, 162n27
security force assistance (SFA) 68, 122, 124–125, 134, 135–136n21
sense of purpose 55, 60
SFA (security force assistance) 68, 122, 124–125, 134, 135–136n21
Shaplen, Robert 177, 178, 179
shared symbols 57
Sharia 198, 199, 219
small-state militaries 121, 122, 125, 126, 134
SMEs, cultural (cultural subject matter experts) 76, 77, 79, 80, 83–85, 87, 89, 90, 91, 92
SMM (Saigon Military Mission) 19
social dynamics: of Islamic State 191, 193, 198; of Norwegian mentoring mission 122, 126–127, 129, 132, 134
social identity 55
social injustice 215
social interactions 128–129, 132, 134
social movements 216
social networks 61
social science 16, 32, 43, 84–85, 91, 168–172, 180; and Israeli Defense Force 100, 106, 110
social solidarity 106–107

social structures 6, 58, 60, 61, 194, 196, 204
sociology 121, 132, 135, 172, 179
Somalia 7, 213–230
Søreide, Ine Eriksen 124
South Vietnam 19–20, 21, 164–186
'spaghetti' slide 76, 77, 88
special forces 5–6, 135n17, 139, 141, 146, 156, 160n9
state legitimacy 6, 15, 164–186
state stabilization 61
Stein, Sir Marc Aurel 35
strategic realism 166
Strategy to Improve the Political Position of the Islamic State of Iraq 7, 200, 202, 203, 207n52
stress, of combat 4, 99, 100, 104, 107, 146
structural violence 43
subcultures, cultural challenges between 92
suffering, in times of adversity 100, 101, 104
Sunni Awakening (*Sahwa*) 192, 200, 202, 203–204, 206n17, 206–207n23
Sunni Islamist insurgencies 3, 55, 56, 62–67, 69
Sunni tribes 6, 7, 64, 191, 194, 196, 198, 199, 202, 205
supernatural, the 17–18, 100, 110
Swidler, Ann 58
SYL (Somali Youth League) 223
symbols: cultural 10, 14–15, 38, 40, 57, 58, 66, 69, 99; military practices as 5, 121; on power point slides 87–88; Prophet Muhammed as 66; religious 39
Syria 28, 29, 40, 45, 65, 102, 141, 191, 192, 199, 204, 205, 206n17

Taliban 38, 140, 141, 142, 144, 154
talismanic functions 4, 97, 101, 102, 104, 107–108, 109
terrain 30, 34, 81, 86, 87, 128, 132; *see also* human terrain; Human Terrain System; Human Terrain Teams (HTTs)
territorial legitimacy 38
terrorism 28, 29, 38, 39, 40, 44, 57, 68, 69n3, 124, 197, 204
theocratization, of Israeli Defense Force 97
theodicy 100, 101
threats 4, 15, 28, 29, 44, 69n3, 142, 194, 204; Al-Shabaab 215, 216, 218; Norwegian mentoring mission 122, 127, 135–136n21
tourism 29, 37, 39, 40, 41

traditional archaeology 41–42
transnational Islamist groups 61, 65
triad of actors 194
tribal Awakening 192, 200, 202, 203–204, 206n17, 206–207n23
tribal code of honor 82, 142, 154, 155, 162n37
tribal dynamics 191, 200, 203
tribal engagement 6, 7, 191–208
tribal inclusion 201
tribal networks 191, 203
tribal warfare 193, 206n20
tribalism, Islamist exploitation of 205
tribe, definition of 193
Trump, President Donald J. 140, 141

UIC (Union of Islamic Courts) 216
ultra-orthodox Jewish community 98
uncertainty of combat 95, 97, 100
unconventional warfare 2, 10, 12, 14, 16, 36, 77, 156
unemployment 217, 226
UNESCO (United Nations Educational, Scientific and Cultural Organisation) 28, 29, 39, 45
Union of Islamic Courts (UIC) 216
United Nations Educational, Scientific and Cultural Organisation (UNESCO) 28, 29, 39, 45
US Department of Defense (DoD) 45, 62, 63, 76, 78, 81
US foreign policy elite
US Marine Corps 4, 60, 76–93
US Special Forces 5–6, 135n17, 139, 141, 146, 156, 160n9
utilization, of material cultural heritage 28

'*Veivalg i norsk utenriks-og sikkerhetspolitikk*' ('Choice of Path in Norwegian Foreign and Security policy') 123
verbal interpretation 82
vernacular religion 4, 95–114
Viet-Cong 2, 21
Vietnam 2, 6, 9, 10, 19–20, 21, 37, 42, 91, 164–186
Viet-Nam: Sociologie d'une guerre 165, 174, 176
Vietnam: The Origins of the Revolution 179
violence 101, 107–108, 127, 129, 155, 220; and collective identity building 55, 58, 65, 69n3; Islamic State 197, 198, 204–205
violent extremism 55
visual representation, of information 86

wand (section system) 152, 153, 162n27
war profiteers 221
warfare: asymmetrical 43, 95–114, 140, 221; conventional 10, 62, 64, 167; counter-guerrilla 16, 166; guerrilla 9, 11, 12–13, 16, 17, 19, 167, 169, 193; irregular 10, 16, 32, 36, 39, 59, 78; post-heroic 100, 101–102, 110; psychological 10, 16, 17; revolutionary 164–186; tribal 193, 206n20; unconventional 2, 10, 12, 14, 16, 36, 77, 156
wargames 87
warlords 216
World War I 32–33, 36, 109
World War II 14–15, 36–37, 91, 100, 109

Xi Jinping, President 39–40

Yemen 40, 226
youth radicalisation 218–219
youth recruitment 213, 214, 216–218